Moral Dilemmas of Modern War

Torture, Assassination, and Blackmail in an Age of
Asymmetric Conflict

Asymmetric conflict is changing the way that we practice and think
about war. Torture, rendition, assassination, blackmail, extortion,
direct attacks on civilians, and chemical weapons are all finding
their way to the battlefield despite long-standing prohibitions. This
book offers a practical guide for policymakers, military officers, lawyers, students, journalists, and others who ask how to adapt the laws
and conventions of war to the changing demands of asymmetric conflict. As war wages between state and nonstate parties, difficult questions arise about the status of guerrillas, the methods each side may
use to disable the other, and the means necessary to identify and
protect civilians caught in the crossfire. Answering these questions
while providing each side a reasonable chance to press its claims by
force of arms requires us to reevaluate the principle of noncombatant immunity, adjust the standards of proportionality, and redefine
the limits of unnecessary suffering and superfluous injury. In doing
so, many practices that conventional war prohibits are slowly evolving into new norms of asymmetric conflict.

Michael L. Gross is professor of political science and chair of the
Department of International Relations at the University of Haifa,
Israel. He is the author of *Ethics and Activism: The Theory and Practice
of Political Morality* (Cambridge University Press, 1997) and *Bioethics
and Armed Conflict: Moral Dilemmas of Medicine and War* (2006).

American River College Library
4700 College Oak Drive
Sacramento, CA 95841

To Stuart
Family and Friend

Moral Dilemmas of Modern War

Torture, Assassination, and Blackmail in an Age of Asymmetric Conflict

MICHAEL L. GROSS
The University of Haifa

CAMBRIDGE
UNIVERSITY PRESS

CAMBRIDGE UNIVERSITY PRESS
Cambridge, New York, Melbourne, Madrid, Cape Town, Singapore,
São Paulo, Delhi, Dubai, Tokyo

Cambridge University Press
32 Avenue of the Americas, New York, NY 10013-2473, USA

www.cambridge.org
Information on this title: www.cambridge.org/9780521685108

© Michael L. Gross 2010

This publication is in copyright. Subject to statutory exception
and to the provisions of relevant collective licensing agreements,
no reproduction of any part may take place without the written
permission of Cambridge University Press.

First published 2010

A catalog record for this publication is available from the British Library.

Library of Congress Cataloging in Publication data
   Gross, Michael L., 1954–
   Moral dilemmas of modern war : torture, assassination, and blackmail in an age of
   asymmetric conflict / Michael L. Gross.
      p.   cm.
   Includes bibliographical references and index.
   ISBN 978-0-521-86615-6 (hardback) – ISBN 978-0-521-68510-8 (pbk.)
   1. War – Moral and ethical aspects – United States.   2. Military ethics –
   United States.   3. Military interrogation – Moral and ethical aspects – United
   States.   I. Title.
   U22.G76 2009
   172'.42–dc22   2009008941

ISBN 978-0-521-86615-6 Hardback
ISBN 978-0-521-68510-8 Paperback

Cambridge University Press has no responsibility for the persistence or
accuracy of URLs for external or third-party Internet Web sites referred to in
this publication and does not guarantee that any content on such Web sites is,
or will remain, accurate or appropriate.

Contents

Preface

I completed this book just as the Gaza War broke out in December 2008. After having experienced the Second Lebanon War as a civilian under fire, I had a sense of déjà vu during this latest war. As the bombing continued, it was soon obvious to nearly any observer that the Israeli Air Force might run out of military targets before Hamas threw in the towel. "Then what?" asked my 16-year-old daughter. "Do we start shelling civilians?"

Her question goes to the heart of this book, as contemporary warfare raises difficult dilemmas about fighting small armies whose soldiers wear no uniforms and who fight in and among civilian population centers. The question, Who do you bomb when there are no more military targets? increasingly occupies state armies as they fight asymmetric wars, but it is not very far from the one guerrillas have asked themselves for decades, namely, Who do you bomb when you cannot reach military targets?

I try to answer both questions by explaining how the idea of civilian vulnerability expands during asymmetric conflict to allow strikes that in traditional wars violate the principle of noncombatant immunity. In Gaza, for example, police officers were among the first targeted in the early days of the fighting. Since when are police officers armed combatants? What nation would want to expose itself to such havoc as comes from destroying the very mechanism that prevents chaos and anarchy? In conventional war, mutual fear of retaliation makes the parties wary about targeting political leaders and agents of law enforcement. In asymmetric war, this convention breaks down very early.

This book is about several different types of asymmetric conflict, including wars against occupation, the war on terror, and wars against rogue regimes. I see it as a practical guide, because it aims to answer the moral and legal questions posed by policymakers, military officers, political leaders, journalists, philosophers, lawyers, students, and citizens as they confront the different tactics, weapons, and practices placed on the table during asymmetric conflict: Are guerrillas honorable foes or criminals? Do they deserve respect or long jail sentences? Are there grounds to torture guerrillas for information or to assassinate them on the battlefield? Is there room to use nonlethal weapons to subdue militants and safeguard the lives of noncombatants? Who are noncombatants anyway? What is the status of all those civilians who shelter and aid guerrillas? Are they as vulnerable as fighters are or do they deserve some measure of immunity? As important, How do things look from the other side? Do guerrillas fighting occupation have any right to attack civilians, particularly those who aid and shelter members of the stronger army? If one side can expand the scope of civilian vulnerability, then why can't the other? Might there be some symmetry to asymmetric war after all?

These are some of the immediate questions of asymmetric war that will bother anyone having the time and inclination to read a daily newspaper. In this book I hope to provide a convincing and dispassionate framework for answering them. This is not always easy. When I wrote *Bioethics and Armed Conflict* several years ago, I believed that living and writing in the shadow of the Montalbano Castle just outside Florence would bring some measure of objective distance. But the idea of objective distance is sometimes naïve. Studying the ethics of war requires a little bit of being both near to and far from the front lines. Studying war also requires some help from friends and family. Here, I want to thank my colleagues who corresponded with me and discussed the many topics this book explores. I owe a particular debt of gratitude to those closer to home. I opened this preface with a piercing observation from my daughter Elisheva. My son Saul, the young soldier mentioned in Chapter 3, carefully read the entire manuscript, and his insights into the dilemmas of asymmetric war were as incisive as they were invaluable. Finally, my hat goes off to my oldest daughter, Daphna, who is pursuing a career that takes human rights seriously and trades academic theory for legal practice. These are the people we hope to guide and inspire with our teaching.

Haifa, Israel – January 2009

Abbreviations

ADS	Active Denial System
API	Additional Protocol I
BWC	Biological Weapons Convention
CAR conflict	Conflict against colonial domination, alien occupation, and racist regimes
CAT	Convention Against Torture
CWC	Chemical Weapons Convention
DDE	doctrine of double effect
EU	European Union
HRW	Human Rights Watch
ICRC	International Committee of the Red Cross
IDF	Israel Defense Forces
IHL	international humanitarian law
IRA	Irish Republican Army
LOAC	law of armed conflict
MOOTW	military operations other than war
MRC	major regional conflict
NLW	nonlethal weapons
PLO	Palestine Liberation Organization
POW	prisoner of war
SIrUS	superfluous injury or unnecessary suffering
UN	United Nations

Torture, Assassination, and Blackmail in an Age of Asymmetric Conflict

Writing in 1992, just after the First Gulf War, military historian Martin van Creveld suggested that important changes in the rules of war were in the offing.[1] For the first time in many years, previously banned practices of war – assassination, hostage taking, and poison gas – were gaining a toehold of support among belligerents, and van Creveld predicted that support for these practices would grow. More than a decade later, we see that he was only partially right. Support has grown, but in a direction he did not predict. Assassination (plots to kill a head of state in the First Gulf War) has emerged as the targeted killing or extrajudicial execution of suspected terrorists. Hostage taking (attempts by Saddam Hussein to protect vital facilities by placing civilians in their midst) is now augmented with blackmail as governments fighting terrorism threaten citizens and their property with catastrophic destruction unless their government reins in terrorists. Poison gas (then used by Iraq to attack Kurdistan and Iran) is now part of a growing arsenal of nonlethal weapons (NLW) developed by the United States and its allies. Van Creveld missed torture. Although torture was a key component of established counterinsurgency warfare in many European colonies following World War II, it did not rise again to prominence until the Iraq War.

Van Creveld's predictions went astray because he focused his attention on a short-lived conventional war against a despot who was willing to sacrifice large numbers of his own civilian population to serve his megalomania. As events would develop, however, Saddam would fall and the war would quickly turn into an insurgency. And, in the way of many insurgencies since the Second World War, the insurgents chose guerrilla warfare and terrorism while their adversaries turned to torture, assassination, and blackmail.

Torture, assassination and blackmail are certainly not new forms of warfare. While such practices have occurred since ancient times, a growing corpus of international law works diligently to prohibit these practices today. Underlying international law is a very strong strand of what Jean Pictet calls humanitarian reasoning:

> A State engaged in a conflict will seek to destroy or weaken the enemy's war potential ... in three ways: death, wound or capture ... . All three are equally capable of eliminating the enemy's strength. Humanitarian reasoning is different. Humanity demands capture rather than wounds, and wounds rather than death; that non-combatants shall be spared as far as possible; that wounds inflicted be as light as possible, so that the injured can be treated and cured; that wounds cause the least possible pain; that captivity be made as endurable as possible.[2]

Humanitarian reasoning, or what I will refer to as simply "humanitarianism," guides combatants in their treatment of one another and of noncombatants and soldiers who are no longer a threat. It infuses the law of armed conflict (LOAC) and international humanitarian law (IHL), and is enshrined in the 1949 Geneva Conventions and the 1977 Protocols (I and II) to the Geneva Conventions. Humanitarianism prohibits torture, summary execution, and weapons that cause unnecessary suffering, while protecting noncombatants from direct attack, pillage, reprisals, indiscriminate destruction of property, and kidnapping. Newly emerging tactics that embrace enhanced interrogation techniques, such as waterboarding, forced stress positions or exposure to cold; nonlethal chemical weapons; assassination; and widespread attacks on civilians impinge directly on these long-standing prohibitions.

The baffling question is why the United States and some of its allies blatantly employ unlawful means of warfare as they wage asymmetric war against national insurgencies, international terror, rogue countries and state-sponsored guerrilla organizations. Sixty years after World War II and the great humanitarian tide of concern for basic human rights, many nations suddenly find themselves resorting to low-tech, primitive, and generally prohibited forms of warfare. Why have liberal democracies now abandoned some of the core principles of humanitarian law as they fight asymmetric wars?

Perhaps the answer lies in the very nature of the conflict. Unencumbered by reciprocity, that is, the ability of an adversary to respond in kind, many military organizations find torture, assassination, and blackmail useful. If they don't, then perhaps they should. According to some views, strong democratic nations are unable to vanquish the weak "because they find it extremely difficult to escalate the level of violence and brutality to that which can secure victory."[3] But brutality is not always the best answer. "If barbarism is employed to achieve military victory," writes Ivan Arreguin-Toft, "any peace that follows will be fragile and costly at best."[4] This is undoubtedly true but certainly depends upon the enemy one faces. The Israelis and Palestinians may want to do better than settle for a fragile and costly peace, but that may not be of concern to a Western country seeking to utterly destroy al-Qaeda, or to a UN multinational force hoping to crush a genocidal regime intent on exterminating its own people. A conflict that seeks political accommodation differs significantly from one that seeks to oust a regime or eliminate a terrorist organization. Different types of asymmetric war demand different tactics.

Thinking about the efficacy and ethics of what many might call restrained brutality sets up the dilemmas in this book. "The logistical parsimony of guerrilla warfare," concludes Gil Merom, "can be met with the parsimony of uninhibited violence, *at least as long as altruistic moral restraints are absent.*[5] Herein is the rub. No democratic society can allow itself an uncontrolled descent into barbarism, but once unfettered by an asymmetry that precludes a reciprocal, in-kind violent response from the weaker party, it is tempting to think how far one might go. The dilemma is real: in some situations, military necessity may demand harsh measures that no nation would or could consider in conventional war. The prospect of success pulls powerful nations to torture, assassination, and blackmail, while deeply ingrained humanitarian norms push them away.

To both justify and restrain harsh measures, military and political leaders make a concerted effort to shoehorn new practices into international law. This does not prevent certain practices, but may contain them at the margins. Thus, torture morphs into "moderate physical pressure," assassination becomes targeted killing and civilian bombing is defensible when directed against "associated" civilian targets, that is, civilians who take some part in the fighting and who bear a measure of responsibility for armed conflict. There are two complementary aspects to these tactics and practices. On one hand, civilians who suffer harm in asymmetric war somehow deserve it, having lost their immunity and protection. On the other hand, those who warrant protection find it when torture saves innocents from ticking bombs, when assassination and nonlethal chemical weapons disable combatants with few civilian casualties, and when blackmail, including terrorism, can enhance security by deterring an enemy from future hostile activity. Torture, assassination, and blackmail, in other words, target the guilty and protect the innocent.

Nevertheless, these practices rarely appear in conventional war. Facing the threat of retaliation, nations remain very wary of targeting enemy soldiers by name, using moderate physical pressure to question enemy prisoners, or attacking civilian targets no matter how much some civilians might contribute to the war effort. Faced with asymmetric war, however, nations, the smaller nonstate groups they fight, jurists, and philosophers are now ready to reconsider deeply held ideas about combatant rights, unnecessary suffering, and noncombatant immunity to lay a foundation for practices that are both militarily necessary and, they hope, humane. Articulating modes of warfare that meet these conditions raises the dilemmas underlying the chapters that follow.

The sections below will address several preliminary questions. First, What are torture, assassination, blackmail, and related practices such as terrorism and chemical warfare? What promise do they hold? Second, How are they different from the practices of conventional war? Close to unlawful, they ascribe responsibility and liability to participants, blur the edge between combatants and noncombatants, and modulate the use of lethal force. Finally, What is asymmetric war? Apart from the all-consuming war on terror, one should not ignore wars of humanitarian intervention, proxy guerrilla wars, and lingering wars of national liberation. Efforts to resolve the dilemmas posed by torture, assassination, and blackmail vary with each type of conflict.

TORTURE, ASSASSINATION, BLACKMAIL, POISON GAS, AND
TERRORISM: A BRIEF RUNDOWN

Torture and Rendition

With the notoriety of Abu Ghraib and Guantanamo Bay, few people
are unaware of torture and rendition. Each is a long-standing counterinsurgency tactic designed to deliver and hold suspects for interrogation. Interrogational torture utilizes extreme physical and
psychological means to extract information from those suspected
of threatening innocent civilians with immediate and catastrophic
harm and/or of threatening national security and the lives of soldiers.
However, interrogational torture does not aim to brutalize a civilian
population into submission by singling out and persecuting political
opponents of the regime.[6] Rendition is an adjunct to interrogational
torture and significantly different from extradition. Extradition is
a legal process that returns criminal suspects for trial in a country
where they committed crimes. Rendition, in contrast, transfers or renders to justice anyone loosely associated with terrorism from one sovereign nation to another for the purpose of interrogation. Warrants
are rarely issued, suspects seldom stand trial, and many detainees
often face long-term incarceration under legally amorphous rules of
administrative detention.[7]

Assassination

Conventional laws of armed conflict deride fingering enemy soldiers
or civilians for assassination or targeted killing. Citing ancient prohibitions against poison and treachery, many still regard assassination
as a despicable form of warfare. For modern jurists, principal among
them Francis Lieber, who codified the laws of war for the Union Army
during the U.S. Civil War, assassination repudiates the innocence
and moral equality of all combatants by naming particular individuals and hunting them down like outlaws. Lieber's firm denunciation
of assassination did not make it into the Geneva Conventions, but its
spirit pervades many military law manuals. This spirit, however, no
longer moves state armies who face guerrilla warfare, where lack of
uniforms makes it difficult to identify, much less disable, enemy combatants. In response, many state armies are investing considerable

resources to develop the intelligence and technical means to do just as Lieber prohibited.[8]

Blackmail

Blackmail, as used here, has many guises and consists of tactics that intentionally or unintentionally harm, or threaten to harm, noncombatants. Blackmailing civilians by both sides to an asymmetric conflict is pervasive because they are generally defenseless. Blackmail may consist of tactics that are large-scale, small-scale, or intermediate in scale. Large-scale blackmail threatens citizens and their property with catastrophic destruction unless their government surrenders or reins in terrorists. Threatening civilians to establish or restore a deterrent capability was one of Israel's and Hezbollah's aims in the Second Lebanon War (2006). Small-scale blackmail extorts collaboration in return for essential services, such as medical care or travel papers. Intermediate measures impose severe restrictions on civilians by using encirclement, siege, banishment, or relocation to distance civilians from the terrorists who depend upon them for support. In many cases the threat is sufficient, but in all cases, the door often opens to implementation when blackmail fails or requires a demonstration of what victims can expect if they refuse the blackmailer's demands.

Nonlethal Warfare

Nonlethal weapons (NLWs) employ optical and acoustic means, energy wave devices, and chemical agents to cause disorientation, discomfort, severe nausea, or temporary unconsciousness to incapacitate opposing forces and minimize collateral harm to noncombatants.[9] While some NLWs repulse an enemy and thereby avoid direct encounters, others temporarily incapacitate an enemy so that the enemy can be overwhelmed and disarmed. In both cases, NLWs provide a force continuum, allowing a wide range of options between using high explosives and doing nothing. Properly deployed, nonlethal weaponry offers advanced military organizations the possibility of temporarily incapacitating enemy forces, controlling crowds, or conducting rescue missions without the need to endanger large numbers of noncombatants. At the same time, however, some NLWs use restricted chemicals and all nonlethal weapons intentionally target un-uniformed combatants and noncombatants alike, a blatant violation of humanitarian law.

Terrorism

Terrorism is the flip side of torture, assassination, and blackmail. It is, as commonly portrayed, the weapon of the weaker side. Some observers continue to draw a significant distinction between terrorism and guerrilla warfare when describing the behavior of such nonstate actors as insurgent and guerrilla groups.[10] While terrorism deliberately targets innocent civilian noncombatants for political gain, and thus is heinous by any understanding of humanitarianism, guerrilla warfare describes the activity of irregular combatants who wear identifying insignia and attack military targets while observing some modicum of the law of armed conflict.

This sharp distinction misses the mark for two reasons. First, it is impractical to apply in the field. Which among the myriad of Palestinian groups, for example, are terrorists and which are guerrilla fighters? Hamas, Fatah, Islamic Jihad, and others meet both criteria. Sometimes they attack civilians, sometimes they strike military targets. Second, the distinction ignores the historical development of twentieth-century guerrilla warfare. Gone are the days of Mao's three-phase program for fledgling guerrillas that exhorted them to evolve from a small group capable of harassing large conventional forces to one capable of defeating an enemy in open warfare. As guerrilla warfare moved from the countryside to the city, first in South America and Africa and later in the Middle East, terrorism, as we now define it, joined the guerrilla repertoire. This did not mark any great ideological change regarding the guilt or innocence of noncombatants, but reflected the tactical need to fight differently in urban areas. Its success remains a matter of debate, but as an emerging tactic there is no doubt that terrorism assumed an increasingly important place in nationalist guerrilla warfare, first among militants fighting for independence against France, Britain, and Portugal in the generation following the Second World War, and then among insurgents in Iraq, Israel, and Sri Lanka.[11] Today, terrorism together with torture, assassination, and blackmail push beyond wars of national self-determination to infuse the war on terror, humanitarian intervention, and proxy wars waged by guerrillas acting at the behest of sovereign countries.

TORTURE, TERROR, ASSASSINATION, AND BLACKMAIL: FUNDAMENTAL CHARACTERISTICS

Torture, terror, assassination, and blackmail depart from the practice of conventional war in several important respects. They are manifestly unlawful, or nearly so, thrive in an atmosphere of limited reciprocity, make judicious use of lethal force, blur the distinction between combatant and noncombatant, presume the guilt rather than the moral innocence of most battlefield actors, and reestablish *jus ad bellum* (just cause of war) as an integral part of the war convention.

Unlawfulness

The law of armed conflict, international humanitarian law, and just war theory generally proscribe torture, terror, assassination, and blackmail. Any number of UN and Geneva Conventions outlaw terrorism.[12] The Convention Against Torture (CAT) expressly prohibits torture and ill treatment as well as rendition or deportation to nations that practice torture. Modern laws of war, as noted, have always taken a very dim view of assassinating combatants, judging it a perfidy of the worst kind. The Chemical Weapons Convention (CWC) (1993) restricts the use of chemical weapons to those riot control agents used by law enforcement officials. This severely limits, if not bans, any use of chemical nonlethal weapons in armed conflict. Finally, a wide variety of international instruments prohibit threatening civilians with harm to pressure their government to behave peaceably or to rein in others.[13]

Limited Reciprocity

In conventional war, parties to the conflict command similar means of warfare and similar levels of destructive power. This often forms the basis for mutual restraint and the impetus for agreements and long-standing conventions that regulate the development, manufacture, and use of various weapons (poison gas or blinding lasers, for example), and protect the rights of combatants and noncombatants alike. No such reciprocity exists in asymmetric warfare. The stronger side, that is to say the state actor or coalition of state actors, utilizes torture, assassination, and blackmail. The weaker side, the nonstate actor, employs terrorism. There are, of course, crossovers. States may terrorize and guerrillas may torture, assassinate, and blackmail. In general, however, democratic states refrain from terrorism for two reasons. First, they have more-refined means at their disposal to harm civilians. Reprisals or incidental harm to civilians during a legitimate military operation, for example, may meet legal and moral tests that terrorism does not. Second, democratic state actors remain constrained by internalized moral norms that prohibit direct and intentional attacks on noncombatants. Nonstate actors, on the other hand, lack the technological means or infrastructure to engage in widespread rendition, detention, torture, and assassination. They are compelled to fight by other means.

Because the sides command different resources and, therefore, choose different tactics as they wage asymmetric war, neither can fight like the other or respond in kind. It is not that they do not wish to follow reciprocal rules, but that they cannot. Neither side, therefore, has any immediate motive for changing the way it fights. Incommensurate abilities and tactics make it difficult to reach mutual agreement about limiting warfare. As a result, each side may choose to ignore the rules of war that gain their legitimacy from reciprocity and mutual self-interest. More precisely, new rules emerge that balance the interests of the participants in a different way. Among these is the judicious use of lethal force.

Judicious Use of Lethal Force

In contrast to conventional war, torture, terror, assassination, and blackmail place less emphasis upon overwhelming destructive power and lethal force. Torture and detention, of course, have no place for lethal force. Their purpose is to extract information. A little-noticed feature of state behavior during asymmetric conflict is the emphasis on capturing, rather than killing, enemy combatants. In conventional wars, the goal is to disable the enemy by death or injury; in asymmetric war, the means of disabling, particularly by the stronger side, are generally less lethal. Many more thousands sit in prison than die on the battlefield. While American forces in Iraq, for example, killed nearly 19,000 insurgents between June 2003 and September 2007, they detained close to 120,000 anti-Iraq forces.[14]

Assassination, on the other hand, is a lethal tactic but one that is often accurate and avoids excessive civilian casualties.[15] Good intelligence, precision-guided munitions, and drones make targeted killing a discriminating tactic. At the same time, many state actors prefer arrest to assassination when this does not overly endanger their troops. This too, limits combatant and noncombatant casualties significantly.

Blackmail, if by this we mean *threats* to civilians to convince their government to take or avoid some particular action is, by its nature, nonlethal. Unfortunately, conventional deterrence of this type can fail, and when it does, it may require a show of strength. The Second Lebanon War is a good example of this phenomenon. When deterrence failed, Israel attacked civilian or mixed infrastructures with deadly force. However, by adhering to newly emerging norms that take note of civilian liability and responsibility (discussed in the following section), these attacks were directed at those civilians claimed to have aided the enemy in some substantial way.

In spite of the prevalence of suicide bombers or "ticking bombs," (that is, any explosive device that presents a grave and immediate threat to life and limb), large numbers of casualties do not always serve the goals of terrorism. Terrorists, as Brian Jenkins famously noted, "want a lot of people watching, not a lot of people dead."[16] However, this is only true of terrorists fighting for national liberation and does not extend to inter-civilian or transnational terrorism where the number of casualties can be exceedingly high. By some accounts, the Algerian War of Independence (1954–1962) took at least 350,000 lives, but only one percent of these were French civilians killed by terrorists. Communists fighting the British in Malaya between 1948 and 1960 killed fewer than three thousand civilians during their 12-year insurrection before giving it up when it proved counterproductive. In Kenya, the Mau Mau insurgency's (1952–1960) highly publicized attacks on British and Asian civilians took about 60 lives, but thousands more among African civilians who supported British policy.

Rebel forces in Cyprus and Basques fighting Spain each caused fewer than five hundred civilian casualties, while Irish Republican Army (IRA) and Palestinian guerrillas (since 2000) have taken fewer than one thousand civilian lives in their respective struggles.[17] These are, or were, struggles for national liberation. In the war on international terror, on the other hand, fears of mass-casualty attacks drive the U.S. war against al-Qaeda.

Just Cause

The traditional law of armed conflict makes no distinction between combatants based on just cause (*jus ad bellum*), that is, which side is right. Excluding an assessment of just cause is fundamental to the rights that soldiers enjoy. Any captured combatant enjoys the rights accorded to a prisoner of war (POW) including humane treatment, freedom from torture, and the right to repatriation when the war is over. No soldier, unless a war criminal (one who gravely violates the Geneva Conventions), is criminally liable for his or her behavior. This is true of a soldier fighting for the most blatant aggressor.

Just wars or noble causes, on the other hand, imply that soldiers on one side are right and just, while their adversaries are evil and unjust. Just cause, therefore, challenges the norm of combatant equality and sets the stage for combatant liability (discussed below). On one hand, many states impute guilt and liability to guerrillas and international terrorists and label them criminals and unlawful combatants. On the other hand, there remains an undercurrent of legitimacy to terrorism when utilized by national liberation movements (Chapter 8). This makes some states hesitant about unilaterally condemning all forms of terrorism. But if terrorism in pursuit of a just cause is sometimes defensible, then those who fight against it, an occupying power, for example, may be criminals themselves.

Just cause also permeates the very idea of humanitarian intervention. Anchored in the UN's right to use military force to protect civilians from rapacious leaders, humanitarian intervention gains credence and demands international support when a rogue government wages unjust war, pursues genocide, or commits crimes against humanity (Chapter 9). If international humanitarian forces are just, then those opposing them, Sudanese regulars, for example, are blatantly unjust and criminal. An air of criminalization, therefore, permeates asymmetric conflict as more and more adversaries view one another as despicable villains rather than honorable foes or brothers in arms. This signifies a sea change in the conventional way of thinking about war and underscores the emerging notion of combatant liability.

Combatant Liability

An important norm of conventional war asserts the moral innocence of combatants on any side. Although they threaten bodily harm, soldiers are not criminals but, in many ways, agents of their state. At the end of the war, as just noted, they enjoy the right to go home and resume their lives without spending time in jail. They do not face trial or punishment for their actions. Asymmetric war challenges this assumption. For state actors, the presumption of liability and, sometimes, criminal guilt, is integral to the practice of torture, terror, and assassination. One reason is functional, the other justificatory. Torture and assassination are tactics of choice because they are cost-efficient practices well suited to technologically advanced armies. Here, it is important to target the right person, not simply someone in uniform, without causing excessive harm to civilians. In each case, the "right" person is the one directly responsible for planning, committing, or abetting a military and/or criminal action. The distinction between military and criminal actions, like that between guerrilla warfare and terrorism, is difficult to define with any precision. Yet criminal guilt or liability of some sort is required to justify or excuse torture and assassination. Combatants may be captured, rendered to justice, detained, and interrogated because there is reasonable evidence that they have committed or are about to commit a crime or act of war.

Moreover, noncombatants are also suspect. Increasingly, state armies are taking military action against "associated" targets, that is, civilians who play a direct or indirect part in war. Attacking civilians judged responsible for injustice is a mainstay of terrorism. But it is never part of conventional warfare, where noncombatant immunity protects any person who does not bear arms, regardless of his or her contribution to the war effort. Nevertheless, asymmetric conflict challenges this norm because it is difficult, if not impossible, to distinguish between soldiers and civilians. This blurs the hard-and-fast distinction between combatants and noncombatant, and subjects the latter to increasing levels of bodily harm.

Combatant-Noncombatant Blur

Ordinarily, noncombatants are innocent: they pose no threat, do not take part in the fighting, and are, therefore, immune from direct harm. But this is changing as civilians assume combatant-like roles in asymmetric conflict. Just as state actors impute guilt and assign criminal liability to guerrillas and those who support them, the logic of liability, responsibility, and guilt also permeates the practice of terrorism and further blurs the distinction between combatants and noncombatants. For guerrilla organizations and conventional armies alike, everyone on the other side is an enemy.

A number of emerging concepts address this change of attitude toward civilians. Collective responsibility assigns liability to anyone actively or tacitly supporting a guerrilla organization or any member of a democratic nation that freely elects a government that manages a colonial or occupying regime. An expanded understanding of combatant status assigns liability to those who actively support the fighting capabilities of either side. These include political leaders, journalists, bankers, teachers, reserve soldiers, and settlers. A broad application of the principle of reprisal allows military forces on either side to retaliate against otherwise innocent civilians as a response to repressive policy by occupying forces or to acts of terrorism. It should not be surprising that civilians find themselves at increased risk in asymmetric wars. Part of the reason, of course, lies in their physical proximity to the fighting. But another part lies in their functional proximity to the fighters. Many civilians look *and act* like combatants.

TYPES OF ASYMMETRIC CONFLICT

As the foregoing discussion might suggest, there are material, legal, and moral dimensions to asymmetric conflict that distinguish it from conventional war between nation-states. Material asymmetry reflects the disparity of arms between the opposing sides. Material asymmetry is common in any war. Nations, after all, go to war when they feel they have the upper hand. But in asymmetric war the material asymmetry is glaring, indeed monopolistic, as the weaker side often lacks sophisticated weaponry, tanks, a navy, an air force or air defense system. Legal asymmetry points to the disparate status of the parties to the conflict. On one hand, sovereign nation-states are the building blocks of the international order and the only legitimate purveyor of armed force. They confront, on the other hand, an array of nonstate actors that include guerrilla organizations or militias representing national groups and wielding some governmental authority such as Hamas or Hezbollah, remnants of a defeated government such as the Taliban, insurgents fighting occupation and their own government like al-Qaeda in Iraq, or international terrorist organizations such as al-Qaeda. Finally, moral asymmetry reflects the power of just cause. The sides to an asymmetric conflict are not morally equal. In wars of humanitarian intervention and the war on terror, moral asymmetry favors the stronger side, reinforcing its material and legal advantage. In wars of national liberation, however, the moral advantage shifts to the weaker side, thereby offsetting its material and legal disadvantage by allowing qualified recourse to some forms of terrorism.

The dilemmas of asymmetric war, therefore, play out differently in various forms of conflict. In each type of conflict, assessments of military necessity, just cause, combatant liability, noncombatant immunity, reciprocity, and concern for future peace will vary. In general, asymmetric conflicts differ as a function of the actors involved, participants' goals or war aims, and the means they use to achieve them. Actors range from guerrillas and terrorists on the weaker side, to states, coalitions of states, and international forces under UN auspices on the stronger side. Goals range from maintaining the status quo to changing it, and from defeating an enemy decisively in pitched battle to simply staving off defeat in the hopes of setting uncontestable conditions for a political settlement. Some conflicts are a series of tactical skirmishes and engagements, while others show signs of comprehensive strategic planning to achieve long-range political goals. The means of war vary considerably. Some are conventional (missiles and artillery) but many other means are unconventional and include torture, assassination, blackmail, terror, and nonlethal weapons. Combining these characteristics with the material, legal, and moral dimensions of asymmetry suggests four kinds of asymmetric conflict: guerrilla wars and insurgencies, wars of intervention, the war on international terror, and proxy guerrilla wars.

Guerrilla Wars and Insurgencies

These are the classic asymmetric wars that Merom and Arreguin-Toft describe and include nationalist insurgencies by a nonstate group fighting against its own government and wars of national liberation fought by small guerrilla armies against a large, well-armed, and technologically superior occupying force. In nationalist insurgencies in Iraq and Afghanistan, guerrilla groups and terrorist organizations battle their own government and the United States, with NATO and coalition forces providing military assistance. Wars of national liberation, defined as struggles against "colonial domination, alien occupation, and racist regimes" (hence CAR conflicts), are the cornerstone of Additional Protocol I (API) (1977), which allows guerrilla organizations to fight occupation under the protection of international law.[18]

As noted, CAR conflicts put the stronger power at a moral disadvantage. The justice of war (*jus ad bellum*) resides with a weak and oppressed national group struggling for self-determination. At best, the stronger side can fault the weaker for aspiring to territory or resources to which it is not entitled (a frequent charge against some Palestinian groups, for example). The stronger group may also fault the weaker for resorting to war when diplomacy remains an option or for employing means that cause excessive casualties or for harming those who enjoy immunity. There is considerable controversy, therefore, about the just means (*jus in bello*) that each side may employ to press its claims. Despite the justice of their claims, no justification of guerrilla warfare allows guerrillas to unnecessarily harm enemy combatants or intentionally harm innocent civilians. This axiom, of course, applies to both sides equally and raises the dilemma of just how far each side can extend necessary and effective means of warfare without running afoul of humanitarianism.

In CAR conflicts, the sides recognize that there is a political horizon anchored in territorial compromise and political accommodation. Armed conflict, therefore, is a painful prelude to a final peace, and this, too, dictates how the sides fight. Generally, neither side can defeat the other militarily. Instead, each uses force to jockey for a political advantage. Unrestrained barbarism by either side may undermine the peace that both sides ultimately hope to achieve. Yet conventional means of war, that is, means the war conventions unambiguously approve, are beyond reach of both sides. The weaker side lacks the means to field a large, modern army. The stronger side can field it, but often finds its enormous firepower is of little use or excessively destructive in fighting at close quarters. The challenge remains to push the envelope without excessive brutality. The answer, in practice, centers on a level of restrained barbarism that each side is willing to accept as the cost of doing business. The outstanding CAR conflict today remains the war between Israel and the Palestinians, while, for example, the Chechnyan and Tamil struggles against Russia and Sri Lanka respectively, are secessionist movements. While the former has gained recognition as an international armed conflict, the latter seek independence from a state that exercises legal sovereignty over the disputed territory. Although the international community is far from granting recognition to every national group that desires statehood, it does recognize that some secessionist movements are internal armed conflicts between state and nonstate adversaries, rather than police actions against criminal elements.

Some nationalist insurgencies may, on the other hand, garner less legitimacy particularly when they fight a lawfully constituted government. But the level of legitimacy can vary considerably. Some organizations in Iraq, al-Qaeda in Iraq, for example, are terrorist groups, while other groups battling the government represent sectarian or foreign interests. Achieving peace with these groups will vary according to their political aims. While there is little chance for compromise with the elements representing al-Qaeda, any viable peace plan will have to accommodate the demands of minority political groups and, perhaps, foreign interests (such as Iran's) as well. Allied and government forces may have to extend similar consideration to the Taliban. In each case, the tactics and brutality each side employs must take into account the postwar gains it hopes to achieve.

Wars of Intervention

Wars of intervention have goals different from those driving wars of national liberation. While the parties to a CAR conflict seek to resolve disputed territorial rights, nation-states intervene in the affairs of sovereign states to address threats to international peace and stability and to rescue embattled civilians from threat of genocide, war crimes, or crimes against humanity. Securing peace and saving persecuted civilians are two distinct causes of war but they often overlap in practice. Fighting in Afghanistan (with UN backing) and Iraq (without UN backing), the United States and its allies have sought to protect vital international and national interests and to restore human rights to a persecuted population. As they confronted a rogue or failing regime, intervening forces also found themselves embroiled in a long-term insurgency with many of the features of a CAR conflict. It was no surprise then that the United States turned to counterinsurgency tactics similar to those other occupying armies use.

Until recently, the world community was reticent about confronting rogue states unless they posed a clear threat to international peace and security. The UN Charter made it possible to raise troops and intervene in the Balkans and the Persian Gulf but only because nations in these areas threatened world peace. But in 2005, and in light of international apathy during the Rwandan genocide, the UN asserted its right to protect citizens of a sovereign nation facing genocide and egregious human rights abuses at the hands of its own government. This provides a more expansive mandate that could allow the world community to intervene in such nations as Sudan, Myanmar (Burma), or similarly troubled areas. The goal of humanitarian intervention is to radically alter the status quo, oust the current government, or otherwise curtail the power of repressive elements and, thereby, preserve the rights of civilians.

The means states have at their disposal to fight a war of intervention may vary considerably depending upon the capabilities of their adversary. What began in Iraq as a conventional war against regular and elite Iraqi troops eventually disintegrated into a guerrilla war and local insurgency. In the former Yugoslavia, Western forces confronted a loosely bound coalition of national militias, paramilitary groups, warlords, and criminal organizations that did not fight for national liberation or to evict occupying forces. Instead, they sought to expand and ethnically cleanse their territory and consolidate local power. Intervening forces, on the other hand, did not fight for territory or for clearly defined military goals, but to create the conditions necessary for humanitarian aid and international oversight as the country reorganized.[19] Employing modern armaments that included air defense systems and artillery, Bosnian Serbs forced some measure of military symmetry replete with hostage taking of UN troops, attacks on safe havens, and artillery bombardments on civilian population centers. Intervening states facing the armed forces of rogue nations may face a similarly well-armed adversary.

Nevertheless, nations facing rogue regimes or remnants thereof are not usually fighting for political accommodation. Facing a relentlessly malevolent government, intervening forces pursue regime change and may be less reluctant to employ torture, assassination, and blackmail than they would in CAR conflicts. Rather than impinging on peace efforts, destroying or severely disabling enemy forces and the support they receive from some segments of the population may be necessary for a postwar settlement that evicts the current regime, restores a working government, and establishes a stable, law abiding state. Similarly, nations fighting against international terrorism are less concerned about forging a postwar peace than utterly destroying their enemy's capacity to wage war.

International Terrorism, al-Qaeda, and the Threat of Weapons of Mass Destruction

Since the attacks on the United States of September 11, 2001, there is a growing understanding that asymmetric conflict includes the war on international terrorism.[20] Unlike CAR conflicts, wars of international terror by such groups as al-Qaeda do not have a nationalist agenda nor are their operations confined to a particular geographic locale. On an immediate level, al-Qaeda and related groups hope to dislodge the United States and its allies from the Middle East and replace moderate Arab states with a fundamentalist Islamic regime. In the long term, they aim to undermine Western interests, destabilize the international order, and thereby lay the foundation for a radical, universal Islam and a revived caliphate.[21]

In this kind of asymmetric conflict, Western and moderate nation-states are arrayed against an international network of interlocking terrorist organizations. Some of these organizations operate freely and independently while others affiliate closely with states that sponsor or support terrorism. Unlike CAR guerrillas, international terrorists do not represent any particular political constituency or territory. Nor is technological asymmetry always as clear and impressive as it is in CAR conflicts. On the contrary, international terror organizations are generally better funded than CAR groups, so that the great concern of many nations is the ongoing efforts of terrorists to obtain chemical, biological, and nuclear weapons of mass destruction. The war on terror, unlike CAR conflicts, admits of no reasonable political solution or compromise. The war is unremitting and long-term and without obvious signposts of success, whether interim treaties, cease-fires, or territorial accommodations.

Asymmetric Proxy Wars

Nations sometimes find it advantageous to let others do their fighting and will, therefore, fund and support local conflicts that they hope will weaken their adversaries. Sometimes these wars are symmetric, pitting two conventionally armed forces against one another, and other times they are asymmetric. Asymmetric proxy wars, the most recent and prominent being the Second Lebanon War between Israel and Hezbollah in July 2006, combine elements of guerrilla warfare and the war on terror. On the face of it, it is asymmetric: a large conventional army sets its forces against a numerically inferior guerrilla force. Unlike ordinary guerrilla organizations, however, Hezbollah forces are armed with sophisticated weaponry that include surface-to-surface and surface-to-sea missiles, advanced anti-tank weapons, night vision, and communications equipment.

Proxy militias fighting at the behest of nation-states, in this case Iran and Syria, do not have the same kind of political agenda as CAR guerrilla groups. Hezbollah has no significant territorial claim against Israel. Rather, it often presents itself as the protector of Palestinian interests while serving the military and political interests of its benefactor states. Proxy wars are a significant development in asymmetric warfare. They superficially resemble CAR conflicts, with the weaker side claiming combatant status while fighting without uniforms, for example. On the other hand, they operate at the behest of a foreign state that supplies them with arms and munitions. In the case of Hezbollah, this severely undermines the nominally sovereign government where the proxy organization operates. For these reasons, Hezbollah is clearly not a party to a CAR conflict.

The threat that proxy wars will pose in the future may grow. The most fertile ground for proxy wars lies in failed or partially failed states that cannot maintain a monopoly over the use of armed force. The conflict in Iraq, which combines elements of an insurgency, a war of humanitarian intervention, and the global war on terror, may also find itself home to a proxy war if government and allied forces fail to exert control over the entire nation. Attacks in Mumbai, India, in November 2008 also combined terrorism, insurgency, and guerrilla warfare in what some saw as a proxy war by Pakistan to use Islamic groups to "weaken India as part of its strategy to return Kashmir to Pakistani sovereignty."[22] In some of these cases, unrestrained barbarism may be counterproductive, but this, again, depends upon who suffers harm and whether the stronger state seeks accommodation and compromise or destruction and dismemberment. Few would complain had Israel taken extreme measures against Hezbollah fighters and destroyed the organization. Hezbollah, however, fought with the support of the local Shiite population making it impossible to take harsh measures without significantly harming the civilian population. The desire for accommodation with the civilian population precludes unrestrained barbarism.

Each type of asymmetric conflict presents a different challenge. CAR conflicts require greater restraint to preserve the possibility of peace. Conflicts involving international terrorism and humanitarian intervention, on the other hand, tend to have urgent short-term goals and so are less prone to settlement. In each case, the perpetrator has no interest in anything its stronger adversary can offer. With no political horizon, unconventional practices of war may prove less threatening to the final peace and, under some conditions, serve to facilitate it. Proxy guerrilla wars and CAR conflicts are, on the other hand, the continuation of politics by violent means. While no participant can ignore the prospect of settlement, lack of reciprocity between the sides will make torture, assassination and blackmail very tempting. In each of these arenas, moral dilemmas, and no few paradoxes, abound.

DILEMMAS AND PARADOXES OF ASYMMETRIC CONFLICT

Moral puzzles, paradoxes, and dilemmas dog war as men and women search for ways to explain, justify, and defend the need to take the lives of others. The tension between the means required to get the job done (that is, military necessity) and the human urge to limit the carnage (humanitarianism) is at the root of our conflicting intuitions about the conduct of war. Chapter 2 presents a puzzle about the moral status of our enemies. During war, many like to think that the good face off against the bad. We are right, they are wrong. We are victims; they are aggressors. Once on the battlefield, however, adversaries often find great confusion. One's enemies, they discover, are not always so bad, but more or less just like oneself, conscripted or enlisting to fight political battles or restore the tarnished honor of their leaders or nation. Yet each side remains wary of its armed enemy; after all, they are out to kill each other. Are they foes or brothers in arms? This question is endemic to war but the modern conventions of war have largely settled it: foes are not friends, but moral equals entitled to similar rights and privileges. Asymmetric war, on the other hand, upsets this tradition and criminalizes adversaries. This affects the conventions of war in very important ways and undermines a great many rights that prisoners of war usually enjoy. Without some element of moral equality, adversaries find it much easier to torture, assassinate, and blackmail their enemies.

An array of paradoxes and dilemmas in war confound us constantly. Some paradoxes make a perfectly reasonable claim but lead to an outcome that seems wholly unreasonable and often counterintuitive. A moral paradox of this kind may call for what seems like bad or evil behavior with the claim that it may bring good and morally commendable results. Reluctance to use nonlethal chemical weapons is paradoxical in this sense. There is an apparently illogical preference for conventional, high-explosive weapons that cause greater harm than nonlethal weapons cause that is difficult to explain. This paradox is the subject of Chapters 3 and 4. Chapter 3 opens Part I – Combatants in Asymmetric War – and lays out the incongruities and contradictions in our understanding of what constitutes excessive harm as adversaries battle. Often defined in terms of superfluous injury or unnecessary suffering, the criteria necessary to set the limits of acceptable suffering in war are elusive. In its discussion of appropriate weaponry for asymmetric conflict, Chapter 4 considers the advantages of nonlethal weapons. Quite possibly the key to waging war without causing excessive civilian casualties, use of nonlethal weapons remains, paradoxically enough, largely proscribed by law and custom.

Unlike paradoxes, moral dilemmas do not lead to counterintuitive outcomes, but to situations that are extraordinarily frustrating. A moral dilemma presents a person with mutually exclusive moral directions. Anyone who strives to respect a fetus's right to life and a mother's right to control her own body, cannot pursue both courses simultaneously. Something must give. Dilemmas such as these are not theoretical exercises, for at the end of the day one must make a decision and act. Inaction has consequences no less shattering than choosing one direction or another. This is particularly true of wartime dilemmas.

Dilemmas intertwine with paradoxes during armed conflict. Concerted action may take us out of a paradox. It is paradoxical, for example, that we think of all soldiers as morally equal when we are convinced that they, or at least their leaders, are nothing more than criminals. Yet soldiers are vulnerable to lethal force while their leaders enjoy protection. Killing combatants is acceptable; assassination is not (Chapter 5). Dilemmas arise when the principles underlying the paradoxes of war collide. The laws of war limit the way one side kills or treats its enemies out of a conviction that even enemies are entitled to respect and dignity. Soldiers lose their right to life but retain their dignity. Why does their dignity matter if their lives do not? This is a paradox. If we somehow resolve it by asserting the paramount importance of human dignity, we are left with a dilemma as we consider torture (Chapter 6). Here, protecting the lives of some (innocent civilians) collides with the dignity of others (suspected terrorists). This is a raw dilemma and perhaps a tragic choice: one cannot meet both moral imperatives and protect lives and dignity at the same time. One or the other must give way.

The immunity of civilians poses a similar puzzle. Soldiers are fair game, no matter how insignificant their role but politicians, journalists, and many civilians are not, no matter how significant their role. Nevertheless, this is changing and Part II – Noncombatants in

Asymmetric War – addresses the shifting status of noncombatants during asymmetric conflict. In principle, we generally have more compassion for enemy civilians than the soldiers they support. Caught up in the machinations of politicians, the civilian population is unthreatening and deserves protection as long as civilians sit on the sidelines while armies fight it out. In reality, however, civilians are not always so innocent. Enemy civilians do not sit quietly on the sidelines. Instead, they often take an active interest in the goings-on while providing succor to their soldiers who are fighting to kill. Yet, the laws of war make it difficult to harm any civilian even as he or she makes a significant contribution to the practice of war. Are at least some civilians legitimate targets, given their growing contribution? The question is particularly pressing in asymmetric wars where there are few unambiguous military targets to begin with. This question, Who do you bomb when there are no more military targets? is at the center of Chapter 7. In the Second Lebanon War, the bank of purely military targets evaporated within days if not hours. Then what? ask military commanders and political leaders. May an army go after civilian targets to bring a government or an army to its knees? If not, must it simply cease fighting and go home? Guerrilla organizations that resort to terrorism have much the opposite problem. They also look askance at the innocence of their enemy's civilians. Operationally, they ask, Who do we bomb when we can't reach military targets? Their answer, described in Chapter 8, is much the same as the answer their adversaries give, namely: civilians.

Although some forms of asymmetric war place civilians in the cross hairs, others strive desperately to save them. In this role, consider the complexities of acting altruistically and working hard to save citizens of foreign nations. We may demand, as the UN now does, that strong nations must aid the persecuted, but then find that those soldiers and citizens who must come to the rescue have no absolute obligation to do so. This often occurs as we ask about our duty to help those beyond our borders. Many believe that humanitarian intervention is obligatory if one nation can save the citizens of another from great harm and at little cost to itself. Little cost means that few soldiers will lose their lives. Fair enough, but may any person, whether citizen or conscript, be *compelled* to risk his life for others when his country's vital interests are *not* at stake? If the answer is no, then no nation can ever go to war on behalf of oppressed civilians in another nation. This is the paradox of humanitarian intervention (Chapter 9). Humanitarian intervention also poses a dilemma for any nation that may have vital interests at stake. As Western nations contemplate intervention in Sudan, for example, other countries like China face a much harder decision. For them, humanitarian intervention may jeopardize significant economic and security interests. When, if ever, do humanitarian imperatives override military or political necessity?

War is a trying and paradoxical business to be sure. Ultimately, I want to pick up the pieces left in the wake of torture, assassination, and blackmail. The discussion leading to the final chapter suggests that norms of war may be shifting in several important ways. First, the practice of war is changing. Fueled by military necessity, such practices as targeted killing, aggressive interrogation, nonlethal warfare, and attacks on civilians are slowly emerging as new norms of war making. Second, moral thinking about war is changing. I have noted how liability and responsibility significantly affect the way combatants and noncombatants treat one another. Fighting at close quarters, lack of uniforms, and the growing role for nonlethal weapons compel such fundamental wartime principles as noncombatant immunity, unnecessary suffering, and proportionality to accommodate the exigencies of asymmetric war. Nations are not simply adopting new practices but also confronting international proscriptions. At the head of this chapter, I asked how the United States and its allies might justify torture, assassination, and blackmail. Their answer is straightforward: torture, assassination and blackmail meet the demands of military necessity *and* humanitarianism.

Reconciling new modes of warfare with international law and, more importantly, with Western nations' sense of what is right and proper military conduct, demands a transparent, public debate. Defensible practices require just that: a defense. A successful defense is a twofold process that first requires convincing evidence that a weapon or tactic is necessary and effective and, second, that it meets humanitarian requirements. The two evaluations are closely linked and it is, therefore, not without cause that the Geneva Conventions understand the laws of armed conflict as "a compromise based on a balance between military necessity [that is, those measures essential to attain the goals of war] and the requirements of humanity."[23] The transition from torture to enhanced interrogation, from assassination to targeted killing, and from attacks on civilians to strikes on associated targets is not merely semantic but reflects an ongoing and serious effort to reconcile military necessity with humanitarian imperatives. The effort is not always successful, but nor does it necessarily fail. These efforts, together with the dilemmas and paradoxes of warfare they raise, inform the chapters to come.

2

Friends, Foes, or Brothers in Arms?

The Puzzle of Combatant Equality

World War I: The Western Front, 1915: Comrade, I did not want to kill you. ... But you were only an idea to me before, an abstraction that lived in my mind and called forth its appropriate response ... . I thought of your hand-grenades, of your bayonet, of your rifle; now I see your wife and your face and our fellowship. Forgive me, comrade. We always see it too late. Why do they never tell us that you are poor devils like us, that your mothers are just as anxious as ours, and that we have the same fear of death, and the same dying and the same agony – Forgive me, comrade; how could you be my enemy?

Erich Maria Remarque, *All Quiet on the Western Front*

Napoleonic Wars: Borodino, Russia, 1812: The French have destroyed my home and are coming to destroy Moscow; they have outraged and are outraging me at every moment. They are my enemies, they are all criminals to my way of thinking ... . They must be put to death.

Leo Tolstoy, *War and Peace*

Questions about the status of enemy soldiers are not the sole purview of asymmetric conflict (or of attitudes about the French). Remarque, speaking through Paul, a World War I German infantryman, presents the classic view of modern war: all soldiers are moral equals and brothers in arms. Each may use armed force to defend himself against attack from the other. Each may kill the other but neither is a criminal. All soldiers, therefore, enjoy the same rights and protections. They may not suffer from weapons that cause superfluous injury and unnecessary suffering. They may not suffer summary execution or torture as they fight their enemy. Upon capture, they enjoy the right to return home when the war is over.

Tolstoy, speaking through Prince Andre, a Russian officer fighting Napoleon in 1812, will have none of this. For him, combatant equality is a charade and illusion: if soldiers are enemies how can they be moral equals? If they are not moral equals then they are nothing but criminals who murder and plunder. They enjoy no right of incarceration but must, instead, be captured and "put to death." Enemy combatants are outlaws in the truest sense, that is, outside the law. Through Andre, Tolstoy pushes this idea to the extreme: if combatants are outside the law, then there is no real meaning to the idea of law-regulated war. Clearly, this is not the way we usually look at wars between nation-states. On the other hand, it is very close to the way many now look at asymmetric war.

While Tolstoy may offer us a glimpse of what we really think about our enemy during war, he does not press the issue with much enthusiasm. Perhaps he believes no one will listen to him. After all, the tradition of chivalry runs deep among the Russian nobility, and chivalry turns on mutual honor and respect among warriors. Andre may also realize that repudiating even the modest rules of war that look askance at categorizing one's enemy as a criminal can be disastrous if warring nations are similarly armed. War would degenerate into anarchy and untold destruction if soldiers could not surrender and expect decent treatment. And while in the end Andre defers to this point, he seriously considers the alternative view: what if war had no rules? What if armies took no prisoners? Would war then be so destructive that no one would fight? Tolstoy thought they might not, a point driven home, perhaps, by the success of nuclear deterrence a century and a half later. Yet while no one is anxious to fight a nuclear war, there are plenty who are more than willing to wage conventional war as destructively as possible. Here, the idea of combatant equality seems oddly out of place.

THE IDEA OF COMBATANT EQUALITY

One way to better understand the difference between Paul and Prince Andre is to turn to the oft-repeated distinction between *jus ad bellum* and *jus in bello*. The first asks, Is war just? The second, Is war fought justly? Paul assumes that the answer to the first question is beyond the ken of the average soldier and, in fact, irrelevant to his status on the battlefield. When Paul and his friends try to divine the cause of the war they are fighting, they first consider insults to national honor and then the amorphous interests of their leaders. In the end, they slowly realize that they have absolutely no idea what caused the war where most of them will lose their lives or what, exactly, makes those they fight their enemy. Andre, on the other hand, is far more perceptive. He has no doubt that Napoleon is the bald aggressor, blatantly violating Russian sovereignty in pursuit of fame and glory. The French soldier is tarred with the same brush of aggression as Napoleon. He is fighting for a loathsome cause and his actions are crimes of the worst and most rapacious kind. Like any heinous criminal, he only deserves death.

However compelling Andre's argument is, the rules of war have taken a different turn. Part humanitarian impulse and part mutual self-interest, the rules of war draw a firm distinction between the justice of war, which rarely concerns soldiers on the battlefield, and the way they wage war, which concerns them greatly. Ordinarily, soldiers are not responsible for participating in a war that is not their making, but they are accountable for fighting badly. But Tolstoy's paradox will not go away. If soldiers fight for their state and their state wages a criminal war of aggression, then how can it be that individual soldiers are not also criminals?

Consider first a definition of aggression. Andre thinks the French are criminals because they are blatant aggressors who invade Russia and "plunder other people's homes, issue false money, and, worse than all, kill my children and my father."[1] The intuitive idea is that a soldier who supports an aggressor nation is far more culpable than one who defends himself or his nation from aggression. Aggression assumes different forms ranging from border violations to genocide, but a middle ground understands aggression as a violation of sovereignty or an attack on vital interests. This includes invasion, bombardment, and blockades of ports or other uses of armed force to deprive "peoples of their right to self-determination, freedom and independence or to disrupt territorial integrity."[2]

The emphasis is on "deprive" and while states fighting in self-defense certainly invade, bombard, and blockade another nation's territory, they are not thereby aggressors. But assigning aggression based on the intention to deprive another people of its rights is extremely difficult. It often seems that every state is acting in self-defense and no state is acting criminally. Paul and his friends consider that possibility:

"It's queer," goes on Krupp, "we are here to protect our fatherland. And the French are over there to protect their fatherland. Now who's in the right?"

"Perhaps both," say I without believing it.

"Yes, well now," pursues Albert, and I see that he means to drive me into a corner, "but our professors and parsons and newspapers say that we are the only ones that are right, and let's hope so, but the French professors and parsons and newspapers say that the right is on their side, now what about that?"

"That I don't know," I say, "but whichever way it is, there is war all the same.[3]

If pressed, Paul and his friends would probably agree that self-defense is a good reason to fight a war and that blatant aggression of the kind that Andre describes is a bad reason. Nevertheless, not everyone striking first is the aggressor. In fact, there may be no aggressor at all. Nations sometimes go to war to settle disputes over conflicting rights. In these cases, war is the court of last resort. Hugo Grotius went as far as to compare some belligerents to litigants: they both may not be right, but each has the right to press his claim on the battlefield, just as litigants do in court.[4] In recent times, the Falklands/ Malvinas War between Argentina and Great Britain fits this mold. After all, claims Argentina, war was only necessary after unsuccessfully spending one hundred years trying to settle the dispute by less-violent means. While the UN recognized a breach of peace in the region and called on Argentina to withdraw its forces, it did not condemn the invasion as a breach of international peace and security nor call on member states to supply troops to enforce the peace and fight the Argentines (as it did following Iraq's invasion of Kuwait).[5] Although some belligerents are like criminals, many others are like litigants, and war allows each an opportunity to assert its right and triumph over its adversary. War, in this view, is a natural extension of diplomacy, politics, and negotiation. When these fail, nations may then choose force of arms.

In these cases, soldiers on each side retain their right of self-defense because there is room to think that both sides might be just. In other cases, belligerents are convinced their adversary is unjust but equally convinced that whatever injustice characterizes a state's behavior, it does not rub off on its soldiers. Paul Bäumer recognizes this immediately as he comforts the dying Frenchman. The correlation between a nation's guilt and its soldiers' guilt is, however, precisely what occupies Andre. If nations are guilty of aggression, suggests Andre, then so are their soldiers; if states act criminally, then their soldiers are criminals. However, this is not the way we usually think of enemy soldiers. A nation, Nazi Germany, for example, may be a criminal aggressor of the worst sort, yet the Allies accorded most German soldiers the right to self-defense and offered every courtesy when they fell captive. Whatever the sins of the nation, they do not taint its citizens or soldiers.

Why is this so? Perhaps soldiers cannot distinguish right from wrong. Unable to recognize that their state acts unjustly, soldiers are not guilty of criminal behavior. The laws of war, however, repudiate this sweeping assumption. While the law would exempt a German soldier from moral and criminal responsibility as he invaded Poland in 1939, it would excoriate the same soldier who shot civilians on orders from above. Why do we expect the offending soldier to exercise moral judgment in one case but not in the other? Is it, perhaps, that he can better understand the consequences of his own action in the latter case or that the moral lines are cut more clearly? Or, is it morally wrong to do either, but simply expedient to exempt soldiers from criminal behavior when they fight in unjust wars? The answer is a combination of moral principles and pragmatism. Combatant equality is, in many ways, a useful fiction in the conduct of conventional war that breaks down in asymmetric conflict.

Recognizing Justice in War

Can soldiers really know whether they are fighting in an unjust war? The assumption in conventional war is no. Soldiers, agents of the country they fight for, neither know nor need to know much of war, whether fighting for Hitler, Saddam Hussein, Roosevelt, or George W. Bush. Many are young and conscripted.[6] Wars, as Kurt Vonnegut so poignantly reminds us, are fought by babies: "When I saw those freshly shaved faces," cries an English colonel, "it was a shock. 'My God, my God –' I said to myself, 'It's the Children's Crusade.'"[7]

Like children, soldiers are exempted from criminal guilt based on their narrow grasp of world events, limited political participation, and susceptibility to political indoctrination. Among conscripts, coercion may also attenuate ascriptions of guilt. This is not to say that soldiers are not responsible for what they are doing. They intend to harm their enemies and gain from it. They are not, therefore, *materially* innocent. Yet, there is an air of *moral* innocence about them. So imagine a child who tries to harm us and it is understandable that we prefer to disable rather than annihilate our enemies without mercy, impose limits on the suffering they might endure, treat them well while in captivity, and repatriate them when the war has ended. These soldiers, babies that they are, go and fight in earnest, convinced of the justice of their cause, just as Paul describes.

This is often understandable, but not always. When nations are aggressors, there is no reason to assume that many soldiers cannot understand the nature of the aggression in which they are participating. The laws of war and our common moral sense hold individual soldiers accountable for violating "manifestly" unlawful orders. Manifestly unlawful orders are those that are so obviously wrong that any reasonable person will certainly know that they are immoral. When soldiers massacred noncombatants in places like My Lai, Vietnam, military courts held them responsible for killing civilians because they should have known that this was unacceptable. In these cases, a "black flag" flies over the actions of the soldiers. Any person "of ordinary sense and understanding" should be able to discern the moral imperative to disobey blatantly unlawful orders.[8] Those who do not must face the consequences.

If this conclusion holds, then there is no reason to assume that black flags do not also fly over war itself. Wars that blatantly violate the territorial integrity of another nation (other than wars of humanitarian intervention) or subjugate a peace-loving people should trigger the same response as a manifestly unlawful order. In both, soldiers and their commanders can turn to a plethora of excuses, justifications, and rationalizations to explain their decision to obey orders and wage war. Nevertheless, we hold soldiers responsible for their actions during war. Otherwise, the rules of war would have no validity whatsoever. The same is true of the rules that govern going to war. If the idea of an unjust or unlawful war is cogent, then common soldiers must take stock of their actions. When war exceeds what persons of ordinary sense and understanding know to be lawful, they should refuse to fight and be held accountable if they act otherwise, just as if they obeyed a similarly unlawful order.

Moral arguments that appeal to their presumed innocence to excuse soldiers from fighting in a manifestly unjust war seem weak. If soldiers have the wherewithal to recognize manifestly unlawful orders about *how* to fight, then they should also know *when* to fight. While we hold common soldiers accountable for their actions in war, we rarely, if ever, demand they judge the justice of the war they are called upon to fight. Although it is difficult to justify this discrepancy morally, conventional warfare offers solid, pragmatic reasons to avoid holding soldiers responsible for the war they support.

Combatant Equality: Less Moral, More Pragmatic

Why make great efforts to release soldiers from moral responsibility when they come to kill us? Why not instead, as Andre demands, hold them directly responsible for their violent crimes against us? There are several answers. One reason for combatant equality speaks to the psychological need to regard one's enemy as a worthy moral opponent rather than a criminal or less than human. Traditional combatants often carry with them a warrior code that demands that they cast their adversaries as moral equals if they hope to maintain their own self-respect, dignity, and sanity as they kill others. "By setting standards of behavior for themselves, accepting certain restraints and even 'honoring their enemies,' writes Shannon E. French, "warriors can create a lifeline that will allow them to pull themselves out of the hell of war and integrate themselves into their society ... . The code is a kind of moral and psychological armor that protects the warrior from becoming a monster in his or her own eyes."[9] French's hypothesis turns the focus inward. The soldier is less concerned with what happens to his enemy and more concerned with what happens to his self-image. This is an important insight in light of the barbarism that often characterizes asymmetric war. "Forget about what we are doing to them, look at what we are doing to ourselves," is a common refrain among soldiers and the citizenry.

Enlightened self-interest resonates during conventional war. When the sides are equally armed and capable of returning measure for measure, it makes good sense to reach agreements based on reciprocity. Just as soldiers fear certain forms of death or treatment at the hands of their enemies, they also fear a war that will never let them return home when it is over. Neither side has any incentive to fight in a way that will sap morale and deny soldiers the option of surrender when their situation is hopeless. While Tolstoy hoped that war fought to the extreme and without the option of surrender would deter soldiers from fighting in any but the most necessary military campaigns, few are willing to give Tolstoy much credence. Instead, mutual self-interest and fear offer good reasons to retain the idea of combatant equality.

Protected by the aura of equality, soldiers know they enjoy certain protections. These protections – the right to surrender, freedom from torture, and benefits of POW status – benefit soldiers on each side. The rules of war cast a net of combatant equality over soldiers on both sides, allowing each to protect its own from unnecessary harm and to instill the morale and courage they need to fight. Soldiers may not fight with much enthusiasm if they fear torture. This provides a powerful incentive to comply. Vague humanitarian interests aside, states care little for the welfare of their enemy's soldiers. But if protecting one's enemies preserves the lives and dignity of one's own, there is a strong incentive to accept combatant equality. At the same time, combatant equality serves to instill obedience and discipline. "If soldiers were liable to legal prosecution for participating in an unjust war," observes Yitzhak Benbaji, "many of them would not immediately follow the orders delivered by the political leadership." Preoccupied instead with figuring out whether their cause is just, they "won't be able to efficiently fight a just war, form a credible deterrent threat or wage a just preemptive attack."[10] Alternatively, combatants who fear they are fighting an unjust war may abandon all restraint knowing they may suffer prosecution no matter how fairly they fight.[11]

Combatant equality, part moral imperative and part mutual self-interest, holds up well in conventional warfare where each side is motivated to bestow its enemy with a degree of moral innocence. Otherwise, each side puts its own soldiers at risk. In asymmetric warfare, however, reciprocity breaks down and when it does, combatant equality is no longer useful. Suddenly, belligerents now hold one another morally responsible. Cries of just cause are endemic, particularly in wars of national liberation against colonial or occupying powers, and wars of humanitarian intervention against rogue, genocidal regimes. Creeping criminalization characterizes the rules of armed conflict. Soldiers on the wrong side of occupation, aggression, terrorism, and genocide face accusations of criminality before they set foot on the battlefield. Here, Andre's accusation of criminal behavior returns with force as belligerents cast aside those conventions of war respecting equality, and target soldiers and enemy civilians alike.

COMBATANT (IN)EQUALITY IN ASYMMETRIC WAR

When war is no longer symmetric and lacks constraints born of mutual fear, loathing for one's enemy resurfaces with a vengeance. Instead of combatant equality, moral and criminal guilt, long banished from conventional warfare, returns to infuse many of the tactics characteristic of asymmetric warfare. As combatant equality disappears, a new question arises. Rather than ask, "How are combatants equal?" we now ask, "How are combatants unequal?" Rather than assume that all combatants enjoy the same rights and privileges, we now assume they merit different rights, privileges, and treatment at the hands of their enemies, depending upon their moral responsibility and the level of threat they pose. The least innocent are the most vulnerable to harm at the hands of their enemies.

Combatant inequality and lack of moral innocence underlie the logic that drives rendition to justice, trial, long-term detention, and execution of combatants long after conventional armies successfully banned these practices from the battlefield. Assassination, for example, is suddenly rearing its head only one hundred and fifty years after Francis Lieber declared it an outrage abhorred by modern law. Condemnation of assassination draws heavily on the moral equality of soldiers. Unless soldiers are, in some sense, criminals, there is no cause to hunt them down and kill them. Without combatant equality, however, there is no reason to be so skittish about assassination, rendition, or detention. Working our way through a justification or condemnation of each of these practices requires some understanding of who combatants are and what they do during armed conflict. Guerrillas fighting a war of national liberation or a proxy war, for example, maintain a firm measure of moral equality that international terrorists or soldiers defending a genocidal regime do not. Terrorists with knowledge of "ticking bombs" are prime candidates for rendition and interrogation. Others without such knowledge are not.

In addition to engaging a wide variety of combatants, asymmetric war must contend with civilian combatants. While many civilians who take no part in a conflict retain their immunity, others lose it when they take an active or direct role in the fighting. In between are civilians who fight "indirectly." They retain but partial immunity. As a result, civilians who enjoy complete immunity in conventional war find themselves increasingly vulnerable in asymmetric warfare because their enemies hold some of them responsible for abetting and participating in hostile action. Adding to this confusion is the inability to clearly distinguish among the many participants because most fight without uniforms.

Distinguishing among combatants, civilian combatants, and noncombatants, assigning responsibility for the threat each poses, and determining each participant's vulnerability are the hardest questions in asymmetric warfare. Because many participants fight without uniforms, it is exceedingly difficult to assess combatant equality or know who is vulnerable to lethal harm, who enjoys combatant rights, who enjoys civilian protections, and who among the vast majority of remaining actors enjoys some of each. Unlike conventional war, asymmetric war boasts of a large population of participants who are neither combatants nor civilians as traditionally defined.

The Status of Modern Combatants:
Who's Who on the Battlefield?

There is colossal confusion as the once hallowed distinction between combatants and noncombatants disintegrates during asymmetric warfare. The following statements are typical:

In the case of Afghanistan, the status of two groups needs to be considered, the Taliban and members of al-Qaeda. In the case of Iraq, there are four such groups: members of the Iraqi armed forces, Iraqis who took up arms to oppose the occupation, foreigners who entered Iraq in order to fight against the coalition, and Iraqis suspected of involvement in "ordinary" criminal activities.

And

Is a person who plans attacks carried out by others taking a direct part in the fighting? What about a person who relays information? What about a person who funds a particular operation? How can you tell whether an alleged planner is engaged in planning or whether he is having a meal with his family?[12]

The first statement, broadly construed, describes combatants; the second, perhaps, noncombatants. These descriptions are far from what one finds in any conventional war. There, the distinction between combatants and noncombatants turns on the simple notion of bearing arms, wearing uniforms, belonging to a military organization, and abiding by the rules of war. These conditions, spelled out clearly in Article 4 of the 3rd 1949 Geneva Convention, define combatant status. While Protocol I to the Geneva Conventions (1977) kept this framework, it made room for a significant exception that allows guerrillas to shed their uniforms when they fight an army of occupation. This single change has profound ramifications for combatant equality and criminalization in asymmetric warfare.

Combatant Equality and the Disappearance of Uniforms

Combatants are obliged to distinguish themselves from the civilian population ... . Recognizing, however, that there are situations in armed conflicts where, owing to the nature of the hostilities an armed combatant cannot so distinguish himself, he shall retain his status as a combatant, provided that, in such situations, he carries his arms openly ... during each military engagement.[13]

This exception, so antithetical to the established norms of armed conflict, has since become the rule. Consider these descriptions from recent conflicts:

- The first Marine to be killed in action died at the hands of an Iraqi dressed in civilian clothes who fired from a pickup truck, not a tank.[14]
- Hamas is adopting a strategy of disappearance: If it wants to, it will clash with the army, in uniform and with weapons. Yet, if it so desires, it can also shed its uniforms, enter houses and pull out the weapons from the cache only once it discovers a military force's weakness.[15]

- "For a guy fighting in Eyta a-Sha'ab, Lebanon, 'withdrawal' means going home, putting your AK-47 under the bed and changing your clothes."[16]
- "Fixed launching positions ... had been built mostly in the orchards of local farmers, who were paid for their assistance by Hezbollah .... The farmers who operated the systems received their instructions by mobile phones.[17]

Lack of uniforms raises the question of combatant equality directly. What is the status of an Iraqi, Hamas, or Hezbollah militant? Is he a combatant and, if so, to what rights is he entitled? If he is captured, what do his captors do with him? How does the fact a participant is also a sometime terrorist affect his status? One answer comes from Protocol I: the Hamas militant is party to a CAR conflict fighting for national self-determination against an occupying power and a combatant entitled to combatant privileges. If he commits acts of terrorism, he is also a war criminal. Nevertheless, he is a combatant first and a war criminal second. However, this is not the way some nations view Hamas, Hezbollah, or the Taliban. Rather, these militants are *never* combatants, but rather are unlawful combatants or criminals from the start. Spurning Protocol I and relying solely on the 1949 Geneva Conventions, the United States defines an unlawful combatant as "a person who has engaged in hostilities ... who is not a lawful enemy combatant (including a person who is part of the Taliban, al-Qaida, or associated forces)."[18] For the United States, *only* Article 4 of the Third Geneva Convention (1949) defines a lawful combatant and demands that he or she wear a uniform, belong to a military organization, and abide by international law. This brings us back to Andre and Paul: are parties to the weaker side criminals or honorable foes? To address this question, it is first useful to understand the rationale behind the exception allowing some guerrillas to fight without uniforms and further understand that it applies only to CAR conflicts, not necessarily to international terror, wars of humanitarian intervention, or proxy guerrilla organizations.

Shedding Uniforms in Asymmetric Warfare

In conventional wars, uniforms mark two distinct classes of actors. Those wearing uniforms are combatants, vulnerable to direct harm;

those not wearing uniforms are noncombatants and protected from direct harm. Combatants, therefore, may not aim at or specifically target noncombatants. Uniforms allow armies to identify one another, disable combatants, and protect, to the extent possible, everyone else. Without uniforms, the safety of noncombatants is precarious. Upsetting this balance, Protocol I makes a provision for guerrillas who might not be able to wear a uniform in some cases. In occupied territory, for example, it would be quite difficult for guerrillas to organize, train, collect intelligence, and mount an attack if they were readily visible to occupying forces. Requiring a uniform effectively denies them any chance of success in a war of national liberation.[19] A "fighting chance" is integral to the just conduct of asymmetric war:

Surprise tactics, ambushes, sabotage, [or] street fighting take the place of war conducted in open country and confrontations between comparable military units. In such procedures, the visible carrying of arms and distinguishing signs may ... be incompatible with the practicalities of the action (for example, if the guerrilla fighters use the population for support or are intermingled with it). Because of this, refusing to allow specific procedures would be to refuse guerrilla warfare. *In order to remain objective and credible, humanitarian law must allow every party an equal chance in combat. If a norm of this body of law is incompatible with this principle and makes it impossible from the outset for one of the parties to have any prospect of victory, it is better not to draft such a norm at all.*[20]

This is an astonishing observation. Here, Charles Chaumont, whose opinion is appended to the Geneva Convention commentary, is making an extraordinary argument: when necessary, groups representing oppressed nations have the right to press their (presumably) just claims by force of arms. Humanitarian law, long considered a mechanism that restricts armed conflict, cannot impede their ability to fight. In other words, oppressed groups as well as nations fighting the tyranny of a rogue state deserve a reasonable fighting chance when diplomacy fails. There are two reasons to support a right to a fighting chance. First, a fighting chance is integral to the idea of just cause. It makes little sense to acknowledge one group's right to fight oppression or another's right to intervene in the affairs of a repressive regime and then use the law of armed conflict to deny either group the means to do so. Second, and perhaps more practically, any state or nonstate party denied a fighting chance by the conventions of war has little reason whatsoever to support humanitarian norms of conduct.

Nevertheless, hard questions about criminality arise when guerrillas condone terrorism (Chapter 7). Do they, too, deserve a fighting chance? Some do because not all nonstate combatants are terrorists. Proxy guerrilla organizations using sophisticated weapons against military targets may harm civilians but cause damage that is only "collateral" and indirect. Many, but not all, Hezbollah attacks on Israeli civilians in 2006, for example, were proximate to military targets. For this reason, many nations, including those in the European Union (EU), accept it as a guerrilla organization whose fighters enjoy combatant equality rather than as a terrorist group whose members are nothing but criminals.[21] Even CAR guerrilla organizations that accept terrorism, the Palestinian Fatah, for example, garner firm respect for their right to a fighting chance. Terrorism is an integral part of their guerrilla strategy. The international community knows it, expects it, and is still willing to extend combatant equality to guerrillas fighting for national self-determination. Fear that emerging conventions extend tacit recognition to terrorists was one reason the United States backed out of Protocol I. As I will elaborate in Chapter 7, the concern was not without foundation. Tacit support for terrorism has long drawn upon the responsibility of its victims by arguing that certain groups of noncombatants are as vulnerable as uniformed, armed soldiers. These not only include political leaders, but also those who sustain military efforts with financial and logistical support. This new elasticity pushes the boundaries of combatant vulnerability and appeals to both sides in an asymmetric war. The result is an entirely new definition of combatant and noncombatant that replaces uniforms and formal affiliation with an individual's real-time behavior.

Defining combatants and noncombatants in asymmetric conflict
Without uniforms and other clear signs of affiliation, a person's participation in the conflict becomes the defining feature of combatancy. Unfortunately, the distinction between participants and nonparticipants is nowhere as clear as the traditional distinction between combatant and noncombatant. As Figure 2.1 shows, the latter is dichotomous while the former maps onto a continuous scale. While

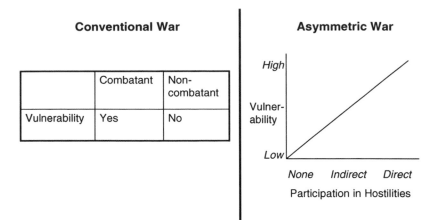

FIGURE 2.1 Combatancy and vulnerability in war.

the left side allows a clear distinction, the right side of the diagram makes it difficult to see where soldiering ends and civilian activity begins.

The left side of the figure depicts the traditional dichotomy: one is either a combatant or noncombatant. Combatants carried arms and served in the army; noncombatants – civilians, wounded soldiers and POWs – did not. In between were isolated grey areas that might include civilians who worked in military installations. They were vulnerable to direct harm, but only when they were present in a military installation (like an arms factory). Outside, they were protected civilians. Questions also arose about civilian leaders, rabble-rousing journalists, and teachers who brainwashed their pupils. Their contribution was significant, but since each side enjoyed their services equally, they remained protected. No side would willingly place its leaders at risk or undermine the role that journalists and teachers play of instilling citizens with the fortitude to make great sacrifices for their country.

In asymmetric wars, there are no longer two dichotomous groups. Instead, there are only participants: actors who play more or less important roles, whether they carry a gun, wear a uniform, hack computer systems from afar, work under contract to the military, or directly or indirectly support armed conflict. There are neither firm criteria for defining direct participation nor any concise list about who falls where along the continuum.

The traditional definition of combatancy depends largely on formal affiliation. Participants in asymmetric conflict, however, eschew the telltale signs of affiliation and thereby make the task of determining other criteria for combatant status all the more urgent. These criteria are functional and focus upon what a person actually does during war rather than upon his or her membership in a particular organization. To this end, the International Committee of the Red Cross (ICRC) sought a difference between war "sustaining" activities and simply support for the war effort. Without this distinction, "every civilian somehow contributing to the war effort could ultimately be regarded as directly participating in hostilities, from a housewife collecting tin cans for the metal industry and a farmer growing crops, to a nurse at a maternity ward who could be said to be raising future soldiers."[22]

What separates war-sustaining activities from support for the general war effort? One suggestion distinguishes "activities that were intended to actually cause harm, from activities that merely built up the capacity to do so." Soldiering is an example of the former, while working in the proverbial arms factory is an example of the latter.[23] Another attempt comes from the discussion in Protocol I: "Direct participation in hostilities implies a direct causal relationship between the activity engaged in and the harm done to the enemy at the time and the place where the activity takes place."[24] This is not far from Gordon Graham's assessment of combatancy in conventional war: "Combatants are those people the purpose of whose activity is to contribute to the threat; noncombatants are those people who do not actively contribute in this sense, although they may constitute part of the relevant causal chain."[25] Graham's suggestion is conceptually useful, but uniforms do the hard work of distinction in the field.

Without uniforms, functional or causal criteria are extremely difficult to apply in practice. While it might be obvious that a civilian firing a gun or operating a missile is as vulnerable as any uniformed combatant, his status is less clear when he goes home, puts the gun under his bed, and goes out to milk the cows. At the same time, there is a vast support network that draws directly from the civilian population whose backing is critical when guerrilla organizations go to war. These "associated" targets – financial, welfare, and communications organizations – are protected by noncombatant immunity in conventional wars because their employees do not belong to the military.

Once we disregard formal affiliation, however, we are left to ask what these people actually do. When we do, it becomes clear that their activities can sustain armed conflict in a most fundamental way. They are, in other words, civilian combatants. This leaves conventional state powers with the task of defining the parameters of direct and indirect participation so they might disable the civilian combatants who pose a risk, while protecting the civilian combatants who do not.

Direct and Indirect Participation in Asymmetric Conflict

To flesh out the idea of participation, it is useful to look at just who state actors see as they peer over the ramparts. U.S. counterinsurgency manuals list several kinds of participants:

- The "leaders and combatants";
- The "political cadre" or "militants of the party," who "assess grievances in local areas and carry out activities that satisfy them;
- "auxiliaries or "active sympathizers" who run safe houses, store weapons, provide passive intelligence, give early warnings of attacks, and provide funding;
- The "mass base" or "supporting populace," that often leads "clandestine lives for the insurgent movement."[26]

Drawing on a number of different sources, an Israeli Court tried to draw a line between *direct* participation – transporting militants, operating weapons, or supervising their operation – and *indirect* participation – selling food or medicine to combatants, providing strategic analysis, logistical support, or monetary aid, and/or distributing propaganda.[27] A working group for the Red Cross adds civilians who aid computer network attacks on enemy infrastructures to the list of those taking a direct part in hostilities. Here there is also room to consider the role of civilian employees of defense contractors who operate weapons systems for foreign or local military organizations.[28] Civilians by affiliation, all are ready to take an active part when called upon.

What is one to make of these lists? Are all those taking a direct part in the hostilities equal in status to uniformed combatants? Or, are some akin to criminals undeserving of combatant rights while others, those taking an indirect part in the conflict, more deserving of protection than harm?

Lists like these have several implications. First, they allow us to evaluate the criteria of direct and indirect participation while discerning certain limitations. Function is important but so is the magnitude of a person's contribution. A person donating a significant sum of money will certainly have a greater effect on the war effort and pose a greater threat to the enemy than someone giving a small sum. The same is true of those providing transportation, supervision, and strategic analysis. Some support is marginal while some provides significant military benefits. At the same time, any consideration of function *and* magnitude renders the categories that define direct and indirect participation both arbitrary and fluid. Providing a good deal of logistical support (indirect participation according to the Israeli list) may sustain the war far more than transporting a single foot soldier to the front (a criterion of direct participation).

Second, any scale of direct and indirect participation has significant ramifications for the idea of vulnerability. In Figure 2.1, both axes are continuous. Thinking about function and magnitude yields a participant a place on the participation scale. But what of his vulnerability? What protection do various participants enjoy? In conventional war, rights are fairly well defined. Noncombatants enjoy immunity from all forms of direct harm and from disproportionate indirect (or collateral) harm. Harm includes death, injury, and/or destruction of property. Combatants are not immune from harm but enjoy freedom from torture, assassination, and unnecessary suffering. How do these protections correspond to different types of participation?

While this question has prompted little discussion, it seems clear that vulnerability increases and protection decreases the higher a person's participation "score." Those near the top of the American list – leaders and combatants – resemble uniformed soldiers who may be killed on sight. Unlike affiliation, the criterion of participation makes no distinction between political and military leaders. Those lower down the list, political cadres and auxiliaries, are direct participants but fall short of being full-time armed combatants. If the impact of their efforts falls significantly short of those of combatants and leaders, then their vulnerability drops accordingly. Practically, this might require conventional forces to use less than lethal force to disable and/or arrest these participants.[29] More troubling are those whose participation is indirect. There is a fine line between civilians who support the war effort and those who indirectly sustain hostilities. What protection do they enjoy? On one hand they have not participated to a sufficient degree to merit direct, intentional harm. On the other hand, their role is not irrelevant and their enemies have a keen interest to disable them. Disabling indirect participants may take one of two forms. First, they are subject to direct but *nonlethal* harm. Nonlethal harm may be physical. That is, indirect participants may find themselves targeted with nonlethal weaponry (Chapter 4). Alternatively, nonlethal harm may aim at their rights and freedom. Apart from arrest and trial, this may include dislocation and expulsion, restriction of movement (siege and curfew), blackmail, and destruction of property. Second, indirect participants may be subject to greater levels of collateral harm. If they get too close to the fighting they may suffer collateral harm as the stronger side seeks to destroy militarily useful targets.

Finally, there is room to ask about coercion. Earlier, I assumed that all civilians "are ready to take a part when called upon." Is this always true? If not, how can parties to an armed conflict know the intention of civilian combatants? The answer, unfortunately, is that they cannot. At best, they judge behavior, and aggressive, threatening behavior merits a disabling response of the varying degrees just described. Nevertheless, there is room to consider the mitigating effects of coercion when civilian combatants fall prisoner. If guerrillas resort to intimidation, one would expect them to try to bully marginally affiliated indirect participants rather than the more ideologically committed direct participants or combatants. Subject to less than lethal force, however, indirect participants are more likely to be captured than killed once they take the field. Once in captivity, a captor can weigh claims of coercion as he or she considers whether to release or incarcerate a civilian who took an indirect role in the conflict.

Direct and Indirect Participation: The Symmetry of Asymmetric Conflict

It cannot go without notice that the principle of participation, rather than affiliation, serves guerrilla organizations just as it serves conventional armed forces. Nonstate actors look at the other side and see civilians taking a direct or indirect part in the hostilities by transporting soldiers, providing medicine and money, and offering logistical support and strategic analyses. Looking further, they may see computer technicians who direct computer network attacks, individuals working for private military organizations, and civilians working for defense contractors. As they assess their adversaries, nonstate actors must also ascribe a level of threat and responsibility to their enemies that their enemies ascribe to them. This offers guerrillas the same choice of targets and may allow them to shed the image of cold-blooded killers of innocent people if they choose their targets based on their participation and contribution to the war effort.

Many of the categories that the parties to an asymmetric conflict utilize will overlap. As a result, numerous actors who thought they were civilian noncombatants will find themselves vulnerable to harm as civilian combatants. None of these actors, whether a direct or indirect participant, is necessarily equal to the other. Each civilian combatant performs a different role, each enjoys certain rights, and each is subject to various and different kinds of harm. Each stands or falls as a measure of his or her own participation. Without uniforms, formal roles are difficult to determine. It is easier and more useful, then, to try to evaluate a participant's vulnerability by fine-tuning the harm he may suffer at the hands of an enemy. The greater one's level of participation, regardless of his or her formal affiliation with a military organization, the greater their vulnerability to lethal harm. The emphasis on personal responsibility marks a significant change in the conduct of asymmetric conflict. In conventional war, all soldiers, regardless of their actual function, are equally vulnerable and equally innocent. None is called to account for his behavior as long as he observes the rules of war. Asymmetric war shifts the focus to an individual's behavior and adjusts its response to a person's responsibility for the threat he or she poses. This principle guides participants on both sides of the conflict. Nevertheless, state actors, unlike their counterparts, face many kinds of nonstate and rogue-state adversaries. As the state actor tries to apply its newfound criteria of participation, it finds that combatant equality will vary significantly from conflict to conflict.

ASSIGNING COMBATANT EQUALITY IN ASYMMETRIC WAR

As they size up their adversary, state actors will ask themselves who among their enemies deserves combatant equality. CAR conflicts of national liberation offer the most promising venue for

combatant equality. Just cause provides sufficient ground to accord
CAR guerrillas the right of self-defense while the international community's tacit acceptance of some forms of terrorism is sufficient to
belie claims of blatant criminality. More importantly, perhaps, there
are pragmatic reasons to extend combatant equality to these nonstate actors even if the state they are fighting remains convinced it
is undeserved. CAR conflicts, unlike international terrorism, strive
ultimately for a political settlement anchored in compromise and
postwar reconstruction. Each side has an incentive to eschew assign-
ments of personal responsibility and criminality and embrace combatant equality insofar as neither side practices war crimes. This
requires the stronger side to take a longer view of terrorism and not
rush to portray every instance of armed nonstate violence as an act
of terror. The weaker side has just the opposite agenda. It must rein
in the worst excesses of terrorism, limit its attacks to responsible parties, and stick to collateral damage (which may, paradoxically, be
more destructive than isolated acts of terror).[30]

No such principles constrain a nation-state's response to international terrorism. Here there is no room for combatant equality. There
are several ways to explain this. First, it may be that international
terrorists are not combatants of any kind, but simply criminals. One
is certainly tempted to see them this way. However, replacing the law
of armed conflict with the rules of law enforcement leads to some
strange outcomes. I will discuss this in detail in Chapter 5, but law
enforcement obligates its officers to make every attempt to arrest suspects, not kill them. Only an imminent and grievous threat to police
officers or bystanders can justify lethal force. This then creates a very
odd outcome if international terrorists (who, as criminals, must first
be arrested) enjoy greater rights than uniformed combatants whom
no one need ever arrest. On the contrary, uniformed combatants are
generally vulnerable to lethal force.

It seems then, that international terrorists should be considered
some sort of combatant. Assume for a moment that they are similar to
Andre's Frenchmen. They come to pillage, loot, murder, and destroy.
They are aggressors of the worst sort and, perhaps, only deserve execution. But when they are Napoleon's troops, there is the very strong
tendency to resist this conclusion. Napoleon's soldiers, after all, fight
for a state pursuing legitimate national interests. Their cause may not

be indisputably just, but it fits in with those that most nation-states agree are legitimate. In these circumstances, soldiers will not question orders. Moreover, reciprocity looms large and, ultimately, Napoleon is looking for political accommodation. If the Russians criminalize and execute the French, the French will certainly follow suit. No side has much to gain (and a lot to lose) by rejecting combatant equality and waging war to the death.

But the war on terror may be just that: a fight to the death. International terrorists can count none among them who aim solely to destroy military targets. Aggression of the worst sort, unmitigated by any nationalist agenda, belies any claim to just cause, while no prospect of a political settlement or response in kind offers any ground for extending combatant equality. The fight will be long, tedious and, most likely, to the death. It appears then, that international terrorists warrant some status that combines criminality with combatancy. This is the proper understanding of unlawful combatant. An unlawful combatant is not a war criminal. War criminals are wayward members of conventional armies or guerrilla groups fighting for national self-determination and include terrorists who belong to either. War criminals are combatants first and criminals second, and therefore vulnerable to lethal harm any time they fight or plan to fight. International terrorists, on the other hand, remain criminals. They deserve no recognition as combatants, but present such an overwhelming danger that they are often treated as combatants insofar as they are vulnerable to lethal harm whenever they pose a threat.

Proxy guerrilla wars present a different challenge to the idea of equality. Proxy guerrillas fighting without uniforms do so in violation of the spirit of the law. As a result, they may lose their equality when they shed their uniforms. While human rights organizations recognized the combatant equality of un-uniformed Hezbollah fighters in the Second Lebanon War, for example, the recognition is ill founded. Although the black letter of the law does not say so, the right to fight without a uniform only has force in situations, notably occupation, that make it impossible to fight in uniform at all. Proxy guerrilla organizations are not armies of national liberation nor, at least in the Second Lebanon War, are they fighting an occupying army. Rather they are a very clever and potentially useful strategic tool of nation-states to project power and protect national interests. There is no reason for proxy guerrillas to fight without uniforms. Once they don their uniforms, they deserve combatant equality assuming of course that the other conditions of lawful combatancy – affiliation with a military organization (rather than a gang of thieves) and respect for the laws of war – apply. If, however, proxy guerrillas continue to eschew uniforms, then they fight perfidiously and in gross violation of any Geneva Convention. These are the acts of war criminals, not combatant equals. This is true even when terrorism is not part of their repertoire.

Wars of humanitarian intervention pose the thorniest problem. The international community asserts the right to intervene when a sovereign state undertakes to exterminate a group of its own citizens. This kind of war only gains legitimacy when the weaker side behaves criminally. Just cause cannot reside with a government engaged in ethnic cleansing, genocide, or egregious human rights abuse. Nor can it reside with those that defend a criminal regime. Soldiers and governments of these types have lost their right to self-defense. On the other hand, babies rushing to take up arms against an invading force defend these criminal states too. Do they not deserve equality if captured? I think the answer is no. In spite of the fact that these soldiers look like ordinary combatants, fight with uniforms, belong to a military organization, and fight according to the rules of war, they do not merit combatant equality. Knowing they are fighting the international community should be sufficient to establish at least minimal awareness that their war is not one of self-defense but something far more odious. As such, soldiers fighting in defense of a genocidal regime would lose their status as combatants and find themselves denied the privileges of prisoners of war. This is a recent phenomenon. Prior to the UN's 2005 recognition of its right to protect persecuted individuals wherever they lived, the international community could only intervene when a state threatened international security. Threatening international security is not necessarily any more criminal than threatening the security of a nation. Although threatening international security may be an act of aggression that damns an aggressor and its troops, there is great ambiguity surrounding criteria of aggression. So much so, in fact, that the International Criminal Court remains unable to offer any firm definition of aggression.[31] There is no ambiguity, however, about war crimes. Soldiers and civilians supporting a criminal regime can have no rights as they fight. Reasonable men and women should be expected to understand this much.

Nevertheless, a hundred thousand Sudanese citizens took to the streets when their government threatened a Jihad to protest the UN's decision to send a military force to Darfur in 2004. Surely, Sudanese soldiers fighting the UN would have thought their war was just.[32] There are two ways to deal with Sudanese troops fighting the UN. The first speaks to a norm of international conduct that has yet to evolve, namely: attacking UN troops exercising the right-to-protect is a criminal act and cannot, by definition, ever be an act of self-defense. The international community has not adequately addressed the status of those fighting for criminal regimes. Alternatively, and although defending forces may not deserve combatant equality, intervening forces may choose to extend combatant rights. If the war goes well and soldiers fight lawfully (strictly according to the laws of war) and surrender, then it is easy to imagine that low-ranking soldiers would be free to join postwar reconstruction efforts. If, on the other hand, the war degenerates into an asymmetric conflict where the weaker side, faced with imminent defeat, embraces guerrilla warfare and terror, and the stronger side responds with torture and assassination as might easily occur in Sudan, then combatant equality will guide no side's conduct. Practice aside, the important moral point is that the weaker side *cannot* enjoy combatant equality in a war of humanitarian intervention. While equality defines the relationship between most nation-states, combatant inequality is the defining attribute of wars of humanitarian intervention. Humanitarian intervention is only justified when the weaker, rogue nation is so egregiously criminal that it is impossible to think their soldiers might somehow retain a measure of moral innocence. We need a coherent doctrine of combatant inequality to justify humanitarian intervention and we cannot justify humanitarian intervention without opening the door to very harsh treatment of belligerents who commit genocide or crimes against humanity.

Asymmetric war pushes combatant equality to the breaking point and it disappears entirely, in fact, in many forms of conflict. The problem begins with lack of uniforms and the widespread involvement of direct and indirect civilian participants. In all conflicts, there are actors who look like or act like conventional combatants. They bear arms, consider themselves full-time members of a guerrilla or other military organization, and enjoy the privileges of rank and affiliation. Of these, some behave criminally. These combatants – international terrorists and defenders of genocidal regimes – do not deserve equality. Combatants party to other conflicts – wars of national liberation and proxy wars – may deserve equality, but might not get it. In conflicts that do not present a political horizon characterized by compromise and postwar reconciliation or are so technologically unmatched that reciprocity breaks down completely – nonstate or rogue-state actors will not always receive combatant equality.

Direct and indirect participation that falls short of full-fledged combatancy presents a more intricate challenge. Lack of uniforms brings state armies to look closely at the function each actor plays and to adjust the means it chooses to disable its enemy accordingly. Not all combatants and participants are equal. The tasks they perform are wildly disparate, making each vulnerable to different types of harm commensurate with their level of involvement and responsibility. Once conventionally defined as noncombatants, they now lose their former protection as they participate directly or indirectly in armed conflict and find themselves the target of direct harm. Such harm may include death, bodily harm, destruction of property, restriction of movement, or curtailment of basic liberties.

The harm that combatants, quasi-combatants, part-time guerrillas, and direct and indirect participants face in war are the subject of the following chapters. Part I focuses on the dilemmas and paradoxes that face participants in asymmetric war, while Part II considers the harm that noncombatants confront. Combatants always face lethal and extreme harm, but in wars between nation-states, conventions constrain the severity of harm combatants endure. Most prominently, they may not endure superfluous injury or unnecessary suffering, attacks with chemical weapons, torture, or assassination. Asymmetric war is breaking these conventions down. When nations find they can develop and use certain weapons with impunity, are there still good reasons to avoid exploding bullets, blinding lasers, incendiary munitions, or chemical weapons?

PART I

COMBATANTS IN ASYMMETRIC WAR

The law of armed conflict (LOAC) and international humanitarian law (IHL) embrace different domains. LOAC focuses on the rights of combatants while IHL, a later phase in the development of the conventions governing the practice of war, addresses the rights of civilian noncombatants and soldiers who have fallen captive or wounded. To apply either set of law and custom cogently, it is first necessary to assign civilians and soldiers to one domain or another. As the previous chapter explains, this is no mean task. Uniformed combatants and uniformed guerrilla fighters fall squarely under the purview of LOAC while innocent and uninvolved civilians enjoy the protection of IHL. Civilian combatants, the other hand, straddle both categories. As they take an increasingly active role in war, they cannot claim complete immunity from their enemy's attempt to disable them. On the other hand, they are not always vulnerable to the same ravages of war that befall full-fledged combatants.

Full-fledged combatants, those fighting in uniform or, at the very least, continuously under arms, enjoy little quarter in battle. Nevertheless, the traditional conventions of war offer them some modicum of protection in prohibiting unnecessary and ghastly harm, torture, and execution. As a practical matter, these conventions led belligerents to exclude particular weapons from the battlefield, prohibit chemical and biological warfare, condemn torture, and avoid assassination. These measures were modest. To warrant prohibition, a weapon or practice must be both fearsome and of questionable military value. Poison gas could cause horrific wounds but also created conditions that made fighting unwieldy and put civilian populations at risk. Torture and assassination might slow an enemy but they also sowed fear and easily sapped morale among soldiers on both sides. In the final analysis, the number of banned weapons and practices was small and whatever tactical void they left was quickly filled by a myriad of armaments that were more useful and often no less terrible.

Asymmetric war, together with striking advances in modern technology, is making room for new weaponry while giving life to some old practices. This is particularly striking in the development of nonlethal weaponry that utilizes advancements in neuroscience and biochemistry. Until the advent of asymmetric war, nonlethal weaponry was an oxymoron. There was neither the need nor the technology to threaten a combatant with anything less than death. But as civilians take the field to either fight with or shield guerrillas, there is growing need to disable combatants and noncombatants as one while trying to hold down casualties. High explosive weapons, however smart or precision guided they are, can cause catastrophic harm in a battlefield environment strewn with combatants, civilian combatants, and noncombatants who are indistinguishable from one another. Nonlethal weapons, however, utilize sophisticated medical technology to incapacitate enemy soldiers and civilians. As they do, they recall the dread of weapons of old that drew on poison, disease, infection, and, indeed, black magic. Yielding to nonlethal weapons brings us to reconsider the limits of superfluous injury and unnecessary suffering that have long characterized conventional war. These dilemmas are the subject of Chapters 3 and 4.

Assassination and torture, on the other hand, are more straightforward. Soldiers die and suffer in war as a matter of course. But just as certain weapons seem beyond the pale, so are certain ways of killing and harming. Assassination is condemned because it is treacherous and does nothing but criminalize an honorable foe. But this is precisely how some forms of asymmetric conflict differ from conventional war. Fighting criminals, there is no reason to avoid assassination. Moreover, assassination has tangible benefits. Reborn as targeted killing it simply does what uniforms once did and allows a state power to properly identify and disable combatants who fight without uniform. The rehabilitation of assassination is described in Chapter 5. Torture, as discussed in Chapter 6, is more odious than assassination and defies rehabilitation. As state armies turn to enhanced interrogation to fight terrorism they find that the number of suspects who harbor crucial information is small, the information they uncover is not always reliable, and, notwithstanding the occasional intelligence-gathering success, the damage done to the moral standing of democratic nations is not easily reversed.

3

Shooting to Kill

The Paradox of Prohibited Weapons

> Parties to a conflict and members of their armed forces do not have an unlimited choice of methods and means of warfare.
>
> Article 35, Additional Protocol I

To fully understand why this is a paradox or at least something of a mystery, consider this story. A few weeks after a young recruit begins his military service he receives an assault rifle. Turning the rifle over, he notices the slot that secures the bayonet. But when he asks his sergeant when they will receive bayonets, the sergeant replies that bayonets violate the rules of war and would not be issued.

Technically, this is incorrect. There is no prohibition against standard issue bayonets. There is, however, a long-standing ban on bayonets with serrated edges. I will discuss the reasons for this in a moment, but for now, it is important to consider the entire episode from the young soldier's point of view. Reflecting on the bayonet ban he asks, Why are the methods of warfare limited? Why can't I use any means necessary to defeat an enemy who is trying to kill me? This question has puzzled people for the longest time. How do we answer it?

There is not one answer to this question but two. First, we avoid certain weapons because our moral intuitions tell us that some weapons are unnecessary to disable an armed adversary or simply inhuman. Appeals to unnecessary suffering and inhuman suffering are two very different but interrelated reasons for avoiding certain weapons. Some weapons cause superfluous suffering and are, therefore, unnecessary.

54

Others cause fearsome suffering and are thereby inhuman. Second, we avoid some weapons because the other side does. Simple self-interest and reciprocity dictate behavior. If an army faces terrifying retaliation in kind, it will avoid particular forms of warfare; if it does not face retaliation, then it is tempted to embrace any weapon regardless of the pain and suffering it brings to enemy combatants.

LIMITING KILLING IN WAR: MILITARY NECESSITY AND MORAL INTUITIONS

The rules of war guide and protect soldiers and their communities. Soldiers must be assured that they are acting justly and with their community's support as they set out to violate their most deeply seated moral principles and kill other human beings. Communities, in turn, arm their soldiers with rules as well as weapons to prevent anarchy. Imagine how quickly law and order might break down if citizens received rifles with no rules or instructions. No society can simply hand out weapons and say, Go fight or, Go defend your country. These rules tell them whom they can harm – soldiers and not civilians – and how they can harm. The "whom" I will take up in later chapters. The subject of this chapter is the "how."

The need to guide whom soldiers kill seems obvious, but why restrict the way they kill enemy soldiers? Why shouldn't soldiers use every means at their disposal to defend their country and, indeed, their very lives? In the middle of the nineteenth century, political leaders began to think about this question as they pondered one of the great technological innovations of the time: the rifle. With a rifled (that is, grooved) barrel it was possible to fire faster and more accurately than with old-style smooth-bore muskets. To increase fatality and injury, arms manufacturers during the U.S. Civil War developed a bullet that would explode inside a man's body a second and a quarter after impact.[1] If the idea makes us wince, it might be because there are, in fact, certain methods of killing other human beings that are inherently objectionable. But are there rational reasons behind this or just a moral aversion to harming people in certain ways?

In truth, there are both. For any number of reasons, many people have a moral aversion to harming or killing other human beings in certain ways. This is not always rational, but represents a deep-seated concern for human suffering and human dignity that many people harbor. No matter how cruel we may think we can treat other people, there is a point where we say, This is no way to treat a dog, much less a human being. However, this is just a gut feeling that defies any easy explanation. Why is killing by bacteria worse than killing by bullets? Why is it permissible to use a straight-edged bayonet but not one that is serrated? What is it about a bullet that enters the body and then explodes that bothers us more than an artillery shell exploding in a man's face? Is one way of killing or disabling really better or more humane than another?

At first glance, it seems obvious that some ways are worse than others. A serrated blade, like a barbed lance, not only disables an attacking soldier, but leaves a gaping wound when the blade or lance is extracted. Does this cause a particularly inhuman wound? Amid the horrors of war, this is a difficult question to answer. One would have to be able to compare the wound a barbed weapon causes with the injuries that other weapons cause and then assess how fearsome each wound is. Clearly, this is very subjective. Searching for more objective criteria of inhuman treatment, we need to ask a different question: Does the second act of wounding (pulling out a serrated blade) serve any purpose? Necessity provides a more objective criterion to assess a weapon. Here one tries to look beyond the mere pain and suffering a weapon causes, to ask about the harm that is necessary to disable an enemy soldier. This was the route diplomats and jurists chose in the mid-nineteenth century as these questions came to the fore.

As the U.S. Civil War ended, the nations of Europe enthusiastically adopted many of its military innovations in logistics, law, medicine, arms, and tactics. Nevertheless, some of these new technologies gave the Europeans pause, and they met in St. Petersburg in 1868 to limit the use of those weapons that made them, too, wince. Addressing the place of "explosive projectiles weighing less than 400 grams" (that is, bullets), the delegates declared:

- That the progress of civilization should have the effect of alleviating as much as possible the calamities of war;
- That the only legitimate object which States should endeavor to accomplish during war is to weaken the military forces of the enemy;

- That for this purpose it is sufficient to disable the greatest possible number of men;
- That this object would be exceeded by the employment of arms which uselessly aggravate the sufferings of disabled men, or render their death inevitable;
- That the employment of such arms would, therefore, be contrary to the laws of humanity.[2]

The St. Petersburg Declaration was a watershed event in the development of the conventions and norms of war. Its point-by-point progression shows how the delegates hoped to tie their aversion to certain weapons to an enlightened idea of humanity, dignity, and necessity. War, they first reasoned, was an act of extreme violence to attain a political goal: territory, allies, resources, and so on. Nations should not fight wars simply to serve the glory of God, annihilate an enemy, and rid him from the face of the earth (as many mistakenly assumed about wars of ancient times). Conceived in this way, the next step was obvious: nations might only pursue those means and methods that sufficiently cripple an army so that it is no longer a political or military threat. This means disabling (not necessarily killing) large numbers of men (that is, soldiers). Anything beyond this point was unnecessary, and the suffering it brought was superfluous and, therefore, cruel and inhuman.

Notice how a weapon is cruel and inhuman not because it causes fearful suffering, but because it causes *any* suffering without purpose. Ulysses S. Grant, Union commander during the Civil War, made the point clearly when he confronted the proliferation of exploding bullets. "When [soldiers] were hit and the ball exploded," observed Grant, "the wound was terrible. In these cases, a solid ball would have hit as well. *Their use is barbarous, because they produce increased suffering without any corresponding advantage to those using them.*"[3] Presumably, if increased suffering did have some corresponding advantage, then explosive bullets would not be so easy to condemn, however terrible the wounds they cause. Thus, we see that the international community is of two minds about the exact nature of the weapons it should ban. Either they are weapons that cause the kind of ghastly suffering we would never inflict on another human being *or* they cause suffering that adds nothing of military value, hitting a man who is already down and disabled. Here, there is no obvious reason to cause him greater suffering. When weapons cause terrible suffering, they violate the laws of humanity. When they cause unnecessary suffering, they violate the laws of war.

These sentiments guide international humanitarian law (IHL) today. As the citation opening this chapter testifies, nations may not use any weapon that comes to hand. In particular, they may not use any weapons that cause superfluous injury or unnecessary suffering. This is a basic principle of modern war and governs the suffering a combatant should have to endure. But what does it mean?

SUPERFLUOUS INJURY AND UNNECESSARY SUFFERING

"Unnecessary suffering" carries two distinct and interconnected interpretations. Emphasizing *unnecessary*, it highlights the superfluousness of certain weapons in particular situations. Emphasizing *suffering*, it highlights excessive human pain and misery that no person should endure in war however necessary or useful it may be. The limits of *unnecessary* suffering are relative. In some situations, nothing more than minimal force may be necessary to disable or dislodge an enemy; in other circumstances, an army may require great force and destruction to accomplish its goals. Depending upon the situation, the same weapon sometimes causes unnecessary suffering and other times it does not. The limits of unnecessary *suffering*, on the other hand, are absolute. A weapon that causes gruesome suffering is never permissible. Here, human conscience dictates just how far one may go and how much suffering one can inflict on an enemy. Where, exactly, do these limits lie?

Trying to flesh out the boundaries of permissible harm, the International Committee of the Red Cross (ICRC) warned belligerents about using weapons that intentionally cause:

(1) Specific disease, specific abnormal physiological state, specific abnormal psychological state, specific and permanent disability, or specific disfigurement, or

(2) Field mortality of more than 25% or hospital mortality of more than 5%, or

(3) Effects for which there is no "well recognized and proved treatment."[4]

By definition, a weapon that produces any of these effects causes superfluous injury and unnecessary suffering. Although the authors do not say so directly, each criterion suggests a different underlying principle. The first criterion speaks to humanity. There are certain wounds that intentionally inflict unspeakable suffering regardless of any military benefit they bring. Intentionality is important. Any weapon can cause disease, disability, or disfigurement, but the ICRC is concerned about weapons specifically designed for these purposes. The criterion is absolute: any kind of disease, disability, or disfigurement is unnecessary or *fearsome* suffering regardless of how effective it might be on the battlefield. This criterion of excessive harm is very close to that which governs the principle of proportionality.[5] Both principles restrain necessity. Although it might be necessary to disable or kill other combatants (or noncombatants), there is a point where the harm they suffer is excessive regardless of the benefit a military operation brings. In this vein, one may concede that explosive bullets are militarily helpful because they wound or kill more soldiers than ordinary bullets, but the price in human suffering for this advantage is just too great.

The second ICRC criterion speaks directly to the level of necessary suffering in war. Since the American Civil War and through subsequent twentieth-century wars, field mortality, that is, the percentage of soldiers who die immediately after being hit, has hovered around 20 percent. Hospital mortality, the percentage of soldiers who die of wounds, on the other hand, has improved significantly in the last century and in recent wars sits at 2.5 percent.[6] In both cases, these numbers point to the casualties necessary to reasonably wage war and secure victory. Casualties in excess of these figures are unnecessary. They exceed what nations historically require to conduct warfare and, therefore, cause superfluous suffering. Notice, however, that this normative argument is weak and speaks only to conventional war. There is no past war whose performance can dictate the norms of future, asymmetric wars. Increased use of nonlethal weapons, precision guided munitions, and, indeed, pinpoint assassination, for example, may bring these numbers down. At this point, however, there are insufficient data to draw any definitive conclusion about the necessary level of field and hospital mortality in future, asymmetric wars.

The last ICRC criterion calls on nations to avoid weapons that cause injuries for which there is no "well recognized and proved treatment."

This, too, echoes the norms of conventional war and reflects the deeply held view that soldiers deserve a fighting chance. Soldiers should have a reasonable chance to repel an attack and recover from the injuries they suffer. A weapon that inflicts untreatable wounds is fearsome, undoubtedly undermines morale, and denies soldiers the opportunity to recover from their wounds and return to battle. Commenting on the exceptional permission to fight without uniforms, I noted how humanitarian law could not deny the prospect of victory to either party from the outset. War, from this perspective, must be a fair contest; using weapons without a recognized and proved treatment denies some soldiers the option of a fair fight.[7] This may not concern the nation-state fighting international terrorism or a genocidal regime, but it may give it pause in a CAR conflict of national liberation or war against proxy guerrillas where both sides ultimately seek political accommodation.

Here reciprocity also creeps in. Warring parties shunning a fair fight from the beginning may care little for their opponent's honor or prospect of victory. "Fair" may be misleading. In reality, parties to an asymmetric war may care little for rules that hamstring their ability to destroy their enemies any way they can. If both sides have access to fearsome weapons, however, simple self-interest may compel the parties to forego them. The rules that bind combatants, in other words, draw heavily on reciprocity. If, on the other hand, only one side has access to certain weapons, the temptation to retain them will be very great.

Reciprocity in Conventional and Asymmetric War

However fearful or unnecessary a weapon may be, no side is going to give it up unless the other side does. Gaining international agreement to relinquish certain weapons (and prevent an expensive arms race) was Russia's primary reason for convening the conference in St. Petersburg. Reciprocity helps explain why nations ultimately agree to forego certain practices and why parties to asymmetric conflict often do not.

War is extraordinarily expensive. It empties treasuries, endangers civilians, devastates property, and takes immense numbers of lives. War often decimates the victors as well as the vanquished, so it is not without reason that nations will try to limit the costs they incur. Costs, however, are only part of the picture. People also find the likelihood of certain kinds of harm inhuman, fearsome, and intimidating. Soldiers do not want to go into battle facing the prospect of wounds that will not heal or having to endure torture if captured. That is, their own aversions come into play as they enter the battlefield. They do not want to suffer dishonorable treatment or abuse. Often, the best way to protect oneself is to protect one's enemy. Hence, one obvious reason for adopting rules about weapons is mutual self-interest.

Limiting the suffering in war often goes hand in hand with limiting the cost of war. Certainly, it makes good economic sense to ban weapons that only offer an insignificant military advantage. Quite often, however, banning a weapon confers a military advantage that both sides covet. Consider again explosive bullets. What Grant really meant is that a mutual ban on the bullets works to everyone's advantage. Certainly, it seems that if one side has a monopoly on a particular weapon, it would not readily relinquish it. Why give up a weapon that demoralizes enemy soldiers, inflicts wounds that require greater medical care and attention, forces quicker evacuation from the battlefield, and, ultimately, causes greater death and suffering than ordinary bullets? Monopoly is the key word. If both sides have access to explosive bullets, then everyone runs scared, thereby leaving each army to commit greater resources to treat and evacuate their wounded. Now, banning the weapon looks sensible. By prohibiting explosive bullets and similarly fearsome weapons, some measure of traditional military rationale is restored. Without dreading the terrifying injuries this ordnance causes, solders can go out and fight as they should.

Why Ban Weapons?

The foregoing discussion provides several different answers for our young conscript. Why do we need laws to limit the means of warfare armies may employ? First, laws prevent anarchy and offer the means to control and oversee those to whom we issue lethal weapons and send to war. Second, a community's moral intuitions about killing, dying, and respect for persons tell us so. Certain injuries are inherently repugnant. They violate the honor and respect we extend to an enemy, exceed the means necessary to disable an armed adversary, or cause inhuman suffering. Finally, combatants adopt rules limiting dreadful weapons because it is in their mutual interest to do so. Anything less exposes one's own to the very injuries they fear most. In conventional war, these three reasons reinforce one another. Combatant equality and respect for an adversary go hand in hand with necessity, shared norms about humanitarianism, and mutual self-interest. In asymmetric war, however, these reasons for limiting access to arms clash with one another. Combatant equality and mutual respect are not regular fixtures of the war on terror or wars of humanitarian intervention. Adversaries may share perceptions of intolerable and inhuman pain and suffering, but military necessity and lack of reciprocity may bring them to ignore the dictates of humanity.

The tension between these principles become clear as we consider the kinds of weapons nations actually ban. Which weapons cause unnecessary suffering on the battlefield? Which does the international community find it prudent to ban absolutely? Are there some weapons, currently banned, that now require reconsideration? In the remainder of this chapter, I want to search for the rationale behind the ban on several types of weapons. In the next chapter, I want to consider whether it might be prudent to lift the ban on nonlethal chemical and biological weapons.

BANNED WEAPONS TODAY

In spite of the weighty arguments that draw on military necessity and humanitarian concern for suffering, the list of banned weapons is very short. Lacking any firm criteria, public officials have successfully banned those weapons that generate sufficient fear among belligerents to remove them from the battlefield. These include explosive and hollow point bullets, explosive charges containing clear glass or other undetectable fragments (which surgeons cannot easily see when treating a wound), poison weapons, asphyxiating gas, serrated bayonets, barbed lances and blinding lasers. Each of these, and often for very different reasons, carries a loaded "wince" factor. But what is it, exactly, that bothers us about these weapons? Are they militarily unnecessary, exceptionally vicious and shocking or are they simply a way of war it makes good sense to ban if all sides agree? For discussion,

I have grouped these weapons into several groups. The first embraces bullets, barbs, and bayonets banned because they cause suffering beyond what is necessary to disable a combatant. Blinding lasers, comprising the second group, and banned before they hit the battle-field, present a different issue. They provoke repugnance because they cause dreadful and fearsome suffering. Weapons like these, as many observers often describe it, "shock the instincts of humanity."[8] This is not necessarily true of poison or poisoned weapons, the third group, whose prohibition has little to do with dreadful suffering and quite a lot to do with treachery, assassination, and perfidious means of warfare. Incendiary weapons, the final group of weapons discussed in this chapter are the exception proving the rule. They cause fear-some suffering of the worst kind and should be a candidate for an absolute prohibition. Nevertheless, they are militarily necessary and nations are reluctant to ban them. Chemical and biological weap-ons are another type of weapon that suggests still other, interrelated concerns. Most prominently, they cause ghastly suffering as weapons of mass destruction. Yet even rendered nonlethal, they raise hackles because they disable adversaries by undermining the human anat-omy in a most insidious way. Nonlethal weapons are the subject of the following chapter.

Serrated Bayonets, Hollow Point Bullets, and Barbed Lances

We overhaul the bayonets – that is to say, the ones that have a saw on the blunt edge. If the [French] catch a man with one of those he's killed on sight. In the next sector some of our men were found whose noses were cut off and their eyes poked out with their own saw-bayonets. Their mouths and noses were stuffed with sawdust so that they suffocated.[9]

This paragraph graphically describes French intolerance of ser-rated bayonets in World War I. Prior to that war there was no ban on serrated bayonets, but as the war progressed it became clear that the French would do everything they could to enforce the ban on the battlefield, a point they eventually made abundantly clear to German soldiers. After the war, a French Inquiry Commission declared these weapons unlawful and contrary to international conventions because they caused horrible wounds.[10] Specific prohibitions against lances with barbed tips appear in U.S. and other military manuals, while the St. Petersburg declaration prohibited explosive bullets (1868) and The Hague Conventions banned hollow point or dum-dum bullets (1899).

The overriding reason for prohibiting these weapons lies in their cruelty. Cruelty, as noted, however, can be ambiguous. It may mean suffering beyond what is necessary to disable another soldier or it may mean dreadful suffering. As General Grant surmised, the emphasis is on the former, that is, explosive bullets add nothing of military value and only increase suffering. Hence, it is rational to ban them. Nevertheless, the link between necessity and suffering is bothersome because it seems that suffering should warrant its own criteria, independent of what is necessary. Once suffering is tethered to necessity, it is easy to imagine battles, if not entire campaigns, where necessity may override any measure of suffering, particularly if one side maintains a monopoly on cruel arms, or the other is willing to inflict great costs on its own troops. To pry the two apart, it might be helpful to think of suffering independently of what is necessary to disable a soldier. The ICRC tries to do this by drawing on statistics that portray a level of permissible suffering in wartime. If, for example, explosive or hollow point bullets increase mortality beyond what is deemed necessary for victory in conventional war, then they should be banned regardless of how effective they may be in any particular situation. Notice, however, that the underlying argument is circular and retains strong ties to necessity. In conventional war, fearsome weapons are not necessary, because belligerents can wage war effectively without the higher mortality these weapons cause. History proves this. As noted, however, the argument is only backward looking. It has no normative force about what will be necessary in the future. If, in the future, a weapon proves effective, then it is no longer unnecessary. If higher – or lower – mortality rates prove optimal in prevailing over one's enemies, then the bar of superfluous injury and unnecessary suffering rises or falls accordingly.

Not all weapons significantly increase mortality. Blinding lasers, for example, may permanently blind an enemy combatant without posing any risk to his life. Nevertheless, it seems abhorrent to inflict a permanent disability on a combatant intentionally. Why is this so? Does it have something to do with combatant equality and innocence, an awful fear of blinding, or disproportionate harm in war?

Blinding Lasers

And the Philistines seized [Samson] and gouged out his eyes, and brought him down to Gaza and bound him in bronze fetters; and he ground at the mill in the prison. (Judges 17:21)

Blinding smacks of the worst kind of barbarism. If Samson was a mortal enemy, then why not kill him on the spot? Instead, the Philistines chose to blind Samson, parade his indignity in the streets of Gaza, and put him to work for all to see. Blinding was a special punishment that humiliated and permanently disabled an enemy (or so the Philistines thought) and denied him an honorable death in battle. Nor was the affront lost on Samson who called to God that he "may be avenged upon the Philistines for one of [his] two eyes."

Confronting blinding today leads observers to ask how, exactly, is blinding a particularly cruel or savage practice? One answer looks to the future and the life a soldier can expect after the war has ended. "If," writes Antonio Cassese, a noted authority on international law, "a weapon by its very nature produces the normal effect of putting men out of action for a period largely exceeding the length of a war, that weapon could be regarded as illegal."[11] What Cassese has in mind is a "window of vulnerability."[12] I will refer to this again when I consider the distinction between interrogation techniques that cause transient discomfort (like waterboarding) and those that cause lasting injury (like genital mutilation), or evaluate the effects of cluster bombs on civilians and the harm these bring long after a war has ended.[13] The idea behind this window is that participants in war may suffer only as long as their suffering serves some military purpose. They are, therefore, only vulnerable as long as the war continues. The enduring effects of some forms of interrogation, the permanent damage blinding lasers cause, and the lasting danger that unexploded cluster bombs pose for civilians violate this constraint.

The obvious response to any attempt to limit suffering to "the length of the war" invokes the horror of any modern weapon whose effects push past the end of a conflict. Apart from the roughly 20 to 25 percent of wounded soldiers who die in battle, roughly two-thirds of the wounded are "walking wounded" who quickly return to duty while the balance require extensive medical treatment. Of seriously wounded soldiers, 15 to 20 percent eventually return to battle,

18 to 25 percent die of their wounds, and most of the others remain disabled long after the war has ended.[14] Modern war, in other words, may kill 25 percent of those hit and leave similar numbers with long-term disabilities including blindness. In the Iraq War, interestingly enough the proportion of deaths dropped compared to many previous wars while the proportion of long-term wounded rose.[15] Due in part to improved evacuation procedures and a new generation of anticoagulants, larger numbers of wounded and fewer numbers of dead will probably characterize other asymmetric wars as the stronger force brings enormous medical resources to bear.[16]

Furthermore, it is clear from the figures that any attempt to limit wounding to the window of vulnerability described earlier is often in vain. High explosives cause horrific wounds that are impossible to contain to the relatively short period that typify many wars. Instead, the argument turns to intent. One should not use weapons that *intend to* permanently disable one's adversary and/or cause horrific suffering. Again, these are two separate arguments. The first speaks to suffering that is unnecessary because it is permanent. This is true of blinding, but also true of many other injuries characteristic of war. The second speaks to suffering that may be necessary to inflict to prevail against an enemy, yet which exceeds what our conscience allows us to do another person.

Excessive Suffering and Permanent Disability

What makes weapons designed to permanently blind a combatant inhuman? It seems very wrong to use a weapon that can disable another combatant only by blinding him for life. But why is this so? Why *not* disable a fighter pilot or guerrilla fighter for life? Why give him or her the chance to recover from his wounds and fight again? Here, combatant equality and reciprocity, two features of war absent in asymmetric conflict, play an important role regulating the use of weapons. The importance of reciprocity is overwhelming. No side wants to see its soldiers incapacitated by fear of inescapable blindness or have expensively trained fighter pilots permanently disabled. For these reasons alone, permanently blinding lasers (as opposed to those that cause temporary blindness) were banned with little controversy in 1995 and before any nation ever deployed them in battle.[17] By some accounts, no such weapon was ever designed. Efforts to ban lasers arose from concerns that laser weapons designed to disable enemy optical systems might cause collateral blindness to those operating them.[18]

Combatant equality and moral innocence make us wary about intentionally harming a combatant in ways that lead to permanent disability. Long-term disability is unnecessary to disable a combatant during conflict and violates his right to return home as whole as possible once the conflict has ended. Soldiers, as noted in the previous chapter, have a special status as killers. Upon capture, they face incarceration until the end of the war and then earn repatriation. If this idea has teeth, then harming a combatant in a way that will inevitably spill over into his civilian life is unnecessary, cruel, and inhuman regardless of whatever military advantage it may confer. Asymmetric war, however, might bring us to think differently about weapons like blinding lasers if we only consider the window of vulnerability. Some of these wars are open-ended and long-term. There is no end-of-war event after which combatants are released and sent home. Instead, some combatants fight on for long periods, oblivious to any desire to return to civilian life. As such, the exigencies of an intractable guerrilla war or enduring war against international terrorism might make it prudent to intentionally disable combatants for life.

These considerations give further cause to disassociate the idea of unnecessary suffering from harm that exceeds what is necessary to disable an opponent and/or that which surpasses the temporal boundaries of war and inflicts future pain. Indeed, simple lack of military necessity does not capture the repugnance associated with blinding. Instead, blinding speaks to a primal fear of losing the ability to see. The ICRC tried to portray this dread as it drew on images of gas-blinded soldiers from the First World War whose plight moved the public far more profoundly than those who suffered chronic and debilitating lung disease or loss of limb. Blindness, for many, is a fate worse than death. "Unlike other injuries," writes the ICRC,

Blinding results in very severe disability and near total dependence on others. Because sight provides us with some 80 to 90 percent of our sensory stimulation, blinding renders a person virtually unable to work or to function independently. This usually leads to a dramatic loss of self-esteem and severe psychological depression. Blinding is much more debilitating than most battlefield injuries. Even if soldiers are not hit by lasers, the silent and invisible

threat created by the presence or suspected presence of blinding lasers in an
opponent's arsenal would increase the occurrence among soldiers of combat
stress disorder and, later, of post-traumatic stress disorder.[19]

This Red Cross description of the horrors of blinding shows suc-
cinctly how the impetus for reciprocal arms agreements stems directly from our aversions to particular kinds of suffering and fear of
attack in kind. Together they set the stage for banning a weapon that
causes superfluous injury or unnecessary suffering. These fears also
show how subjective assessments of serious and disabling injuries are.
Attempts to empirically study suffering and to quantify quality of life
make it clear that it is very difficult to distinguish between permissible and forbidden weapons based solely on the kinds of wounds and
injuries they cause.

Measuring Suffering and Quality of Life

Intense suffering of the kind that exceeds what people ought to ever
bear is very difficult to define with any precision. As U.S. policymakers considered interrogation during the second Bush Administration,
for example, they waffled from one extreme that compares intense
suffering to that accompanying organ failure and death to that which
simply shocks the conscience of the court. In between were attempts
to anchor suffering in a vague assessment of its intensity and duration.[20] Similarly, armies look for definitive criteria to define the kind
of suffering that no weapon should ever cause. Rather than applying
vague criteria, however, it is generally easier to identify a particular
weapon and point to widespread revulsion at the suffering it causes.
This explains the unilateral condemnation of weapons causing
blindness or the effects of poison gas.

Disability states, however, are subjective and fluid and they constantly confound health planners as they struggle to allocate resources
to alleviate suffering. Assessments of disability vary considerably
with age and culture and, in many cases, disabilities do not preclude
patients from living relatively full lives.

To assess health states, policymakers may use a table similar to
Table 3.1.[21]

Health states reflect disability states and distress rather than specific loss of function. Disability ranges, for example, from no disability (1) to severe limits on one's choice of work and the inability to

TABLE 3.1 Map of Health States

Disability	Distress			
	A None	B Mild	C Moderate	D Severe
1. No disability	1.000	.995	.990	.967
2. Choice of work severely limited	.964	.972	.942	.870
3. Confined to wheelchair	.875	.845	.680	.000
4. Confined to bed	.677	.564	.000	−1.486

do more than light housekeeping (2) to confinement to a wheelchair (3) or to a bed (4). While disability states are objective determinations, distress states are considerably more subjective. Health care professionals, patients in general, and/or patients facing treatment rank distress and pain on a scale from none to severe.[22]

The numbers express the relative health state of patients with certain disabilities and indicate the number of normal life years they are willing to trade for their disabled life. A score of 0.845 (state 3B), for example, means that a person who is confined to a wheelchair and suffers mild distress rates the quality of his present life at 84.5 percent of a normal life. To put it differently, this patient is prepared to exchange 10 years of his present life for no less than 8.45 years of a normal life without disability or distress (a negative score, on the other hand, signifies a life worse than death). Many people, it turns out, are happy just to be alive and often unwilling to significantly shorten their present lives to gain a life with no disabilities. This leads directly into the present discussion. How much suffering do blindness and related disabilities cause?

"Sighted people," writes one disability activist, "notoriously overestimate the disruptiveness of being blind. ..."[23] Ordinary people do this because they do not always appreciate that a person's assessment of his or her health state includes disability *and* distress. Poor health becomes intolerable when a person suffers severe pain and can no longer interact with others, pursue a career, take care of herself, and get around. Injuries caused by weapons – whether hollow point bullets, serrated bayonets, blinding lasers, or ordinary high explosives – are subject to assessment by the same standards of distress and disability. Here, we see several things. First, quality of life varies considerably among individuals. It is very difficult to generalize about the disability and distress a particular injury will cause. The Health Utilities Index, for example, assigns a value of 0.61 to a life encumbered by blindness where zero is dead and 1.0 reflects perfect health. But other studies are more optimistic, observing that "individuals with visual impairment and blindness who remain in the community have a higher quality of life than might be expected [and] ... likely adapt over time.[24]" This is consistent with the variability of suffering that those who lose important functions may experience. Second, relatively few health states are sufficiently severe that individuals are willing to trade away many years of a disabled life for fewer years of a life free of disease or disability. Finally, neither quality of life nor disability states correlate well with the severity of injuries associated with different weapons. Judging by the behavior of the world community, the unilateral ban on blinding lasers indicates that blinding is surely one of the more agonizing injuries imaginable. By the same token, the failure to ban a wide array of high-explosive weapons suggests that maiming, burning, and paralysis are less egregious injuries. Yet blindness, by many accounts, is less disabling than paralysis or burn wounds. The value of a visually impaired life may be 60 percent that of a perfectly healthy one, but the same index indicates that a life burdened by moderate pain, confinement to a wheelchair, and limited use of the hands, merits only 42 percent of the value of a healthy life.[25] Why then ban blinding lasers and permit other weapons?

This question shows how criteria based on suffering and disability offer little chance to meaningfully distinguish between the wounds caused by those weapons that are banned and those that are not. Is the ICRC's assessment about blindness, then, right or wrong? It probably depends upon whom you ask. The blind may think that loss of sight is probably the least dreadful of those injuries just described. But the blind don't go to war and it is noteworthy that the sighted overestimate the disruptiveness of blindness. For the sighted, blindness causes suffering far worse than other harms in war. This is fortuitous: blinding lasers happen to elicit a sufficient level of dread so that nations are quick to ban them. This shows the willingness of nations to ban certain weapons when the injuries they inflict exceed a threshold of perceived disability. Push this too hard, as I have done above, and it quickly becomes clear that this threshold is illusory. Based on suffering alone, it is difficult to establish cogent criteria to permit or ban certain weapons. However, this shortcoming may not always matter. Suffering, in most cases, is only a handmaiden to necessity. W. Hays Parks, former General Counsel to the U.S. Department of Defense, suggests, for example, that the controversy over blinding lasers had little to do with superfluous injury and everything to do with military necessity and fear of uncontrolled deployment. For Parks, therefore, the Protocol against blinding lasers was "an arms control agreement rather than a law of war treaty.[26]" An arms control treaty is born of necessity while the laws of war make room for humanitarianism. In the case of blinding lasers, necessity and self-interest motivated nations to ban a weapon before any nation could deploy it. Necessity and self-interest also explain the reluctance to ban dreadful weapons that are useful. This is the lesson of incendiary weapons.

Incendiary Weapons

Incendiary weapons highlight the ambivalence that nations have about weapons that cause extreme but useful suffering. Incendiary weapons set fire to material objects, such as fuel depots and military targets, or disable combatants by burning them. Burning results from flames and intense heat (from flamethrowers or napalm, for example) or from a chemical reaction as is common with white phosphorous. The burns these weapons cause are particularly horrific.

Phosphorous has the quality of gluing to the body when burning and cannot be scraped off, but must be cut out leaving frightful wounds. Furthermore, it is said to be highly toxic, poisoning the liver, kidneys and the nervous system after absorption through the wound.[27]

Napalm burns rapidly affect the underlying muscles, tendons and bones which greatly complicate the surgical problem. Reconstructive surgery to treat such conditions requires a long series of operations over several years.[28]

In words not far from those used to recount the misery of permanent blindness, doctors describe how "patients with extensive deep burns suffer the greatest trauma to which the body can be exposed."[29] It seems clear from the above descriptions that the severe wounds phosphorous and napalm cause go well beyond what is necessary to disable a combatant, as they poison internal organs and destroy bones, tendons, and muscles. The suffering is intense and often extends well beyond the length of the war.

Yet, the international community has not unconditionally banned incendiary weapons as it has blinding lasers. In fact, they are perfectly acceptable weapons provided an armed force uses them solely against military targets and takes special precautions to protect civilians. This means that belligerents cannot use air-delivered incendiary bombs (such as napalm or phosphorous bombs) against any military target located within "a concentration of civilians" or use other incendiary weapons unless the "military objective is clearly separated from the concentration of civilians and all feasible precautions are taken with a view to limiting the incendiary effects to the military objective and to avoiding, and in any event to minimizing incidental loss of civilian life."[30]

The concern here is not the fearsome and/or unnecessary suffering incendiary weapons inflict on other *soldiers*, but on noncombatants. International humanitarian law strives to protect noncombatants. Ordinarily, an air force can bomb a military target (say a munitions dump or training facility) located near a civilian population fully expecting that it will also inflict collateral harm on civilians. Incendiary weapons, on the other hand, always cause excessive and inhuman harm. One reason is that the collateral effects are difficult to control. This occurred as the Allies firebombed German cities in World War II. Beyond this, however, is proportionality: civilians should never suffer the injuries that incendiary weapons cause regardless of any military advantage they confer. Their suffering is both excessive and inhuman.[31]

Nevertheless, it is not necessarily inhuman to use incendiary weapons against soldiers. So now we face a contradiction. Soldiers are human and if incendiary weapons cause forbidden, inhuman wounds then soldiers, too, should enjoy protection from their effects. But because of the need to balance military necessity with the woeful harm that incendiary munitions cause, combatants remain vulnerable to these weapons. As nations consider the advantages incendiary weapons offer, humanitarianism drops to the wayside. Only the necessity argument remains. The United States, for example, never ratified

Protocol III restricting the use of incendiary weapons, because, in its opinion, incendiary weapons are weapons of choice if the military target is a munitions dump or biological facility (where the high temperatures resulting from an incendiary attack can destroy microorganisms). As a result, President Clinton refused to support the Protocol banning incendiary weapons because "incendiary weapons have significant military value, particularly with respect to flammable military targets that cannot so readily be destroyed with conventional explosives."[32] Similar concerns by other nations removed the restriction prohibiting the use of incendiary weapons against combatants. The rule of customary warfare stated in the Protocol, then, evolved into something of a loose guideline that prohibits incendiary weapons "unless it is not feasible to use a less harmful weapon to render a person *hors de combat*."[33] In practice, soldiers do not always look for the less harmful weapon. Rather, the evolving norm prohibits incendiary weapons from use against soldiers without cover. Those in fortified positions remain vulnerable to attack.[34]

By 2005, ICRC observers could voice encouragement in light of very few reports of armies using napalm or other incendiary weapons.[35] The emerging norm, however, rested squarely on military necessity, leading the United States to use white phosphorous weapons against military targets in Fallujah, Iraq, in 2004.[36] In this instance, American forces confronted armed combatants and it was not clear that they thought much about first using a less-harmful weapon to disable enemy fighters. At the same time, the U.S. did not face a threat in kind. Lack of reciprocity, again, sums up the challenges that asymmetric warfare present to any effort to ban weapons that cause superfluous injury or unnecessary suffering.

SUPERFLUOUS INJURY AND UNNECESSARY SUFFERING IN ASYMMETRIC WAR

The impact of asymmetric warfare on the use of weapons that cause unnecessary suffering is to undermine any ban that draws on military necessity. In asymmetric war, military necessity may recommend recourse to weapons that the conditions of conventional war belie. Necessity, as noted, comes in many forms. Very often, military necessity means choosing weapons that advance one's cause and avoiding those that retard it. Necessity also speaks to the level of casualties that conventional war requires if either side is to have a fighting chance. At a more personal level, necessity prohibits hitting a man when he is down or harming him after a war has ended and he is no longer a soldier. Conventional armies often ask, What military advantage can come from an injury that afflicts a former enemy who is no longer a threat? The answer is none. This alone may offer a good reason to avoid harming a combatant well into the future. However, this reasoning only has bite when it is reasonable to suppose that the war will not last long and that peace will reign in its wake. This is not true in some asymmetric wars, particularly the war on terror. These wars may go on indefinitely and long-term disability may not be unnecessary or superfluous. Nor is there any reason to extend a fighting chance to those parties pursuing international terrorism, genocide, or crimes against humanity.

In conventional wars, military necessity often turns on reciprocity between nations. Nation-states fighting one another often have a mutual interest to avoid inflicting injuries that severely demoralize troops, make treatment more difficult, and return too few soldiers to duty. They would gladly inflict these injuries on their enemies but for the prospect of facing a response in kind. This constraint breaks down early in most asymmetric wars: wars of intervention, wars of national liberation, and wars against proxy guerrillas. Sophisticated weaponry – airplanes, bombers, guided missiles, drones, and incendiary weapons, for example – are beyond the weaker side's means in most asymmetric conflicts. The stronger side has no fear that their adversary may use a weapon that will undermine their troop morale or cause wounds that are difficult to treat. They may have an incentive, however, to avoid weapons that cause grievous injury to their opponents if this impedes the prospect of peace. In some wars, therefore, particularly in CAR conflicts of national liberation, parties may restrain their behavior if peace is on the horizon. But in wars against international terrorism and wars of humanitarian intervention, for example, the stronger side has no incentive to avoid weapons that cause extreme suffering among its enemies. Proxy wars present difficult issues as guerrillas often draw certain classes of civilians into the conflict. In the Second Lebanon War, Israel did not hesitate to bomb civilians it accused of actively supporting the war, deploy drones to assassinate guerrilla combatants and terrorists, and make liberal use of cluster bombs against all three. Nor was it any accident that incendiary weapons surfaced in Iraq and chemical weapons found their way into Russia's war against Chechnya.[37]

Nevertheless, asymmetric war should not affect our intuitions about cruelty and suffering. Relieved of the fear of like-kind harm in asymmetric conflict, states and humanitarian organizations search for independent criteria of suffering. This is very difficult to articulate with any consistency. Although cruel and fearsome weapons merit an absolute ban regardless of military necessity, it is extraordinarily difficult to define the limits of permissible suffering with any accuracy or agreement. There is no logical reason why blindness should be any more an egregious injury than injuries caused by high explosives or incendiary weapons.

"Fearsome" and "cruel" are subjective intuitions about what members of a particular community find especially dreadful. We cringe as we contemplate permanent blindness or the slow agony of dying by asphyxiation, incurable disease, or extensive burns. Searching for ways to prevent these harms from befalling *us*, we appeal to unnecessary suffering, which is, in reality, *our* horrific suffering. Later and over time, these norms are internalized, expand in scope, and sometimes prove relatively resistant to change.[38] Sometimes, a community can successfully impose its norm of suffering on the practice of war as France did when it formally banned serrated bayonets in World War I. Other times, a nation may thwart the imposition of a norm of suffering as the United States did when its military interests in Iraq overrode whatever reticence it had about using incendiary weapons. There is no denying the repugnance that the injuries caused by some weapons evoke, but it seems clear that feelings of revulsion are highly subjective and more importantly, subject to the dictates of national interest and military necessity. This makes it even more difficult to appeal to unnecessary suffering in restricting weapons during asymmetric conflict.

Different weapons carry different degrees of prohibitions and restrictions. The world community prohibits serrated bayonets and blinding lasers but for very different reasons, the former because they cause superfluous harm and the latter because they bring cruel injuries. Incendiary weapons (and as described in the following chapter, chemical weapons), on the other hand, face only restrictions rather than prohibitions. In accounting for this, it is important to see that necessity and humanitarianism are important but sometimes conflicting principles. Necessity precedes the test of humanitarianism. In conventional war, necessity dictates the non-use of fearsome weapons. In asymmetric war, necessity may dictate their use. Humanitarian law can only make a very weak case to restrict the use of certain weapons. Based on suffering alone, there is rarely a compelling reason to prefer one kind of weapon to another. Soldiers, vulnerable to harm in the course of battle, will suffer accordingly. Necessity and humanitarianism can, however, protect noncombatants more effectively than soldiers. Although, harming noncombatants is sometimes unavoidable it rarely brings significant military benefits. This is precisely why it is called "incidental" harm. Finding little room for the kind of inhuman but militarily useful harm that combatants may encounter, the international community has successfully banned or restricted landmines, incendiary weapons, and, most recently, cluster bombs.

The idea of superfluous injury and unnecessary suffering has a similar impact on assessments of chemical and biological weapons. While international treaties ban biological weapons absolutely, they only restrict the use of chemical weapons. The logic is peculiar. Formal agreements ban chemical weapons from the battlefield but permit law enforcement officials to use certain classes of nonlethal weapons such as tear gas, to control riots. Humanitarian norms, in other words, permits nations to use chemical weapons against civilians but not soldiers. At the same time, successful efforts to restrict chemical weapons block deployment of nonlethal chemical weapons, leaving nations no choice but to deploy lethal weapons rather than those that might cause less suffering and injury. Imperiling anyone caught up on the battlefield, lethal weaponry presents dangers particularly acute in asymmetric war where combatants and civilians fight indistinguishably from one another and at close quarters. Nonlethal weapons seem particularly appropriate for asymmetric warfare, yet remain the subject of considerable controversy because many believe that they, too, cause superfluous injury and unnecessary suffering.

4

Shooting to Stun

The Paradox of Nonlethal Warfare

> In many instances, our forces are allowed to shoot somebody and kill them, but they're not allowed to use a nonlethal riot-control agent ... There are times when the use of nonlethal riot agents is perfectly appropriate, although legal constraints make for a very awkward situation.
>
> Donald Rumsfeld, former U.S. Secretary of Defense[1]

Rumsfeld has a point. How can modern war make it easy for soldiers to kill one another with bullets, shells, and bombs but make it hard for them to incapacitate their enemies with chemical or biological agents, sound waves, blinding lights, or electromagnetic pulses? Indeed, it seems paradoxical that international law allows, if not encourages, adversaries to kill one another by the most horrible means imaginable, while forbidding them from employing an array of weapons that will only temporarily disable enemy soldiers.

Nonlethal weapons (NLWs) are not weapons of mass destruction. They are specifically designed to temporarily incapacitate rather than kill. They do not inflict intense suffering. They produce no effects that extend beyond the time of war. Nor do they cause wounds that are especially difficult to treat. They seem, at first glance, to offer means that are both militarily useful and relatively friendly on the battlefield. So, is Rumsfeld right? Should advanced nations embrace nonlethal weaponry to both wage war effectively and reduce its suffering? Taking up Rumsfeld's challenge requires another look at NLWs (especially those he calls "nonlethal riot control agents"), their

TABLE 4.1 Nonlethal Anti-Personnel Weapons

Category	Type	Effects
Biological	Viruses and toxins	Respiratory/ gastrointestinal disease
Optical	Lasers, strobes	Temporary blindness, disorientation
Acoustical	Audible or infra sound	Incapacitation, nausea, vomiting
Chemical	Calmatives	Unconsciousness
	Irritants: tear gas and pepper gas	Tearing, choking
	Psychotropic drugs	Hallucination, disorientation
	Gastroconvulsives	Nausea, vomiting, incapacitation
Electromagnetic	Active Denial System (ADS)	Intensely painful burning sensation
Neurological	Radio frequency (RF)	Incapacitation
	fMRI	Detect mind states
	Transcranial Magnetic Stimulation (TMS)	Alter mental status

place in asymmetric warfare, and the arguments of those who oppose them.

THE NATURE OF NONLETHAL WEAPONS

World War I first presented the possibility of using chemical weapons to incapacitate rather than kill enemy soldiers. Since then, researchers have proposed and developed an astonishing array of NLWs. Today, there are many NLWs on the drawing boards, at various stages of development or since abandoned. Table 4.1 lists the many types of NLWs and their effects on human beings. These do not include chemical and biological agents affecting material and equipment, herbicides and defoliants, nor NLWs such as rubber bullets or landmines that can cause permanent disability.

Biological weapons, categorically banned by the Biological Weapons Convention in 1972, were the subject of considerable attention following the First World War. Some utilized anthrax, small pox, and botulinum toxin, virulent pathogens that made for weapons of mass destruction. Scientists and doctors also devoted considerable energy to weaponizing nonlethal pathogens to incapacitate enemy soldiers by causing severely debilitating, but not life-threatening, illness. Today, research continues apace in other fields. Optical weapons – lasers and flash grenades – cause temporary blindness and disorientation. Acoustical weapons, still unperfected, employ inaudible infrasound that can resonate in body cavities to bring on disorientation, nausea, vomiting, and bowel spasms.[2] Calmatives, chemical agents that depress or anesthetize the central nervous system, cause unconsciousness or incapacitating hallucinations. Finally, the Active Denial System (ADS) developed by the U.S. Army utilizes electromagnetic millimeter waves that penetrate just below the surface of the skin to cause a painful burning sensation without permanent damage. Far from science fiction, NLWs are a growing part of an advanced army's arsenal as it confronts the difficult logistics of asymmetric warfare and the war on terror.[3] In Iraq and elsewhere, for example, NLWs hold promise for such difficult tasks as "securing populated areas, preventing infiltration, and avoiding civilian casualties."[4]

Of these many weapons, I will focus on three: chemical and biological (CB) weapons that temporarily incapacitate enemy troops, the Active Denial System ADS that utilizes electromagnetic waves to repulse large crowds that threaten military installations, and, finally, neuroweapons that alter mind states to reduce or eliminate lethal threats. Chemical weapons and the ADS are, in one form or another, nearly operational. Neuroweapons, on the other hand, are still on the drawing board and no army will be using them anytime soon. Until then, we are left to ponder whether, indeed, we have discovered a method to harm human beings in a way that was hitherto unimaginable.

Chemical and Biological (CB) Weapons

Weaponizing CB agents has made tremendous strides since the Germans opened a canister of chlorine gas on April 22, 1915, and let it waft over Allied positions. By the end of the twentieth century weapons engineers had designed artillery shells and bombs to aerosolize pathogens and chemical agents that human targets inhale or absorb through the skin and eyes. Nonlethal biological weapons employed bacteria and viruses to cause incapacitating rather than life-threatening illness. These include brucellosis, Q-Fever, and Venezuelan Equine Encephalitis (VEE). VEE, for example, is particularly debilitating, causing headaches, high fever, and several weeks of fatigue.[5] Mortality is less than one percent, making it a particularly attractive nonlethal virus, and both the United States and the USSR successfully weaponized VEE as an incapacitating agent before ending their biological weapons programs.[6] Q-Fever and brucellosis have similar effects on humans and were also candidates for incapacitating biological weapons. Considering the casualties of a biological attack on a civilian population of five hundred thousand, the World Health Organization estimated that Q-Fever would leave 150 dead and 125,000 incapacitated while brucellosis would leave five hundred dead and over one hundred thousand incapacitated. In contrast, a similar attack with weaponized anthrax could kill up to 95,000 people.[7]

While the Biological Weapons Convention (BWC) prohibits biological weapons of all types and left most nations to destroy their lethal and nonlethal weapons, the Chemical Weapons Convention (CWC) (1993) only *restricts* chemical weapons development. While the convention prevents nations from "developing, producing, otherwise acquiring, stockpiling, retaining or using" chemical weapons, including incapacitating agents, it does allow nations to use and develop "riot control agents" for the purposes of "law enforcement".[8] These permissible exceptions are less than airtight and show the way through which advanced nations will push their nonlethal chemical weapons programs.

Law enforcement agents currently use a number of nonlethal chemical agents that include tear gases and irritants. These "harassing agents" cause extreme discomfort but only for as long as people are exposed. The effects disappear just after contact. Until then, those affected stay busy "removing themselves from exposure."[9] Except in very high doses, harassing agents are generally not lethal and those exposed do not usually require medical attention. Agents such as CS (2-chlorobenzalmalononitrile) and CN (2-chloroacetophenone) are irritants that cause coughing, choking, severe headaches, nausea, vomiting, and pain. In the best cases, law enforcement agencies will use harassing agents to control crowds that threaten public safety. In other circumstances, however, CS and CN sometimes enjoy military use. While the U.S. Army brought CN and CS to Vietnam as incapacitating agents, American forces often used them in conjunction with lethal weaponry, a turn of events that led critics to charge that irritants aggravated casualties as troops would flush out and then attack the Vietcong with conventional weapons.

Vietnam also saw the Americans deploying the psychotropic agent BZ against North Vietnamese troops in 1968.[10] BZ, the hydrochloride salt of 3-quinuclidinyl benzilate, is an incapacitating rather than a harassing agent. Unlike individuals exposed to harassing agents, those exposed to an incapacitating agent are often unaware of their predicament and are unable (nor inclined) to flee its effects. Although the effect may be prolonged, medical aid is not usually required.[11] Exposure to BZ causes dizziness, confusion, hallucinations, and unpredictable behavior and renders troops unfit for combat for as long as 72 hours. Although the CWC bans BZ specifically, the appeal of finding a nonlethal "bullet" to disable enemy troops without killing them has not waned. As a result, the search continues for incapacitating agents that weapons designers can shoehorn into the CWC provisions that allow riot control agents.

Today, there are new classes of chemical weapons, such as the calmative agent fentanyl and its derivatives, that may meet CWC guidelines. Calmatives are potent anesthetics that are dispersed in the air or administered through the skin and render anyone exposed immediately unconscious. Calmatives cannot break up threatening crowds nor do they kill or injure enemy forces. Rather, they knock them out. Impressed with their potential, the National Research Council (USA) endorsed the development of calmatives and other chemical NLWs that "offer the theoretical possibility of peacefully incapacitating combatants/agitators, reducing the need for the violence that is frequently associated with many of the current methods."[12] Once they incapacitate their enemy, attacking troops must sort them out and send the civilians home and enemy combatants to prison. Status tribunals of the kind established by the Geneva Conventions offer an appropriate vehicle for doing this. In the aftermath of war or battle, enemy combatants often intermingle with refugees, and conquering armies must determine the status of each. During the First Gulf War, for example, U.S. forces conducted 1,196 tribunal hearings recognizing 310 persons as enemy POWs and the others as displaced civilians and refugees.[13] There is no reason that similar tribunals cannot establish the status of a mixed group of civilians and un-uniformed combatants disabled by calmative weapons.

Active Denial System

Unlike chemical weapons, the Active Denial System (ADS) emits electromagnetic waves. Looking like a large radar screen mounted on the back of a truck or field tripod (see Figure 4.1), the system emits 95 GHz millimeter-wave-directed energy. These millimeter waves penetrate to a depth of 0.4 mm and heat the skin to $55°$ C, a temperature that "exceeds the pain threshold but does not exceed the threshold for tissue damage."[14] Although blistering may result when exposure is longer than one minute, people will instinctively flee the beam after a few seconds, making the ADS an effective system to disperse violent crowds.[15]

The U.S. expects to deploy the ADS in counterinsurgency and peacekeeping missions to protect facilities from attack and clear the battlefield of noncombatants. Common riot control agents, such as tear gas, principally affect the eyes and airways and while often a useful form of crowd control, they are neither quick acting enough nor always effective when armed combatants intermingle with civilians and don protective masks. When tear gas fails, the only option is to use live ammunition or, at best, rubber bullets. Each may cause permanent injury. ADS, on the other hand, may allow U.S. forces to effectively and nonlethally disperse a mixed crowd threatening a check post or base perimeter. The U.S. Army also envisions a significant role for ADS when troops must attack a position occupied by combatants and noncombatants. In this situation, "the ADS is employed first to deny the enemy effective use of their weapons" and second to "delay/disrupt the counterattack's maneuver upon friendly forces." In the process, civilians are expected to flee, thereby leaving only combatants to face armed troops. "The ADS," concludes one Army assessment, "will disrupt enemy movement and remove neutral civilians from the battlefield."[16] In these circumstances, the weapon is designed to reduce civilian casualties and protect noncombatants by

FIGURE 4.1 The Active Denial System. Photo by Airman 1st Class Gina Chiaverotti, January 26, 2007. Courtesy of the U.S. Army (http://www.army. mil/-images/2007/01/26/2124/).

inflicting less than lethal harm. If the system proves itself, it will play a central role in an increasing number of military missions during asymmetric conflict.

Neuroweapons

"There is increasing military interest in the development of techniques that can survey and possibly control and manipulate the mental processes of potential enemies," write Neil Davison and Nick Lewer." One of these is transcranial magnetic stimulation (TMS). TMS technology is painless and "focuses an intense magnetic field on specific brain regions, and can affect thoughts, perceptions and behaviors that are dependent on those regions." With TMS it might then be possible to alter a person's feelings about others and to change hostility and hatred into trust and cooperation. Although the

TMS device is small, it currently requires an operator to pass a small electric coil directly over a person's head. Future applications, however, may allow for long-distance operation.[17] TMS may then enable an armed force to painlessly and nonlethally alter an enemy's state of mind and behavior, and thereby make it all the easier to subdue that enemy.[18] Alternatively, it might be possible to soften up detainees and make them more amenable to interrogation.

In addition, there is fledging interest in incapacitating weapons that use radiofrequency (RF) radiation to control the release of neurotransmitters in the nervous system. Early research indicates that RF radiation can cause the adrenal glands to produce excessive amounts of neurotransmitters, which, in turn, may serve to immobilize or otherwise incapacitate those affected.[19] The results are far from implementation, but the idea is to produce an incapacitating weapon similar to chemical weapons without the attendant legal difficulties of using a chemical agent that flirts with the CWC restrictions. At the same time, RF radiation would not be subject to fluctuating atmospheric conditions or difficulties of delivery that plague airborne chemical weapons.

Finally, consider the possibilities of functional magnetic resonance imaging (fMRI) so named because it maps brain activity with an MRI device while a person is performing a cognitive task or function. FMRI does not alter behavior, but it can detect deception by watching brain activity when subjects are asked to identify photos of possible confederates, hideouts, or weapons. FMRI may then be a useful tool for interrogators who suspect that a detainee has specific information about a terror attack or knows the perpetrators.[20] Larger and heavier than a TMS apparatus, the fMRI is pushing researchers to search for a small portable model that can map the brain from a distance. This might allow an armed force to detect and identify combatants who are otherwise indistinguishable from civilian noncombatants.[21] Physiologically, the technology is harmless and painless (assuming the subject cooperates), but like all neuroweapons, fMRI confronts us with the prospect of invading the recesses of the human brain. Neuroweapons, like many other NLWs, sharpen the debate over the type of harm we permit ourselves to inflict on other human beings. ADS skillfully exploits a body's physiological safety zone between pain and tissue damage. Chemical weapons deaden neurological responses, biological weapons undermine the body's physiological defenses in a most fundamental way, and neuroweapons push their way into a person's brain and alter his behavior.[22] This is, perhaps, the final assault on human dignity and free will, but the fundamental puzzle of nonlethal warfare remains: Why is any of this worse than shooting an enemy dead?

TMS, RF radiation, and fMRI open a new frontier in nonlethal weaponry. They, together with chemical agents and millimeter-wave systems offer a technologically sophisticated military organization the means to incapacitate, identify, and interrogate potential enemies while hoping to prevent overwhelming harm to those civilians who do not threaten them. The hurdles facing all three kinds of NLWs are both legal and moral. However, the first test of any weapons system, which many people often forget, is effectiveness. A weapon must work and confer some military advantage at the lowest possible cost. Only then can we ask whether it conforms to existing legal guidelines, whether it brings disproportionate harm to noncombatants, and whether it causes superfluous injury or unnecessary suffering to combatants.

CAN THEY WORK? THE ROLE OF NONLETHAL WEAPONS IN ASYMMETRIC WAR

During the Second Lebanon War (2006), the Israeli air force attacked a convoy fleeing the village of Marwahine following a warning to evacuate within two hours. Twenty-three people died in the attack. On review, both the United Nations Human Rights Council and Human Rights Watch (HRW) condemned the attacks for causing excessive, disproportionate, and unnecessary civilian casualties.[23] In response, Israel argued that un-uniformed Hezbollah fighters were taking advantage of civilian convoys to escape and regroup. The UN answered by declaring, "Even if there were Hezbollah members among the civilians who left the villages in convoys, this does not justify the attacks as they would be utterly disproportionate."[24]

This far-ranging interpretation of proportionality is not unreasonable in the context of international law.[25] There is certainly an intuitive feeling that killing 21 or 22 innocent civilians solely to eliminate one or two militants is excessive. Notice, however, how the

UN's interpretation of proportionality prohibits nearly any attack on convoys containing civilians no matter how necessary or successful a means to cripple enemy forces. Nine hundred thousand Lebanese civilians fled the fighting during the war and it would have been an easy thing for the five-to-seven thousand Hezbollah militiamen to mix among them (at a ratio far exceeding 22 civilians for every militant), escape, and reorganize their forces. If attacking these convoys causes disproportionate harm, then no matter how convincingly a nation proves that enemy forces are using civilian convoys to conceal the transportation of rockets and weaponry, no attack is permissible for fear of harming too many civilians.[26] Enemy forces are then immune from attack. Clearly, this is a sweeping claim with important ramifications for asymmetric warfare. It implies that in some instances, no proportionate response to an armed threat is at all possible.

High explosives, however smart they are, cannot solve this problem. The Marwahine attack was, in fact, a pinpoint strike. Only after the fact was it clear that the air force attacked a civilian convoy. Could NLWs have done any better? Perhaps. Earlier in the war, the Hezbollah surprised Israel by launching a surface-to-sea missile, severely damaging the flagship of Israel's navy. There was reason to fear similar attacks, and by some reports, military officials feared that this convoy, if that was what it was, had taken up a position to spot for Hezbollah gunners. If so, a portable ADS might have allowed troops to disperse the crowd and buy time for a full investigation. Alternatively, calmative or neuroweapons might have incapacitated them, allowing ground forces to move in and capture them all. In either case, NLWs might have spared civilian lives while meeting operational demands.

While the early impetus for developing nonlethal weaponry came from a keen desire to limit the horrendous casualties of modern warfare and, perhaps, naïvely wage war without death, it was the changing nature of contemporary armed conflict that challenged weapons designers to develop alternative forms of weaponry.[27] Fighting in built-up areas against forces intermingled with noncombatants, as was the case in southern Lebanon and in Iraq and Afghanistan, large conventional armies find it impossible to bring their enormous firepower to bear. On one hand, it is difficult to use massive, high-explosive munitions without causing extensive civilian casualties. On the other, the inability to distinguish between noncombatant and militants who fight without uniforms puts civilians at risk no matter what kind of weapon an army uses. This led the National Research Council to embrace calmatives in 2003, the Council on Foreign Affairs to encourage the U.S. Army to accelerate the development of acoustical, millimeter-wave, and optical incapacitating weapons, and scientists and researchers to probe the potential of neuroweapons.

Putting aside the early results, which are so far mixed, the motives that many advocates of nonlethal warfare profess are professional and humanitarian. Neither professional soldiers, nor the armies that field them, fight well when civilians are constantly at risk. This problem is particularly acute in asymmetric warfare. Opposing forces are relatively weak and small compared to the size of the army they face and compared to the size of their own population. A million Lebanese live in South Lebanon but Hezbollah forces probably never numbered more than a few thousand. Militants are difficult to ferret out, pure military targets are few and far between, and civilians often perform quasi-military roles. This is true in any number of new wars where well-armed states must intervene to prevent massacres of innocent civilians and restore political stability (as in the former Yugoslavia and Darfur), to fight states sponsoring terrorism (as in Afghanistan), to suppress insurgency (in Iraq), or to settle political disputes violently (between Israel and the Palestinians, for example). Short of harming everyone or no one, NLWs may offer the possibility to spare civilian lives and provide military organizations with a force continuum with which to respond to various levels of threats without causing indiscriminate or excessive civilian casualties. If conventional warfare only offers military planners one of two options – responding with overwhelming military force or doing nothing at all – NLWs significantly augment military strategy.

In contrast to conventional forms of warfare, nonlethal warfare offers the novel strategy of shooting first and asking questions later. NLWs, in other words, are deliberately indiscriminate, a fact that worries critics but is the very nature of the beast. Because it is often so difficult to distinguish military from nonmilitary targets, NLWs target them all. Calmative agents may subdue a threatening crowd that friendly forces must then capture and interrogate (using a noninvasive and painless fMRI). The ADS will repulse a similar crowd and, hopefully, inflict a measure of pain that will persuade noncombatants to exit the field thereby leaving only the militants to fight. In each of these cases, civilians face nonlethal harm to save them from the greater harm of conventional weapons.

In spite of these optimistic scenarios and high expectations, there are very little firm data about how NLWs will actually perform in battle. Some of the recent attempts to use chemical weapons against Vietnamese guerrillas or Chechnyan terrorists point to a number of possible pitfalls as armies use chemical weapons. ADS and neuroweapons remain untested in battle, but they too raise concerns that all might not go as nonlethally as one might hope.

Drawing on the American experience in Vietnam, critics describe how the U.S. military used irritants, harassing agents, and psychotropic drugs to drive North Vietnamese soldiers from tunnels and underground bunkers and then, once exposed, shelled them with artillery and cannon fire.[28] Here, nonlethal agents function as a force multiplier to increase the lethality and effectiveness of conventional weapons. At the same time, high concentrations of tear gas killed Vietnamese civilians during tunnel flushing operations to root out North Vietnamese soldiers. Military doctrine may be able to differentiate between conventional and nonlethal warfare in theory, but in practice, argue critics, the two are merely different sides of the same lethal coin. In neither case did U.S. forces use NLWs to minimize casualties. On the contrary, they joined the arsenal of lethal weaponry to disable an enemy and attain military victory.

The fact is that no proponent of nonlethal warfare advocates deploying troops without recourse to conventional arms. In many scenarios, lethal force backs up NLWs. The ADS, for example, may drive off noncombatants but then leaves the field clear to attack guerrillas with lethal force. This worries some observers who fear that a mobile ADS will "incapacitate fighters who will then be more susceptible to lethal fire."[29] This may pose a difficult problem. On one hand, soldiers flushed from tunnels or routed at a check post by ADS may remain a lethal threat. A soldier who is only confused or disoriented but not disabled remains a threat and a reasonable target for lethal force. In this situation, a system combining ADS and, say, artillery fire becomes another lawful lethal weapons system assuming it does not inflict unnecessary suffering nor indiscriminately harm civilians. On the other hand, the tenor of humanitarian law dictates minimal use of disabling force, urging combatants to capture rather than kill their enemy when possible. Certainly, there seems something very wrong with killing soldiers incapacitated by a calmative agent. Yet asymmetric war presents gray areas that require case-by-case analysis. The Israeli army, for example, routinely "confirms" the death of wounded terrorists (that is, kills them) out of fear they may blow themselves up as troops approach.[30] In the only military use of a calmative agent to date, the Russians cited similar fears when they killed unconscious Chechnyan terrorists in Moscow. In both cases, the targets were incapacitated but remained a lethal threat.

Nevertheless, the evidence is far from entirely convincing and the Moscow debacle just mentioned is a case in point. When Chechnyan guerrillas seized a Moscow theatre in 2002 and held 850 hostages, the Russian authorities decided to subdue the insurgents by pumping the calmative fentanyl (or a fentanyl derivative) through the ventilation system. Everyone in the theatre lost consciousness immediately. Unfortunately, 129 hostages also died, as did all fifty terrorists who were shot dead before they could regain consciousness. What happened? Clearly, the chemical concentration that incapacitates most people may kill others. Critics charged that the episode points to the lethality of calmatives and the inability to control dosages and effects in a relatively confined space (not to mention on the open field).

Calmative chemicals are not inherently nonlethal. They are only nonlethal in low doses. The difference between the lethal and nonlethal dose is the chemical's therapeutic or relative safety index. The greater the index, the more likely the weapon will remain nonlethal. Usually, these indices are very high. The index for fentanyl is 300, that is, a fatal dose is 300 times the dose required for incapacitation. For other calmatives, such as carfentanil, the index is 10,600, making it a superior nonlethal chemical agent.[31] The problem, however, is that no one really knows whether this is high enough when using calmatives under battle conditions. In the Moscow theatre, for example, the Russians risked delivering a lethal dose to those close to the ventilation ducts so they could deliver an incapacitating dose to those far away. If delivery is difficult in a closed theatre, imagine what it will be like on the battlefield.

Uncertain atmospheric conditions have always plagued airborne NLWs and for this reason the ADS, radio frequency devices, and other electromagnetic systems are attractive. But Moscow is definitely not the last word on calmatives. Supporters of nonlethal chemical weapons note the Russian penchant for secrecy, never divulging the name of the calmative they used. Russian authorities kept their own medical personnel in the dark. As a result, they had very little of the proper antidote on hand. Under better conditions, the outcome might have been much more favorable.[32] At the same time, work continues apace on a calmative bullet that will deliver a chemical agent directly through the skin of an enemy soldier.[33]

The debate over effectiveness and lethality requires considerably more data that can only come from battle testing. There are a great many aspects of nonlethal warfare that we simply don't know much about. Will calmatives prove effective in battle? Will they save civilian lives or simply expose them to greater risk, as the doses necessary to incapacitate soldiers prove lethal to children, the elderly, and the infirm? What will really happen when millimeter- wave weapons take aim at a hostile crowd? Will they flee the beam or run the wrong way? Will the operator turn off the beam to spare some or keep it going to keep the crowd from reforming? No one yet knows. There is simply too little evidence. Nevertheless, let us assume for the moment that the systems will work as planned, that NLWs will provide the force continuum that military planners seek and will significantly minimize harm to noncombatants. This alone does not make the case, for as Secretary Rumsfeld complained, legal constraints still make things awkward.

ARE THEY LEGAL? NONLETHAL WEAPONS AND
CHEMICAL WARFARE

There is no shortage of disagreement about whether nations may legally deploy NLWs as they fight guerrillas, insurgents, or terrorists around the world. The Chemical Weapons Convention (CWC) allows officials to use riot control weapons to enforce the law, not fight a war. This immediately raised two questions. The first, almost entirely unanticipated in the last days of the Cold War, is, What is war and what is law enforcement? Rather than think of them as two distinct categories waged by armies or police forces, there is a growing tendency to see them as two poles of a spectrum with a wide variety of military-like operations in between. Second, What are riot control agents, exactly? Technology waits for no treaty and a vast new pharmacopoeia of chemicals, including calmatives, is now available that may, or may not, qualify as riot control agents. These are just two of the questions that plague the issue of NLWs. Nor are the disagreements confined to chemical or biological NLWs. The ADS does not utilize chemicals but controls crowds with a beam of millimeter waves, a hitherto unknown nonlethal weapon.

What Is War?

International treaties are clear about one thing: nations may use chemical agents in law enforcement but never in war. Beyond this, we are in the dark because law enforcement and war remain undefined. Clearly, this was not always the case. Until recently, law enforcement was a domestic affair. Law enforcement officials gain their authority from the state; their job is to serve and protect. When unruly crowds violate the law and disturb the peace, police officers have ready access to tear gas and other means to restore order. They do not seek to disable or kill criminals or unruly citizens (as armies seek to kill the enemy) but rather to subdue and peacefully arrest them. For law enforcement officials the idea of using a chemical agent as a force multiplier is, usually, unthinkable. The goals of warfare, however, are much different. Wars protect vital national interests; they do not enforce the law. Soldiers draw their authority from their states but they fight other states that recognize a different authority and a different set of laws (unlike criminals and police who are all subject to the same legal system). And, of course, soldiers may shoot to kill. For soldiers, lethal force is the rule, while for law enforcement officials who must respect a suspect's right to life and due process, it is the exception.

Events of recent years, particularly those surrounding the war on terror and asymmetric warfare, have muddied this (relatively) clear distinction. States now speak of international law enforcement as they battle terrorists or weigh humanitarian intervention and peace enforcement. Battling a technologically less sophisticated and numerically weaker opponent, states fight to bring terrorists to justice, topple rogue regimes, and/or save the innocents from the genocidal hands of rapacious despots. Some call these "new wars"; while evolving military doctrine in the United States preferred MOOTW – military operations other than war. But before MOOTW, there was Vietnam. There, Secretary of State Dean Rusk introduced the idea of "situations analogous to riot control:"

We do not expect that gas will be used in ordinary military operations. Police-type weapons were used in riot control in South Vietnam ... and in situations analogous to riot control, where the Viet Cong, for example, were using civilians as screens for their own operations.[34]

Rusk's arguments would later resonate in military operations other than war. MOOTWs are not bloodless operations, but nor are they wars in the traditional sense of one nation fighting another to protect vital national interests. Instead, MOOTWs look to the proactive use of force and focus "on deterring war, resolving conflict, promoting peace, and supporting civil authorities in response to domestic crises." Although MOOTWs look something like war, employ many combat capabilities, and undertake "preemptive, retaliatory, and rescue operations," their overriding goal is to "prevent, preempt, or limit potential hostilities."[35] Military operations other than war include combating terrorism, offering military support to civilian authorities, evacuating noncombatants from war zones, performing peacekeeping operations, and providing humanitarian assistance. As the war in Iraq and Afghanistan intensified, the U.S. military dropped the term MOOTW and distinguished between "major operations involving large-scale combat" and "a crises response or limited contingency operation" to describe a wide array of operations from Iraq and Afghanistan to Somalia, Bosnia, and Panama.[36] These operations are not quite war and not quite law enforcement. May the military capabilities of an army engaged in these conflicts include riot control agents or other NLWs? There is growing support for just this development.

What Are Riot Control Agents?

While the CWC permits riot control agents for law enforcement, it restricts the use of toxic chemicals. Riot control agents are any chemical that rapidly produces "sensory irritation or disabling physical effects which disappear within a short time following termination of exposure."[37] Toxic chemicals, on the other hand, cause death, temporary incapacitation, or permanent harm. So where do calmatives fall and when can they be used? It seems that the framers of the Convention expected everyone to understand that a calmative agent that attacks and depresses the central nervous system is more a toxic chemical than a riot control agent whose effects disappear very quickly. Every nation, however, is free to make its own determination as it interprets the Convention. If a nation classifies calmatives as riot control agents, then a military organization can only use them to enforce the law, preserve public order, and protect their security forces.[38] In the United States, however, a 1975 Executive Order permits U.S. forces to use riot control agents in some combat operations, just as they did in Vietnam. These include rescue missions and "situations in which civilians are used to mask or screen attacks."[39] In both cases, calmatives may reduce civilian casualties as U.S. forces carry out combat-related missions. But this is not the end of the story. A state may concede that calmatives are toxic chemicals, but still insist that it is permissible to use calmatives for military purposes other than "warfare." This brings us back to MOOTW. "If the Pentagon interprets the term 'toxic chemicals' to include incapacitating NLWs [nonlethal weapons], such as calmative agents," write Coppernoll and Maruyama, "their utility in MRC [major regional conflict] is questionable. The sole operational utility of chemical-based anti-personnel NLWs will then be in MOOTW [military operations other than war], not MRC."[40]

Nor is this the end of the story either. When the Russians used calmatives in 2002, they pushed the envelope right off the table. What is striking about the Russian operation was the silence, that is, the acquiescence, it met with from the rest of the world. The Russians were not fighting international criminals but battling guerrillas in a war that the Russian government previously recognized as a "non-international armed conflict."[41] The Russian war against Chechnya was not a law enforcement operation but part of a civil war, somewhere between a military operation other than war and a major regional conflict . It was new territory for calmative weapons and one that the international community seemed ready and anxious to accept.

The longing for NLWs is not confined to calmatives but embraces the entire arsenal of chemical, acoustical, optical, and electromagnetic technologies. Unlike chemical weapons, neither the ADS nor neuroweapons are subject to specific conventions that restrict their use. As science leaps forward it may simply be easier to bypass existing conventions by turning to alternative technologies that do not use chemical agents. This strategy may work well, but for the general restriction on superfluous injury and unnecessary suffering that applies to all weapons. Even under the most optimal conditions, NLWs cause harm and they do so in the most unconventional ways. Although the harm is short lived, does it, nonetheless, cause unnecessary suffering?

What Is Superfluous Injury and Unnecessary Suffering?

Finding it difficult to define unnecessary suffering with any precision, we saw in the previous chapter how most international conventions make do with prohibitions on certain kinds of weapons that cause fearsome suffering: hollow point bullets, poisoned weapons, asphyxiating gas, serrated bayonets, and blinding lasers. NLWs, however, do not cause injuries nearly this serious. Instead, they attack the body in more subtle and perhaps more menacing ways.

With this concern in mind, the International Committee of the Red Cross (ICRC) suggested that weapons inflict "superfluous injury and unnecessary suffering" when they cause "specific disease, a specific abnormal physiological state, a specific abnormal psychological state, or specific and permanent disability or specific disfigurement.[42] Permanent disability or disfigurement is neither the common nor the intended result of NLWs, but many NLWs do cause abnormal physiological or psychological states. NLWs are, therefore, *medicalized* weapons and herein lies what may be their insidious character. The weapons surveyed here do not use high explosives to cause blunt traumatic injury, but instead turn to pathogens, chemicals, and radio, sound, and electromagnetic waves to undermine the body's defenses from within. Medicalized weapons exploit medical knowledge to harm and disable.

A restriction, therefore, that defines superfluous injury and unnecessary suffering in terms of an abnormal "physiological or psychological state" undercuts any medicalized weapon no matter how nonlethal it is. For this is what medicalized weapons do: they interfere with normal physiological and psychological processes and target the human anatomy. Humanitarian organizations find this particularly galling because "most people," writes Robin Coupland of the ICRC, "consider warfare waged with weapons developed in laboratories by biomedical scientists unacceptable." "The primary effect [of weapons]," he continues, "should not be to target a specific part of the human anatomy, physiology or biochemistry."[13] With this in mind, the ICRC's 2006 *Guide to the Legal Review of New Weapons, Means and Methods of Warfare* cautions against any weapon that "would cause anatomical injury or anatomical disability or disfigurement *which are specific to the design of the weapon.*"[14] This means that a weapon specifically designed to disfigure the human body, depress the central nervous system, trigger convulsions, induce unconsciousness, or heat the skin to painful temperatures is one that inflicts unnecessary suffering and superfluous injury and violates the Geneva Conventions regardless of the magnitude or permanence of the harm it causes. This is a sweeping claim that deserves attention.[45] If valid, it forbids any medicalized nonlethal weapon whether it utilizes chemicals, electromagnetic waves, or radio frequencies. The ICRC does not specifically mention injury to the brain, but changing the brain's chemistry to alter behavior seems especially sinister and dehumanizing. But why are bacteria (or any other nonlethal technology) any worse than bullets? I confess no easy answer to this question.

One way to evaluate the Red Cross claim is to think about the first meaning of unnecessary suffering noted in the previous chapter. Here, the criticism of medicalized weapons is straightforward: they cause harm that is not militarily necessary. Framed in this way, however, the objection is off the mark. The purpose of NLWs is quite the opposite. They aim to prevent the grievous harm that lethal weapons and high explosives cause. Nevertheless, one might raise legitimate concerns that NLWs lead to, rather than cause, unnecessary suffering. Critics of chemical NLWs often make this point when they recommend NLWs that do not use chemical agents. This was precisely the view of the Council on Foreign Relations in 2004.[46] They were not so much concerned with the harm calmatives may cause, as with the likelihood that any permissible chemical weapon, no matter how nonlethal, will open a door to allow nations to repudiate the hard-won CWC and build chemical weapons of mass destruction.[47] This is no simple matter. How does the international community protect existing treaties and conventions that successfully outlaw certain weapons? Moreover, do we really want to open the door to a new array of weapons that bring previously unimaginable types of harm, however nonlethal they may be?

Answers to these questions are elusive. Neither international law nor the warfare it regulates is static. Emerging technologies offer an array of weapons hitherto unimaginable, and the exigencies of asymmetric warfare (some of which were also unimaginable) force us to constantly reevaluate and reinterpret many subjects. Discussions about the nature of war will undoubtedly raise questions about international law enforcement, the war on terror, and the many forms of insurgency. These discussions will spill over into an examination of other instruments of international law. There is currently no agreed-upon definition of rogue or unlawful combatants, just as there is no consensus about the nature of law enforcement or the scope of military operations other than war. As the international community wrestles with these issues there is no reason to think it will slide down a slippery slope rather than construct firm red lines about the use of different weapons in various situations. The CWC is not an outright ban but a convention restricting chemical weapons. As technology develops and as circumstances demand, the parties to the convention will inevitably work to redefine its restrictions. Note that however cogent the fear of proliferation may be, it only pertains to chemical nonlethal weapons and not to those NLWs that utilize other technologies.

Another way, to evaluate Red Cross concerns is to think about the second meaning of unnecessary suffering. Rather than being militarily unnecessary, we might ask whether the suffering that combatants and noncombatants suffer at the hands of nonlethal, medicalized weapons inhuman? Here, it seems that the ICRC harbors a stronger, yet unarticulated, fear of weapons that manipulate the human body in ways that are, perhaps, unnatural. In his novel *Saturday,* Ian McEwan describes a chance encounter between a mugger and a surgeon. The mugger is desperately ill and the surgeon knows it, and just as the potential for violence escalates, the assailant understands that his victim can help him. The situation then changes dramatically. Now, writes McEwan, "they are together ... in a world not of the medical but of the magical. When you're diseased it is unwise to abuse the shaman."[48] So, the mugger backs off.

This brief description of medicine in an isolated episode of hostility and conflict suggests that the problem of NLWs may not be one of suffering in the sense of unendurable or frightful pain but of something far more subtle. Jonathan Moreno asks whether neuroweapons that modify the brain do not put us into "special territory" where we are "overstepping some natural line and jeopardizing our essential nature or personhood."[49] This is a real fear. When weapons push beyond blunt trauma, blood loss, and death, and can cause a genetically engineered viral disease, interfere with neural networks, depress the central nervous system, shut down sight, or induce hallucinations then they have, in some sense, moved from the medical to the magical. Medicalized weapons are, in this sense, magical weapons, the most fearsome of all. They inflict harm that is not merely painful but in some way insidious. McEwan raises the specter of shamanhood. Every society entrusts health care professionals with the means to prevent sickness and stall death. Because these same means may serve malevolent ends, the medical community must reassure us with oaths and rituals that it will not cross the line. Otherwise, we cannot give doctors our trust. The lay community, too, must remain on guard and wary lest the shaman garner more power than he already has.

These fears are not entirely groundless, but they pale before the possibility of using NLWs to significantly reduce civilian casualties during asymmetric war. It is true that the medical community plays a role in weapons development that it has never played before. Because it is impossible to develop NLWs without medical expertise, members of the medical community will find themselves involved in war making. Whether this will significantly undermine the practice of medicine is just one question that will only find an answer once these weapons hit the battlefield. The same is true of the novel harm that NLWs cause. Will soldiers and civilians prefer incapacitation, fleeting pain, or neurological intrusion to death or loss of limb? It is not unreasonable to think that many would.[50]

THE FUTURE OF NONLETHAL WEAPONS

There are many unanswered questions about NLWs. We don't know whether they will meet their operational demands and reduce casualties, and whether military organizations will resist the temptation to use NLWs as force multipliers. We don't know whether nations will avoid the slippery slope and unravel the hard-fought ban on chemical weapons of mass destruction. We don't know whether we can confine the members of the medical community to their traditional role as guardians of health while carefully regulating their role as its destroyer. In short, we simply do not know yet whether NLWs will really save civilian lives from the ravages of contemporary armed conflict. There is much to learn that can only come with the trial and error of deployment.

We do know something, however, about the devastation that conventional high-explosive weapons bring. We also know something about the effects of asymmetric warfare. We know that in a war between a powerful nation-state and a relatively small but heavily armed enemy widely dispersed among civilian population centers, it is easy to kill civilians. We know that the intent and design of NLWs is to reduce harm to noncombatants while maintaining combat readiness. Never before did armies design weapons with this purpose in mind. This is something new, and should not be overlooked in our zeal to preserve existing treaties and conventions. As NLWs make their way to the battlefield, a host of legal and ethical questions will arise. Some, the subject of this chapter, we can anticipate, others await actual deployment of weapons in the field.

To paraphrase *New York Times* columnist Thomas Friedman: "Some things are true even if Donald Rumsfeld believes them." There are times when the use of NLWs is perfectly appropriate. It was not surprising that the United States and other nations allowed Russia to set an important precedent when they responded to Chechnyan guerrillas with calmatives. Russian behavior and international acquiescence will slowly bend legal barriers and lay the groundwork for important changes in international law. One such change will dramatically affect the way we treat civilians during wartime. Unlike ordinary weapons, NLWs deliberately target civilian noncombatants in a way that blatantly violates the principle of noncombatant immunity. In conventional warfare, civilians may suffer collateral damage to the extreme, but never direct harm. To defend such a radical change of policy we must begin to think in terms of a lesser evils test that compares a small amount of direct harm with a greater level of indirect or collateral harm that comes from using high explosives. If the former is significantly less than the latter, then there are firm moral grounds for targeting civilian noncombatants with NLWs regardless of fears that we may offend human dignity by invading hitherto private reaches of the brain. The lesser evil calculation also goes to the crux of many of the bioethical arguments against nonlethal weaponry. Chemical agents or electromagnetic waves do cause unusual and bizarre harm to human beings. Calmatives may short circuit neural pathways, electromagnetic waves simulate a sense of burning, while TMS manipulates brain activity. It is a heady mix, but if we discount our primal fear of the shaman and his magic, then it is difficult to understand how nonlethal incapacitation is worse than permanent disability, disfigurement, and death.

In a changing geopolitical environment characterized by fierce ethnic rivalries, regional conflict, terrorism and asymmetric war, scientific and medical technology will offer policymakers and planners a huge array of weaponry. As it does, we have to watch carefully: first, to verify that weapons are effective and then to be certain that they do not bring more harm than they hope to prevent. This is true of any military innovation, whether technologically sophisticated nonlethal arms or the oldest, low-tech weapons of them all: assassination and torture.

5

Murder, Self-Defense, or Execution?

The Dilemma of Assassination

> **Lieber Code (1863), Section IX: Assassination:** The law of war does not allow proclaiming an individual belonging to the hostile army an outlaw, who may be slain without trial by any captor, any more than the modern law of peace allows such international outlawry; on the contrary, it abhors such outrage. The sternest retaliation should follow the murder committed in consequence of such proclamation, made by whatever authority.[1]

Francis Lieber, the renowned German jurist whom President Abraham Lincoln recruited to formulate a comprehensive law of war during the U.S. Civil War, has stern things to say about assassination. The Lieber Code, with its innovative laws addressing the rights of prisoners of war, immunity for noncombatants, medical neutrality, and permissible weapons, had an enormous impact on the development of international law. Although the Geneva Conventions did not expressly adopt his unequivocal condemnation of assassination, his ban did make its way into the military manuals of many nations in language very close to Lieber's original.[2] But what is Lieber talking about when he denounces a nation for slaying the enemy without a trial? After all, isn't this what soldiers do?

Fast-forward one hundred and fifty years. During the post–9/11 war on terror, the United States uses unmanned drones and specially trained teams to hunt guerrillas. In Yemen, there is spectacular success as intelligence successfully identifies the whereabouts of militants responsible for attacking the USS Cole in 2000 and killing 17 sailors.

In November 2002, a precision-guided missile zeros in on their car and kills the mastermind of the Cole attack and five other al-Qaeda operatives. Elsewhere in the Middle East, the Israeli army rolled out its policy of targeted killings to identify, track, and kill Palestinian guerrillas planning attacks on Israeli military and civilian targets. Clearly impressed, the American Army shook off the stigma of its widely condemned Vietnam-era Phoenix program that targeted thousands of Viet Cong insurgents, and quietly built a small elite force to capture and liquidate first Ba'athist dissidents and later insurgent members of al-Qaeda in Iraq.[3] Despite the immediate success of many of these missions, some nations were soon defending themselves against charges of assassination, secret paramilitary death squads, perfidious conduct during war, and extrajudicial execution.[4]

What prompts such vociferous condemnation? Assassination has the singular virtue of substantially reducing collateral damage and harm to noncombatants while eliminating grave, military threats. In an age when low-intensity war is increasingly replacing conventional armed conflict, and pinpoint attacks against combatants are preferable to indiscriminate assaults on mixed populations of civilians and soldiers, assassination should be particularly attractive. Time-tested, it is the paradigmatic "smart" weapon: identify your prey, hunt him down, and kill him. But for reasons that are often difficult to articulate, assassination evokes particular revulsion. Morally odious, it seems to violate a deep-seated and inviolable norm. "The most imperative military necessity," wrote J. M. Spaight in 1911, "could not justify the use of poison, or the torture ("inhumane treatment") of a prisoner of war (POW), or *assassination*.[5] As a tactic of war, assassination is certainly most puzzling.

WHAT IS ASSASSINATION AND TARGETED KILLING?

Many acts of wartime violence go under the name of assassination. One is the murder of a high-ranking enemy political leader in the hopes this will deliver a crippling blow and hasten the end of the war. Military planners who thought about assassinating Hitler had this in mind. In other cases, more relevant today, assassination may effectively allow a conventional power to topple a rogue regime without the devastating costs of armed intervention. Prior to the Iraq

American River College Library

War, there was open discussion about the benefits of killing Saddam Hussein.[6] Although these are interesting cases, they are not what Lieber or many nations usually have in mind. A political leader is a civilian and traditionally immune from killing during war. Lieber, on the other hand, directs our attention to enemy soldiers who have no such immunity. Here, he argues that enemies may not assassinate one another, although they may certainly shoot each other dead for simply wearing a uniform. What is the difference? What is it about assassination that raises so many hackles?

Assassination in Lieber's time was little different from targeted killings today. In each case, a particular combatant is singled out by name, declared an outlaw or unlawful combatant, and then hunted and killed, often in stealth. Framed this way, the problem is not hard to see. Either soldiers are criminals or they are not. If they are not outlaws, then there is no cause to declare them criminals or kill them covertly. If they are criminals, however, then they should be charged, arrested, tried, and sentenced, not shot on sight. Killing criminals without the benefit of trial smacks of extrajudicial execution. Today, this is potentially a huge problem, precisely because many believe that guerrillas and militants who take the field against Western forces are unlawful combatants and nothing more than criminals. If true, they are outside the laws of war (that is outlaws) and the laws of war hardly apply.

It is noteworthy that Lieber and Lincoln resisted the temptation to criminalize their enemies as Lincoln faced an army of Southern rebels. It would have been easy enough to brand soldiers of the Confederacy as outlaws and dispense with any conventions of war. But this is not what Lieber did. Instead, he brought them all under the umbrella of the law. This was a seminal contribution to the laws of war. It meant that no combatant, solely by virtue of his intent to kill his enemy, is a criminal, and that all combatants enjoy the presumption of innocence. Innocence does not mean that soldiers pose no mortal threat, but it does mean that no soldier faces arrest, trial, and punishment for killing enemy soldiers. For this reason, as noted in the first chapter, captive soldiers are not in the same category as jailed criminals. Rather, they are combatants who have been disarmed and forcibly prevented from returning to duty. Unless they have committed war crimes, they are free to go home when hostilities end.

This is the way of modern war and is consistent with disabling one's enemy rather than annihilating him. Once we name soldiers for killing, however, we upset this innocence with precisely the argument that Lieber presents. Naming names assigns guilt and, as Lieber suggests, proclaims soldiers outlaws. In doing so, assassination, as Lieber describes it, places war itself beyond convention. If one side can declare another's soldiers outside the law, then others are free to follow suit. The war convention disintegrates, and armed conflict is no longer amenable to Lieber's effort to regulate war by the force of enlightened principles of reason. This was Lieber's great enterprise and to work, every participant in war had to enjoy equal status under the law. To declare ordinary soldiers outside the law would upset the grand plan.

Today it is worthwhile to think again about Lieber's logic as we consider the question of targeted killing. By most accounts, targeted killings are named killings. They consist of compiling lists of certain individuals who pose specific threats and then killing them when the opportunity presents itself during armed conflict. The targets are usually terrorists or guerrillas, that is, those who operate at the behest of known terrorist or insurgent organizations. As noted throughout this book, however, the category of terrorist or guerrilla is not discrete or compact. There is no clear line between guerrilla and terrorist, or between these two groups and civilians who take an active part in the hostilities. Targeted killings thrive in this environment and rarely occur in any context other than asymmetric war. Bolstered by reciprocity and material symmetry, and unconsciously aware, perhaps, of Lieber's admonitions, few military planners ever suggest targeting or naming ordinary, i.e., regular, combatants in conventional war.

Is targeted killing a justifiable tactic in modern war? Answering this question depends upon how we answer several others. First, Who do targeted killings target? What is their status? Are they criminals, terrorists, guerrillas, or ordinary combatants? Second, What paradigm should regulate our behavior? Two paradigms justify the use of lethal force: war or law enforcement. War permits combatants to use lethal force against enemy soldiers with relatively few restrictions. Law enforcement, on the other hand, permits police officers to employ lethal force against suspected criminals but remains tightly circumscribed. Police officers may kill in self-defense in unusually threatening and dangerous circumstances, but they may not otherwise harm a criminal in the absence of due process. Once we focus upon the criminal dimension of terrorism, the paradigm shifts from war to law enforcement and with it to the restriction that the latter places upon using lethal force. Lieber advises us to put criminality aside and this will prove to be a good idea in some forms of asymmetric conflict where it is useful to preserve combatant equality. Finally, we have to ask whether targeted killings are effective and cost-efficient. What are targeted killings supposed to accomplish? Some say they thwart terrorist attacks. Others point to the deterrent effects, while still others suggest they are nothing but punishment for past misdeeds. Does targeted killing accomplish any of these ends and, if so, at what cost?

The Targets of Assassination: Combatants or Criminals?

Who are the targets of assassination? During World War II, U.S. intelligence uncovered plans for Admiral Isoroku Yamamoto, commander of the combined Japanese fleet and chief architect of the attack on Pearl Harbor, to inspect his forward positions in April 1943.[7] Knowing his flight plan, it was a simple matter to intercept and destroy Yamamoto's plane. While this certainly seems like a legitimate act of war and little different from bombing his military headquarters or barracks, Yamamoto's killing provoked some soul searching. If the Japanese thought that the United States had acted dishonorably or perfidiously, they might respond by assassinating high-ranking Allied officers or officials. These fears convinced American military planners to keep the episode under wraps until well after the war ended. Yamamoto's was one of the rare cases of targeted killing by the Allies in the Second World War. The repercussions of assassination are much feared.

Today, nations worry little about a response in kind from their adversaries and, therefore, have little to fear and, perhaps, much to gain from assassinating their enemies. At the same time, international law obscures the status of the weaker side to an asymmetric conflict. For no few observers, guerrillas are either criminals undeserving of protection under the law of armed conflict, or in an innovative twist of logic, they are civilians who take an active part in the hostilities. In both cases, they are not ordinary combatants. Condemning targeted killing as extrajudicial execution, human rights activists are quick to point out how international law straightjackets the way we must define some battlefield actors. "Armed Palestinians are not combatants according to any known legal definition," writes Yael Stein, of B'Tselem, The Israeli Information Center for Human Rights in the Occupied Territories. "They are civilians – which is the only legal alternative – and can only be attacked for as long as they actively participate in hostilities."[8] Stein's remarks highlight the problem of shifting identity that plagues the definition of combatant that I noted in Chapter 2. It seems that terrorists and guerrillas maintain two statuses. On the battlefield, they are something like combatants; off the battlefield and at the time they are targeted, they are something like civilians or some other form of noncombatant.

Granting guerrillas a shifting status can lead to peculiar and counterintuitive conclusions. Like human rights organizations, the Israeli Supreme Court also viewed guerrillas as wayward civilians when the court ruled on targeted killings in 2006. Civilians, reasoned the Court, merit protection only as long as they remain on the sidelines. Once they take a direct part in the hostilities, they lose their immunity. Once they cease fighting, they get it back again. While there are lengthy debates about whether a civilian driving a supply truck for militants or a farmer storing missiles in the barn are taking an active or direct part in the hostilities, there is no doubt that an armed militant attacking a military base or a suicide bomber making his way to a shopping mall is actively making war. It is, therefore, extremely odd that court justices and human rights activists would view the latter as civilians of any sort. Many guerrillas may not wear uniforms but they assume combatant status when they take up arms and fight as members of a guerilla organization. They are not civilians who lend an occasional hand to partisans or guerrillas, but fighters who maintain their hostile status off the battlefield as they prepare for battle, lay plans, tend to their weapons, and maintain their fighting capability.

Whatever the original framers of humanitarian law had in mind when they considered the status of civilians taking an active part in hostilities, it is hard to imagine that they were thinking about full-time militants fighting without uniforms rather than the civilians who sometimes supported them. Only by ignoring this not-so-subtle distinction could the Israeli Supreme Court write, "Among the military means, one must choose the means whose harm to the human rights of the harmed person is smallest. If a terrorist taking a direct part in hostilities can be arrested, interrogated, and tried, those are the means which should be employed."[9] Philip Heymann and Juliette Kayyem draw up similar policy recommendations that limit targeted killings to "situations in which it is necessary to prevent a greater, reasonably imminent harm or in defense against a reasonably imminent threat to the lives of the targets of the planned terrorist attack."[10] A targeted killing, in other words, must be an unavoidable, last resort measure necessary to prevent an immediate and grave threat to human life. These are exactly the same rules that guide law enforcement officials. They, too, may only employ lethal force when it is "absolutely necessary to protect persons from unlawful violence, effect a lawful arrest or quell a riot or insurrection."[11] This approach, like that of the Israeli courts, therefore, leans heavily on the assumption that targeted killings must conform to the rules of law enforcement when a nation fights criminal terrorists. Viewed in this way, arrest, trial, and other principles of law enforcement are the rule, while lethal force is the exception. Abiding by guidelines like these avoids the stigma of extrajudicial execution, but at the cost of viewing everyone on the battlefield as a civilian of one sort or another.

However, this is the wrong direction entirely if terrorists, guerrillas, and insurgents are combatants rather than some odd breed of civilian. If they are combatants, there is no call to arrest, interrogate, and try terrorists, guerrillas, or insurgents rather than kill them. Ordinary combatants, if that is what they are, may be shot and killed solely for facing their enemy in wartime. Following the rules of law enforcement would extend greater rights to guerrillas and terrorists than regular combatants enjoy. This is counterintuitive to the extreme, particularly if one attributes a measure of guilt and liability to terrorists and guerrillas but confers innocence on conventional combatants. Something is amiss; returning to a war or self-defense paradigm may help right things.

In contrast to the paradigm of law enforcement, the war paradigm carries far fewer restrictions when facing an armed threat. Combatants are vulnerable regardless of the immediate threat they pose. Yet, here too, there are different kinds of combatants. War criminals, like any criminal, retain the right of due process. Sometimes, however, there is a tendency to use targeted killing to punish terrorists for past deeds. "*Terrorists Responsible for Dolphinarium Attack Liquidated*" read the headline of one Israeli newspaper on November 1, 2001, referring to an attack that killed more than twenty youngsters earlier that year in Tel Aviv. "Liquidation" is execution. Capital punishment without trial is beyond the pale of justifiable killing compelling officials to claim that these same terrorists are planning future attacks and, therefore, liable for targeted killing.

If terrorists are war criminals, then they have lost no rights to due process that would permit authorities to try to execute them under the guise of self-defense. On the contrary, capturing wanted war criminals requires authorities to make an effort to arrest and bring them to justice. This is true, however, only insofar as those wanted no longer pose a lethal threat. Facing a force that counts war criminals among its members, no attacking army can be required to try to arrest them first. These war criminals, like terrorists, are combatants first and criminals second. When they pose a deadly threat, they are subject to lethal force; when they have laid down their arms, they face arrest, trial and incarceration. Unlike ordinary combatants, they will not go home when the war is over. They have no rights that put them in a position superior to ordinary combatants.

This has us thinking again about the assassination of ordinary combatants that Lieber forbids. To preserve the rules of conventional war, Lieber does not want to disturb the equality of soldiers. Rather than focus on equality of soldiers, however, it is best to understand targeted killing as an adaption of the war convention that permits soldiers to kill one another in the absence of uniforms. While the war convention assumes that soldiers can identify one another by uniform or insignia, guerrillas participating in an asymmetric war rarely oblige us in this way. Can the stronger force just use lists of names to identify their enemy? In this case, names on a list serve the same function as a uniform: they determine affiliation. Then, once a state army knows that a particular person is a member of an enemy military organization, nothing stands in the way of disabling him when the opportunity presents. This might be the best way to understand the morality of targeting un-uniformed soldiers without upsetting combatant equality as Lieber fears.

Affiliation: Using Names Instead of Uniforms

The importance of uniforms is one of the pivotal issues that targeted killing addresses during asymmetric warfare. In conventional, symmetrical war, soldiers are vulnerable solely because they are members of their nation's armed services. This has nothing to do with the threat they pose personally. Instead, they are part of a collective, organizational threat that waxes and wanes during warfare. The traditional war convention assumes a clear, consistent, and fixed definition of the combatant and, ordinarily, a uniform or insignia is the sole indication of organizational affiliation. We have already seen how this unravels in asymmetric warfare. Un-uniformed combatants can change status almost at will and, as a result, enjoy a unique advantage during a guerrilla war or insurgency. On the battlefield and bearing their arms openly, they are combatants. Off the battlefield, they hide their arms and seemingly revert to noncombatant status. Without uniforms or insignia, it is impossible to identify un-uniformed militants as combatants.

Although un-uniformed guerrillas seem to shed and shift their status with ease, no fighting force can maintain that they are no longer combatants simply because they leave the scene of a battle and discard, as it were, the only earmarks of combatant status. Once a combatant, by whatever criteria, including the lax conditions of Protocol I, guerrillas, militants, and insurgents remain combatants whether on the battlefield or off. They never leave the armed forces that are party to the conflict. As such, the problem is primarily one of properly identifying combatants in the absence of uniforms or other markings. Here is where "naming" is useful: if one cannot determine organizational affiliation by uniforms or insignia, it is reasonable, indeed imperative, to turn to alternative methods. Naming does not imply criminal guilt or outlaw status but establishes affiliation in the same way that uniforms do.[12] Naming combatants is considerably more difficult than recognizing them by uniform and so demands careful intelligence to assemble a list of individuals affiliated with the enemy's armed forces. Armed with this list, it is possible to establish combatant status. Anyone listed is a combatant and as vulnerable as one in uniform. Each may be killed or wounded, and need not be arrested and tried.

Slowly, then, we are working our way out of Lieber's challenge. As written, his paragraph 148 is an odd prohibition. The objection

to targeted killing cannot be that enemy soldiers are simply slain
without trial, for that is the way of war. Rather, it is the presumption
that specific enemy soldiers are, in some way, guilty of outlawry that
rankles Lieber. To name and target a uniformed soldier imputes
criminal behavior where there is none. Killing a uniformed soldier
is permissible but branding him an outlaw and condemning him to
death undermines the law of war and makes a travesty of soldiers'
innocence. But name an un-uniformed soldier to establish affiliation,
and the problem disappears. Naming does not single out ordinary
soldiers for execution. Rather it uses names instead of uniforms to tag
them as combatants.

Armed with an accurate list of guerrillas, military planners may
now ask whether targeted killings are the best way to disable their
adversaries. They will want to choose a method that is effective while
avoiding superfluous injury to soldiers and civilians alike. As they
deliberate, however, policymakers must remain aware of unusual
problems associated with targeted killing that do not often plague
other forms of warfare. Unlike ordinary killing in war, naming and
hunting guerrillas, usually with the help of local collaborators and
traitors, often provokes a deep sense of moral outrage. The indignation of victims of treachery and duplicity is not easily appeased and
can often lead to escalation and brutality that serves no reasonable
military purpose. The laws of war are well aware of this problem and it
is one of the striking ironies of war that it cannot long tolerate perfidy
and breaches of trust between enemies.

Perfidious Warfare

Assassination and targeted killing highlight the dilemma posed by
perfidy and treachery. While the laws of war protect civilians, prisoners of war, and the wounded, they offer very few rules about how one
side can kill, maim, and wound soldiers on the other side. One prominent rule, discussed in Chapter 3, restricts weapons to those that do
not cause superfluous injury or unnecessary suffering. Soldiers may
use no more force than necessary to get the job done. But what about
deceit and ruses or spies and collaborators? Can an army trick the
enemy in some way? It certainly seems that it can, and war is a long
history of ambushes, ruses, feints, and misinformation. Nevertheless,
there are limits to the tricks enemies can pull. In particular, they

cannot abuse the trust they need to fight one another. But what trust can there possibly be in war?

Think of the classic violations of wartime trust: a soldier lays down his arms and waves a white flag. As the enemy approaches, the surrendering soldier (or a friend hiding behind some trees) grabs his gun and shoots them down. This is perfidy. It abuses a convention of war and violates the fragile trust that characterizes the relationship between enemies during war. The approaching enemy soldiers trust the surrendering soldier not to harm them. At the same time, the surrendering soldier trusts that his enemies will not kill him. Otherwise, surrender is impossible. Why do enemies agree to this convention? Keeping in mind that sometimes they do not (and this is a recurring problem in asymmetric war), there might be two reasons: the aversion to shooting an unarmed man and simple self-interest. While some enemies might recoil at shooting an unarmed man at close range, the overriding reason is self-interest. War, if we go by the standards of international law, is not a fight to the death. Rather, sides fight until they have disabled one another and forced the other side to surrender. Surrender is the key here. During war, soldiers must have the option of surrendering if their situation is hopeless. Nevertheless, it is an extremely tricky business and requires that each side trust the other in the way I have just described. One false move, and the entire venture collapses into mutual recrimination and violence. Imagine how much more difficult it would be if one side or the other abuses the inherent trust the convention requires. No one could ever surrender and soldiers would fight to the death.

Assassination violates trust in war in the same way. How many instances like the following have repeated themselves in history?

> Under the pretense of arranging a permanent treaty, Hengist asked for a meeting with the elders of the Britons, unarmed, on the first of May at the 'Cloister of Ambrius.' However, treacherously, Hengist ordered his men to hide their long knives (the *seaxes*) in their leggings, and at his signal, '*Nimet oure saxes*,' they fell upon the Britons, killing four hundred and sixty.[13]

Here, too, the author denounces "treachery" and the flagrant breach of faith during war by Hengist and his men. Modern philosophers of war are similarly incensed, concerned that such disregard would only increase the suffering in war and make peace all the more difficult. Taking the long view of events like these, Emer de Vattel, the eighteenth-century Swiss jurist, condemned assassination in the strongest terms. "What scourge could be more terrible in its effects on the human race," he wrote in 1758, "than the practice of securing the assassination of one's enemy by means of a traitor?"[14] The scourge of assassination lies in the fear that it might easily undermine efforts to end war through intimate peace negotiations. Without surrender and without peace negotiations, war might continue interminably. Targeted killing, as we will see below, may have these very effects on peace in the Middle East.

If the driving force behind the aversion to assassination is the mutual interest in preserving some element of trust during war, what happens when self-interest makes assassination look good? Hengist took a calculated risk, hoping to change the political landscape in one stroke and end the war on his own terms. In 1811, the Egyptian ruler Muhammad Ali, invited the Mamluk chiefs to negotiate peace, only to murder them all after dinner. In each case, the assassins consolidated their hold on power. In asymmetric warfare, as in the instances just described, victims of assassination cannot respond in kind. They may respond with terror and attacks against soft targets, but the wherewithal of targeted killing is beyond them. Why then shouldn't nation-states use targeted killing against their weaker nonstate enemies? It certainly will not upset any fragile trust between enemies, for little, if any, exists. It will affect surrender but little, because terrorists, militants, and guerrillas have few opportunities to take prisoners. So we are back to the question, Does it work and what does it cost?

TARGETED KILLING: AN EFFECTIVE TACTIC OF ASYMMETRIC WAR?

Accepting targeted killing as a legitimate form of warfare does not preclude a careful assessment of its necessity, civilian costs, and military benefits. Are targeted killings necessary to meet the threat from armed insurgents? Are they effective? Do they limit or exacerbate harm to civilians? There is no easy way to answer these questions because criteria are so elusive. Some observers believe that a reasonable hope of success is sufficient to justify targeted killing.[15] Certainly, this is true, but what does it mean? More importantly, what of the cost? Given sufficient firepower, one can always find a tactic that offers a reasonable hope of success.

The Cost of Collaboration

Targeted killings do not take place in an intelligence vacuum. On the contrary, copious amounts of reliable intelligence are necessary to sustain a comprehensive program of targeted killing. While electronic means provide some information, most comes from human intelligence sources: informants and collaborators. For this reason, targeted killings carry costs not typically associated with ordinary killing during wartime.[16] The legitimacy of naming to determine affiliation does not allay these costs, many of which are inseparable from the process of identification. Un-uniformed militants are difficult to identify without extensive intelligence that comes largely from a well-watered network of informants, collaborators, and traitors. By all accounts, Ibrahim Bani Odeh, a Palestinian bomb maker, was decapitated when the headrest of the car he borrowed from his cousin, a known collaborator, exploded. Fatah leader Hussein Abayyat was assassinated after being fingered by four informers, and Yahiya Ayyash, the famous "engineer" assassinated in Gaza in 1996 when his cell phone blew up, was set up by a colleague's relative-turned-collaborator.[17] Informants and collaborators are similarly crucial to U.S. counterinsurgency efforts in Iraq:

During COIN [counterinsurgency], intelligence organizations at various levels usually infiltrate the opposing side and obtain inside information. When a population is of divided allegiance, there are usually opportunities for infiltration. Almost certainly, Sunni insurgents gain inside information from the Iraqi government and the Iraqi Army. Similarly, U.S. and Iraqi intelligence organizations cultivate informers among the insurgents.[18]

In war, but particularly in asymmetric wars against un-uniformed combatants embedded deep among the civilian population, information is the key. Beyond their own lives, nonstate actors present very few strategic or military targets that a state power can target effectively and without excessive civilian casualties. "With information and intelligence," explains British General Rupert Smith, "the individual insurgent becomes the target and escalation is measured in his sense of an increased threat to his own worth."[19] To gather information, counterinsurgent forces must cultivate informants and collaborators. Informants are of two types. Some are "members of the conspiracy [that is, insurgents and militants themselves] who can be threatened, enticed, or cajoled into becoming informers."[20] This brings to mind law enforcement officials who enlist informants from the criminal gangs they are trying to destroy. But many other informants are not at all like police informers who are either criminals themselves or concerned citizens anxious to rid their neighborhood of criminal elements. Instead, many collaborators are ordinary citizens who are also threatened, enticed, or cajoled and cooperate following threats of imprisonment and torture, or offers of money, medical care, or travel permits.[21] Others turn to collaboration to exact revenge and settle scores. The numbers are not trivial and estimates of collaborators and informants among Palestinians, for example, range widely from 40,000 to 120,000 individuals (1–4 percent of the population).[22]

The effects of collaboration are pervasive among an occupied people. "The Palestinian collaborator in the Israeli strategy," notes Abdel-Jawad, for example, "serves the purpose of creating mistrust, spreading confusion and undermining collective self-confidence within Palestinian society.[23]" Once facilitated by spies, informers, compromised friends, and family members, assassination subverts strongly held beliefs about integrity, trust, honor, and loyalty that hold traditional societies together. And, it creates a vicious cycle of violence:

Every time a wanted individual was captured, wounded, or killed, the public immediately suspected the work of an informer. It was the beginning of a vicious cycle in which the wanted individuals were hunted by the security forces, while the suspected collaborators were hunted by the wanted, who held them responsible for the death or capture of their comrades.[24]

Clearly, this is not a healthy situation for any society. Targeted killing provokes a fierce reaction against both collaborators and those who recruit them and, at the same time, rend the moral and social fabric of the community. This is part of the scourge that so preoccupied Vattel and may explain, at least in part, the violent response that often follows targeted killing fueled by collaboration, a response that brings additional civilian casualties and makes it that much more difficult to forge peace.

Civilian Costs

Apart from the costs of collaboration, troops also injure and kill bystanders when they attack un-uniformed combatants. In fighting between September 29, 2000, and August 31, 2008, Israeli troops successfully targeted 232 named combatants while killing 154 civilians.[25] Are these collateral civilian casualties excessive or reasonable? We saw in the previous chapter just how difficult it is to quantify disproportionate casualties.[26] On the face of it, it seems that a ratio of less than 1:1 is reasonable, particularly if one considers that the 232 militants did not wear uniforms and operated well entrenched among civilians. The real test of targeted killings, however, is the military advantage that Israel gains from the deaths of these combatants. On one hand, targeted killings should deplete enemy ranks; on the other, it should save civilian lives. Each outcome is difficult to evaluate with any precision. Targeted killing depletes the ranks but it also motivates new recruits to join. The real advantage may lie in eliminating highly qualified personnel rather than simply large numbers of militants. Expert bomb makers are difficult to replace and their deaths may set an organization back for some time. Targeted killings may also prevent civilian deaths by deterring others from taking part in suicide missions. However, counterfactual claims, that is, estimating the number of deaths or suicide missions that do not occur following a successful targeted killing, are difficult to assess. As we will see in the following section, there is conflicting evidence about the effects of targeted killings. Nevertheless, if there is a reasonable expectation that the deaths of 232 militants saved many Israeli lives, then 154 civilian casualties do not seem excessive, particularly as Israel makes considerable efforts to limit civilian casualties. While some isolated missions cause excessive casualties, it seems that the policy as a whole is proportionate.[27] If, on the other hand, targeted killing increases casualties among those it is trying to protect, then the policy is misguided.

Do Targeted Killings Save or Endanger Lives?

Are targeted killings effective? Do they enhance security, disable the enemy, and improve the prospects for eventually ending armed conflict? Commenting on a secret American plan to "locate, target, and kill leaders of al-Qaeda in Iraq, insurgent leaders, and renegade militia leaders," Bob Woodward suggests that the plan's success is partly responsible for the impressive turn of U.S. fortunes in Iraq. After mid-2007, security improved considerably and by April 2008, coalition casualties and insurgent activity were both down significantly. Although targeted killings were a crucial part of American strategy, Woodward also attributes the decreased violence in Iraq to the surge of U.S. forces that increased troop numbers in Baghdad from 17,000 to 40,000 soldiers, to the "Anbar awakening" that led Sunnis to oppose extremists and assist U.S. and Iraqi forces, and to the decision of the Madhi Army to stand down after heavy losses in Karbala in August 2007 following confrontation with Iraqi forces.[28]

In Israel, the correlation between targeted killings and security is more difficult to determine. There, critics charge that targeted killings only incite further attacks and often slide from interdiction to retaliation, retribution, and revenge. Proponents argue that the situation has improved. Here, too, firm criteria are lacking. Daniel Statman, for example, describes how in January 2004, "the situation is much better ... than it was in March 2002, when Israel was facing two to three terrorist attacks a day, resulting in the deaths of more than a hundred Israelis in one month."[29] While March 2002 was, indeed, a watershed that prompted sweeping military action in the West Bank to root out terrorists, it is not obvious that the situation two years later was much better. Targeted killings were a fixture of the fighting since November 2000 and it is not clear whether they reduced the threat of terror.[30] In the 18 months following Israel's reinvasion of the West Bank in the summer of 2002, the number of Israelis killed by terrorists within the pre-1967 borders has held steady at about 50 in each six-month period.[31] Subsequently, however, the situation improved and the number of casualties decreased, a fact that is probably attributable to the separation fence that kept guerrillas out of Israel and led the Palestinians, particularly Hamas, to pursue long-range missile attacks that were not nearly as lethal as suicide attacks.[32]

In the years before the separation fence effectively prevented Palestinians from freely entering Israel, there was considerable concern that targeted killings only provoked terror attacks.[33] In late November 2001, after a relative lull in the fighting, Israeli forces assassinated Mahmoud Abu Hanoud, a high-ranking Hamas commander. Palestinian leaders accused Israel of provoking militants to scuttle American mediation efforts and warned of Hamas-backed retaliation.[34] Bloody terror attacks following Hanoud's death left forty Israelis dead. The same scenario repeated itself a month later following the assassination of Tanzim leader Raed Karmi. In the aftermath, ten civilians died in publicly announced retaliatory terror attacks that eventually led the Israeli army to reoccupy the West Bank for the first time since the outbreak of hostilities. Lawrence Freedman, on the other hand, remains convinced that targeted killings are the "most effective means the Israelis had to bring down the number of successful suicide attempts." He cites the Hamas demand for a cease-fire that came 11 months after Hamas's founding leaders, Sheik Ahmed Yassin and Abdel al-Rantissi, were assassinated in March 2004.[35]

The empirical evidence, however, supports the impression that targeted killings result in more terror bombings. One has to distinguish between the number of terror attacks and the number of resulting civilian casualties. While researchers do not agree about whether civilian casualties increase or decrease following targeted killings, many are convinced that targeted killings increase motivation among guerrillas and, as a result, the number of raids, successful or not, increases following a targeted killing.[36] Targeted killing triggers high emotions and draws significant numbers of new recruits that replenish the terror stock, that is, the cadre of men and women willing to undertake suicide bombings or launch Qassem missiles from Gaza (an activity that, too, is often suicidal). The result may be a greater number of terror and missile attacks, thereby feeding a cycle of targeted killing and terrorism.[37] The parties are not ignorant of these outcomes and constantly try to fine-tune targeted killings and terrorist attacks to gain maximum advantages. Guerrillas will want to kill maximum numbers of civilians and provoke targeted killings severe enough to bring in fresh recruits, but weak enough so as not to devastate their higher ranks. Counterinsurgents, on the other hand, will try to carry out targeted killings that are severe enough to remove an immediate threat and destabilize terror organizations, but not so brutal as to motivate enemy civilians to join the guerrilla ranks.[38]

In the Palestinian-Israeli conflict, therefore, results remain mixed. For Israelis, targeted killings provide a visceral sense of potency when there often is no effective response to terror attacks. They believe that targeted killings, particularly the killing of important enemy military leaders, will bear fruit. Targeted killing satisfies a sense of justice or even vengeance as terrorists get their due. Israelis find proof of their effectiveness in the recurring demand that Palestinians make to stop the killings as a price for peace or quiet. On the Palestinian side, targeted killings provoke moral outrage and cries of revenge. In their wake, young Palestinians rush to join radical movements and give their lives attacking Israelis or launching missiles that they know will cause little damage.[39] More than torture and more than innocent civilian deaths, targeted killings provoke a particular kind of outrage that flares violently in war and is not easy to assuage in the peace that follows. Targeted killings reduce enemy capabilities but easily instill a stronger will to fight.

The U.S. and Israeli cases highlight the place of targeted killing in counterinsurgency warfare. In Iraq, targeted killings eliminated high-ranking extremists and helped U.S. and Iraqi forces provide security for the local population. Protecting the local population is, perhaps, the first goal of successful counterinsurgency because it secures the good will of the inhabitants, distances them from guerrillas, and denies support and refuge for militants. In Iraq, targeted killings and security operations went hand in hand. Targeted killings did not increase motivation among Sunnis who turned their backs on the brutality of the insurgents. At the same time, the United States and Iraq ramped up troop numbers providing the wherewithal to protect the local population. In Israel, on the other hand, guerrillas do not terrorize the local Palestinian population nor does the local population suffer from lack of security. Eliminating guerrillas does not enhance Palestinian security but only exacerbates feelings of dissatisfaction, repression, and *in*security under occupation. In this climate, it is no surprise that targeted killing is far less effective than in Iraq or other intervention sites.

REASSESSING TARGETED KILLING

Lieber assumed it was impossible to make the argument for targeted killings without unacceptably turning combatants into outlaws. Given the conditions of warfare in his day and, indeed, in most of the modern period, he was probably right. Soldiers wore uniforms and insignia and were easy to identify. Naming names added nothing to their vulnerability nor did it render any person a more legitimate target. On the contrary, it only presupposed an element of moral culpability that Lieber found loathsome. Today, lack of uniforms makes targeted killing an essential tool for combating nonstate actors. It need not and, indeed, should not imply criminal guilt.

This should address the concern that targeted killings are a form of extrajudicial execution perpetrated by paramilitary death squads. Concern about extrajudicial execution arises because the status of targets is ambiguous. If, as many human rights organizations claim, targeted militants are civilians and not regular combatants, then they enjoy the right of due process. No military or police force may shoot them on sight. Were their status so dubious, this might be true. The militants targeted, however, are very far from civilians and very far from the rare cases the framers of the Geneva Conventions had in mind when they voiced concern about the rights of civilians taking a direct part in hostilities. Militants, insurgents, guerrillas, and terrorists are regular combatants in everything but uniform. Protocol I exempts guerrillas from uniforms to give them a fighting chance, not because their status as combatants is any different from someone wearing a uniform. On the contrary, the overriding intent of Protocol I is to grant guerrillas and insurgents exactly the same status as any other combatant. International law extends nonstate actors the right to fight without uniforms as a way to offer militants operational mobility, not to hide their identity forever.

In the absence of a uniformed adversary, state armies are left to identify the combatants among the indistinguishable and hostile mass of people they face. The obvious method is to gather intelligence and make a list. Anyone on the list is as affiliated with an enemy military organization just as surely as if he or she was wearing a uniform. Establish affiliation and the law enforcement paradigm has no force. There may be war criminals among militants just as there may be war criminals among a uniformed army. When they fight as part of either organization, they are first combatants, subject to lethal force. When they lay down their arms, they enjoy the rights of any criminal suspect.

The great weakness of assigning affiliation based on any list, however, is the veracity of the list itself. Those lists the American

Army used in Vietnam were riddled with errors. By some estimates, 90 percent of those killed were civilians, without any connection to the Viet Cong.[40] In Israel, there seems little concern about mistaken identity among watchdog human rights organizations. Charting the escalation of targeted killing in the Palestinian conflict, B'Tselem, The Israeli Information Center for Human Rights in the Occupied Territories, maintains two sets of figures: "Palestinians killed during the course of a targeted killing" and "Palestinians who were the object of a targeted killing."[41] The former figure includes all those killed in an attack, noncombatants and combatants alike; the latter, only militants. When asked, B'Tselem had no doubt that the intended objects of targeted killings were all members of one military organization or another.

Effectiveness in the short and long term remains the lynchpin of any justification for targeted killing. The evidence from Israel and Iraq suggests two different trends. In Iraq, preliminary reports describe how U.S. forces cultivate informers among insurgents and civilians who are anxious to rid their towns of al-Qaeda in Iraq. In Iraq, collaboration does not seem to have the same corrosive effect that it has among Palestinians. Instead, targeted killing in Iraq has the potential to provide benefits to the many parties anxious to destroy the al-Qaeda infrastructure. Targeted killing may hold similar potential during a military intervention under UN aegis as intervening troops work to dismember a genocidal regime. Unless encumbered by grave mistakes of identity, an assassination policy aimed at al-Qaeda militants does not threaten postwar rehabilitation.

In the Palestinian-Israeli conflict, however, the reality of a national liberation struggle creates a different set of circumstances. Here, there are significant costs to a policy of targeted killing that feeds on coerced collaboration and treachery. These costs limit its effectiveness. At worst, targeted killings radicalize the population, undermine social stability, encourage recruitment to militant organizations, and increase terror attacks and civilian casualties. At best, they may have some short-term success as militants struggle to regroup. Although targeted killings may reduce enemy capabilities, they intensify the motivation to fight and die. In a CAR conflict of national liberation the long-term effect of targeted killing cannot be but to undermine efforts at postwar peace and reconstruction. These costs should force belligerents to carefully consider the overall benefits of targeted killing. This is not to say that there will not be instances where a targeted killing is the only or least costly way to thwart an imminent threat. Targeted killing, once shorn of the stigma of extrajudicial execution and perfidy, joins the litany of weapons an army has at its disposal. One great benefit of targeted killings, at least as they emerge in Israel and Iraq in recent years, is their accuracy and relative lack of accompanying civilian casualties. Coupled with the additional advantage of significantly disabling enemy operatives, targeted killing will always be attractive. Add the cost of collaboration and the prospect of terrorist reprisals, however, and a sweeping policy of targeted killings in a CAR conflict becomes counterproductive.

With increased interest in targeted killing, it may also be that uniforms will continue to lose their significance. They certainly would not protect anyone deemed a sufficiently serious threat from a targeted killing. While it is difficult, in other words, to depart from the war convention and justify targeted killing without raising the otherwise insurmountable difficulty that non-uniformed combatants pose, it is quite likely that this link to old conventions will soon be forgotten. Targeted killings will offer another avenue for waging war. The costs might be high, but this only tends to limit naming to extreme situations and overwhelming threats that cannot be met by other means.

If this is the correct way of looking at targeted killing, one cannot preclude any side from adopting similar tactics when the benefits justify the costs. Lack of any capacity to respond in kind by the weaker side gives the stronger side a virtual monopoly on targeted killings. But this may change and if it does, no one should be surprised if guerrillas one day decide to pursue targeted killing and, for example, target young pilots whether in the field or at home on leave. Based solely on the threat they pose to civilians, bomber pilots are no less menacing than terrorists are. Should guerrillas or insurgents ever achieve the means to respond in kind, states fielding conventional forces might then find cause to desist and restore the convention that forbids targeted killing. Bomber pilots, after all, are considerably more expensive to train than suicide bombers. Unfortunately, once this particular genie is out of the bottle, it might not be that easy to get it back inside again.

TORTURE AND ASSASSINATION

As the title of this book suggests, torture and assassination seem to complement one another. If assassination is but another form of legitimate killing in warfare, then one might be tempted to say that torture and rendition are just another form of interrogation and intelligence gathering. As we will see in the next chapter, however, the issues at stake are far different. Targeted killings do not fly in the face of an absolute prohibition. Rather, targeted killing properly understood as named killing rather than perfidious assassination offers a solution necessitated by the lack of uniforms among combatants. Without the ability to establish affiliation based on lists of names rather than insignia, the *stronger* side's right to an equal chance in asymmetric combat suffers. Targeted killing restores a certain element of equilibrium.

Some may see rendition, torture, and harsh interrogation in a similar light. Like targeted killings, these unconventional interrogation methods offset the menace of terrorism and ticking bombs. Both torture and assassination merit consideration when the weaker side cannot respond in kind. There is something to this argument. In fact, it drives much of the torture debate. Nevertheless, torture – banned absolutely and unequivocally by international law and worldwide consensus – faces considerably more opposition and controversy than targeted killing.

6

Human Dignity or Human Life

The Dilemmas of Torture and Rendition

> The senior leadership at the CIA understood clearly that the capture, detention and interrogation of senior al-Qa'ida members was new ground – morally and legally.[1]
>
> George Tenet, Director of the Central Intelligence Agency (1997–2004)

There are two torture dilemmas. The first is the dilemma of torture; the second the dilemma of the torture debate. The first asks whether and under what conditions we may lift the universal ban on torture to save the lives of innocent civilians. Some thoughtful commentators reject torture in any form and for any reason, while others, like George Tenet, are more tolerant, if not more urgent, about probing the limits of interrogation. They will want to know if torture in the face of murderous terrorism is not the lesser evil. The second dilemma asks whether we do harm merely by discussing exceptions to the ban on torture. When democracies talk about exempting themselves from long-standing norms of behavior, repressive regimes are not far behind. They will want to know why they, too, cannot practice torture to prevent terror. How do we answer each of these challenges?

The debate about permissible torture in a democracy is not new. It preoccupied the British in the 1960s and 1970s and the Israelis in the 1980s and 1990s and the Americans since Abu Ghraib. Successive arguments build on the old, and in spite of marginal innovations, the contours of the debate have remained virtually unchanged since the British grappled with their methods of fighting insurgents in the colonies and Northern Ireland. There are several important elements to this debate. First, there is considerable sympathy for harsh interrogation techniques in the war on terror. In spite of vociferous indignation in some quarters, most Western nations support rendition, that is, U.S. requests to hand over terror suspects knowing they may face harsh interrogation. Second, public and judicial scrutiny has confined harsh or "enhanced" interrogation techniques to national intelligence agencies and there it continues to enjoy support. In this context, many defend torture to save large numbers of lives. Third, emerging, although relatively scant, evidence that enhanced interrogation techniques do not work (because they produce false or stale information) or carry great costs when they work occasionally (because they leave innocent victims or widespread fear and mistrust in their wake) or that other methods (such as cultivating trust or using informants) work better, does not belie the possibility that torture may sometimes save many lives. In spite of the efforts of many scholars to ascertain the effectiveness of torture, the evidence remains insufficient to prove otherwise and, given the secrecy of the agencies that practice torture, comprehensive evidence might never be forthcoming.

In the absence of firm, empirical evidence denying the effectiveness of torture, there remain adequate arguments for some forms of interrogational torture. I will describe these below. Any defense of enhanced interrogation, however, demands a clear distinction between interrogational torture (to obtain information) and terroristic torture (to brutalize or intimidate political opponents), between unlawful terrorism and lawful internal dissent, and between moderate physical pressure or "torture-lite," and cruel or vicious torture.

Supporters of enhanced interrogation overwhelm opponents in the first part of the torture debate. Foreign governments comply with American requests to arrest and transfer suspects to American jurisdiction. Public opinion is often supportive. Intelligence agencies take heart from their ability to prevent catastrophic terrorist attacks, and defenders of enhanced interrogation find nearly unassailable refuge in the lesser evil. However, advocates fare poorly in the second debate. Failing to convincingly distinguish between the harsh interrogations that democracies may practice and the brutal torture that repressive regimes may not, leaves the latter to equate the two. If democracies can torture terrorists, why can't other regimes torture their political opponents? Providing a convincing answer without running afoul of charges of hypocrisy is not easy. In the end, democracies face giving up the practice of torture or instituting safeguards to prevent egregious abuse.

THE TORTURE DEBATE TODAY

Torture is slow to come out of the closet and the best impression of its modern practice is that we still do not know much about it. Philosophers, jurists, and politicians continue to debate the definition of torture, possible justifications, and its best effects. So much of the debate depends upon whether torture works, and despite a burgeoning literature, torture remains shrouded in secrecy. For every case analysis of ineffective torture,[2] is the intelligence officer with the story of the one that didn't get away and of how torture produced the right information at the right time to prevent a catastrophic attack on innocent civilians. However, information remains sparse. No intelligence service has, nor likely ever will, open up all its files. No outside analyst has or likely ever will examine the 90 ticking bomb cases that Israeli officials say required enhanced interrogation.[3] Nevertheless, torture remains relatively rare. The 90 cases just cited account for perhaps two percent of investigations in Israel. In the United States, the number of cited cases is about 30.[4]

Thinking about ticking bombs, real and imagined, sets the stage for a lesser evil argument: if enhanced interrogational measures can save lives, then torture is less evil than letting many people die. This is the most prominent argument in support of torture. Against it are two camps. There are those who continue to attack the many premises of the ticking bomb scenario. Rather than producing the information necessary and sufficient to avert a calamitous terror attack, torture only delivers misleading, stale, or piecemeal information. At the same time, there is nothing to prevent terrorists from planning for operatives falling captive and making any number of contingency plans to move their device and reschedule their attack.[5] At the very least, opponents weigh in with unseen dangers: perhaps torture can save lives, but it carries significant costs that are impossible to ignore. These include harm to mistaken victims, the growing use of torture in law enforcement, and the erosion of civil liberties. The second camp of opponents eschews the complexities of ambiguous data and takes a more absolute viewpoint. When asked, Does torture work? one human rights activist simply answered, "We don't know and we don't care." Torture is always wrong no matter how many lives it might save. A person should no sooner torture another for life-saving information than rape him.

To evaluate these arguments, I will first map several key aspects of the debate. These include the definition of torture, an assessment of its effectiveness, and an evaluation of common justifications. In the second section, I look at the torture debate from on high and consider its place in the world today.

What Is Torture?

There is no single definition of torture. It is common, first, to distinguish between interrogational torture and terroristic torture. "The idea that torture is a cruel and ugly practice," writes Judge Richard Posner, "confuses torture as a routine practice of dictators ... with torture as an *exceptional* method of counterterrorist interrogations."[6] Terroristic torture is the way of repressive regimes. Its purpose is to terrorize the citizenry and stifle political opposition. Interrogational torture, on the other hand, is an adjunct of asymmetric war. It embraces harsh measures to elicit information from terrorists, militants, and insurgents who threaten national security. Contrary to widespread opinion, this is not the ticking bomb scenario often described. There are few cases where interrogators expect a single suspect to provide all the information necessary to avert a catastrophic attack on civilians. In practice, authorities use interrogational torture to save innocent, civilian lives *and* to prevent attacks on soldiers and military installations. Any justification of torture that leans heavily on the innocence of terror victims must contend with the messy fact that interrogational torture is a way of war, not solely a means to protect the innocent. It must also contend with the exigencies of modern intelligence gathering. Ticking bomb scenarios are not prevalent. Rather, the complexity of outsourced and decentralized terror networks makes it unlikely that information is concentrated in the hands of any one person.[7] Interrogation, therefore, lends itself most often to the slow accumulation of large quantities of piecemeal, low-level information that security forces require to fight terror networks and insurgencies.[8] U.S. General John Keane, former army vice chief of staff, refers to this as network mapping: the "tedious reading and sifting of interrogation reports, tactical operations, signal intercepts, other human intelligence reports, [and] captured documents."[9]

If this is the right way to understand interrogation in asymmetric conflict, then the central question of the debate is somewhat more mundane than the prospect of ticking bombs: Is it permissible to use enhanced interrogation techniques to obtain important military information? Framed in this way, one readily sees just how old and worn the question is. No military organization has raised it seriously in modern times for the simple reason that no party to a conventional war had much use for any military technique that its enemy can use with such demoralizing force. Asymmetric warfare, however, changes this equation. Guerrilla forces lack the means to capture more than a few enemy soldiers, while state military organizations expend considerable resources to capture and interrogate large numbers of guerrillas. Once states are insured of a virtual monopoly, interrogational torture is up for consideration.

Nevertheless, the debate is carefully circumscribed. No proponent of enhanced interrogation defends terroristic torture or torture in the hands of law enforcement officials. Moreover, advocates draw a line between different techniques, justifying only those that cause less than severe harm. This reframes the central question again: Is it permissible and is it effective to use harsh but not brutal interrogation techniques to elicit militarily important information? The next section, Acceptable and Unacceptable Interrogation Techniques, addresses the question of permissible techniques; and the following section, Is Torture Effective? examines the question of effectiveness.

Acceptable and Unacceptable Interrogation Techniques

Table 6.1 describes three broad categories of interrogation techniques: those that everyone accepts, those that everyone rejects, and those that many dispute.

Acceptable techniques that govern questioning by law enforcement and military officials appear in army and police interrogation manuals.[10] These are built around establishing rapport, gaining

TABLE 6.1 Acceptable and Unacceptable Interrogation Techniques by Agency

Interrogating Agency	Interrogation Techniques
Acceptable to police or army	*Law Enforcement Techniques* 1. psychological pressure 2. deception 3. good cop – bad cop 4. isolation
Acceptable to intelligence services only	*Enhanced Techniques: Moderate Physical Pressure or "Torture Lite"* 1. blindfolding 2. stress positions 3. loud music 4. sleep and sensory deprivation 5. waterboarding
Never acceptable for any agency	*Extreme, Brutal, and Severe Techniques* 1. severe beating 2. maiming or mutilation 3. sexual abuse

confidence, and working to identify a detainee's "primary emotions, values, traditions, and characteristics and use them to gain the source's willing cooperation."[11] However, investigators can also employ deception (leading a suspect to believe his interrogator is someone other than a U.S. official); psychological pressure (manipulating fear of incarceration or fear of never seeing one's family again); procedures that undermine a suspect's perception of his "loyalty, technical competence, leadership abilities or soldierly qualities" (without becoming degrading or humiliating); good cop/bad cop routines; and, in some cases, physical isolation.[12] Unacceptable techniques include those intuitively brutal to the extreme: severe beatings, maiming and mutilation, rape and sexual abuse. These techniques exceed the bounds of defensible torture and cause a degree of intense suffering that U.S. government legal advisors have compared to the pain "accompanying serious physical injury" or that which "shocks the conscience."[13] Whatever the exact definition, no democratic nation permits any of its police or security forces to use these brutal means. Between acceptable and unacceptable techniques, are those that have earned a variety of euphemistic descriptions such as torture lite, enhanced interrogation techniques, or moderate physical pressure. They include hooding or blindfolding, exposure to loud music and temperature extremes, slapping, starvation, wall standing and other stress positions and, in some cases, water boarding.

None of these latter techniques is new to democratic nations. When the European Court of Human Rights (1976) considered the lawfulness of these interrogation techniques, they echoed the majority view of two British government committees in the early 1970s, which, in turn, reached back into British history for a precedent. These techniques, noted the Parker Report, "have been developed since the [Second World] War to deal with a number of situations involving internal security in Palestine, Malaya, Kenya, Cyprus, British Cameroon, Brunei, British Guiana, Aden, Borneo/Malaysia, and the Persian Gulf."[14] The European Court respected this long tradition and slowly drew it out of the shadows while dismissing claims that these techniques necessarily constituted torture.[15] These were the same techniques an Israeli commission would approve in 1987 as it accepted the European Court's distinction between the combined use of the techniques, which constitute torture, and the techniques themselves, which, while inhuman and degrading, are free of the stigma attached to "deliberate inhuman treatment causing very serious and cruel suffering" and, therefore, did not "occasion suffering of the particular intensity and cruelty implied by the term 'torture'"[16]

Following 9/11, the American government would turn to all of these decisions, reports, and papers as it, too, employed enhanced interrogation techniques to fight terrorism. Banned for use by law enforcement and military officials, enhanced interrogation is the sole purview of intelligence agencies. In the United States, enhanced interrogation was reserved for terror suspects and other unlawful combatants but is beyond the pale for interrogating common criminals. These methods include shaking, slapping, beating, exposure to cold, stress positions, and, in the United States, waterboarding, a technique that simulates drowning by submerging the suspect.[17]

What, if anything, distinguishes one set of techniques from another? Are some significantly different from others or are all just part of a continuous spectrum of interrogation techniques? Those techniques we consider repugnant are usually the most brutal, impinge upon a person's dignity in a most extreme way, and cause extreme suffering, particularly long-term future suffering, that is entirely gratuitous and unnecessary. At the other end of the spectrum, interrogation does none of this. Severe questioning may be unpleasant and humiliating but it causes no immediate or long-term physical pain and suffering. One may ask why police officers may browbeat, threaten, or humiliate a prisoner and the answer seems to be that a) the level of humiliation does not exceed a threshold that undermines a person's dignity, b) the probability that a person committed a violent crime tempers the respect we owe another human being, and c) this disrespect is short-term. True, police interrogations may violate these conditions too, but when they do, interrogators are subject to disciplinary measures. Those who work for intelligence agencies, on the other hand, rarely face disciplinary action.

Intelligence agencies have wider latitude. Whether this is defensible is a separate question I will consider in a moment. First, I want to ask how the enhanced techniques of intelligence officials differ from extreme or brutal practices. One answer might be that the harm suspects suffer is not invasive or direct. Rather there is something passive or indirect about hooding, wall standing, sleep deprivation, loud music, or starvation. These "soften up" rather than directly harm a person in the way beating or electroshock or burning or drowning does.[18] Second, the intensity of pain that moderate physical pressure causes seems reasonably less than the pain that extreme physical pressure causes. Finally, the pain of hooding and stress techniques is transient and of limited duration. It does not extend much, if at all, beyond the time needed to elicit information. Once the hood comes off or the suspect may stretch his limbs, the detainee's body returns to normal functioning.

There is no great body of empirical evidence to support any of these assumptions conclusively. Often the pain of enhanced interrogation can be intense. Sometimes the psychological and physical sequelae last a lifetime. Nevertheless, moderate physical pressure, as defined earlier, does not seem to depart from what is necessary to get information from terror suspects. And, it seems significantly less extreme than the pain most people associate with torture. Commenting on the combination of these techniques, Darius Rejali writes:

Detainees who emerged from the Shabeh [combination of techniques] interrogation had "little physical proof of their experience. The few signs left on the prisoners' bodies evaporated after a shower, uninterrupted sleep and standard prison rations." When prisoners had clear wounds of torture, "the community understood why they broke down." But lacking clear wounds, they could not explain their weakness. Nor could they explain why they refused to continue their nationalist activities, a damaging move in a society in which political struggle was a measure of social worth. "The associated feelings of shame, remorse, and guilt can even cause severe mental trauma that would not have been experienced had the subjects been physically scarred." Shabeh combines a thousand clean practices to create a *social* death.[19]

There are two ways to read this description. For some, it shows something qualitatively different about moderate physical pressure that many people recognize. It is not as harmful as extreme interrogation. After all, a social death cannot be as bad as a real one. For others, the passage may suggest that a social death is just as bad as a physical death. What reason, then, is there to think that psychological pain is any less harmful or long lasting than pain inflicted on the body?

Perhaps there is none and, indeed, many firm opponents of torture argue that it is objectively impossible to distinguish between the harms that moderate techniques cause and those more brutal. Notice, however, that this argument cuts both ways. If it is difficult to distinguish between the effects of moderate and extreme physical pressure, then one may also argue that no less pain and suffering awaits a suspect or convicted felon in many jails in the United States or elsewhere in the free world. In other words, the harm that comes from landing in police custody (and being subject to "ordinary" interrogation and/or incarceration) or in the hands of a domestic intelligence agency moves along a continuum that is difficult to break into discrete categories. There is no place to draw a line based solely on the effects incarceration or questioning may have on the individual. Being suspected of violent crimes is not good for one's health. Some people may suffer from good cop/bad cop routines; others may persevere in the face of extreme physical duress. Moreover, these are the endpoints on the interrogation scale. In between, the middle is very muddy.

All this takes us back to a cultural view of cruel and unusual punishment. I asked this question in Chapter 3: Why are the effects of poison gas or blinding lasers worse than injury by high explosives that can equally kill or maim one for life? One answer, of interest in the context of interrogation, focuses on the window of vulnerability during war. Soldiers are vulnerable only as long as they pose a threat. Deliberately causing harm that persists far after hostilities have ended is unnecessary and therefore gratuitous and superfluous.

Extreme interrogation techniques that cause harm persisting far into the future is particularly objectionable. But long-term harm, particularly psychological harm, may also result from moderate physical pressure or lawful interrogation and incarceration. The persistence of the harm alone does not allow us to clearly distinguish between acceptable, questionable, and unacceptable techniques.

As a result, I suspect the reason for resisting extreme techniques but accepting the moderate ones is not so easily quantifiable. Instead, much turns on our intuitions about what is too cruel to do to others no matter what the consequences. Here a certain respect for human dignity takes over. This may not be the suspect's dignity but our own, and reflects a self-imposed vision of human worth that does not allow reasonable people to act in certain ways. As described in Chapter 4, many people agree about what kinds of suffering are superfluous and unnecessary or shock the conscience as the constantly evolving American view of severe torture now puts it.[20] Mustard and chlorine gas evokes ghastly images of suffering even though they are far less lethal and disfiguring than artillery shells, bullets, and hand grenades. Incendiary weapons cause horrific wounds but are often no less disabling than shrapnel. Yet many recoil from the former and tacitly accept the inevitability of the latter. Blindness is not fatal but particularly repugnant. In the case of torture, it seems that the worst excesses are not those that necessarily cause the most pain but those that mutilate or disfigure the human body or target specific physiological or psychological systems. This view would suggest prohibiting extreme torture, medical experimentation, or deliberately inflicting disease on suspects. These are precisely the kinds of effects that the ICRC has excluded from legitimate weapons development. Nevertheless, the reasons for excluding these harms while accepting others are difficult to sustain with any objectivity. None of this denies the brutality of torture, but it does offer some insight as to why moderate physical pressure seems significantly different from extreme torture to many people. No technique, however, is ever acceptable if it proves ineffective.

Is Torture Effective?

Some may argue that we would be more effective if we sanctioned torture or other expedient methods to obtain information from the enemy. They would be wrong. Beyond the basic fact that such actions are illegal, history shows that they are also frequently neither useful nor necessary.[21] (General David Petraeus, former Commander of U.S. forces in Iraq)

General Petraeus's skepticism notwithstanding, the question of effectiveness remains vexing. No intelligence agency is ready to supply details of successful investigations so the evidence is largely anecdotal.[22] Some documented torture cases are subject to scrutiny, and scholars have closely questioned claims about effective torture in Algeria, the United States, and elsewhere.[23] Accompanying this argument, however, are two others that deserve closer consideration: first, torture provides very poor information and second, informants provide better information.

Investigators recognize that information obtained under torture or the threat of torture is problematic. Investigators prefer a gradual approach to interrogation that builds rapport and gains trust. Harsh interrogation techniques lie in the background first as a threat, then if necessary, as reality. At the same time, data from independent sources – sometimes human, sometimes electronic – supplement the information that suspects supply. To get a grasp on the quality of information that torture provides, Rejali turns to the American army's Phoenix counterinsurgency program during the Vietnam War. Phoenix operatives first attempted to identify and then kill members of the Viet Cong. Rather than try to answer the question Is torture effective? based on individual cases, Rejali offers a novel approach by examining a large-scale application. Drawing on recent data from Stathis Kalyvas and Matthew Kocher, Rejali emphasizes that of 10,700 documented targeted killings, fewer than one thousand were confirmed Viet Cong. The rest were most likely innocent civilians.[24] While Kalyvas and Kocher attribute this remarkable lack of accuracy to the extreme violence attending a civil war, the tendency of counterinsurgents to liquidate a victim on less-than-convincing evidence, and the unreliability of informants who often want to settle personal scores, Rejali also attributes it to the unreliability of torture U.S. forces used to extract information about the Viet Cong.

In Vietnam, torture may well have yielded inaccurate information. But if targeted killing is a test case for effective torture, then a more successful counterinsurgency program belies Rejali's claim. In the previous chapter I described an Israeli policy of targeted killing that owes no small measure of its success to aggressive intelligence gathering. Civilians lost their lives in the course of operations but few casualties, if any, were the result of mistaken identification.[25] Rather, civilians suffered collateral harm in the course of targeting correctly identified militants. By this standard, then, interrogation proved exceptionally effective.

As I noted in Chapter 5, targeted killing is problematic for other reasons, but lack of reliable information was not one of them. Instead, targeted killings can achieve spectacular success in asymmetric war. Unfortunately, this very success may only exacerbate conflict and complicate postwar reconstruction. Assassinating Palestinian militants did little to reduce (and probably increased) the rate of terror attacks. Nor can one overlook the cost of collaboration as authorities threaten ordinary citizens to turn informant (as discussed in the previous chapter). Collaboration, as Rejali suggests, can often yield better information than torturing militants. However, collaboration is morally problematic and certainly no alternative to torture as Rejali and other opponents of torture suggest. Few informants come forward willingly. Some, or their families, face the threat of torture and physical violence. Many harbor personal grudges or accept bribes to turn informer, while still others agree to collaborate rather than risk the loss of travel passes or access to medical care. Collaboration does not replace aggressive interrogation; it merely supplants it. And, if Israel's policy of targeted killing is any indication, the two together may yield very reliable information.

As we evaluate the torture debate to date, it is difficult to conclude unequivocally that torture, the threat of torture, or enhanced interrogation techniques do not work. The odds of gleaning important information may be small, but given the overriding fear of terrorism in an atmosphere of overwhelming uncertainty, even democratic nations may find ways to justify interrogational torture.

JUSTIFYING INTERROGATIONAL TORTURE

The inability to agree on just what torture is and evidence that it is sometimes more effective than opponents claim, give life to the debate. The first line of defense is to deny that torture lite or moderate physical pressure is significantly worse than the kind of interrogation we permit law enforcement agencies to use on hardened criminals. Once officials define torture in terms of a threshold of severe pain and suffering in excess of what their interrogations cause, as American, British, and Israeli officials often try to do, then they are not practicing torture. Under these circumstances, they are employing legitimate interrogation techniques that by definition do not violate a suspect's rights. All that remains is for each nation to draw up a list of justifiable and preapproved techniques. During the second Bush Administration, American officials did just that for the CIA.[26] But this argument is disingenuous. No democratic nation permits law enforcement agencies or its military to use enhanced interrogation. Enhanced techniques are restricted to intelligence agencies and only when questioning those suspected of terrorism. What justifies more extreme means when the suspect is a terrorist?

Life, Dignity, and the Lesser Evil

Although there are many ways to frame the torture debate, the core dilemma remains the same: How do you balance the dignity of some and the lives of others? Viewed in this way, the answer seems easy: life trumps dignity and respect for self-esteem.[27] After all, the terrorists suspected of planting a bomb stay alive, a little worse for wear, perhaps, but still alive. His or her victims, on the other hand, die a gruesome death. Torture, in this view, is the lesser evil, offset by saving many innocent lives from catastrophic harm.

The lesser evil argument is largely about weighing the consequences of moderate physical pressure, and leaves advocates and opponents trying to sort out the costs and benefits of enhanced interrogation. This is not easy, particularly in the absence of reliable data. Will torture give authorities the information they need, when they need it? Are less-harmful means of interrogation available? Does torture present a long-term threat to all citizens by eroding concern for liberty and human rights? Or, closer in time, how should we factor in mistaken victims who suffer torture but who turn out to know little or nothing of impending terror attacks?

Gathering all this information into a neat cost-benefit equation is difficult. Rational agents with the best of intentions have a hard time making life-and-death decisions under conditions of risk or uncertainty. Because thoughtful people inflate the danger of catastrophic and unfamiliar scenarios, they routinely fear terror more than automobile accidents, for example, even though the latter are far more prevalent. Terror provokes fear and dread, fatal auto accidents are an unpleasant fact of life, a risk we all assume for the convenience of easy travel. If rational agents misjudge the risk of terrorism when the odds of dying in a terror attack are common knowledge, they are all the more skittish when probabilities remain unknown and outcomes uncertain. Guards at a check post do not know if the ambulance approaching is a car bomb, nor do interrogators often know the odds that the suspect before them conceals important information.

When the odds are unknown, some try to estimate them based on past events. This can be highly subjective. Others, lacking relevant information, will assign equal probabilities to each outcome and assume an equal chance the suspect holds crucial information. Moreover, because the cost (and fear) of a terror attack is so great in the minds of most people, one only requires a relatively small chance that torture will prevent terror to adopt extreme measures. The ticking bomb scenario, so prevalent in the literature and uppermost in peoples' minds, need not be on the table. Rather it is enough, as many investigators claim, that there be a reasonable chance (which may be objectively quite small) that harsh interrogation will provide important information for uncovering and defeating terrorists who intend harm to soldiers or civilians. In the end, all these fears and inflated probabilities easily overwhelm the immediate (but comparatively lesser) harm that torture inflicts on a terror suspect and the long-term (but heavily discounted) harm that may befall a democratic society that accepts harsh interrogation.

It is no surprise that human rights organizations despair of ever refuting ticking bomb or less-urgent scenarios of terrorism. Terrorism trades on abject fear, not statistics. Terrorists, therefore, have a keen interest in exaggerating the imminent threat they pose. They cannot stand before interrogators and then try to downplay the severity of the menace they present. Everyone plays into the other's hands. Terror suspects need torture to legitimate their claims and instill fear in their victims. Interrogators need terrorists and ticking bombs to defend harsh interrogation. This makes it doubly difficult for critics of harsh interrogation to claim that they have misjudged the odds.

Nevertheless, blunt calculations of costs and benefits, even if miscalculated, present moral challenges that cannot be ignored. If we are to avoid terror at all costs then why stop with moderate physical pressure? Why not torture passersby or others who are not themselves terror suspects but chance upon crucial information? Why not torture a terrorist's child if this will force a detained suspect to speak? Why not torture common but heinous criminals – mass murderers, serial rapists, and pedophiles – if that will stop their crimes? Those who rely on the argument of the lesser evil alone cannot easily answer these questions. To answer them, defenders of enhanced interrogation must invoke the rights of interrogees to construct safeguards they hope will regulate or constrain torture.

Regulating and Constraining Enhanced Interrogation

Democracies hope to avoid the worst abuses of interrogation by prohibiting inhuman techniques that cause severe, long-term, and unnecessary harm. At the same time, some democracies also try to put legal or judicial safeguards in place. The best-known example is the attempt by the Israeli Supreme Court. Ruling that democracies must fight with one hand tied behind their backs, the Israeli Court glossed over the distinction between torture and ill-treatment, and demanded that a "reasonable investigation is necessarily one free of torture, free of cruel, inhuman treatment of the subject and free of any degrading handling whatsoever."[28] That is, the Court specifically rejected any attempt to force a dichotomy between torture and moderate physical pressure. Both are unlawful, both violate a person's basic right to respect for dignity and freedom from torture. Nevertheless, torture and ill-treatment may be defensible if necessary to save innocent lives. When the right to life of one group collides with the human dignity of another, the latter gives way. This is the necessity defense and recognizes both the integrity of the torture victim's rights and the need to violate them under exceptional circumstances.

To the Israeli court, torture is at best only defensible. After all is said and done, an interrogator must stand before the bar and explain how he violated the law to avoid "consequences ... which would have inflicted grievous harm or injury."[29] He must show that his actions met the threat of grave and unavoidable harm with a proportionate, effective, and last-resort response. On paper, this is what the necessity defense should look like. In practice, however, investigators have rarely stood trial.[30] "As long as interrogators act in a reasonable manner," declared Israel's state prosecutor in 2002, "they will not be tried on criminal or disciplinary charges for their actions even if jurists define these actions as unjustified."[31] Instead of having to defend themselves after the fact, investigators received prior authorization from senior officials based on the threat they thought a suspect posed. But there was never any judicial follow-up. No one had to show that torture was necessary to get the information needed to prevent a terror attack. What began as a carefully controlled exception gradually morphed into an acceptable rule of conduct demanding little in the way of accountability or defense. Nevertheless, the glare of publicity and the prospect of judicial intervention has reduced the severity and frequency of torture complaints in Israel and led the United States to suspend enhanced interrogation techniques in 2009.[32]

These safeguards do nothing, however, to ensure that innocent persons are not tortured or that police interrogators do not use torture in their investigations of common criminals. The first is more a philosophical than a practical problem. Most people will agree that it is wrong to torture a terrorist's child to force him to reveal important information. The child is innocent of wrongdoing and has done nothing to jeopardize his right to life or freedom from torture. This is obvious, perhaps, but it requires that we put the necessity defense in a slightly different form: *Torture is permitted as a last resort to save innocent lives as long as the innocent are not tortured.* Even ticking bombs do not override the life of the innocent. This is a common intuition: few would sacrifice an innocent person to transplant his organs to save the lives of four or five patients who would otherwise die. Similarly, the rights of the innocent would also protect a nonterrorist – cook, passerby, or spouse, perhaps – who chances upon important information. Each is as innocent as the child is but for the fact that they know something and the child does not. Why not torture the cook for what he knows? If he is innocent, why shouldn't he reveal the truth? Some take reticence as a sign of guilt, place the reluctant cook in the same category as the terrorist, and conclude that authorities may question both with equal severity.[33] This would be mistaken, however; people do not speak for many reasons and fear is foremost among them. The cook may choose to remain silent to protect himself or his family from reprisal. Under these circumstances, his rights deserve the utmost respect.

This reasoning does not help us with those guilty of crimes less heinous than terrorism. If the greater good drives defensible torture of terror suspects, then why not torture ordinary criminals? There are different answers to this question. Anyone consistently concerned with the rationale of the lesser evil may, indeed, agree that torturing criminals is sometimes as defensible as torturing terrorists. In both cases, many innocent lives may be saved. Yet, the costs of torturing criminals are unacceptably greater than the costs of torturing terror suspects. Torture may easily undermine the criminal justice system where ordinary criminals face trial and, therefore, should be vigorously condemned. Interrogational torture, on the other hand, has been the purview of specific intelligence agencies and an isolated, dedicated military court system. Taken with the fact that many tortured suspects are "outsiders," that is, noncitizens, it is easy to see how the costs of torturing them will not have the same ramifications as torturing ordinary criminals. By design, many democratic nations have successfully kept these outsiders out. This is precisely the point of confining enhanced interrogation to intelligence agencies and trying suspects before military tribunals. There is little evidence to suggest that torture in Britain, Israel, or the United States leached into the local criminal justice system and affected the prosecution of ordinary criminals.

It is important to see that the dilemma of torturing cooks and criminals arises because we have yet to define interrogational torture as a tactic of war limited to combatants. In fact, this is precisely what differentiates terroristic torture from interrogational torture. The former is a feature of civil society in a despotic regime and draws no distinction between political, criminal, or military threats. Interrogational torture, on the other hand, arises only in the context of asymmetric conflict and has no truck with criminals or political opponents of the government. These civilians are beyond the law of armed conflict, and the ways of war should not affect them. Instead, the evolving norm confines interrogational torture to combatants, however difficult they are to define. Therefore, the question is never Why not torture children, cooks, and criminals? but Why not torture commandos and other combatants? In ordinary, conventional warfare the answer is the same as we give to the question Why not assassinate enemy combatants? namely, it does not pass the test of military necessity. The fear and demoralization that comes from exposing one's own troops to the prospect of enemy torture offsets any military advantage that enhanced interrogation techniques confer. In asymmetric war, however, the weaker side lacks the means to capture and torture large numbers of uniformed combatants.[34] On the contrary, some guerrilla organizations, like Hamas or Hezbollah, find it far more profitable to hold the few soldiers they capture for lopsided prisoner exchanges. In the absence of reciprocity, harsh interrogation is much more cost-effective for the stronger side than it is in conventional war.

At the same time, torture is not foreign to democratic states. Torture, like other tactics discussed here, is entering the arsenal because it saves friendly lives (military and civilian), targets only the potentially guilty, limits collateral harm, and benefits from the weaker side's inability to respond in kind. Previously held in check by reciprocity, nations banned torture from the battlefield. But it was rampant in colonial warfare[35] and is now cut loose when stronger nations do not fear that their soldiers face significant danger from the other side. This explains the sudden proliferation of support for torture, support that no one would dare voice in the immediate post–World War Two era. Moreover, it explains worldwide support for rendition.

RENDITION AND INTERROGATION: INTERNATIONAL COOPERATION AND SUPPORT

Rendition to Justice

Capturing and detaining an enemy rather than killing him or her is a far more prevalent tactic in asymmetric war than it is in conventional war. In conventional wars, enemy soldiers are disabled by death or injury; in asymmetric war, they are captured, incarcerated, and interrogated. Information, not a body count, is the key to defeating many terrorist and guerrilla organizations. The overwhelming need for information, usually low-level and fragmentary, coupled with the nonexistent threat of reciprocal torture, set the stage for rendition and enhanced interrogation.

Rendition to justice describes a procedure for bringing a criminal suspect residing in one country to another country for incarceration, interrogation, and trial. Unlike extradition, that is, a formal legal process anchored in an outstanding arrest warrant, rendition usually targets suspects who may harbor no more than information and for whom no arrest warrant is issued. "One of the purposes of extraordinary rendition," write Weissbrodt and Bergquist, "appears to be to hold persons outside of the recognized judicial procedures for extraditions and criminal trial."[36] As with torture and assassination, the presumption of guilt drives rendition, but there are no warrants or authorization beyond those provided by the intelligence organizations of the countries involved. At the request of one country, usually the United States, a suspect residing elsewhere is arrested by local authorities and delivered to American custody for interrogation and prosecution.

What sullies rendition, however, is not the forcible transfer of a suspect from one country to another, but the prospect he or she may face torture. In fact, the legality of rendition depends entirely upon the prospect that the suspect will face torture. A summary prepared for the U.S. Congress makes this point clearly:

Under US regulations implementing CAT (the Convention Against Torture), a person may be transferred to a country that provides credible assurances that the rendered person will not be tortured. Neither CAT nor implementing legislation prohibits the rendition of persons to countries where they would be subject to harsh interrogation techniques not rising to the level of torture.[37]

Human rights activists, on the other hand, are quick to point out that rendition violates a number of human rights that have nothing to do with freedom from torture. These include the right to counsel, the right to an impartial tribunal, as well as protection from forcible transfer and arbitrary arrest. The Geneva Conventions also impose strict prohibitions on the transfer of civilians and prisoners, a prohibition the United States has skirted by placing unlawful combatants beyond the purview of the Geneva Conventions and interpreting the Conventions to allow the temporary transfer of persons for the purposes of interrogation (in Iraq, for example).[38]

Nevertheless, many nations accept U.S. assurances that American interrogation techniques do not violate the provisions of CAT or the 1949 Geneva Conventions (Article 3) that ban torture. As a result, rendition enjoys the support of a great many nations including Canada, Russia, Sweden, Germany, the UK, Indonesia, Bosnia, Poland, Thailand, Italy, Pakistan, Egypt, Jordan, Morocco, Saudi Arabia, and Uzbekistan.[39] In these instances, suspects are sought for questioning, not trial, and states cooperate when there is reasonable suspicion that crimes of terror have been committed. There is little in international law to prohibit cooperation between states, while many of the restrictions that might prevent states from transferring suspects to another state can be suspended in times of public emergency such as the war on terror, broadly construed.[40]

Obviously, this is not the way that nations at war treat ordinary combatants. In conventional war, combatants face capture and incarceration until the cessation of hostilities. Unless accused of war crimes, they cannot face trial for the mere fact that they are soldiers who kill their enemy. At the same time, each side, fearing abuse of its own soldiers, usually refrains from torture. In asymmetric warfare, all this breaks down. On one side, soldiers are no longer captured and held for the duration of the hostilities, but are "kidnapped" and held incommunicado in exchange for other prisoners. On the other side, combatants fighting with groups like the Taliban, Hamas, and al-Qaeda are declared unlawful combatants and deprived of the privileges ordinary POWs enjoy. They are rendered to justice, incarcerated without due process, and sometimes tortured to obtain information. In many cases, torture begins with rendition. This is the sticking point for many nations. But once assured that interrogation is lawful, they have few qualms about turning suspects over to U.S. authorities.

None of this, however, precludes public criticism or judicial intervention. In 2003, the Committee Against Torture chastised Sweden for its role in rendering Ahmed Agiza to Egypt. Sweden's participation in rendition was not the issue, rather its failure to ensure that the suspect would not face torture, as CAT requires.[41] In June 2007, 26 Americans (mostly CIA agents) went on trial in Italy accused of kidnapping an Egyptian national in Milan, taking him to a U.S. base, and flying him to Egypt for interrogation.[42] In 2005 German prosecutors investigated the CIA kidnapping and mistaken rendition of a German citizen, Khaled el-Masri, and in 2007, issued warrants for the arrest of 13 CIA agents.[43] In 2007 a UK Parliamentary Commission reproached the U.S. over its rendition policy and expressed its concern that suspects face torture. In response, the British government accepted assurances from Secretary of State Rice that "the U.S. respects the rules of international law, does not authorize or condone the torture of detainees, does not transport, and has not transported, detainees from one country to another for the purposes of interrogation using torture."[44] Because interrogation techniques remain classified, Britain and other governments relied on President George W. Bush's guarantee that American methods "comply with the obligations of the United States under Common Article 3," and "do not include murder, torture, cruel or inhuman treatment, mutilation or maiming, intentionally causing serious bodily injury, rape, sexual assault or abuse, taking of hostages, or performing of biological experiments."[45] As the Obama and subsequent administrations reevaluate U.S. policy, they will have to issue similar guarantees about American interrogation techniques. If foreign governments accept U.S. assurances, then one will expect to see support for rendition and the interrogation techniques that come with it. The same is true of popular support.

Popular Support for Rendition and Torture

Commenting on interrogational torture, Richard Posner is perplexed. "It is especially odd," he writes, "to issue an unqualified condemnation of a practice that almost everyone accepts the necessity of resorting to in extreme situations."[46] Public opinion polls, on the other hand, paint a picture of a world divided on the question of torture. In a 2008 poll, most people across the world (57%) favor "clear rules against torture." Nevertheless, large numbers (35%) believe that "terrorists pose such an extreme threat that governments should now be allowed to use some degree of torture if it may gain information that saves innocent lives." This is more support than a similar poll found in 2006.[47] The poll does not define torture nor distinguish it from less abusive forms of interrogation. In a poll among Americans, however, researchers found that support for torture increased 50% when defined as humiliating treatment or mental torture and nearly doubled when defined to include the threat of torture.[48] Finally, the percentage of individuals polled who oppose torture (57%) is considerably less than those opposing restrictions on a free press (81%), racial discrimination (90%), and discrimination against women (86%).[49] Unqualified support for or opposition to torture is clearly problematic for many individuals. This does not lend support to Posner's contention that almost everyone supports interrogational torture, but neither does it mean that almost everyone repudiates torture as they do other violations of basic rights. They are, at best, ambivalent.

With no small measure of popular and political support, democracies interrogate terror suspects using procedures they would never think to use on ordinary criminals or on ordinary combatants. This alone might be cause to think that torture belongs neither to law enforcement nor to war, but is instead a deviation from both. However, torture is best understood in terms of how armies may treat enemy combatants: permissible harm on the battlefield is a function of military necessity, reciprocity, and humanitarianism. Military necessity entails an evaluation of short-term effectiveness and long-term costs. If, in the past, military planners believed torture ever worked, they were held in check by the prospect of a threat-in-kind. Faced with the deleterious effect torture might have on their own forces, armies were right to reject torture based on military necessity alone. No humanitarian evaluation was necessary.

Today the story is different. Once military planners think a tactic has military benefits, it must pass the test of humanitarianism. This explains the preoccupation with "torture lite" or "moderate physical pressure." Even as some judicial systems demand a necessity defense, that is, a reaffirmation of the test of military necessity, they draw the line between permissible ill-treatment and prohibited tactics. The Israeli Court never says as much, but it is understood that the necessity defense cannot aid an investigator who mutilates, maims, or rapes a detainee. As democracies wrestle with permissible torture, the distinction between forbidden techniques, techniques suitable for ordinary suspects, and techniques suitable for terror suspects is very much on their minds. Sorting out this hard question in an open society requires the active participation of the public, the press, the courts, the military, and the politicians. The torture debate is important, but it can also be dangerous.

THE DILEMMA OF THE TORTURE DEBATE

To study national security issues, asymmetric conflict, and the war on terrorism, African and Asian military and law enforcement officials often visit Western nations. As they do, representatives from China, Nigeria, and Zimbabwe listen closely to arguments that may justify harsh interrogation and inevitably wonder whether they, too, might successfully use enhanced techniques to question their adversaries. Accused of torturing captured militants in the Ogaden, Ethiopian officials, for example, insist that they only use harsh interrogation to help fight off militants.[50] In response, Western officials are quick to draw their attention to the important difference between interrogating ruthless terrorists and persecuting political dissidents and between torture lite and torture not-so-lite. But the Chinese, Nigerians, Zimbabweans, and Ethiopians are not so easily swayed. Faced with accusations of human rights abuses, they say the Western response is hypocritical. After all, they declare, "We are fighting terrorism too."

Hearing this, absolutists will feel vindicated. Torture, they say, is always and unequivocally wrong. Any exceptions undermine the hard-earned international support for its universal prohibition and open the door to all kinds of brutality by unenlightened regimes. But does absolutism go too far? Isn't there a difference between American interrogators in Guantanamo Bay and interrogators who practiced torture in Rwanda, in junta-era Chile and Argentina, or in apartheid-era South Africa? The answer, hopefully, is yes and it depends crucially on the distinctions between interrogational and terroristic torture, terrorism and internal dissent, and moderate physical pressure and brutality as just described. But the justifications for these distinctions that draw from lesser evil arguments backed up with a vigorous grasp of human rights are not, as this discussion has shown, easy to articulate. If we dispute them at home, how can we explain them to the less-developed nations of the world without looking hypocritical or, at least, allowing them to paint us as such? There are two answers to this question. One is to put significant safeguards in place so that torture in democracies is never mistaken for the torture practiced in repressive regimes. The other is to abandon torture entirely.

Safeguards

Regulating torture requires several safeguards. First, an intelligence agency must garner the support of the citizenry whom it is charged to protect. Citizens need not venerate domestic intelligence officers, but they must be secure in their belief that their intelligence service will not turn against them. I doubt China, Nigeria, or Zimbabwe or most nondemocratic nations can make this claim. This kind of faith only grows from a strong tradition of democracy and liberal norms. I do not think that support for severe interrogation would approach fifty percent in the United States unless Americans had more than just a modicum of faith in their security services.

Second, the courts must scrutinize the activity of intelligence agencies before, during, and after armed conflict. In many nations there remains a vestige of Cicero's old saw: "During war, the law is silent." Keeping the courts out of armed conflict may be useful when conflicts are short and well defined. But this is not happening anytime soon. The war on terror is ill defined, enemies are nebulous, and the effort is open ended. There is considerable room for real-time legal supervision of military action, court review of ongoing operations that involve torture, and hearings to evaluate the behavior of investigators. The necessity defense demands a defense. Interrogators who act unlawfully must defend their actions before their peers and before the bar. Yet, they rarely do. This undermines public faith in both intelligence agencies and the bodies designated to oversee them.

Finally, there must be a central role for human rights organizations that take absolutism seriously. They are the watchdogs of democracy. They carry on the role that pacifists from the historic peace churches play in wartime. They, too, are absolutists who repudiate war in all its forms. Condemning war, but realizing the futility of preaching to the converted, absolutists prefer instead to "bear witness" so that by drawing the public's attention to the brutality of war they hope to have some small influence at the margins and prevent the worse of excesses. And, in some countries, they are successful. Following court appeals by human rights organizations, there has been a significant change in the severity and frequency of enhanced interrogation techniques used to question Palestinian detainees, for example. Interrogators shackle detainees' hands less uncomfortably,

cover their eyes with opaque glasses rather than wrap their head with
a filthy bag, and no longer subject detainees to loud music.[51] These
are small gains but human rights organizations keep the debate in
focus and force all of us to wrestle with the inherent evil of war and
torture, even as we make exceptions for ourselves. But why wrestle?
Why not just abandon enhanced interrogation entirely?

An Absolute Prohibition?

Writing in 1997, Daniel Statman observed, "The moral danger of torture is so great, and the moral benefits so doubtful, that in practice
torture should be considered as prohibited absolutely."[52] Statman
is only half right. The moral benefits are, if not doubtful, relatively
marginal. Tortured suspects may provide information about ticking
bombs or hostile acts that saves many innocent lives. Nevertheless,
the information they provide is often incomplete and obtainable by
less-controversial means of questioning. There is a wealth of information waiting for U.S. interrogators to mine from detainees in Iraq, for
example, but little, if any, seems to require enhanced techniques.[53]
Needed instead are greater numbers of well-trained interrogators to
gather and evaluate the many bits and pieces of data they obtain.
None of this means, of course, that enhanced techniques will not produce vital information. Yet even the most ardent supporters acknowledge that enhanced techniques are a last resort and infrequently
used. They are not the bread and butter of successful interrogation.

At the same time, there is no overwhelming evidence that the costs
of torture in a democracy are intolerable. Interrogational torture
has yet to prove the cancer some feared. Outside the philosophical
literature, neither ordinary criminals nor the children of terrorists
face harsh interrogation, nor do interrogators use obviously cruel
and inhuman techniques, nor has interrogational torture slid into
terroristic torture. In short, democracies have kept enhanced interrogation in check by confining it to a specific and well-defined group
of individuals: unlawful combatants. While the concept of "unlawful combatant" lacks clarity, some belligerents, namely those fighting
terrorism, invest the notion of unlawful combatancy with great significance. It defines for them those whom they may torture and those
whom they may not. The line might be somewhat arbitrary, perhaps

even indefensible, but it does stand firm in a democracy, augmented by an array of judicial institutions that keep terror suspects and insurgents far from a nation's criminal justice system.

This conclusion is likely to rile opponents and supporters of torture, alike. Opponents remain convinced that the costs of enhanced interrogation are high and the benefits low, while supporters trumpet its benefits, more than slightly exaggerated by vagaries of rational decision making under uncertainty, and downplay its costs. Both have only half the issue right. Compared with nonlethal warfare, targeted killing, terrorism, and constant assaults on civilians in asymmetric warfare, torture is a marginal phenomenon. It is infrequent and neither benefits nor costs democracies greatly. Outside of democracies, however, the equation changes dramatically. Torture is a staple of repressive regimes, infiltrates civil society, terrorizes civilians in war and peace, and undermines peaceful coexistence among nations. Democratic nations might contain torture and keep it well within the confines of excusable conduct, but their behavior echoes well beyond their borders. Whether they institute safeguards or abandon enhanced interrogation, it is unlikely that a democratic nation's policy at home will sway repressive regimes one way or another. Abandoning torture will, however, provide the grounds democracies need to condemn terrorism, extend protections to civilians during war, and justify humanitarian intervention on behalf of those suffering torture, blackmail, and genocide at the hands of despotic regimes. Terrorism, war on civilians, and humanitarian intervention together with the dilemmas and paradoxes they raise in asymmetric conflict are the subjects of the second half of this book.

PART II

NONCOMBATANTS IN ASYMMETRIC WAR

In Part I we have seen how asymmetry of means leads to asymmetry on the battlefield. First, there is a glaring tendency for combatants to criminalize one another. How usefully this serves the interests of the combatants varies relative to the conflict. In some conflicts it is useful to criminalize one's adversary, while in others it is considerably more beneficial to extend equality. Second, asymmetric conflict undermines an entire range of conventional practices by scrutinizing the long-standing concern to avoid superfluous injury and unnecessary suffering and by raising the prospect of nonlethal warfare, torture, and assassination. Absent fears of retaliation, combatants are again asking what kinds of weapons they may use. In many cases, the logic of conventional war no longer dictates strict restrictions on various tactics. Targeted killing, calmative agents, and millimeter-wave weapons will all find increasing use. Torture, too, is up for consideration in many democratic nations, although the controversy it provokes exhausts great reserves of moral energy and prevents judicious discussion of other, more urgent topics.

Some of these topics are the subject of the second half of this book. While asymmetry of means produces radical asymmetry on the battlefield, treatment of civilians by either side remains remarkably symmetrical. Conventional armies ask, Whom can we attack when we have exhausted our bank of military targets? Guerrillas ask, Whom can we attack when we cannot reach military targets? The answer is the same for each, namely civilians. This raises critical problems for both sides,

because the long tradition of just war and the laws governing armed
conflict prohibit direct attacks on civilians. I have already noted how
nonlethal warfare challenges this very basic tenet. Nonlethal warfare,
however, does not kill. Civilians suffer incapacitating harm to save
them from lethal harm. Terrorism and strikes on civilians by a conventional force, on the other hand, deliver grievous and irreversible
harm to civilians.

Chapter 7 addresses the dilemma of conventional state armies
as they confront their inability to strike at a sufficient number of
military targets to overwhelm a guerrilla force that is indistinguishable from and often supported by a civilian population. Chapter 8
addresses the mirror image of this difficulty and looks at guerrilla
organizations that face a superior military force with well-protected
and relatively inaccessible military targets. Searching for legitimate
targets to strike, guerrillas and conventional armies bring three strik-
ingly similar arguments to bear. First, the sides will try to distinguish
between direct and collateral harm, arguing that civilians may often
suffer the latter but never the former. This is a stock argument of
conventional armies, but surfaces among guerrilla groups as well.
During the Second Lebanon War, for example, Hezbollah claimed
that it aimed many of its missiles at military installations. Civilian
casualties resulted from mistakes, operational errors and inaccuracy,
not direct attacks on the innocent.

Second, many on each side will set collateral concerns aside and
ask specifically about targeting civilians who bear some responsibility
for the conflict. Guerrillas will acknowledge direct strikes on civilians, but impute a strong measure of responsibility and criminality
to the people they harm. State armies, too, assign responsibility to
justify attacks on civilians who take a direct or indirect role in the
fighting. Fighting insurgents, conventional armies draw up detailed
lists of civilian or quasi-combatants who provide aid, store arms,
contribute money, or provide logistical support. State actors, like
guerrillas, claim that the civilians they attack are not innocent, but
are instead accountable. Finally, both sides may set their sights on
innocent civilians as they think seriously about undertaking reprisals and about threatening civilians with disproportionate force to
compel their enemy to surrender. In contrast to conventional war,
civilians take a greater role in the fighting during asymmetric war

and quickly replace purely military targets as the target of choice and opportunity.

Unexpectedly, the world community is waking up to the catastrophic harm that governments can bring to their own citizens. In light of the way that asymmetric war endangers many citizens, particularly those who take a direct or indirect role in the fighting, it might seem odd to see a growing concern for truly innocent civilians. But this sentiment, yet to receive overwhelming material support, sits firmly behind the United Nations right-to-protect doctrine. International willingness to intervene militarily on behalf of persecuted peoples across the globe is an unprecedented development that represents extraordinary concern for ordinary individuals facing brutal genocidal and criminal regimes. This is the subject of Chapter 9.

In the final analysis, asymmetric war cuts in several directions at once. On one hand, and regardless of treaty law, practice is changing in significant ways. Despite the legal disagreements surrounding calmative weapons, for example, the international community tacitly endorses this new class of weapons. Treaty change is probably not far behind. Although controversial, there is also growing support for targeted killing, enhanced interrogation, and rendition, although they remain counterproductive in some circumstances. Similarly, the scope of noncombatant immunity is shrinking as belligerents find support for attacking civilians when they are not entirely innocent and take some part in the fighting. Many of these practices are discriminatory, that is, they deny combatant equality and focus upon those whose responsibility or suspected responsibility is weightier than others. All told, these changes relax existing laws and conventions to account for the exigencies of asymmetric warfare and the right of each side to maintain its fighting chance.

On the other hand, the world community is ever cognizant of the overwhelming harm that innocent civilians suffer in war. Isolated attempts to outlaw weapons that have little military value but present great dangers to civilians are often successful. The necessity of humanitarian intervention coupled with the desanctification of state sovereignty is slowly taking hold. Ironically, these two trends go together. Fighting wars of humanitarian intervention, like other forms of asymmetric conflict, requires novel tactics that force reinterpretations of combatant equality, the idea of proportionality, superfluous injury and unnecessary suffering, targeted killing, and civilian immunity. The previous chapters described how these changes affect combatants; the remaining chapters investigate the effects of asymmetric conflict on civilians.

7

Blackmailing the Innocent

The Dilemma of Noncombatant Immunity

Blackmail, or more precisely, extortion, is an act that threatens civilians with egregious harm to pressure their state or nonstate government to bring an end to war and/or deter them from war in the future.[1] It is not foreign to armed conflict. In asymmetric war, the problem is particularly acute because each side's ability to solely target military objects is limited. When guerrillas cannot reach military targets and choose to target mixed or civilian targets instead, they face fierce condemnation. The stronger parties, too, face a similar problem and similar condemnation. When they exhaust their bank of military targets, their hands seem tied regardless of the intensity of the threat they confront. Each side asks how to continue fighting when military targets are either inaccessible or are few and far between. In each case, they turn to civilian targets.

In conventional war, soldiers, regardless of the role they play, are fair game. Civilians, regardless of the threat they pose, are not. There are many good reasons for adhering to this convention. For many nations, it protects their civilians from excessive harm and pushes the field of battle away from population centers. "Thanks to this convention," writes Yitzchak Benbaji, "the soldiers' family members are safer, released soldiers would have safer places to return to, and wounded soldiers would have protected healing spaces."[2] This is probably true, assuming we are talking about the Western Front circa 1917. But often, and particularly in asymmetric warfare, the convention breaks down. The stronger side does not always fear for its civilian population, while the weaker side, fighting within civilian population centers, does not have a safer place, far from the battlefield, to retreat. More significantly, the importance of affiliation is lost entirely. As noted in Chapters 2 and 5, fighting without uniforms makes it difficult to establish affiliation. As a result, greater emphasis is placed on actual behavior, the threat one poses, the harm one causes, and the contribution a person makes to the war effort. While guerrillas are as vulnerable as combatants are and civilians taking little or no part in the war are as protected as noncombatants, the great challenge is defining other participants by meaningful criteria of contribution rather than inapplicable criteria of affiliation. Guerrillas and conventional armies look beyond affiliation and ask themselves which civilians are vulnerable to what kinds of harm? In the olden days, the answer was, virtually, none. Today, it is many.

Without targeting civilians, it may be well impossible for either side to prevail in an asymmetric conflict. This is a stark reversal of conventional thinking. In 1868 representatives of the major European powers optimistically declared: "The only legitimate object which States should endeavor to accomplish during war is to weaken the military forces of the enemy; for this purpose it is sufficient to disable the greatest possible number of men" [that is, soldiers]. Among other things, they assumed that there is never any need to deliberately harm civilians to win a conventional war; "weakening military forces" and disabling soldiers will always suffice. Civilians may certainly suffer in war, but only in the course of necessary military operations where the harm befalling them is unavoidable, proportionate, and indirect. This article of faith now seems quaint. It is difficult to decide any war without directly harming some civilians. Determining which civilians are vulnerable is the very hard question at hand.

NONCOMBATANT IMMUNITY AND CIVILIAN VULNERABILITY IN ASYMMETRIC WAR

Civilians suffer many forms of harm. These are summarized in Table 7.1.

The first two groups are increasingly common to asymmetric war and include those civilians taking some part in an armed conflict. While some civilian combatants may be full-fledged fighters, others

TABLE 7.1 Vulnerability of Civilian Actors

Civilian Actor	Level of Participation	Type of Harm	Purpose of Harm
1. Civilian combatant	Direct	Direct and lethal	Disable actor
2. Civilian quasi-combatant ("associated" target)	Indirect	Direct and nonlethal	Disable actor
3. Civilian noncombatant (proximate to actors 1 and 2)	None	Collateral harm: lethal, indirect, and proportionate	None
4. Civilian noncombatant	None	Disproportionate force: direct and lethal or nonlethal	Punish, coerce, deter, and/or demoralize

participate directly but only undertake military activities part-time. These civilians are on par with military targets, enjoy no immunity, and remain subject to direct and lethal harm. The second category is extremely problematic and includes indirect civilian participants, those who provide intelligence or monetary, medical, or logistical aid. They are quasi-combatants and often part of a guerrilla organization's political wing. But by any traditional account, these are civilians who should enjoy complete immunity from direct harm. In asymmetric conflict, however, they emerge as the next target of opportunity. In the Second Lebanon War these targets were termed "associated structures," that is, civilian targets associated with and supportive of the Hezbollah war effort. These were not military targets in any traditional sense. All military targets had been destroyed very early on. Nevertheless, associated targets were subject to direct attack. This is a controversial tactic and while there is general agreement among many observers that civilian combatants are vulnerable to lethal harm, it is not clear exactly what level of participation triggers this vulnerability or what level of force belligerents may use to disable civilian quasi-combatants whose role is indirect. While quite often these attacks were lethal and devastating, I want to argue for an obligation to meet these threats with less than lethal force first.

The third and fourth group of civilians includes those taking no active part in the war. They are civilian noncombatants. Those in category three represent civilians who are close to the fighting but not part of it. They find themselves subject to collateral or incidental harm that befalls them as the unintended but unavoidable outcome of a necessary military operation aimed at guerrillas and civilians in categories one and two. While the law of armed conflict gives wide berth to belligerents causing incidental harm to civilians, it puts a stop to things when the harm becomes disproportionate or excessive. However, it is often difficult to keep incidental harm within the limits of proportionality, particularly in asymmetric warfare. Setting the threshold too high leaves little room for permissible collateral harm and may deny the parties to an asymmetric conflict (usually the stronger one) "an equal chance in combat" and "prospect of victory" that Charles Chaumont noted. Setting the bar too low relaxes the standards of proportionality and callously endangers civilians. Very often, there is also a great temptation to punish or try to demoralize civilians when a war cannot be won by disabling military and associated targets. This is blackmail. These civilians (category four) may be close to the fighting or far from it. They are targeted in an effort to compel an enemy government to cease hostilities. This is the doctrine of disproportionate force, and it is gaining a sympathetic hearing among some parties to the enduring Palestinian-Israeli conflict. Attacking associated civilian targets, broadening the scope of disproportionate civilian harm, and attacking civilians to alter their government's behavior are endemic to asymmetric warfare and pose a stiff challenge to conventional moral and legal theories of war. Each is a subject of the following discussions.

Attacking Civilian Combatants

Civilian Combatants are not necessarily rank-and-file militants, that is, the leaders and day-to-day members of a guerrilla organization who train and fight on a regular basis. Rather, civilian combatants are often part-time guerrillas. Recall the description of Lebanese civilians who operated missile batteries from their barns or stored munitions in their sheds. These are civilians taking a direct part in the fighting. As they do, they are vulnerable to direct and lethal harm. There is little dispute about this; the harder question is to assess their status when they are not fighting.

When not fighting, conventional thinking demands that belligerents treat civilian combatants as civilians and make every effort to first arrest them. This norm recognizes that civilian combatants are not full-time combatants and, therefore, do not pose a constant threat. When they are not firing or storing weapons, they regain some element of their immunity. The principle is correct but with certain caveats. First, civilians taking a direct part in the hostilities must constitute the exception rather than the rule. In modern legal analysis, jurists and human rights organizations have taken a marginal category of armed civilians and extended it to all the military forces on the weaker side. By Israeli thinking, for example, all Palestinian militants are civilians taking a direct part in the hostilities. None is a lawful combatant. This only undermines the spirit of the law and denies combatant status to the many guerrilla fighters who deserve it. Second, the category must remain relatively marginal. If the stronger side cannot use it indiscriminately, neither can the weaker side turn civilians into a large-scale military force. If they do, then civilian combatant units simply become an auxiliary force and a legitimate military target. This is especially true if the civilian combatant force assumes strategic importance. If, for example, a guerrilla organization has a force to call on in the future and, perhaps, to use to deter its enemy from taking belligerent action, then this reserve force is a constant threat. Its members, therefore, are vulnerable all the time. It is, in other words, difficult to limit vulnerability to those times when a civilian takes an active part in the fighting. Although part-time participants, civilian combatants can be a full-time threat. This is also true at the local level. A civilian who fires a missile from his barn must also guard the missile battery, protect it from the elements, and, perhaps, move it from place to place. He is, in effect, constantly on call and, therefore, constantly vulnerable. Quasi-combatants, or those taking an indirect role, pose somewhat different problems. They enjoy widespread immunity but fulfill an increasingly important role in asymmetric war.

Attacking Quasi-Civilian Combatants and Associated Targets in the Second Lebanon War

The Second Lebanon War was a watershed for the conduct of hostilities during asymmetric war. Unlike many previous conflicts in the Middle East or elsewhere, the Second Lebanon War was not a war of national liberation, nor were Hezbollah forces fighting an army of occupation. Rather, the war saw a small, well-armed guerrilla army acting in the interests of a state power and seriously threatening civilian population centers with long-range ballistic missiles, all the while claiming the right to fight under the cover of its own civilians. During the war the Israel Defense Forces (IDF) directly attacked military, dual use, and associated targets. Not all of these conform to traditional targets in armed conflict. While military targets included armed fighters, weapons stores, and transport, many were not Hezbollah members at all, but civilian combatants who fought as part-time guerrillas, provided transport and logistical support, or lent their property for storing weapons.[3] There were no military bases to speak of and the only military targets were Hezbollah command posts and homes and long-range missile sites. These numbered only 83, accounted for less than 5 percent of the seven thousand airstrikes, and were destroyed by the fifth day of the war.[4] This then left the army two options. First, the search went on for military targets with varied success. Second, policymakers expanded the scope of civilian vulnerability to include associated structures.

During the war, Israel targeted associated structures hoping that their destruction would bring a concrete military advantage. Associated targets are the immediate answer to the question, Whom do you bomb when there are no more accessible military targets? They also address the question about direct and indirect participation in the war. Apart from Hezbollah fighters, homeowners who rented their property to store weapons, and other civilian combatants taking a direct role in the fighting, there are hosts of actors who support the organization. These neither are military targets in any traditional sense nor are they dual use targets such as bridges, roads, or power plants. Instead, associated targets include financial, law enforcement, welfare, political, educational, and media institutions that support the war-fighting capabilities of a guerrilla organization. These institutions indirectly support guerrilla military activities and provide personnel, funds, and other nonmilitary services.

Defining Associated Targets

Outside the norm of conventional warfare, any definition of associated targets remains at the discretion of the warring parties. The

final report of the Israeli commission of inquiry into the Second
Lebanon War makes an ambiguous allusion to "power centers and
infrastructures directly identified with Hezbollah and their war making capabilities."[5] Human Rights Watch (HRW) in their 2007 report,
however, investigated a number of these targets and documented
attacks on banks, homes of Hezbollah civilian officials, Hezbollah
charitable organizations, and TV stations.[6] In response, the IDF
spokesperson was candid:

In the war on terror in general, it's not just about hitting an army base, which
they don't have, or a bunker. It is also about undermining their ability to
operate. ... That ranges from incitement on television and radio, financial
institutions and, of course, other grass-roots institutions that breed more followers, more terrorists, training bases, and obviously, schools.[7]

Obviously, this raised intensely problematic moral issues. First,
in what way are these targets legitimate? Second, what does destroying them achieve? Third, how much harm can an army cause as it
destroys these targets? Finally, what of reciprocity? If it is legitimate
for a stronger power to target banks, welfare agencies, financial
institutions, and schools, why can't guerrillas attack these same
targets?

Supporting institutions like newspapers and TV, schools and financial organizations have always presented a problem for traditional
theories of just war. There is no doubt that they contribute to the
war effort in a very significant way, although no one working in these
institutions is a member of the armed forces or bears arms. In spite
of their enormous contribution to the war effort, nations have found
it useful to subscribe to agreements that protect those who work for
these institutions. By protecting civilian targets, even those that significantly support the war effort, belligerents hope to place all civilian targets out of bounds and prevent a slide down a slippery slope
that may lead to attacks against many less-threatening civilians. At
the same time, a sweeping definition of noncombatant immunity
might hope to confine fighting to the battlefield and away from civilian population centers.

In asymmetric war, however, the home front easily becomes the bat-
tlefront. Moreover, any injunction to protect all civilians might confer
such widespread immunity on the weaker side that fighting would be

impossible. Without attacking some civilians who participate in or support the war, the stronger side quickly runs out of targets. The result is a statement like that of the IDF spokesperson. The weaker side takes a similar view as it casts around for legitimate civilian targets. At one point, it no longer serves the interests of the parties to an asymmetric conflict to extend legal protection to many hitherto protected civilians. This change reaches far into the territory of noncombatant immunity as traditionally understood.

Attacking Associated Targets

Attacking associated targets demands two things. First, the attack must be effective, and second, the attacker must use no more than the force necessary to disable the facility. These are the standard ethical demands of any military operation. During the Second Lebanon War, Israel assumed, for example, that the destruction of media targets would significantly disrupt Hezbollah operations, but Israel never successfully silenced Hezbollah TV, so this hypothesis remains untested. Destroying banks, too, may deliver an important blow to operations, although it does not seem that this slowed things down much in the month-long war. Perhaps over a longer period this tactic is effective. More likely is the assumption that destruction of associated targets makes life miserable for civilians who cannot get to the bank, avail themselves of welfare service, get up-to-date news or entertainment, or attend school. These attacks then become part of a campaign to punish the civilian population (as discussed further below). It is hard to understand how the destruction of schools in a month-long war will prevent more followers from breeding. Some observers, for example, describe how after intense disillusionment among Lebanese with Hezbollah at the beginning of the war, the organization steadily gained support.[8] There is nothing in the foregoing discussion, however, to suggest that all attacks on associated targets are ineffective. It does mean that the attacking power must be reasonably certain that the destruction of the target confers some military advantage. If it does, the way is open to ask about how much force is necessary to disable these targets.

When military sites are the target and civilians are not in harm's way, there are few limits on the level of force that an army may use.

Associated targets present a thornier problem because those who work and support these institutions are not armed. In this sense, they may bear some relationship to civilians who work in an arms factory or drive a supply truck. The status of the arms worker is not entirely clear. On one hand, the facility has important military value and the person working there is knowingly and actively supporting the war. On the other, the workers are unarmed civilians. Therefore, an army may try to destroy the facility while giving thought to sparing the employees, not because they are innocent but because they are useless once the factory is destroyed. The vulnerability of these actors is the subject of much debate. The truck driver or munitions expert can find work elsewhere just as soon as a truck or workshop is available. Some observers believe that actors like the truck driver or munitions worker are vulnerable all the time (just like soldiers) while others contend they are only vulnerable while driving their truck or working in the factory. The difference of opinion turns on whether one views the truck driver or munitions worker as a direct threat to life and limb, or as one who only contributes to the capacity to cause harm without causing harm himself.[9]

Regardless of how one views the truck driver or munitions worker, no side shows compunction about attacking a munitions facility or vehicle laden with military supplies. It is clearly a military target. They show far more restraint about attacking banks, welfare organizations, and educational facilities. These facilities may have military value, but in a symmetric war fear of retaliation forces belligerents to rigidly define and protect one another's civilian institutions. They will attack arms factories but will continue to wage war without touching financial, welfare, media, or educational facilities. In asymmetric war, however, there is no fear of significant retaliation and there are few other institutions to attack.

Turning to associated targets does not mean, however, that they may suffer the same degree of harm as an arms factory. By all accounts, associated targets are second-tier targets. They contribute to a nation or group's war-making capability but they are not as important as arms factories or military bases. This alone should make us think twice about the force required to disable them. At the same time, it seems that while only high explosives can destroy an arms factory, there are less-destructive ways to disable associated targets.

For example, military organizations may disable a bank, welfare office, school, or TV station by cutting off electricity, blocking access, or hacking the computers. There are also less-than-lethal methods for restraining or neutralizing their employees. These might include the use of nonlethal weapons accompanied by arrest and incarceration, siege, or expulsion. There are no grounds, necessarily, for using lethal force. Associated targets are midway down the participation scale. Their employees are not as vulnerable to lethal harm as civilians taking on a combatant role. Nevertheless, they are considerably more vulnerable than civilians taking little or no role in the fighting. Moderate participation demands moderate disabling methods. This condition reflects two moral mainstays of armed conflict and demand that the belligerents use the least lethal means to disable an enemy and inflict no more harm than necessary.

The option of targeting associated targets is not limited to the stronger side. Reciprocity creeps in as guerrillas consider their targeting options (as discussed in the next chapter). They may justify direct and deliberate harm to civilians on the same grounds that the stronger side uses. Searching for targets to disable their enemy, guerrillas, too, recognize that some civilians underwrite the war effort in a significant way. But as guerrillas aim for schools, banks, government offices, welfare organizations, and media outlets, their weapons will be cruder than those the stronger side uses for the same purposes. Inaccurate missiles put large numbers of non-combatants at risk while, at the same time, less-than-lethal means (including arrest, incarceration, siege, or deportation) might not be available to guerrilla forces. As a result, they may resort to increasingly lethal means to achieve the same result that conventional armies can accomplish by less-lethal means. When they do, quasi-combatants and noncombatants may suffer disproportionately and unnecessarily. At one point, guerrillas and conventional forces must (but rarely do) ask whether the harm they bring is excessive. When harm becomes disproportionate, they will find their hands tied. Proportionality, however, remains a vague and difficult idea to implement. Is proportionality capable of restraining the sides during asymmetric warfare? The short answer is yes, but only after adjusting the standards of proportionality to meet the exigencies of asymmetric conflict.

REASSESSING PROPORTIONALITY IN ASYMMETRIC CONFLICT

In Chapter 4 I described an attack on a convoy of civilians that killed 23 people. Since Hezbollah used civilian convoys to transport men and materiel, and civilians had been warned off the roads, the Israeli army attacked the convoy on the assumption that it was a military convoy or a civilian convoy giving cover to militants. The UN response to the attack, as noted, was fierce. In their view, the attack was disproportionate, violated the principle of distinction, and could not be justified on the basis of the convoy being a military objective. This was true "even if there were Hezbollah members among the civilians."[10] In Chapter 4 I used this case to introduce nonlethal weapons. Here, I want to use it to look at proportionality in asymmetric warfare.

Describing the international reaction to the Second Lebanon War, Harel and Issacharoff recount how, "The Europeans talked mostly about proportion and were unable to equate the dozens of Israelis killed by Hezbollah Katyusha rockets with the hundreds of Lebanese citizens killed by the IDF."[11] As viscerally lacerating as it is, comparing civilian casualties has nothing to do with the idea of proportionality in warfare. Instead, proportionality refers to incidental loss of life that is excessive. Incidental in this context means necessary but indirect, that is, collateral, damage:

[Those who plan an attack shall] refrain from launching any attack which may be expected to cause incidental loss of civilian life … which would be excessive in relation to the concrete and military advantage anticipated. (Article 57 (2) (iii).[12]

Disproportionate casualties occur in the context of necessary military operations where the loss of civilian life is both unavoidable and indirect. Proportionality is an ends-means relationship. It does not speak to relative losses on each side; n casualties on one side coupled with $20n$ on the other do not necessarily render a war or military action disproportionate. Instead, proportionality compares the harm one causes to the good one expects to attain. Disproportionate harm is too much harm, raising the question, How many casualties, then, are too many, that is, "excessive in relation to the concrete and military advantage anticipated?"

To answer this question, consider an arithmetic rule for figuring disproportionality:

If the nation is trying to prevent terrorist attacks like those of September 11, 2001, then tragic though the result will be, and assuming the nation makes serious efforts to minimize collateral harm, it may kill *somewhat more* enemy civilians if that is unavoidable in saving a smaller number of its own.[13]

Now consider an intuitive or gut feeling approach to the same problem. Here, legal historian Geoffrey Best suggests that we compare disproportionality to a manifestly unlawful, superior order that soldiers and officers should refuse to carry out when it exceeds the intuitive limits of morality and law. "Although [a manifestly unlawful order] may be tricky and embarrassing to define in advance," writes Best, "the reasonable man or woman knows one when he receives one."[14] By the same token, a reasonable man or woman knows disproportionate harm when he or she sees it.

Unfortunately, neither formulation gets us very far and each shows just how incoherent and unworkable the principle of proportionality can be. The arithmetic approach founders for two reasons. Conceptually, there is no reason to weigh the number of enemy civilians harmed solely against the number of compatriots saved. Concrete military advantages not only include saving the lives of compatriots, but also restoration of a deterrent capability, preservation of civilian and military infrastructures, or successfully securing territory. These are difficult if not impossible to quantify against the lives of enemy civilians.

But the algorithm is unworkable even if its sole consideration is the number of individuals harmed or saved from harm. To see this, it is only necessary to think about a single missile that can only be destroyed while causing civilian casualties. How many casualties are too many? To answer, we first have to calculate the number of civilians saved by destroying a single missile. While one missile may kill, for example, 10 or more people, one must consider whether that missile will harm anyone at all. The probability that a single missile will kill anyone is often very low. In the Second Lebanon War, the figure was close to one Israeli death per one hundred missiles.[15] If there is a one percent chance a missile will do damage, then at best, we are saving a tenth of a person by destroying a particular missile ($10 \times 1\%$). To destroy this missile, an attacker is permitted to cause somewhat more enemy civilian casualties. What could this mean? For the sake of argument, let us say that half a person is somewhat more than a tenth of one. Since persons are not readily divisible, the minimum casualty is one person, and one casualty is a disproportionate casualty (because it is more than "somewhat" more) when trying to destroy a missile that has but a one percent chance of killing anyone. If an army cannot destroy one missile (because there is no level of permissible collateral damage), then it cannot destroy any, whether the enemy has one missile or ten thousand. This cannot be right.

Let us consider the ten thousand missiles collectively. Figuring half a person killed per missile would allow an army to cause five thousand collateral casualties to destroy them all. Does this sound right or does it seem to be too many? If it does not make sense to base proportionality on the threat of each missile individually, it does seem morally correct to tolerate some number of incidental (collateral) casualties based on the total threat. But notice that we accept this total number of five thousand or some other number because it feels right rather than on some calculation of how many die on one side and how many live on the other. This is the tenor of the Geneva Conventions. Commenting on proportionality, Additional Protocol I (API) offers an easy case of disproportionality to help guide our judgment:

Some cases [of disproportionate harm] will be clear-cut and the decision easy to take. For example, the presence of a soldier on leave obviously cannot justify the destruction of a village.[16]

While this is probably obvious to most individuals, it is equally obvious that it is necessary to include the words "on leave" to remove any doubt about proportionality. Omit them (and assume that the soldier is on active duty) and the case is no longer obvious. In fact, it becomes quite complex if the soldier is armed with a portable missile.

This brings us back to Best's intuitive criterion of proportionality. It is interesting that Best compares disproportionality to a manifestly unlawful order. His insistence on knowing a violation of proportionality "when you see it" is entirely consistent with those military manuals that remind soldiers to obey all superior orders except those "a man of ordinary sense and understanding would know to be unlawful."[17] For assessing proportionality, however, this formulation is not helpful.

If it is not easy to exercise one's sense of justice and recognize an infraction when an order is manifestly unlawful, it must be exceptionally difficult to grasp when an order is disproportionate. An unlawful order is wrong because combatants deliberately murder civilians. A disproportionate order, on the other hand, occurs in an entirely different moral atmosphere, one where killing civilians is generally permissible. Disproportionate casualties are incidental, that is, necessary and unintentional (and, therefore, permissible) but remain, in some vague sense, excessive. Can we expect a man of ordinary sense and understanding to evaluate excessive or disproportionate (but otherwise permissible) harm, as readily as we expect him to discern intentional and unnecessary harm?

Let us assume the answer is yes: reasonable individuals can discern gross violations of proportionality. Granting gut feelings of disproportionate harm, however, wreaks some havoc in asymmetric conflict. Killing 20 or 22 civilians to disable a single militant fleeing in a civilian convoy seems excessive to the extreme. Attacks on houses thought to house short- and medium-range missiles also brought condemnation as many civilians lost their lives. Multiply these cases by the tens, if not hundreds, of similar instances as militants fought or fled under the cover of civilians, and the harm wrought on noncombatants cries to the heavens. These cases undeniably elicit the appropriate intuition of disproportionate harm. At the same time, however, warfare becomes impossible if civilian deaths in these instances are disproportionate. The question is whether asymmetric conflict demands alternative standards of proportionality.

REASSESSING PROPORTIONALITY IN ASYMMETRIC CONFLICT: THE PROBLEM OF HUMAN SHIELDS AND INACCURATE WEAPONRY

Under the going rules of proportionality, one weighs enemy civilian casualties against expected military advantage. In asymmetric war, the destruction of some military targets is proportionate by these standards. For example, destroying most of the long-range missile launchers in the Second Lebanon War caused about 20 civilian casualties, while attacks on dual use targets (that is, civilian objects that serve the military including roads, bridges, airports, power stations, and refineries[18]) killed approximately 40 civilians.[19] But what happens when it is difficult to gain any military advantage without harming larger numbers of civilians? What if the weaker side has no option but to place mobile missile launchers in populous neighborhoods? One question is whether this is a cynical use of human shields.

Proportionality and Human Shields

While international law prohibits using civilians to shield military installations, Anthony Cordesman observes, "A nonstate actor is virtually forced to use human shields as a means of countering its conventional weakness."[20] What exactly are human shields and may a guerrilla organization use them as Cordesman suggests? International law prohibits intentionally using civilians to render areas immune from enemy attack.[21] This is distinct from failing to take reasonable and feasible precautions to protect civilians from harm during war. An egregious example of the former occurred in Iraq as Iraqi soldiers placed civilians in front of their convoys to ward off attack.[22] There is less agreement regarding Hezbollah's conduct in the war. The Israeli government claims Hezbollah deliberately fired from populated areas to prevent attacks on missile launchers; HRW claims these same acts merely constitute the failure to take sufficient measures to protect civilians, a lesser crime of war.[23]

Evaluating these conflicting claims is difficult. Human shielding in Lebanon did not take the form of placing civilians in front of missile launchers at gunpoint. But what does it mean when human rights activists agree that Hezbollah did not take feasible precautions to protect civilians? Should they have warned civilians away from the launch sites or placed the sites farther from populated areas? Civilians who freely aided Hezbollah by storing missiles or accepting instructions to launch missiles compound the problem.[24] Presumably, the core of Hezbollah was too small to do all the work itself and had no choice but to enlist the help of civilian combatants and quasi-combatants. I think this is how best to read Cordesman's statement. At issue is not placing babies on the fenders of half-tracks, rather the necessity of enlisting the aid of civilians who live and work in populated villages. If Hezbollah had no choice but to expand their capabilities in this way, then it would not be feasible to protect innocent noncombatants short of wholesale evacuation prior to the commencement of hostilities. Charges of cynically using human shields are off the mark.

Nevertheless, the presence of civilian noncombatants does not deny an enemy force the right to attack the military targets in their midst. Quite the contrary. The inability to take feasible precautions actually *expands* the range of permissible, proportionate harm precisely because guerrilla forces cannot take further steps to protect the civilians close by. The permissibility of using human shields does not affect the duty of the stronger side to observe proportionality as it attacks the weaker side.[25] However, it does affect the scope of proportionality. If guerrilla organizations have a right to place offensive missiles in densely populated civilian centers, then the stronger side must have a similar right to disable these missiles without necessarily causing disproportionate harm. Since a strategy of human shields will probably endanger many civilians in a way that is disproportionate by prevailing standards, something must give in the proportionality calculation to make room for proportionate responses against targets in close proximity to noncombatants. To see how this works, it is useful to see how the inaccuracy of weaponry can broaden the scope of proportionate harm for the weaker side.

Proportionality and Weapon Accuracy in Asymmetric Conflict

Think about two nations attacking a similar target. Nation A has sophisticated weapons and can destroy the target with n number of unavoidable civilian casualties. But Nonstate B has cruder weapons and can only destroy the target with twice or three times the casualties Nation A causes. The same holds true for associated targets that Nation A can disable with nonlethal means but Nonstate B cannot disable without causing civilian casualties. As A and B attack similar targets, the military advantage each hopes to gain is similar. This may mean, for example, that the destruction of the target saves the lives of the same number of compatriot civilians. Yet the cost of saving these lives is different. Nation A kills somewhat more enemy civilians than the number of compatriot civilians saved, while Nonstate B harms many more enemy civilians. By any arithmetic or intuitive account of proportionality, A's act is proportionate and B's is not. The problem reverses itself when attacking convoys. When stronger Nation A tries to capture or kill fleeing militants who hide among civilians or attempts to destroy missile launchers close to civilian populations, many more than "somewhat more" enemy civilians may have to die. In contrast, a guerrilla attack on a large, military enemy convoy may necessitate no civilian casualties whatsoever.

In response to this incongruity, the weaker side would justifiably claim that its cruder weapons broaden the scope of proportionality and allow it more collateral harm than the principle traditionally permits. The stronger side would claim that military targets nested deep in civilian population centers (or in convoys) would loosen the principle of proportionality in the same way. In neither case is it feasible to protect civilians further. The weaker side is unable to obtain more accurate weapons and neither side is able to protect civilians close to launch sites. Guerrillas cannot evacuate them and conventional armies find that warnings do not easily clear an area of civilians. Any alternative answer to the problem of proportionality severely impinges upon the ability to fight at all. This might require the stronger Nation A to use nonlethal weapons (NLWs) and the weaker Nonstate B to desist entirely (assuming it cannot obtain NLWs).

Neither solution, however, solves the problem entirely. NLWs are a good choice for Nation A, but as noted in Chapter 4, they remain relatively undeveloped and subject to an array of practical and legal obstacles. Nonstate B, for its part, is unlikely to stand down. It will argue, as might Nation A in circumstances similar to the attack on the convoy fleeing Marwahine, Lebanon, that proportionality, as traditionally understood, must be bankrupt if it prevents one side or another from fighting at all. As a result, it should be possible to think about redefining the limits of proportionality. Here, it is particularly important to distinguish disproportionate harm from that which is unnecessary or deliberate.

Reassessing Proportionality in Asymmetric Conflict

Reassessing proportionality requires us to abandon any notion of an arithmetic or intuitive approach and take a serious look at the empirical relationship between necessity and the military advantage that acts of war are supposed to secure. Proportionality acts as a constraint on a necessary military operation. Once we understand the kind of casualties that most necessary military operations cause, we might then get a baseline for excessive casualties. This baseline serves as a guide to disproportionate harm so that anything in excess violates the principle of proportionality. This is not unlike the attempt by the Red Cross, described in Chapter 3, to quantify unnecessary suffering by condemning weapons that cause soldiers to suffer a mortality rate in excess of 25 percent. The baseline mortality rate of 25 percent is just beyond what has been the norm in 200 years of warfare. Anything beyond that is excessive or superfluous. Ascertaining the boundaries of proportionate harm requires a close study of the casualties that different types of asymmetric war bring. For this purpose, the Second Lebanon War offers some preliminary insights.

Civilians were killed in Lebanon during a) attacks on Hezbollah combatants and strongholds in the countryside, b) attacks on missile dumps and missile launcher sites, c) attacks on Hezbollah military headquarters in Beirut, and d) attacks on Lebanese infrastructures. To assess these casualties, it is first important to distinguish between unnecessary, disproportionate, and direct harm. Civilian casualties are unnecessary when they are entirely unrelated to any military advantage. This happens when they are not required to achieve a military goal, might be avoided while successfully pursuing the same goal, occur after a nation achieves its legitimate war aims, or occur in pursuit of military goals that are not feasible. In the Second Lebanon War, for example, there are good reasons to think that Israel's legitimate war aims – restoration of calm to its northern border, displacement of Hezbollah forces to the north and their replacement with Lebanese forces – were largely achieved with the G8 (Group of Eight nations) declaration of July 7, 2006, ten days after the war started and certainly once the first UN resolutions were drafted on August 2, 2006, roughly ten days before the war ended. If true, then any casualties incurred after these dates were unnecessary rather than disproportionate. If a nation has not yet achieved its war aims, unnecessary casualties may also result when military goals are not feasible. Aerial bombing razed entire sections of Beirut in an attempt to destroy Hezbollah military headquarters, but was it possible to destroy Hezbollah military headquarters in Beirut? If the answer is no, given the limits of the bunker busting bombs Israel chose to use, then any casualties are unnecessary.

Legitimate questions about proportionality arise in the context of attacks on militants and missile launcher sites. Many of these attacks, as noted above, resulted in relatively few civilian casualties and did not raise charges of disproportionality. Attempts to destroy short-range mobile launchers, on the other hand, were far less successful. This led planners to try cluster bombs and hope that by saturating an area with high explosives some would hit their targets. Cluster bombs are single artillery shells that contain hundreds of small bomblets that disperse over a large area. In contrast to the successful destruction of long-range launchers by aerial bombardment, however, cluster shells did nothing to reduce the number of short-range missile attacks in Lebanon. Events proved that it was simply not feasible to destroy missile launchers in this way. Accompanying casualties were superfluous. Similarly, civilian casualties coming after the fighting ended are also unnecessary. Although cluster bomblets explode in the air or on impact, a dud rate of about 14 percent left one million unexploded bombs scattered across southern Lebanon. Through December 2008, more than two years after the war, twenty Lebanese civilians died and 197 were injured after triggering unexploded ordnance.[26] These deaths have no military purpose. Without purpose these casualties are unnecessary, not disproportionate.

Assessments of proportionality only arise when attacks are necessary and are most problematic when trying to evaluate civilian casualties that occur in pursuit of identifiable and legitimate targets nested in densely populated areas. Here, proportionate harm rises to the number of civilian casualties that are unavoidable and necessary to destroy these targets. The number is going to be larger than "somewhat more" compatriot civilians that military attacks can put at risk under conventional circumstances and may very well reach numbers similar to those in the Marwahine example. In its 2007 report, *Why They Died, Civilian Casualties in Lebanon during the 2006 War*, HRW provides detailed data of the circumstances surrounding many of the 1,109 Lebanese combatant and civilian casualties. Their descriptions provide some clues about disproportionality in asymmetric conflict.

With clear evidence of militants using villages for cover, HRW does not raise the charge of disproportionality when as many as 9 civilians died as airplanes struck a village after Hezbollah fired rockets nearby (July 18, 2006). HRW was also tolerant of civilian casualties as the

Israeli army targeted militants. This included 5 civilians who died in an attack that killed 17 militants (July 19), and 4 civilians who died in an attack that killed 3 militants (August 3–4).

Other operations, however, drew criticism. The United Nations Human Rights Council condemned the Marwahine attack when 22 or 23 civilians died. HRW criticizes the IDF for failing to halt the attack when it became clear that the target was not a military target (in spite of legitimate initial suspicions). While it is not clear how HRW might have reacted had some of the passengers been military personnel, other cases offer some indication. On July 24, 2006 an air attack killed 15 civilians along with 2 militants, while an August 13th strike killed 36 civilians and 4 militants. In addition, an attack on an apartment complex in response to hostile fire killed 39 Lebanese civilians (August 7). Each case drew charges of disproportionality. In the third case, HRW acknowledged the possibility of hostile fire but asked whether the high number of civilian casualties was proportionate. In the second case, HRW went on to note, "It is unlikely that Israel would have launched such a massive strike to kill such low-ranking Hezbollah officials. More likely, it had faulty intelligence that senior Hezbollah leaders were present at the complex."[27]

UN and HRW data, however incomplete, offer some preliminary directions for thinking about proportionality. First, the last case suggests that 36 civilian deaths to disable 4 combatants might be proportionate if senior militants are the target. Coupled with the other cases described, it suggests that 9 or 10 civilian casualties could be necessary to disable a military target and, therefore, are not disproportionate. Second, aggregate numbers matter. An attack that kills 9 in pursuit of a single military target does not elicit the same condemnation as an attack that kills 36 in pursuit of 4 combatants. Although the cost per military target is identical, calculations of proportionality cannot ignore the impact of aggregate numbers. Regardless of military necessity, attacks that caused more than 20 or 25 casualties brought criticism. Third, 81 of the 94 attacks cataloged by HRW caused 10 civilian casualties or fewer. The sides dispute the circumstances of many of these attacks, but none drew charges of disproportionate harm. This tacit understanding of proportionality may have led Israeli forces to try to preserve this intuitive limit of proportionate harm. It is noteworthy that among 5 documented cases causing more than 20 deaths, an aggregate number of casualties that immediately brought charges of disproportionality, 4 may have been the result of faulty intelligence or operational errors.[28] This reinforces the fourth point: in war, and particularly in asymmetric war fought among civilians, mistakes can be catastrophic and more civilians will suffer from unnecessary rather than disproportionate harm. It is peculiar that just war theory pays scant attention to mistakes and operational errors, focusing instead on the Dresdens and the Hamburgs where Allied forces targeted large numbers of civilians directly in World War II.

The numbers, of course, are very rough and limited. In the future, additional data may come from a better understanding of the events surrounding civilian casualties in Afghanistan and Pakistan. There, U.S. and NATO operations have caused significant numbers of non-combatant deaths that have risen from 477 in the first eight months of 2007, to 577 in the same period in 2008. The United Nations has yet to call these disproportionate largely because sufficient data are not available.[29] Nevertheless, the UN calls upon pro-government forces in Afghanistan to conduct timely and transparent investigations of high-civilian casualty incidents to assess compliance with international law and allay public fears of indiscriminate and disproportionate force in the fight against al-Qaeda and the Taliban.[30] As the database grows with comprehensive data from these and other theatres, there should be growing evidence that proportionality is bending and corresponds to what might be the average number of casualties necessary to fight under the conditions of asymmetric war.

Common attempts to quantify proportionality do not take into account the asymmetry of arms or the extreme risk that guerrilla tactics impose on civilians. Both of these factors affect proportionality in asymmetric warfare and widen its scope. These factors allow each side reasonable latitude and a way to fight without constantly running afoul of disproportionality. Disproportionate harm, like collateral harm, is often unintended and leads many states to heartfelt expressions of remorse. Although many nations try to limit excessive harm, they do not always recognize when they benefit militarily from collateral damage, as discussed in the following chapter. Guerrillas are sometimes more candid and often endorse attacks on civilians to take revenge on their enemy or demoralize their population. Stronger powers, on the other hand, are supposed to repudiate attacks of this sort. Sometimes they do, but they, like their adversaries, often find themselves bereft of military targets. As this happens, each side considers the benefit of deliberately harming civilians whether to restore or maintain a deterrence capability or demoralize the civilian population. This is the doctrine of disproportionate force, an increasingly common, but unwelcome, phenomenon of asymmetric conflict.

DETERRENCE, DEMORALIZATION, AND PUNISHMENT: THE DOCTRINE OF DISPROPORTIONATE FORCE

Commenting on the strategy necessary to win an asymmetric conflict like the Second Lebanese War, retired general Yaakov Amidror proposed this line of attack:

The determination of Israel's government to respond and to retaliate is a very important factor in restoring deterrence. Now those around Israel understand that Israel has certain red lines and that if these lines are crossed, Israel's retaliation will be intentionally disproportionate. As a small country, we cannot allow ourselves the luxury of reacting proportionally.[31]

Here, Amidror describes an intentionally harsh response that is not limited to conventional military targets. On the contrary, the emerging doctrine of disproportionate force draws on the complicity of civilian combatants and quasi-combatants. General Gadi Eisenkot, Israel Defense Forces commander of the Northern Front, spoke plainly: "We will wield disproportionate power against every village from which shots are fired on Israel, and cause immense damage and destruction. From our perspective, these are military bases."[32]

The doctrine of disproportionate force hopes to strip civilian noncombatants of their immunity and coerce the civilian population to exert pressure on military and political leaders to end the war and/or think twice about supporting militants in the future. The doctrine makes a moral and empirical claim. Morally, a small country or nonstate actor must intentionally harm an enemy's civilian population; otherwise, its very existence may be at stake. Empirically, harming civilians and destroying their infrastructures enhances one's deterrent capability or bestows some other military advantage. Disproportionate force, therefore, causes direct rather than incidental harm to civilians. Both the moral and empirical claims are problematic.

Short of supreme emergencies, that is, genocidal threats, no one argues it is morally permissible to attack civilian targets directly.[33] Whether these emergencies allow one to throw off the constraints of international humanitarian law and strike at civilian noncombatants remains a contentious issue. In most asymmetric conflicts, however, few of the warring parties face the threat of genocide so that under ordinary conditions of asymmetric war it remains impermissible to target civilians directly. Nor can there be any talk of "forcing surrender by means of attacks that *incidentally* harm the civilian population," as Protocol I rightly declares.[34] As I will argue in the following chapter, incidental harm that brings military benefits is on a par with direct harm. Both deliberately target civilians and should remain prohibited in the strongest terms.

Empirically, the claim that bombing demoralizes civilians has been subject to withering criticism. It did not work in World War II, it does not work in limited reprisal operations, it does not work for terrorists, and it does not work for larger armies facing a guerrilla organization.[35] In fact, terrorism, demoralization bombing, and other direct attacks on the civilian population tend to stiffen resolve. Nonetheless strategists sometimes consider that while punishing civilians may not break their resolve in the current war, the attack may sit in the back of their minds and serve to deter their leaders from future acts of aggression. In the Second Lebanon War, missile fire into Israel and massive destruction of civilian infrastructure in Lebanon did nothing to demoralize the sides or push their leadership toward giving up, though each side earnestly thought it would.[36] Nevertheless, the consequences of that war might certainly figure into plans for waging the next.

While some attacks may have deterrent value of this sort, it remains questionable whether this should allow any side to gut the concept of noncombatant immunity entirely and permit attacks on civilian noncombatants whenever this is militarily useful. Although the stronger side to an asymmetric conflict does not face the same kind of threat to its civilian population that it may face in a conventional war, it may nonetheless face missile or terror attacks. The prospect of retaliation and reprisal may be sufficient reason to respect noncombatant immunity.

Nor can any theory of vulnerability in wartime ignore the rights of the innocent. This is particularly true of the participation scale that I have outlined in previous chapters. Judging vulnerability by participation makes it clear that the more a civilian participates, the less innocent he is and the more vulnerable to harm. Combatants face lethal harm, while associated quasi-combatants remain vulnerable to direct, albeit nonlethal harm. Farther down the line, a civilian taking no part in any hostility should enjoy complete immunity from anything but proportionate, collateral harm. Subjecting innocents to direct, lethal harm to demoralize their government places innocent civilians at greater risk than a quasi-combatant who takes a more active role in the fighting. If the participation scale has any validity whatsoever, lower levels of participation cannot imply greater vulnerability.

The rule of noncombatant immunity is present in all forms of warfare. In symmetric warfare, however, the sides have a mutual interest to restrict vulnerability to those affiliated with their armed forces and to protect those civilians who are not necessarily innocent. In asymmetric warfare, on the other hand, the sides abandon this restriction and reinstate the vulnerability of a wide range of citizens who take part in the fighting. However, this should not include civilians who are not combatants.

Although directly attacking civilians may be effective for future deterrence, these attacks cross the same line that prohibits the use of certain weapons, however effective they might be in a particular situation. In spite of pragmatic arguments to the contrary, observers (at least realists) are often astonished when the world community invokes deeply held norms to underwrite humanitarian intervention or distance itself from chemical weapons, landmines, and cluster bombs.[37] Inflicting direct and grievous harm on civilian noncombatants remains anathema. Many nonstate guerrilla organizations often fail to grasp the repugnance they elicit with indiscriminate terror attacks on noncombatants. They find that terrorism taints their cause no matter how unjust their opponents, while their opponents find themselves condemned by world opinion when too many entirely innocent civilians die in the fighting. No explanations about lack of alternative means or of guerrillas hiding behind human shields will suffice. Good public relations and ethical conduct go hand in hand.[38] No nation can or should permit harm to large numbers of individuals guilty of nothing more than being citizens of a state at war.

As state and nonstate actors become increasingly sophisticated and struggle with the paucity of military targets characteristic of asymmetric conflict, they will develop a more nuanced grasp of civilian vulnerability that tries to articulate criteria for direct and indirect participation and in a way that will open the door to attacking associated targets. Parties to the conflict will push the envelope on noncombatant immunity to allow themselves a fighting chance. Asymmetric war will broaden the scope of proportionate harm but the warring parties remain accountable for unnecessary harm to civilians and for direct attacks that serve no other purpose but to punish or deter civilians. Enemy civilian noncombatants have done nothing to lose their right to life to allow an enemy to take it callously.

Charges of disproportionate harm will continue to dog asymmetric conflict but as the parties strive to conform to the changing criteria of proportionality, they must also realize that many more civilians suffer unnecessary and gratuitous harm that comes from unfeasible military operations, operational errors, and misguided attempts to demoralize. These casualties should be preventable. If humanitarian law is to have any bite at all, then a substantial portion of the civilian population must warrant its protection. At the same time, the conditions of permissible and proportionate harm cannot be so strict that it would never be possible to lawfully and humanely wage war. As conventional armies grapple with the limits of asymmetric warfare, they will benefit from but also chafe under these changing restrictions. This is no less true for guerrilla organizations who also contemplate attacking enemy civilians.

8

Killing the Innocent

The Dilemma of Terrorism

BAGHDAD, Iraq, February 2008: Two mentally disabled women were strapped with explosives Friday and sent into busy Baghdad markets, where they were blown up by remote control, a top Iraqi government official said. The bombs killed at least 98 people.[1]

This is an unusually horrifying act of terrorism. Ordinarily, we are accustomed to seeing terrorists do their own work. Those they recruit for suicide missions are not, as many studies have shown, religious zealots, economically deprived, illiterate, or mentally unbalanced. Instead, they are like grass-roots political activists who are willing to use extreme means to achieve their ends.[2] But sending two mentally disabled women seems "demonic," as some U.S. officials put it to describe a particularly repugnant form of terrorism that crosses all the red lines.

Interestingly, an incident like this forces us to think hard about terrorism. If some forms of terrorism are demonic or particularly reprehensible, it seems that other forms are more acceptable. Some cross the red lines, others stay within certain boundaries and are, to some extent, tolerable or at least understandable. Former Israeli Prime Minister Ehud Barak once declared, "If I were a Palestinian at the right age, I would have joined one of the terrorist organizations." Barak is saying what many people think: I may not agree with terrorism, but I can certainly understand the motivation that leads those to join terror organizations. And, if I were in their shoes, I might certainly do it too.

178

In this chapter I want to frame the question facing a guerrilla organization as exactly the same one confronting a strong, conventional army as the two face off: Whom do you attack when there are no viable military targets? In asymmetric war, conventional armies often exhaust their bank of military targets early on while guerrilla armies lack the wherewithal to effectively target them at all. Guerrillas, therefore, face a dilemma of their own. On one hand, they seek political goals – independence and self-determination – that they cannot achieve without armed struggle. On the other hand, armed struggle may require attacking nonmilitary targets and harming innocent civilians. We will see that they confront their dilemma in much the same way as the conventional armies who fight them. Either they turn to military necessity to justify the use of violence against civilians, or they deny that those they target are entirely innocent. The first draws a parallel between terrorism, collateral damage, and reprisal while the second upends the traditional idea of noncombatant immunity. Before delving into this dilemma, a few words are necessary to clarify the place of terrorism in guerrilla warfare. Today, we often assume that terrorism is the be-all and end-all of guerrilla organizations. This is not entirely true. Instead, terrorism is part of the repertoire of armed force that guerrilla organizations use to press their political aims in asymmetric war.

GUERRILLA-ISM AND TERRORISM

Today a pejorative, "terrorist" was once a badge of honor. Albert Camus's Czarist era protagonists exult in their terrorism: "We are resolved to carry on the reign of terror, of which this bomb is the beginning, until the land is given back to its rightful owners, to the people," affirms one terrorist. "Do you understand why I asked to throw the bomb? To die for an ideal – that's the only way of proving oneself worthy of it. It's our only justification," declares another.[3] Nevertheless, Camus's just assassins would not kill children, calmly accepted their criminality, and waited fervently for their own execution to expiate their guilt. A halo of sorts floated above their heads. By the post–World War II period, the tactics changed as women and children slipped into in the cross hairs. Still, many terrorists fighting for national liberation gained an almost mythic status. Interviewing

Saadi Yacef, an Algerian leader who fought the French during their war of independence, *New York Times* reporter Daniel Williams describes Yacef as a "rebel" and "resistance leader" whose "terror tactics are part of the national mythology." Yacef himself is unrepentant: "[Terror] was not just a tactic. It was part of a whole strategy that included mass participation. It was specifically targeted at occupiers, not just anybody ... . We killed women, yes, and took fetuses out of their wombs. But ours was for liberation. This was our only means against a cruel enemy."[4] This sentiment is common to the many definitions that describe terrorism as acts of violence that intentionally target civilians in pursuit of a political goal.[5]

As guerrilla warfare moved from the countryside into the city, terrorism gained ground and insurgents adapted their strategy accordingly.[6] In contrast to rural insurgencies, urban guerrillas turned to terrorism because they could no longer retreat to the countryside, build forces slowly, and harass enemy troops. At the same time, the close-quarter fighting of urban conflict made it difficult and often impractical to target military forces alone. Postwar urban terrorism plagued British rule in Palestine, Cyprus, Aden, Malaya, and Kenya, and French rule in Algeria[7]; and assumed a prominent place among South American insurgents. Terrorism included attacks against enemy civilians, government officials, police officers, collaborators, and sympathizers among the local population. For some guerrillas, terrorism offered a short cut to Mao's arduous program of patiently building rebel forces from a militia capable of sporadic hit-and-run attacks to a conventional army capable of overwhelming enemy forces in open warfare. For others, terrorism was a necessary tactic given the fighting terrain and limited number of forces available to insurgents. For most, terrorism aimed to weaken civilian morale among the enemy, compel the government to recognize guerrilla demands, place their national cause firmly on the international agenda, and garner support for militant groups at home.

Terrorism, however, does not stand alone but forms an integral part of urban and other forms of guerrilla warfare. Terrorism is most successful when combined with programs to build mass popular support rather than used in isolation.[8] The combination of guerrilla warfare and urban terrorism will likely constitute a potent form of asymmetric warfare in the near future. At its most effective, terrorism is not a different kind of warfare, nor a criminal activity void of any political purpose. Although many commentators try to draw a clear distinction between despicable acts of terror and noble acts of guerrilla warfare, the former preying on the innocent and the latter fighting an armed adversary, terrorism and guerrilla warfare are often inseparable. Terrorism is a guerrilla tactic necessitated by circumstance: local terrain, demography, popular support for guerrilla activities, and enemy capabilities. Terrorism, at least in the hands of national liberation movements, is anchored in the same ideological motives that underlie guerrilla behavior in general. It is but another means to achieve a just end. Opponents of nationalist terrorism question its means, but not often its ends. This is not necessarily true about other forms of terrorism.

Since 9/11, it is common to distinguish nationalist terrorism from the transnational or millennial terrorism of al-Qaeda and other radical Islamic movements. Nationalist terrorism is a carryover from anti-colonial warfare and is among the violent means that guerrilla organizations use against the reigning political power to achieve independence or self-determination. Secessionist movements fighting to escape gross injustice and severe human rights abuses may also include terrorism in their repertoire.[9] Transnational terrorism, in contrast, does not usually speak to any national goal but, instead, to a pan-religious or pan-national ideal that looks beyond the boundaries of the traditional nation-state. Nevertheless, the exact difference between these two kinds of terrorism is difficult to pinpoint.

On one hand, the difference is obvious. National guerrilla movements strive for a just cause. Many may take issue with their tactics, but their causes seem noble enough, particularly when the people they represent are suffering great hardship and injustice. Transnational movements, on the other hand, are about subjugation, not freedom. They thrive on discord and disruption and seem to seek nothing more than the ruin of Western interests. Without just cause of any kind, there is certainly no room to express any understanding of their methods. On the other hand, there is no compelling moral reason to think that organizations striving for national goals are morally superior to those that transcend parochial nationalism in favor of some transnational or pan-religious entity. If, by some accounts, millennial Islamic groups pursue the interests of the Islamic religious nation, the *umma*, then there is no reason to think that their cause is any less just than those who pursue independence for Chechnya, Palestine, or Kosovo.[10] All are Islamic; some look to the nation-state, others look beyond it.

How the two forms of terrorism affect one another remains debatable. Robert O. Keohane, for example, suggests that 9/11 has delegitimized transnational terrorism and united many nations in an effort to eradicate Islamic terrorism just as they united two hundred years ago to fight piracy. As a result, support for Palestinians and Kashmiri rebels has dropped, while Russia gained a freer hand to fight Chechnyan militants.[11] Nevertheless, some guerrilla organizations like Fatah have disassociated themselves from the militant Islamic ideology that tars Hamas, and thereby regain no small measure of legitimacy. Nor did some non-Islamic terrorists, Tamil or Basque separatists, for example, necessarily suffer from delegitimation in their respective conflicts.

These trends reinforce the differences between nationalist and transnational terrorism and set up the problem at hand. Just as the distinction between ordinary terrorism and demonic terrorism lends a measure of support for the former, the distinction between nationalist terrorism and transnational terrorism also grants a measure of legitimacy to terrorism undertaken in the name of national liberation.

JUSTIFYING THE HEINOUS

Intentional harm to the innocent in the pursuit of a political goal is the hallmark of terrorism. Is it possible, however, to look at terrorism as an extreme form of armed violence that, like any similarly destructive weapon, has its use in armed conflict under certain circumstances? If so, then, like any weapon, terrorism must be an effective, necessary, and proportionate response to aggression, while only targeting those who take some part in the hostilities. There seems to be no obvious reason why terrorism cannot sometimes meet these conditions. Of course, terrorism targets noncombatants directly and, in doing so, seems to fail the test of just and lawful warfare. But the conventions of war do not always prohibit direct harm to noncombatants. Civilian reprisals, not entirely discredited today, turn on direct harm to noncombatants when one side violates the laws of war. Alternatively, supporters of terrorism may seek to expand the sphere of combatant targets to include political leaders and/or civilians who directly, indirectly, or potentially support the armed forces. This is certainly what conventional forces are doing. Finally, one must face the simple argument that intentionality may not matter much. Terrorists face condemnation because they intentionally kill civilian noncombatants. But if killing civilians under the guise of collateral damage is nothing but a moral smokescreen, then some forms of terrorism may not be as far from conventional wartime killing as one might think.

Some of these arguments can carry considerable weight. When it came time to ratify Protocol I, the United States refused, convinced that international law was on the verge of legalizing terrorism. Protocol I, argued Abraham Sofaer, legal advisor to the State Department in the Reagan Administration, created two classes of combatants: "those fighting [against colonial domination and alien occupation and racist regimes who] obtain prisoner-of-war status if captured, and immunity from prosecution from belligerent acts" and "those fighting for less-favored political causes ... [who] would not receive POW status or immunity of prosecution from warlike acts."[12] For the Reagan and all subsequent U.S. administrations, this meant that Protocol I, the most current and widely accepted codification of the Geneva Conventions, condoned terrorism in the hands of those fighting for national self-determination.

On the face of it, the accusation is false: Protocol I clearly condemns terrorism. Yet it would be naive to assume that lawmakers were blind to the reality of colonial conflict. Which groups among those fighting colonial, alien, or racist regimes did not attack some civilians indiscriminately or violate the Protocol's prohibition of engaging "in acts or threats of violence the primary purpose of which is to spread terror among the civilian population"? Certainly not the Algerians, Greek Cypriots, the Mau Mau, the Irish Republican Army (IRA), or the Palestine Liberation Organization (PLO). As a result, the UN General Assembly has always been of two minds about terrorism, condemning it on the one hand, but understanding that eliminating terrorism depends on removing its root causes: colonialism, racism, alien domination, occupation, and "massive and flagrant violations of human rights and fundamental freedoms."[13] Naturally, one can ask whether it is acceptable to use terrorism to do just that. It is no wonder then that Finnish jurist Jan Klabbers candidly declares, "The criminalization of terrorism has not been (and cannot be) complete; in the corners of the minds of the members of the Security Council ... there is still a tiny voice whispering that not all violence is by definition criminal because, after all, violence can be used for the noblest of purposes."[14] This tiny voice does not seem to go away. Ehud Barak seems to have heard it loud and clear when he thought about an alternative life as a Palestinian.

Excusing Terrorism under Extreme Conditions

Think about the relatively rare but morally unproblematic questions. Might Eastern European Jews attack and kill German civilians to forestall the Holocaust? Might Kurds have attacked Iraqis to prevent further gas attacks on Kurdish civilians? Many people would, undoubtedly answer yes: a persecuted people may use terrorism to avert genocide. Terrorism, in this case, is the lesser evil. Faced with an overwhelming, existential threat (a great evil) and no alternative means to avert catastrophe, necessity will excuse acts of terrorism (a lesser evil) if they are an effective means of last resort. Terrorism remains reprehensible because it directly targets innocent noncombatants, but excusable under these circumstances. Perpetrators of terror must defend themselves and convince their peers that no less-harmful means are available to save the lives of innocent victims facing genocide or crimes against humanity.

The scenarios as I briefly presented them have no historical basis. Each is a figment of idle speculation about alternate history. In their time, the Jews and Kurds did not, nor could they, terrorize their enemies; they simply perished in droves. Nevertheless, the fictional scenario raises a number of issues that course through discussions about terrorism. First, it points to the unease that many observers feel about an absolute ban on terrorism.[15] Second, it sets certain conditions for excusable terrorism while at the same time raising a number of important questions. First, what magnitude of harm must a threat pose before a people may use terrorism? Must a people face genocide or may they respond with terrorism to press a claim for self-determination or redress some lesser form of political oppression? Second, what magnitude of harm may one inflict? Must the acts of terror that Jews or Kurds undertake bear some relationship to the acts others perpetrated against them? Terrorism, even in the most extreme cases imaginable, must meet the test of necessity and effectiveness. Must it also be proportionate? Finally, what of justice and responsibility? I have painted a brief picture of excusable terrorism, but who are its legitimate targets? May one use terror to punish innocent civilians for their government's misdeeds? This is the logic of reprisal. Or, may guerrillas attack those either directly or indirectly responsible for the repression their people suffer? These questions course through any attempt to justify terrorism.

Justifying Terrorism in Asymmetric War

When asked about the use of terror, Mohammed Dahlan, commander of Palestinian security forces in Gaza in 2002, warned Israel "whoever harms civilians must expect similar responses."[16] Representatives of al-Qaeda make similar statements to justify terrorist attacks against American targets. Unpacking his argument, Dahlan has several things in mind:

1. *Intentionality and the idea of collateral damage do not matter.* The standard response to Dahlan's argument is echoed in the words of an Israeli mother whose child was severely injured in a terror attack: "The Palestinians," she said, "aim to hurt our sons and rejoice at their injuries, while neither we, nor our army, *intend* to hurt them."[17] In response to the claim that guerrillas intentionally harm civilians, Dahlan may move in one of two directions. He can claim that intentionality does not matter, and that Israel or any similarly situated state actor remains responsible for the unintentional deaths of innocent civilians resulting from an intentional military operation. Or, he may argue that Israel intentionally harmed Palestinian civilians even while claiming it did not. In neither case are the arguments trivial for they suggest that the stronger state's actions are morally blameworthy and may invite legitimate reprisals.

2. *Israeli (or American or European) citizens are the legitimate targets of reprisal.* While international law increasingly frowns on reprisals, there is no firm consensus that reprisals are wrong. Indeed, there is a long history of Israeli reprisal raids in the 1950s in response to Arab attacks on Israeli civilians. Why, the Palestinians seem to be asking, can they not do the same? Why can't they deliberately attack innocent civilians in response to injustices the Israeli government perpetrates? In a larger sense, Dahlan may also be appealing to a broader principle of collective responsibility. Reprisals are strictly proportionate, their justification lies in a response in kind and the hope that they will prevent an enemy from attacking civilians further. The principle of collective responsibility, however, turns its back on proportionality and aims to punish anyone who threatens another people or nation. Since complicity can cast a wide net, it is easy to see how "whoever harms civilians" may include the military personnel, political leaders, and no small number of civilians as well.

3. *Extreme conditions excuse terror attacks on civilians as a measure of last resort.* Guerrilla organizations may not only hope to deter future attacks but may also hope to break local morale and exert pressure on the government to acquiesce to their political demands. This recalls the doctrine of disproportionate force noted in the previous chapter and takes us back to the first question raised above: What is genocide? Is the physical threat of annihilation or some lesser military or political threat sufficient to justify intentionally harming civilians if no other means, or targets, are available?

Each of these arguments merits careful consideration. To reject them out of hand will also hamstring stronger nations as they fight weaker forces and find themselves with no better option than to harm civilians as they prosecute their war. They, too, will want to know whether intentionality matters, whether they may take reprisals against innocent civilians, and who, among the many enemy civilians they face, may have lost their immunity in asymmetric conflict.

Intentionality

Does intentionality matter or is it a gimmick? In the tradition of just war, intentionality is central and supplies the moral foundation for harming civilians in wartime. Direct harm violates the principle of noncombatant immunity, but collateral harm leaves room for considerable devastation under certain conditions often known as the doctrine of double effect (DDE). The DDE reiterates the importance of intentionality and allows combatants to kill civilians when their deaths are an unintended, although foreseen, side effect of a necessary military operation that produces less harm than one reasonably hopes to forestall. It is a double effect because the goal, or first effect, of a military operation is to destroy a military target. Sometimes, however, an armed force cannot accomplish its aims without harming civilians who live or work close to a military target. Civilian deaths are a secondary effect, one that an attacking force clearly foresees but cannot avoid. Nevertheless, the goal of the action is not to harm civilians. In this way, civilian deaths are unintentional but foreseen.

In practice, the weaker parties to an asymmetric conflict may be excused for thinking that the antipathy toward direct harm only favors those who can cause sufficient harm indirectly. Collateral damage, although unintended, carries certain benefits, and deterrence has always been chief among them. Pondering the ethics of nuclear deterrence, for example, Paul Ramsey remained convinced that it was morally wrong to target Russian civilians with nuclear weapons. So, in what seems a moral sleight of hand, Ramsey made room for indirect harm. As a matter of avowed policy, U.S. military planners aimed their missiles at military installations, not civilian population centers. Atomic weapons were nevertheless sufficiently destructive to destroy military installations and annihilate millions of civilians who happened to be living nearby. But it was the latter, indirect threat that did all the strategic work and was sufficient to deter the Russians from a nuclear first strike.[18] In this way, indirect harm is not necessarily unintentional. In asymmetric war one may exploit collateral damage for similar purposes: "The deaths of women and children during IDF (Israel Defense Forces) operations against wanted men has become routine," writes a *Ha'aretz* newspaper commentator in 2002, "but this week a senior officer was even quoted, in response to the civilian deaths in Al Bureij (fighting in the Al Bureij refugee camp killed 10 Palestinians and wounded 20), as saying that a 'large number of casualties has deterrent value.'"[19] These are collateral casualties; no one suggests that any armed force may kill civilians directly. Nevertheless, these indirect casualties are not necessarily unintentional.

Collateral harm that backs up a deterrent capability or brings other military benefits is no longer unintended harm. Civilian casualties may be a by-product of a legitimate and necessary military operation, but it is an intended by-product that serves a military purpose. Civilians suffer harm for military purposes and one is left to ask how collateral harm of this sort is different from the intentional harm that terrorists cause. Philosophers, too, have had a difficult time with the idea of intentionality. It seems obvious enough: One may not intentionally harm a civilian during war. But what does this mean? Does it simply reflect the state of mind of a soldier or pilot? If it does, the outcome will be strange. Think about two pilots who perform exactly the same act, bombing an arms factory, for example, and killing exactly the same number of civilians living nearby. One bomber did his best to hit the factory and felt remorse over unavoidable civilian casualties, but the other hoped to teach civilians a lesson as he destroyed valuable munitions. Do we condemn one and praise the other? It seems not.

Scenarios such as these lead philosophers to look beyond someone's state of mind and ask whether there is any military purpose to killing civilians.[20] If their deaths serve a military purpose then they are not incidental or collateral. The acid test is whether an attacker profits from the death of civilians in any way.[21] Susan Uniacke calls this the test of failure: Would the mission fail if civilians did not die? On the face of it, a NATO bomber pilot attacking guerrilla positions in Afghanistan can claim that the scores of dead civilians contributed nothing to his purpose. If so, their deaths were truly incidental. Terrorism, on the other hand, cannot succeed without killing innocent civilians.[22] As a result, terrorists intentionally cause harm and their acts are reprehensible.

Unfortunately, this dichotomy is none too neat. As the citations noted above attest, conventional armies often acknowledge the benefits of collateral damage and, in fact, may depend upon them to effectively deter their enemy from future aggression. When conventional (or nuclear) strategy violates noncombatant immunity in this manner, we may respond in one of two ways. One is to condemn the state actor for abusing the latitude that the DDE and principle of collateral harm allows.[23] Collateral damage cannot allow a state or nonstate actor to benefit militarily from the civilian deaths its military operations cause. Alternatively, we can recognize that intentional harm inevitably seeps into any practical application of the DDE and admit that armies exploit and gain from incidental harm. Unfortunately, any such recognition also allows guerrillas the same latitude we extend to states, and now permits both to hide intentional harm behind the mask of the double effect. Whether this opens the door to excessive civilian casualties remains a difficult question to answer. In conventional war, reciprocity and mutual self-interest may hold noncombatant harm in check despite the elasticity of both the DDE and the idea of collateral damage. This may not hold true in asymmetric conflict.

Collateral and Intentional Harm in Asymmetric Conflict

In asymmetric conflict, an odd and paradoxical dynamic may take hold that makes it difficult to curb harm to civilians in the context of international law. Consider the following scenarios:

Attacks against Civilian Targets

Guerrillas have the technological means to fire a missile of limited range and accuracy. The only target within range is a small town (Town A) that they periodically shell. In a seven-year period, their attacks kill 20 people and wound scores of others in the town and outlying areas.[24] Guerrillas also have the ability to dispatch suicide bombers into civilian population centers. These attacks manifestly violate noncombatant immunity and draw charges of war crimes by some international human rights organizations.[25] For the most part, the stronger state's response is relatively restrained. Armed forces make every attempt to target the perpetrators while large-scale artillery bombardments of guerrilla infrastructures that cause significant civilian casualties remain the exception. In these circumstances terror attacks do not ordinarily elicit an overwhelming military response.

Attacks against Military Targets

Guerrillas have the technological means to fire a missile of limited range and accuracy. The largest target within range is a medium-sized city (City B) with several strategic installations. They periodically shell the city causing a number of casualties. The DDE allows a guerrilla organization to attack a military target insofar as the collateral damage is not disproportionate. If the missiles are technologically unsophisticated and inaccurate, then they may cause a significant, but necessary, number of civilian casualties as guerrillas claim to pursue a military target. In response to these attacks, the stronger state launches a major ground operation that takes over one hundred lives.[26]

Notice how the circumstances of the second case give guerrillas extremely wide moral, legal, and tactical latitude. There are, however, limits to this strategy. First, a weapon that is inaccurate to the point where it is impossible to differentiate between civilian and military targets will draw charges of indiscriminate use. Second, any direct attack on civilian population centers violates noncombatant immunity. These accusations are severe, but they are couched in the language of armed conflict, not terrorism. In the Second Lebanon War, Hezbollah ran afoul of both charges even as it claimed to aim solely at military targets and confine civilian harm to collateral damage or operational errors.[27] Nevertheless, attacking military targets permits guerrillas to significantly harm civilians under the guise of unintentional, collateral damage. The paradox, of course, is this: guerrilla attacks on City B are no longer acts of terrorism, but acts of war that can cause significantly greater harm than intentional attacks on civilians did. As a result, they precipitate a far more destructive response. Paradoxically, *fewer civilians suffer harm when intentions matter than when they do not.* As guerrillas obtain more powerful and sophisticated arms, they begin to fight more like conventional armies. Their status and image may improve, but war now escalates significantly under the cover of unintentional collateral damage. And, for many on both sides of an asymmetric conflict, it is just that: a cover that is difficult to take seriously. Using the DDE to excuse heavy casualties but condemn lighter losses guts the concept of its usefulness.

Two difficulties, therefore, come from placing undue emphasis on intentionality and intentional harm. First, there is a misguided tendency to equate intentional and direct harm. Second, focusing on intentionality might favor attacks that cause greater rather than lesser harm. Ordinarily, we think that intentional and direct harm are synonymous. Yet, indirect harm, that is, the second effect of a military operation, can be intentional if it provides an acknowledged military benefit. Once military planners recognize that collateral harm is useful, it is no longer unintended the next time around. As a result, both the collateral and direct harm that guerrilla or conventional military organizations cause is often intentional. Intentionality does not condemn or justify harm during war. This comes from understanding the status and rights of the target population and a tactic's effectiveness (which seems entirely lost in the discussion). With the exception of reprisals, civilian noncombatants are not legitimate targets. When civilian *combatants* are the target, what matters is effectiveness and proportionality, not intentionality.

Reprisals

As the cases above suggest, it is often difficult to defend collateral harm to civilians, particularly when it benefits the insurgents' or counterinsurgents' cause. Benefits, as noted earlier, are a sure test of intentionality leaving the sides to explore other avenues to justify harm to civilians. One of the most time-tested is reprisals and they can serve guerrilla and state army interests alike. Reprisals represent one of the rare instances that allow belligerents to harm civilians directly. Civilians retain their protected status but the unique logic of reprisals allows one side to override noncombatant immunity and deliberately target civilians.

The Logic of Reprisal

Claims that terror attacks are reprisals for indiscriminate collateral damage or that attacks on terrorists are reprisals for terrorism are not easily disentangled. The principle of self-help anchors reprisal and the right of a belligerent to violate the laws of war in response to a prior violation by the other side.[28] Violations and reprisals are generally "in kind." Harm to one side's civilians (or prisoners of war, or wounded, or hospitals, for example) is met with similar harm perpetrated by the other side. Reprisals are not acts of ordinary self-defense, for they are an inherently unlawful response to past unlawful acts. Retribution and vengeance are not the primary purposes of reprisal, although many guerrilla organizations justify reprisals as just that. Rather, reprisals aim to force states or nonstates to comply with international law by harming their civilians, other noncombatants, or protected facilities. Nor should reprisals cause harm that exceeds the number killed and wounded in the initial infraction. Reprisals, therefore, form a carefully circumscribed form of warfare restrained by strict proportionality. Even in this limited form, it is easy to see how the logic of reprisal may serve the interests of guerrillas and state actors alike. Justified by an unlawful act of war, but unlawful acts themselves, reprisals hold forth the prospect of lawfully inflicting direct harm on civilians during war.

Reprisals against Civilians

Civilians have not always enjoyed protection from the strong urge to attack them when their nation or army violates the laws of war. While the 1949 Geneva Conventions safeguard the lives of civilians in occupied territories, only the 1977 Protocols to the Geneva Conventions, Articles 51–58, protect civilians in unoccupied, enemy territory from reprisal. Yet some nations, particularly the powerful industrial nations of the West, have been slow to relinquish the right of reprisal. The United States, for example, refused to ratify Protocol I partly because, "the total elimination of the right of reprisal ... would hamper the ability of the United States to respond to an enemy's intentional disregard of ... the Geneva Conventions of 1949."[29] Britain, Italy, France, and Germany, on the other hand, ratified Protocol I, but each reserved the right to retaliate against the civilian population of any nation egregiously violating noncombatant immunity.[30] In the final analysis, write Henckaerts and Doswald-Beck in their encyclopedic compilation of customary humanitarian law, "it is difficult to conclude that there has yet crystallized a customary rule specifically prohibiting reprisals against civilians."[31]

In theory, reprisals remain attractive for several reasons. One is efficacy: military planners often assume that reprisals against civilians are an effective tool for forcing nations to observe international law. Another attraction is the oft-repeated reference to *lex talonis*, retaliating with evil for evil. This is the simplest reading of Dahlan's warning cited earlier: you kill our civilians and we will kill yours. Although modern treatises on reprisal gloss over *lex talonis* on the assumption that it is but a remnant of primitive law, there is no doubt that targeting civilians in reprisal for unlawful acts of war, particularly those aimed at civilians to begin with, retains a certain appeal based on vengeance and simple justice. At the same time, reprisal, like revenge, also rests on the idea of strict proportionality that many might find attractive. Like revenge, one side aims at inflicting no more harm than it suffered at the hands of the other.

In practice, however, reprisals remain extraordinarily problematic. Far from self-limiting, they often spiral into infinite cycles of tit-for-tat. Nor are the parties inclined to keep their response proportionate to the original infraction. "You don't understand the logic of vengeance," Monteverdi admonishes Nero's offended wife in the *Coronation of Poppea*, "on every slight pay back in blood and slaughter."[32] This lesson is lost on no one, least of all adversaries caught up in the cycle of reprisal and retribution. Nor do reprisals necessarily break morale or lead citizens to convince their government to change its ways of war. On the contrary, reprisals, like disproportionate force, only harden civilians' resolve to fight and survive.[33] And, apart from these difficulties, reprisals remain morally and legally problematic. If civilian immunity is to have any meaning whatsoever, then ordinary civilians cannot pay for the crimes of others regardless of the actions of their state or the nonstate forces to which they give allegiance. Nor can one justify killing one group of civilians today to prevent the killing of another group in the future. In neither case has the targeted group lost its right to life. This is the single strongest argument against civilian reprisals and should thoroughly repudiate any attempt by either side to justify civilian reprisals.

Nevertheless, this view has yet to overwhelm the international community. If reprisals remain on the table, one is left to think about effectiveness. Are acts of terror and reprisals effective? The answer depends, in part, on what perpetrators are after. Reprisals, traditionally understood, focus on short-term goals. For guerrillas, restoration of sullied honor, that is, revenge, is the simplest goal for them to achieve. It requires no tactical victory, only a solid belief that a terror attack somehow restores a group's honor by exacting a blood price. These are not the short-term goals, however, that the doctrine of reprisals brings to mind. Instead, reprisal seeks an immediate change of behavior on the part of one's adversary. Like the restoration of honor, the perception of behavioral change is often entirely subjective and difficult to evaluate. Many Hamas leaders are no doubt convinced that their attacks on Israel forced the cease-fire that prevailed until December 2008. Israel believes its attacks in response to

indiscriminate shelling forced the lull. Each side had its cease-fire
and each was convinced that reprisals accounted for its success.

The long-term effects of reprisals and terrorism in general are
more difficult to evaluate and the results are decidedly mixed. Some
observers are entirely convinced that terrorism provided the means
for guerrillas to defeat the French in Algeria, the Israelis in Gaza, the
Americans in Beirut, and to successfully wring significant concessions
from the United Nations and the world community.[34] A more modest
assessment admits that while terrorism has gotten them where they
are, many guerrilla organizations have not gotten very far at all in
terms of achieving their national aspirations.[35] More likely, terrorism
is responsible for their many missed opportunities that Abba Eban
made so much about. Terrorism, observes Michael Ignatieff, is a form
of politics that "aims at the death of politics itself."[36]

Ignatieff's assessment requires some focus. International terrorism
in the hands of al-Qaeda certainly aims at the death of politics if by
politics we mean a dynamic process of confrontation that strives for
compromise and accommodation. Nationalist terrorism, on the other
hand, is wholly political. Inordinate emphasis on terrorism suffers
from the same defects as inordinate emphasis on reprisals and demoralization bombing in the hands of a conventional army. Strict and proportionate reprisals sometimes carry short-term benefits, particularly
if the side employing them is quick to change strategy and jettison
reprisals or terrorism when they start to solidify its enemy's resolve and
precipitate harsh responses stemming from the fierce moral indignation that attacks on civilians usually bring. In the long term, however,
reprisals, terrorism, disproportionate force, and direct or collateral
attacks on civilians are doubly problematic: they strengthen rather
than weaken a nation's determination to fight and often trigger a
fierce response in kind. For these reasons, they often fail.

Nevertheless, reprisals remain attractive to many nations that are
reluctant to agree to an outright ban. Support for reprisals, however,
opens the door to support for terrorism because both trade on harming civilians directly. Guerrillas sometimes muddy the waters by exult-
ing in vengeance, formally the wrong motive for reprisal but popular
among their constituency. Conventional armies often eschew reprisal
in favor of language anchored in collateral harm, but glean military
benefits from civilian casualties nonetheless. Directly or indirectly,

then, both sides can benefit from the moral and legal framework of reprisal. Reprisals reflect a sanctioned exception to the conventions that prohibit directly killing civilians when one side grossly violates the principles of international law and the law of armed conflict. And, this is precisely what guerrillas and conventional armies often claim, particularly as they criminalize the actions of the other. As I noted in the first chapter, nationalist terrorism does not always generate enormous body counts and may constitute a measure of proportionate harm if necessary and effective to fight gross injustice. Critics will condemn the deliberate nature of the harm terrorism brings, but direct harm is an acceptable feature of reprisal.

The argument for reprisal is attractive because it puts terrorism and other forms of direct harm to civilians into a justificatory framework firmly anchored in international conventions. If there is any difficulty with the argument, it is, perhaps, too attractive. In conventional warfare, reprisals are not the rule but the rare exception. Elevating reprisals to a common way of warfare that makes room for terrorism on the weaker side and direct harm to civilians under the guise of collateral damage on the stronger, will probably give many people pause because it effectively does away with noncombatant immunity. Asymmetric warfare is, as Rupert Smith so aptly puts it, a war among the people.[37] A sweeping doctrine of acceptable reprisal offers the people no protection whatsoever. Reprisal, therefore, should not be the moral and legal framework of choice to justify attacks on civilians in asymmetric war. Instead, adversaries will seek to expand the sphere of vulnerability and target those military and civilian agents responsible for the threat each side faces while trying to protect those civilians who sit quietly on the sidelines.

Targeting Those Responsible: Expanding the Sphere of Vulnerability

Protocol I sanctions, and perhaps even encourages, the use of armed force by "peoples [who] are fighting against colonial domination and alien occupation and against racist regimes in the exercise of their right of self-determination." Who are legitimate targets in this struggle? "A person is morally justified employing terrorism," writes J. Angelo Corlett, if among other things, "he directs terrorist activity ... only against those clearly guilty of committing acts of significant injustice" and uses terrorism "to best achieve a cessation of the conditions of injustice which might justify the use of terrorism in the first place."[38] This assertion makes three assumptions. First, the idea of "significant injustice" casts a net far wider than the prevailing norms imply. Protocol I feeds a norm sympathetic to guerrillas who use terrorism to fight against colonial, alien, and racist regimes in pursuit of national self-determination. There are other significant injustices in the world – among them, poverty, gender discrimination, and child abuse – but these do not seem sufficiently egregious to justify terrorism. And, there are greater injustices – genocide and ethnic cleansing – that the norm permitting terrorism might want to include as it makes room for struggles against occupation. Second, terrorism, like any other tactic of armed conflict, must be effective. It must achieve what it sets out to accomplish. Terrorism is not an isolated means to end occupation but part of a comprehensive strategy that encompasses civil unrest, military operations, and attacks on enemy civilians. Here the jury is out. As I noted above, there are conflicting assessments about the effectiveness of terrorism as a tactic of guerrilla warfare. Nevertheless, effectiveness is not enough; defensible terrorism must also target those responsible.

Among those who may be responsible are those who benefit from the unjust state of affairs and/or support the government's policy and/or can influence and change government policy.[39] This group can be large and reaches beyond uniformed soldiers to embrace political leaders and other civilians who actively and effectively support the war effort. Guerrilla organizations face the same cohort that conventional armies do when they look into the enemy camp and see civilians and bureaucrats running the machinery of occupation, settlers or other civilian personnel who establish their nation's presence on the ground, reservists and off-duty soldiers. Further from direct military involvement are those whose contributing role is central: journalists, educators, students, and employees of welfare organizations or financial institutions who extend logistical support to the military or, more generally, provide political, ideological, and religious backing for occupation, intervention, or other policies guerrillas oppose. They are the mirror image of civilians taking a direct or indirect part in the hostilities that counterinsurgent forces target. Both, traditionally, are noncombatants, but focusing squarely on responsibility pushes many into the combatant camp. Guerrillas, no less than those fighting them, take responsibility seriously. Modern justifications of terrorism, just described, pursue this route. Otherwise, they are deliberately lending support to killing the innocent. To justify attacks that inflict harm directly, vulnerable targets must bear some responsibility for the threat or injustice guerrillas (or counterinsurgency forces) face.

Still, it is difficult to escape the impression that terrorists seek out those whom everyone agrees is innocent so their attacks can achieve the greatest impact. In principle, urban terrorism does not rule out attacks on civilian noncombatants and they figure prominently in places like Sri Lanka, Chechnya, and elsewhere. Indeed, guerrillas perceive these attacks as necessary to provoke the disproportionate response that will attract sympathy to their cause. States respond most ferociously when their innocents suffer great harm. Innocence, therefore, and not responsibility, is often a prerequisite for victimhood. This clearly puts a crimp in the terrorists' desire to paint all their victims as responsible for grave injustice.

Here, even sympathetic observers should part company with guerrilla agendas. Aside from the limited appeal of reprisal, no one advocates directly harming the innocent. At the same time, support for a norm of collective responsibility that embraces all citizens, or all who vote or could vote, is eccentric. While Barry Buzan claims that democratic citizens get the government they deserve and, as a result, bear direct responsibility for its action, this ignores the fact that a great many people do not vote for their government or they may support the government based on unrelated issues.[40] Nevertheless, Jeff Goodwin suggests that guerrillas assess responsibility or complicity based on the political order of the regime they face. Facing an autocratic or oligarchic regime, guerrillas hold only the political and business elite responsible. Facing a democratic regime, however, particularly one where military conscription is law, the entire body politic comes under fire.[41] In practice, however, this distinction is crude and reinforced by racial, cultural, and nationalist agendas. Palestinians, for example, face a democratic regime where all adult citizens participate in a sophisticated, representative political process. Do guerrillas hold everyone responsible or just Israel's Jewish citizens? My guess is the latter. Conscription, too, is an equally dubious premise on which to base complicity. While conscription may mean that many citizens are soldiers, potential soldiers, or reserve soldiers, it also means that young men and women who otherwise have no truck with guerrilla organizations, suddenly find themselves in the firing line. One would think that thoughtful terrorists would have much more sympathy for common conscripts than for the elite commandos who fill the ranks of many counterinsurgency forces.

Moreover, imputing responsibility to all citizens, regardless of regime type, is potentially dangerous to guerrilla organizations themselves. They, too, need the idea of innocence to protect *their* citizens. Otherwise, they face an enemy who may readily brand all of their compatriots as combatants. If guerrillas wish to appeal to some measure of noncombatant immunity to protect their own, they must maintain some semblance of respect for enemy civilians. Nor does this seem unrealistic. Guerrillas who employ terrorism need not tar all their adversaries' citizens with the brush of complicity. Rather they, like the nation-state they face, can stake out grounds that will enjoy a firm level of support if they look beyond armed enemy combatants and only target those who have a hand in the aggression that insurgents are fighting to overcome. These quasi-combatants include no small number of enemy civilians that humanitarian law currently defines as noncombatants, and while defensible terrorism cannot target the polity at large, it may allow insurgents (and counterinsurgents) to intentionally harm quasi-combatants while exposing the truly innocent to collateral damage. A mix of tactics that bring intentional harm to quasi-combatants and collateral harm to noncombatants is the hallmark of asymmetric warfare. These tactics mark an emerging norm that recognizes the many instances when combatants have no viable option of restricting their attacks to military targets. It is a new norm for nation-states and guerrillas alike. What does this emerging norm look like?

THE LIMITS OF DEFENSIBLE TERRORISM

Michael Ignatieff eloquently describes the limits of a nationalist struggle:

If we believe that their oppression is such that it justifies turning to violence as a last resort, then the ethics of their struggle passes out of human rights and into the laws of war. These rules expressly forbid the targeting of civilians … . To be sure, this limits the struggles for freedom. You cannot fight dirty; you must take on military targets, not civilian ones.[42]

In one sense, this seems hopelessly naïve particularly when a group cannot take on military targets because there is none in range or they are too well protected. It is also normatively problematic if guerrillas merit an equal chance in combat and a reasonable prospect of victory.[43] Confronting this dilemma leads to a steady revision of what it means to fight dirty. This is true as we assess torture and assassination and as we consider terrorism and other attacks on civilians. Fighting dirty does not exclude attacks on all civilians. Rather, it only excludes attacks on civilians who are not combatants or quasi-combatants. In the course of strikes on combatants or quasi-combatants, innocent civilians find themselves subject to collateral harm when an attack is unavoidably necessary, effective, and proportionate. Necessity, effectiveness, and proportionality are, of course, the watchwords of just and lawful war and it might sound perverse to apply them to terrorism. Nevertheless, they lay the foundation for defensible terrorism. It bears repeating that these principles combined with the evolving concept of the civilian combatant also help counterinsurgents defend torture, assassination, and blackmail.

The first and hardest test to pass is, as always, effectiveness. Terrorism brings mixed results. Short-term tactical gains are transient and meet with a brutal response. Long-term strategic gains are more difficult to pinpoint. Nontactical gains – honor, glory, or martyrdom – have little effect on the resolution of conflict. Following an assessment of effectiveness, terrorism, like any military tactic, faces the test of humanitarianism. Any means, however effective, must also be discriminating and proportionate. Attacks must distinguish between the direct harm they cause combatants and quasi-combatants, and the indirect suffering that noncombatants must bear. Nor can guerrilla attacks cause disproportionate harm to the latter, however necessary and unavoidable it may be. In this context, it is possible to address the oft-repeated argument that terrorism, if ever justified, ought to be only a last resort in the most dire of circumstances. Only groups facing imminent genocide may turn to terrorism if that is the only means available to stave off extermination.

This argument is peculiar, for once we understand terrorism as a defensible tactic of asymmetric warfare, there is no reason to think in terms of a last resort. Guerrillas certainly do not think that way. If terrorism, understood as direct attacks on civilian combatants, is legitimate, it is subject to the same criteria that guide all forms of armed conflict: necessity, effectiveness, and proportionality. Military necessity does not demand that belligerents search for alternative or more peaceful means to accomplish a military goal unless those means are more effective and less costly. If a tactic or operation only attacks those vulnerable (as soldiers and civilian combatants and quasi-combatants are) and takes reasonable care to avoid excessive harm to noncombatants, then the cost/benefit analysis is straightforward: Did a particular military operation achieve its goal at reasonable cost? In this context, "last resort" is not applicable. Resorting to terrorism does not require that other means are unavailable and that only terrorism can work, but that terrorism affords a reasonable chance of gaining a military or political advantage.

The overriding question remains, however, whether terrorists really preserve the distinction between quasi-combatant and noncombatant, as the evolving norm defines them, and take pains to target the former and protect the latter. The answer is: only sometimes. Sometimes terrorist rhetoric combines the language of reprisal (intentionally killing innocents in response to a similar act against their citizens) with the language of collective responsibility (all adult citizens of nation X are responsible for their government's policies). This casts far too wide a net and fails to preserve any principle of discrimination. At other times, however, we find that guerrillas concede the innocence of certain groups and only target those whom many can agree are responsible. While many Palestinians, for example, overwhelmingly support armed attacks on soldiers and settlers, many voice reluctance about strikes against Israeli civilians living inside the pre-1967 borders.[44] However, these attitudes seem to change with the circumstances. If there is going to be a hard-and-fast rule that regulates terrorism, then it must be a variation of Ignatieff's: terrorists must avoid attacking civilians understanding, however, that this category excludes a great many quasi-combatants who previously enjoyed the protection of noncombatant immunity. Terrorism is only defensible when it is discriminating.

This observation addresses the question raised by the paradox of intentionality: Are terror attacks that cause small numbers of intended casualties morally preferable to conventional attacks that bring larger numbers of incidental casualties? Might a guerrilla organization choose the former as part of an ongoing war of attrition rather than engage in a larger-scale battle that will bring a devastating response? The best answer is that both are wrong. The small-scale attacks are unjustifiable because they derive a military benefit from violating the right to life that civilian noncombatants enjoy. The large-scale attacks are simply ineffective. Similar considerations rein in military action on the stronger side. This does not deprive either side of a fighting chance but does constrain the way warring parties do battle. To meet this constraint, guerrillas must adopt a principle of discrimination that is astonishingly close to the same principle state armies must adopt as they, too, take aim at civilian combatants and quasi-combatants.

FIGHTING IN THE SHADOW OF HARM TO CIVILIANS

The place of civilians in asymmetric warfare is precarious. Guerrillas without uniforms mix freely among civilians and many civilians actively aid guerrillas. Counterinsurgents may be uniformed and armed, but the civilians they protect contribute in important ways to the wars they are fighting. As each side casts about for targets when they cannot strike at military objects, there are really only two options: increase the bank of military targets or attack civilians who support the war.

Increase the Bank of Military Targets

When one side or another runs out of military targets, one option is to expand the bank of military targets while acting to reduce incidental harm to civilian combatants. For the stronger side this means gathering better intelligence and using precision bombs and nonlethal weapons. For the weaker side, it inevitably means gaining access to military targets and this, too, requires better intelligence and more sophisticated weapons. These efforts will be only partially successful. Weaponry will remain asymmetric and most guerrilla organizations will not have the means to put their adversary's military capabilities at significant risk. Guerrilla organizations will continue to nest their military installations among civilians and depend on civilians to take some part in the fighting. Their best hope is not losing and here they often prove remarkably successful. The stronger army will never have its pick of the kind of military and strategic targets that are vulnerable in a conventional war. As a result, each side may test the limits of conventional war law by resorting to reprisals or by broadening the range of vulnerable civilian targets while, at the same time, trying to avoid indefensible terrorism, that is, deliberate attacks on the innocent to punish, demoralize, or deter.

Associated Targets and Participating Civilians

Between less-than-promising attempts to increase the bank of military targets and the indefensible option of indiscriminately harming the innocent, lie strikes on an array of civilian facilities. These can be permissible targets if their destruction brings a significant military advantage and the civilians who run these facilities do not suffer substantial lethal harm. The idea of associated structures does not make a mockery of noncombatant immunity. Rather, it marks an important step in the struggle to understand the scope and limits of asymmetric war. If either side is to command the ability to prosecute a war or engage in armed conflict, the distinction between associated targets and noncombatants is crucial, as is the imperative to disable rather than destroy these same targets.

Meeting these conditions poses a stiff challenge. For guerrilla armies it certainly puts many targets out of bounds. Targeting structures or civilians that do not support the military in any obvious way is simple terrorism, a charge that applies to both sides equally. While many guerrilla organizations often seem to miss this point, philosophical justifications of terrorism are keenly aware that only those civilians who support some form of political injustice are vulnerable to direct attack.[45] Few such theorists have given thought to the means, lethal or nonlethal, that guerrilla organizations may employ to disable these targets. Nor is there much of an effort to distinguish among various forms of participation. State actors, on the other hand, are sensitive to the immorality of attacks on innocent civilians, but do not usually recognize that any military operation that benefits from harm to innocent civilians is akin to terrorism.

Expanding the range of permissible direct harm in warfare grows from the need of each side to press its claims by force of arms. Morally, there are limits to permissible direct harm but they do not come to the fore in a mere dichotomy between combatants and noncombatants, the former vulnerable and the latter immune. Instead, the emerging norm discards "combatants and noncombatants" for "participants." The acute challenge for both sides is defining these participants with precision and consistency. This is precisely the thrust of the Red Cross's Expert Meetings described in Chapter 2.[46] Participants are vulnerable to varying degrees of direct harm, sometimes lethal, sometimes nonlethal. And while agreement may emerge on this point, guerrilla organizations will argue that they lack nonlethal weapons, smart bombs, or the means to detain those who work in banks, government offices, welfare organizations, or the media – just as conventional armies may complain that these less-than-lethal measures are not feasible or risk the lives of their soldiers. In some cases these complaints are reasonable, in others, just excuses. Limited means may require guerrillas to choose a strategy of threats, warnings and nonlethal violence to intimidate civilians working in associated structures and disrupt public services that support the enemy's war effort. Belligerents on each side must show that the destruction of the target they choose will significantly slow down an enemy's war making capability and that its choice of means was the least destructive and most effective available. This will allow guerrillas to cause collateral harm while targeting military targets and disable civilian combatants and quasi-combatants by lethal and other means. The world community will judge this display in the same way it evaluates disproportionate harm or manifestly unlawful orders. As it does, new norms of conduct emerge that will obligate both sides to an asymmetric conflict.

The idea of associated targets expands the range of potential targets significantly but still raises the question, What if disabling these targets cannot decide the outcome of the war? Is it permissible to target innocent civilians to try to force capitulation or to establish a deterrent capability? This is the same question as, What if conventional arms cannot decide the outcome of the war? Can nations then resort to banned weapons such as poison gas, nuclear weapons, or anti-personnel landmines? The answer is no. There are going to be limits beyond which the world community will unequivocally condemn attacks. But the norm is certainly changing. Faced with lack of military targets and the growing role that civilians play in asymmetric war, increasing numbers of individuals are going to find themselves at risk for direct and/or collateral harm.

Questions about the vulnerability of civilians are central to proxy guerrilla wars and CAR conflicts of national liberation. In the war on terror, however, the questions do not arise in the same way. Unlike proxy guerrillas or those fighting for independence, a terrorist force like al-Qaeda is fighting a war shorn of any justice. Without any semblance of just war, no measure that al-Qaeda adopts can be just, much less proportionate. Any discussion of proportionality is simply irrelevant. Moreover, the supporting role of civilians in al-Qaeda's war of terror is dubious. In many (though clearly not all) wars of terror, there are few civilian participants. This makes it harder for terrorists to claim that they must recruit civilians to wage war. This, in turn, makes it more difficult for the stronger side to broaden the scope of permissible proportionate harm as it goes after associated civilian targets in densely populated areas. On the contrary, given the innocence of many civilians living under a reign of terror, there is a strong imperative to take particular care to protect them. The same is undoubtedly true of wars of humanitarian intervention. Genocidal regimes have no place to think about proportionate harm; *any* harm they cause is beyond the pale. At the same time, local civilians do not wage war against the intervening force, but look to it for salvation. In a war of humanitarian intervention, the weaker side cannot claim a need to enlist local civilians to support their fight.

Asymmetric war challenges the world community to ensure an equal chance in combat for those pressing just claims and to protect noncombatants caught in the crossfire. Nowhere is the imperative to defend innocent civilians more clearly stated than in the UN's right to use force against despotic regimes. In practice, however, wars of humanitarian intervention confound intervening nations and their soldiers. Before a nation takes on a criminal regime, it must ask whether intervention might endanger its vital national interests. Their soldiers ask a similar question: Why must they risk their very lives for those who live beyond their borders?

9

Risking Our Lives to Save Others

Puzzles of Humanitarian Intervention

Confronting a wide array of difficulties that often have little to do with national defense, states contemplating humanitarian intervention face hard dilemmas. First, there is the immediate question of intervention. Facing massive human rights abuses in authoritarian and/or failing regimes, states must nonetheless ask whether their own national interests legitimately prevent them from intervening. Observers often speak of pure humanitarian intervention, that is, military action that defends the rights of another nation's citizens but offers the intervening nation no tangible benefits. In other instances, however, intervening nations have conflicting interests. The rights of the persecuted make one demand, while national interest or "reason of state" makes another. As nations work through this dilemma, they may very well decide to intervene. This leads to the paradox of intervention: a state may recognize an obligation to intervene but remain unable to demand that its citizens risk their lives for others. While many moral theories recognize the duty to rescue others, the cost must be reasonable. Dying, however, is not a reasonable cost for anyone. As a result, no individual has any obligation to join an intervening force even when his or her nation has the obligation to provide one.

THE DILEMMA OF HUMANITARIAN INTERVENTION

The dilemma of humanitarian intervention is often phrased as follows: Does the duty to respect state sovereignty trump the responsibility of the international community to take action when the people of a nation are at risk?[1] While a difficult question, the international community has finally answered no; national interest and state sovereignty in the twenty-first century are no longer sacrosanct. However, this understanding is very recent. As late as 1993, Samuel Huntington condemned the United States's ill-fated mission to stabilize Somalia. "It is morally unjustifiable and politically indefensible," he wrote, "that members of the Armed Forces should be killed to prevent Somalis from killing one another ... The military should only be given military missions which involve possible combat when they advance national security interests and are directed against a foreign enemy of the United States."[2] Underlying opposition to wars of humanitarian intervention is the commitment to self-defense and the protection of national interests as the sole justification for using armed force. In the absence of vital military, national, or strategic interests, no state may risk the lives of its soldiers whatsoever.

Until recently, the United Nations maintained a similar position. Under the UN Charter (Article 43), the UN the authority to obligate its members to contribute "armed forces, assistance, and facilities ... necessary for the purpose of maintaining international peace and security" but nothing more. In practice, the UN has two roles: peace *enforcement* and peace*keeping*. To enforce the peace, the UN authorizes military action against states threatening international security. In the Korean War and the First Gulf War, for example, UN troops under U.S. command served as combatants and fought in military units against the armed forces of a sovereign nation. The UN also authorized peace enforcement operations in Somalia, Bosnia, Haiti, Rwanda, eastern Zaire, Albania, the Central African Republic, Kosovo, and East Timor. In Afghanistan and the former Yugoslavia, NATO troops exercised their right to collective self-defense as they intervened against rogue regimes. Peacekeeping operations, on the other hand, police and monitor treaty obligations and may provide buffer forces between belligerents flirting with a fragile peace. By law, peacekeepers are noncombatants and may only use their weapons in personal self-defense. Currently, peacekeeping operations are underway in Haiti, Cyprus, and the Golan Heights to name just a few.[3] Keeping the peace is a diplomatic mission; enforcing it is a military mission. Peace enforcers are full-fledged combatants and at risk for their lives. Peacekeepers are police officers, at risk for bodily harm but generally present to enforce the law.

In cases of peace enforcement, humanitarian intervention can hitchhike on security interests. The key justification for answering the UN call to enforce the peace lies in national or collective self-defense. When a ruthless regime brutally violates the rights, dignity, and person of its own citizens, violence inevitably spills over its borders and threatens the security of other nations. If confronting massive human rights abuses with armed force also ensures international peace and prosperity, prevents rogue regimes from fomenting terrorism and international crime, and removes the incentive for large-scale and sudden emigration that can destabilize peaceful nations, then humanitarian intervention can piggyback on wars of self-defense. Here, nations fighting to protect human rights and the lives of those far from their own borders, are also fighting to defend vital national interests.

When national interests are not at stake, justification turns on an appeal to universal human rights. "If we deny the moral duty and legal right to [intervene]," writes Fernando Tesón, "we deny not only the centrality of justice in political affairs, but also the common humanity that binds us all.[4] Tesón is correct. Rights do not exist without the concomitant obligation to secure and protect them. If the idea of universal human rights is to have any bite at all, then someone, somewhere has the obligation to defend those who face egregious injustice. If one's own government cannot do it, then the duty falls to those who can."[5]

This claim has always been controversial for the very reasons that Huntington suggests. But in 2005, the UN World Summit startled many observers. Confronting past inaction in the face of genocide and ethnic cleansing in Africa, the world community asserted its "right to protect" and resolved to take military action "should peaceful means be inadequate and national authorities are manifestly failing to protect their populations from genocide, war crimes, ethnic cleansing and crimes against humanity."[6] The right to protect is not sweeping. Mindful of critics concerned about the inability to articulate legal norms or moral principles of intervention in a way that will not lead to rampant abuse, the UN Summit regulated intervention in two ways. First, the UN was careful to confine military intervention to preventing gross human rights abuse rather than effecting regime change or democratization. Second, the Summit demanded international consensus before undertaking military action, rather than permitting unilateral action by a single state. Nevertheless, this is a remarkable sea change because it undermines the sanctity of state sovereignty when states fail to meet the minimal obligations they owe their citizens. And, it extends the mandate of the UN to enforce the peace when human rights rather than international security are at stake. The UN right-to-protect helps to answer one question when national and humanitarian interests clash. In contrast to Huntington's claim, nations have a prima facie obligation to defend the persecuted when there is no immediate national interest to do so. What happens, however, when a nation has an interest *not* to intervene, that is, when intervention might harm its interests? This is a much more difficult problem and the reactions of China to calls for intervention in Sudan and Myanmar (Burma) illustrate the difficult dilemma nations may face.

Chinese Interests in Sudan and Myanmar

Sudan presents one of the most pressing cases for humanitarian intervention. UN resolution 1769 (2007) mandating UN and African Union troops to protect the lives of noncombatant Sudanese and international aid workers reflects the kind of humanitarian intervention the right to protect invokes. Formally, the UN is enforcing the peace under Article 43 (Chapter VII) of the UN Charter, but by massacring and dislocating its own citizens the Sudanese government poses a far greater threat to human rights than to world peace. In Myanmar, calls for intervention arose following egregious human rights abuses, forced labor, involuntary relocation, and violent suppression of basic liberties as the military government cracked down on dissidents, most recently in 2007. Later, when a catastrophic cyclone created a humanitarian emergency in 2008, calls for intervention resounded once again.[7] In the first case, the debate turned on intervention to force a *change* of regime to protect human rights; in the second, to *bypassing* the regime to offer humanitarian aid when the government proved inept. In neither case did substantial military action ensue.

Human rights abuses in Sudan or Myanmar do not pose a threat to international security. For some nations, this means that intervention offers no material or military benefits. For other nations, however, intervention might *adversely* affect economic, political, and/or security interests. While lack of material benefit was once sufficient reason to eschew intervention, the emerging norm of intervention now requires nations to carefully weigh their duty to protect foreign nationals. Nations who have little to gain economically or militarily may not back off when citizens of foreign nations face persecution. But what of those nations with something to lose? The weight of humanitarian intervention is not overriding. Nations have to consider whether they may suffer for their efforts. This is precisely what seems to have been on the mind of China as it confronted the indignation of its colleagues at the United Nations.

The Chinese have significant military, political, and economic interests in Myanmar. Rejected by the West, the Burmese military junta turned to China to acquire training programs, weapons, and advanced technology, thereby making the Burmese Army one of the largest in Southeast Asia. In return, the Burmese government has proved relatively compliant. They share intelligence with the Chinese and by some accounts have allowed the Chinese to establish listening posts and, possibly, a military presence on Burmese territory. Economically, China imports timber, agricultural products, and gemstones and exports military hardware, machinery, and consumer goods to Myanmar. A very large population of ethnic Chinese living in Myanmar supports this trade. Viable energy resources and a suitable and secure infrastructure to bring natural gas and oil to China via Myanmar are overriding concerns. Any change in the Burmese government, therefore, is cause for Chinese unease. A government headed by opposition leader Aung San Suu Kyi that an intervening force might install would be far less sympathetic to China and far more eager to establish ties with the West. Chinese interest in Myanmar is part of a larger geopolitical strategy to offset the growing influence of the US and other powers. Closer to home, Myanmar's other large neighbor, India, finds itself in a similar bind. Hoping to wean Myanmar from Chinese influence, India cannot afford to antagonize the Burmese government by criticizing its human rights record. Rather it hopes to win Myanmar over by quieter and more positive means. China, for its part, is not reluctant to use its veto power in the UN to stymie human rights resolutions condemning Burmese abuse.[8]

Intervention in Sudan and Myanmar

How, if at all, might a nation consider humanitarian intervention if military action on behalf of others threatens its vital interests? Expansive theories of humanitarian intervention generate a prima facie obligation to prevent war crimes, crimes against humanity, genocide, and ethnic cleansing. Can national interests ever offset these concerns? Looking at Myanmar, for example, it might be possible to sidestep this question. Human rights abuses and political suppression in Myanmar are severe but it is not clear that these approach genocide, ethnic cleansing, or crimes against humanity. In the Karen district of Myanmar, Amnesty International finds "widespread and systematic commission of violations of international human rights and humanitarian law on a scale that amounted to crimes against humanity. Destruction of houses and crops, enforced disappearances, forced labor, displacement and killings of Karen villagers were among the abuses."[9] Other observers give this careful consideration, but conclude that the "persecution and forced relocation of ethnic minorities in Myanmar do not sufficiently sustain allegations of genocidal intent.[10] Instead, Marek Pietschmann and Jeremy Sarkin advocate intervention to resettle and protect refugees, establish safe havens to end forced labor, distribute aid, and combat the drug trade.

Assume for a moment that the international community has the right to mobilize forces to prevent these evils, whether crimes against humanity or lesser evils. What then are the obligations of a nation like China to support intervention in Myanmar? In part, the answer depends upon how intervention affects Chinese interests. If intervening troops undertake to establish safe havens, protect refugees, or distribute aid by bypassing the central government, nominally recognizing their sovereignty and then leaving once they accomplish their purpose, then it is difficult to see how Chinese interests are threatened. This seems particularly true of calls to intervene after the Burmese government thwarted rescue efforts following a devastating cyclone that killed close to one hundred thousand people, left fifty-three thousand missing, and adversely affected the lives of 2.5 million others.[11] The government was at best inept and at worse maliciously obstructive. Intervening forces would merely bypass the government and then leave. They would not irreversibly threaten Burmese sovereignty. Would the Chinese have cause to oppose intervention in these circumstances? They might, if they fear that intervention will jeopardize their influence in Myanmar or that foreign forces will ultimately seek to depose the current regime. Either of these events would significantly undermine Chinese geopolitical interests. To assuage Chinese fears would require the international community to establish a blueprint for surgical and short-term intervention, a difficult challenge given the complexities of past interventions in places like the former Yugoslavia. Nevertheless, these guarantees are essential to convince recalcitrant states to support intervention.

The question is harder when regime change is unavoidable as it may be in Sudan. There a 2005 UN Commission found evidence of crimes against humanity including "killing of civilians, torture, enforced disappearances, destruction of villages, rape, pillaging and forced displacement," while the head of the government in 2009 stood accused by the International Criminal Court of war crimes and crimes against humanity.[12] Intervention in Sudan faces the formidable task of protecting refugees, preventing displacement and disappearance, and providing safe areas. While fighting in Myanmar may be minimal (particularly if the goal is distribution of humanitarian aid), far more violence may accompany military intervention in Sudan. Intervention will not be surgical but will bring great political upheaval and, quite possibly, regime change. This would affect some foreign interests significantly.

As in Myanmar, Chinese interests in Sudan coalesce around energy and arms. Spurned by the West, Sudan turned to China to buy large quantities of weaponry and sophisticated aircraft.[13] China's place in Sudan's oil economy is overwhelming. In 2007, Sudan sold 40 percent of its oil to China (accounting for 6 percent of all Chinese oil imports) and was the largest Chinese overseas oil investment.[14] Sudan, like Myanmar, is a niche market that China can enjoy with little competition from Western nations reluctant to ally themselves too closely with repressive regimes and pariah states. Sudan, nevertheless, is far from the Chinese border and outside its direct sphere of influence. As a result, Chinese interests are far more economic than strategic or political. At the same time, the threat to human rights in Sudan is far more serious than in Myanmar. This combination of factors eases the dilemma between humanitarian and national interests. In fact, China may be well on its way to partially resolving the dilemma itself.

Until recently, there was consensus that "Beijing's intransigence in the Security Council was essentially linked to its oil interests."[15] By 2006, analysts could point to China's support for United Nations and African Union troops in Darfur as well as criticism of Myanmar crackdown on dissidents. China's interests remain economic – the sale of arms and purchase of oil are paramount – but China is beginning to understand that egregious human rights violations, subsequent Western condemnation, and international calls for intervention can undermine these economic interests. The result is an attempt by China to moderate the worst excesses of states like Sudan and Myanmar with an eye to ultimately protect and advance Chinese interests. However, these same interests make it unlikely that China would support aggressive intervention in either country.

Faced with a choice between protecting bald economic interests and putting a stop to crimes against humanity, the moral imperative favors intervention. Yet it is doubtful that the Chinese see it that way. For the same reasons they would oppose intervention in Myanmar, the Chinese fear severe and irreversible economic harm should Western forces intervene in Sudan. Coming with China's efforts to pressure the Sudanese to reform, there is a growing understanding that the West can do a better job to assuage Chinese fears. Writing in *Foreign Affairs* in 2008, Stephanie Kleine-Ahlbrandt and Andrew Small called on Washington to "hold detailed discussions with Beijing to reduce its concerns about possible state collapse, political upheaval, or other major crises ... reassure Beijing about the implications of political transitions and to enlist its help in facilitating them."[16] Addressing economic concerns, Western nations try to convince the Chinese that regime change will not harm its interests. To do this, the world community may incorporate protection of Chinese oil interests into any future political settlement, make provisions to replace lost oil supplies, and/or guarantee revenues. Unlike strategic interests, economic interests are significantly more fungible and leave the door open to creative thinking that might remove impediments to support for military intervention. This may not mean countries like China will actively support armed intervention but it may go a long way to muting their opposition.

The foregoing discussion sets the stage for humanitarian intervention under those conditions the UN right to protect lays out. When a nation has no countervailing interests other than the cost of intervention, then it has a prima facie obligation to intervene. We will see below that the cost of rescue is carefully circumscribed and must be "reasonable." When humanitarian welfare is at stake but intervention endangers significant national interests, nations must carefully evaluate the effects of armed intervention. If intervention is "regime bypassing," these interests may face no long-lasting harm. If intervention is "regime replacing," intervening bodies such as the UN must make a concerted effort to protect endangered interests or reasonably compensate the affected state for damage it suffers. Compensation, in turn, obligates the affected state to join the intervention or, in the very least, refrain from thwarting it. The hardest problems will arise when intervening to put an end to overwhelming human rights abuses conflicts with overriding geopolitical interests that cannot be set aside. Neither Myanmar nor Sudan is such an example. In such a case, the world community may simply have to ride roughshod over the dissenting state. If that state is a Security Council member and its refusal paralyzes the UN, other collective defense bodies such as NATO or the European Union (EU) might have to take the reins.

If this discussion offers some guidelines about when nations should consider humanitarian intervention, it says nothing about the obligations of citizens serving in the armed forces of these countries to risk their lives to rescue others. This is a difficult problem with no obvious answer. While nations may be obligated to put treasure and blood on the line, the same is not easily said for the individual soldier who must risk his life to protect others. This is the paradox of humanitarian intervention.[17]

THE PARADOX OF HUMANITARIAN INTERVENTION

Strategic considerations notwithstanding, the Allied refusal to bomb the rail lines running to Auschwitz has met with harsh criticism. Surely, the Allies could have spared the few planes necessary to damage or destroy the death camps that were exterminating tens of thousands. Bombing the rail lines would have been a humanitarian gesture, designed to save the lives of noncombatant victims of war crimes while achieving little or no strategic gain. Potential gains were great while likely costs were low: to save thousands from murder only few needed to risk their lives. So, we argue, the Allies had a moral obligation to save innocent lives. No less an argument condemns military inaction in Rwanda and Darfur.

But if states and armies have an obligation to use their military forces for the sake of humanity, what of the soldier who must die in the line of that duty? Is there the same duty to risk one's life and die for humanity that there is, generally, to risk one's life for the state? Unless there is some vital national interest at stake, many, like Huntington, think not. It is no wonder, for example, that the International Commission on Intervention and State Sovereignty candidly advises intervening nations "... the risk to personnel involved in any military action may in fact make it politically imperative for the intervening state to be able to claim some degree of self-interest in the intervention, however altruistic its primary motive might actually be."[18]

When humanitarian intervention intertwines with a nation's vital interests, there will be little compunction about risking the lives of members of its armed forces. But when the UN calls on a nation to contribute forces purely for humanitarian intervention, there will be room to ask what price a nation's soldiers should pay for the welfare of others. "Rescuing others," writes Fernando Tesón, "will always be *onerous*.[19] The big question is, however, just how onerous their duty to rescue should be. Here, supporters of intervention hedge. "Our duty to respect [human] rights," declares Allen Buchanan "carries a presumptive duty to help ensure that all persons can live in conditions in which their basic rights are respected, *at least if we can do so without excessive costs to ourselves*."[20] Buchanan's qualifying clause goes to the heart of the problem. If humanitarian intervention imposes a duty on democratic states that they *"owe* to victims of internal crises and crimes" as Stanley Hoffmann demands, then someone, namely the soldiers of the state that intervenes, must bear the cost of protecting other human beings from genocide, enslavement, ethnic cleansing, and wanton rape and murder.[21] These costs are not trivial because some of these soldiers will die. But unless we are prepared to assume them, humanitarian intervention will fail.

This sums up the paradox of humanitarian intervention: How can it be that a state often has an obligation to intervene and risk soldiers' lives, but individual soldiers are not similarly obligated ?[22] Low costs, great benefits, and the prospect of relatively few casualties obligate the state to intercede. High costs and the prospect of death, on the other hand, seem to release each citizen from the very same duty when his own nation's interests are not at stake. The inability to resolve this paradox successfully can only undercut bold attempts to take on humanitarian intervention. What remains of the state's obligation to tender aid if those who must fulfill the state's duties are under no obligation to act?

Working our way out of the dilemma takes two forms. The first looks at the individual rescuer and asks whether he must risk his life for others in the same way he risks his life when his country is threatened. If not, then perhaps states must ask their citizens to volunteer for humanitarian intervention. The latter solution has its adherents but is ultimately not viable: it is not possible to anchor the state's obligation to intervene in the voluntary actions of its citizens. Rather, the problem requires a second look that abandons our initial concern with the individual rescuer and focuses on the collective ability to do good when a nation is capable of mounting an intervention force.

The Duty to Aid Others

Every man is bound to assist those who have need of assistance, if he can do it without exposing himself to sensible inconvenience. (Jeremy Bentham)[23]

When costs are low, the moral obligation to undertake easy rescue is intuitively compelling. But when costs rise, we begin to ask how much inconvenience a person must endure to help others. This may depend on the benefits of rescue. When the benefits of rescuing a persecuted people are significant, there is a greater onus on those capable of providing rescue. Rather than sensible inconvenience, a rescuer may be required to bear "considerable inconvenience short of fundamental changes in the fabric of his life."[24] Nevertheless, neither "considerable" nor "sensible" inconvenience can compel individuals to give their lives to aid others. No person can be forced to give up his life no matter how many lives this may save.

On the other hand, it seems reasonable to suppose that a few lives lost are reasonable from the state's perspective. Moreover, when states go to war, they compel their citizens to risk their lives all the time. In the very least, might not states compel their soldiers to assume the burden of intervention? Here, too, the answer is no. Humanitarian intervention does not generate the same obligation as national defense. For some philosophers, in fact, the obligation to die for the state is highly problematic. "Indeed," points out Michael Walzer, "the great advantage of liberal society may simply be this: that no one can be asked to die for public reasons on behalf of the state."[25] If they cannot die for the state, how can they possibly die for those who live beyond their state?

To explain the obligation to die for the state Walzer turns to philosophers like Jean-Jacques Rousseau to see how citizens in the modern state set aside individual interests in favor of a shared, collective vision of the good. Understanding that the state and community provide the identity, fellow feeling, and mutual support necessary for a full and meaningful existence, its citizens are willing to risk their lives for something more than their own security. However, Rousseau's understandings do nothing to solve the problem of humanitarian intervention. The obligation to die for the state draws from the strong bond between those who die and those whom they die for, a bond that flourishes, at best, to the edge of the nation-state and then seems to disappear. While Rousseau offers us a vision of an emerging super-personality that reached its grandest form in General Will, he could not push beyond national borders to embrace all of humankind within a universal, cosmopolitan order. On the contrary, Rousseau placed great emphasis on the small city-state and could not imagine educating good citizens without the religious, historical, and linguistic ties that bind them to one another.[26] Citizens may die on behalf of their state, but are unwilling, in fact unable, to risk their lives for anything more. If the state represents a natural stopping point for the political obligation to sacrifice one's life, then it is impossible to conceive of any obligation to risk dying for humanity. At best, there is only the obligation to risk one's life when humanitarian intervention also protects the security of one's own state. But if rogue states threaten the lives of no one but their own citizens, then the best we can do is to ask for volunteers to stop them.

Volunteering for Humanitarian Intervention

Volunteering replaces a state-imposed obligation with one that is self-imposed. This then allows states to undertake humanitarian intervention without the worry of forcibly imposing undue risk on particular individuals. It is no accident, therefore, that humanitarian intervention is often compared to law enforcement and that its most ardent advocates agree that only volunteers can comprise its forces. Just as police officers and firefighters voluntarily risk their lives to serve and protect other members of their community, volunteer humanitarian forces accept similar risks to defend citizens of foreign countries. Therefore, concludes Buchanan, "The moral justification for supporting armed humanitarian intervention need not depend upon the problematic assumption that risking our lives does not count as an excessive cost. So, even, if it is true that the natural duty of justice does not require us to risk violent death for the sake of protecting other persons' basic human rights, it still obligates us to support institutions for armed intervention ... so long as these institutions only entail a risk of violent death for those who accept it *voluntarily*."[27]

In this context, the obligation to risk death or injury is not a political obligation, but a professional obligation that comes with the particular vocation that police officers, firefighters, and soldiers choose. Yet law enforcement and humanitarian intervention are not analogous. While humanitarian intervention remains a contentious subject of debate, any social contract is going to make firm provisions for police and fire protection, and while volunteers are desirable, they are not necessary. Lacking sufficient volunteer forces, no nation has second thoughts about using military troops, whether conscripts or enlistees, to assist law enforcement officials or fire fighters in a public emergency. These troops do not need to consent. More broadly speaking, one can certainly imagine a group of individuals setting up a state who simply assign police or firefighting duties on a rotating basis or by lot if no one volunteers. The reason is simple: everyone needs police and fire protection and they expect the state to provide it. Fairness demands that either police or firefighters volunteer and receive adequate compensation, or are conscripted in a way that distributes the burden equally; nothing allows the state to sidestep its obligation to protect its citizens should no one volunteer. Yet this is precisely what would happen if insufficient numbers volunteer for humanitarian intervention. The state has no obligation to conscript forces when voluntary enlistment fails. Rather, as Buchanan suggests, the state has only an obligation to support those who have already agreed to assume substantial risk. If none does, the state's obligation collapses.

Humanitarian intervention remains, therefore, a peculiar obligation that, at best, places states in a supporting role, but cannot compel them to act when individuals refuse to bear the cost of risking their lives. Depending only on volunteers, no state may conscript its citizens to fight for others as it sometimes does to fight fires or enforce the law. This means that among nations whose armed forces depend primarily upon conscript forces (such as Germany, Greece, Finland, China, and Bolivia), none has grounds to commit its troops to humanitarian intervention; their obligation to undertake humanitarian aid never gets off the ground. States fielding volunteer armies (such as the United States, UK, France, and Italy), on the other hand, will see their obligation to aid crumble if insufficient numbers volunteer for service or if they are unable to deploy their volunteers for all forms of military service.[28] One may reasonably ask whether American soldiers, for example, volunteer for humanitarian duty when they swear to "support and defend the Constitution of the United States against all enemies, foreign and domestic." There is nothing here to suggest that soldiers agree to fight against foreign armies that do not threaten American security. Without volunteers who consent specifically to humanitarian duties, states have no choice but to refuse their international obligations.

In the final analysis, it is impossible to anchor the obligation to die for those beyond our state in the same obligation to die that we owe our compatriots. It is equally problematic to depend upon individuals consenting to risk their lives, for this undermines the collective obligation when insufficient numbers volunteer. More than a paradox, there is a deep and irreconcilable inconsistency if collective obligations depend upon the voluntary behavior or the professional obligations of individuals. Instead, resolving the paradox requires that we focus first on collective obligations and only then on individual duties.

OVERCOMING STATE BOUNDARIES: THE LURE
OF COSMOPOLITANISM

The obligation to aid others at the cost of our very lives founders because it cannot cross the divide between individual and collective obligation. The vehicle for crossing over thrives on mutual consent to protect one another or threats to vital national interests that endanger us all. Simply put, neither materializes when those just over the border face merciless persecution. No agreement binds the stronger nation to the weaker, nor do the stronger nation's citizens face any danger as the persecuted suffer. Nevertheless, the stronger, wealthier nation has the means to help. Perhaps the answer to the paradox demands that we reverse the order of our inquiry. Rather than try to draw the collective obligation from an individual duty to aid others, a duty that never seems to get off the ground, it might be more fruitful to skip over individual obligations and focus first on the knowledge that collectively a strong, powerful nation can, in fact, aid others in distress. Christopher Kutz, for example, offers a framework of rescue that may ease the problem and help establish grounds for an obligation to risk one's life to rescue others.[29] Kutz only describes a case of easy rescue; whether rescue must necessarily remain easy or may grow to embrace supreme sacrifices, is the question at hand.

Dying for Others: Looking Beyond the State and Individuals

Deliberately eschewing national boundaries, Kutz envisions two arbitrary groups, the Blues and the Reds, separated in the desert by some distance. The Blue group, significantly smaller than the Red, loses all its water to bandits. Noting that Red can replenish Blues' water at little cost to each individual member, Kutz wants to think first about Reds collective obligation to Blue before thinking about each Red member's individual moral obligation. Instead of characterizing the relationship between the two groups as a "network of obligations running each to each," as it is customary to construe rescue, Kutz ponders the claim of each member of the endangered group against the rescuing group as a whole. This becomes apparent as one thinks about a single Red who refuses to give up his water. While other

Reds may complain that the recalcitrant Red did not join the group effort of providing water, the Blues find that Red, as a whole, has met its obligation, "They," writes Kutz, "answered my call for help."[30] Regardless of individual holdouts, the Red community has met the claim of every Blue. With this intuition, Kutz hopes to overcome the problem that has plagued us all along, namely an individualistic conception of obligations that "denies the agency of all by focusing on the agency of each." Kutz's plan is to ground individual obligations in collective obligations, a stark reversal of the way we have been considering the duty to rescue. The idea seems simple: "If we are to satisfy our collective obligation to aid others, then I ought to do my part."[31] This is much different from saying "If I have an individual obligation to aid others, then we can all do our part."

Embracing the former, we can address the intervention paradox directly by starting with a collective obligation and then drawing out the individual obligation to aid others in need. To see the significance of the collective obligation, it is important to understand that there are two very different forms of rescue: those that individuals can achieve alone and those that require collective action. Saving a drowning child is a case of individual rescue. Here, one person alone can achieve great good and has an obligation to act when the cost is reasonable. It is a mistake, however, to think that a collective obligation simply aggregates many individual obligations so that if the latter fail, the former collapses. We can see this by looking at collective rescue. When more than one person is necessary to carry out a rescue, the emphasis shifts to what only a *group* can do. It makes little sense to start with an individual's obligation because, quite often, no individual alone can rescue anyone. He or she is powerless no matter what sacrifice he or she is willing to make. If "ought" implies "can" (that is, if we are only obligated to do what we can do), and in many cases of rescue no individual can effectively act alone, then there is no room whatsoever to speak of an individual obligation to rescue until we see what the group can do. The group, on the other hand, can make a difference and accomplish considerable good when all its members work together. This capacity for successful collective action dictates the shared obligation to aid those in distress. Meeting this obligation demands that the group mobilize the critical mass necessary for action. The group may agree to ask for volunteers but its collective obligation does not disappear if there are no volunteers. If no one volunteers, then the group may also adopt a coercive, but fair, scheme (such as conscription) to recruit the manpower necessary to meet its collective obligation. Volunteers, therefore, are neither morally nor practically necessary to meet the collective duty of humanitarian intervention.

The argument from collective responsibility now makes room to claim what many interventionists want to say: if a state has an obligation to undertake humanitarian intervention, then its citizens have the obligation to risk their lives for humanity. To see this, think about an overwhelming attack on Blue that only Red can repel. Red can fend off an attack and rescue Blue with few casualties. Blue, therefore, has a claim against the Red community as a whole, while Reds have an obligation to get the job done together. Blue will not care if one Red refuses to cooperate or another loses his life. Instead, Blues will thank Red collectively if they can save Blue (or most Blues). And, most likely, Red can. So, then, as Kutz concludes, does each of us recognize an "obligation to do our part of together helping the Blues?" If the source of our individual obligation lies in our understanding that we have a collective obligation that cannot get off the ground unless we all cooperate, then the answer is yes. Alone, no one can help, but together, everyone can save Blue. The first obligation is the collective duty. The collective then passes the obligation through to its members whether it asks for volunteers, draws straws, or coerces them all fairly and equally.

The Force of Collective Obligations

The force of collective obligations stands out as we look again at Auschwitz. There is a world of difference between a commander who says to his pilots, "Gentlemen, we have an opportunity to attack the rail lines feeding this infamous camp. The target has no strategic value but we can save many lives. However, some of you will lose your lives in this mission. Do I have any volunteers?" And one who says, "Gentlemen, we've got more men, more money, and more materiel than any army on earth and we can use a small portion of our resources to save many lives by attacking the rail lines feeding this infamous camp. Casualties will be light." In the first case, the obligation starts with the individual pilot. It also ends there if no one volunteers. In the second case, the capabilities of the group dictate the shared obligation to aid those in distress. No one need be asked to volunteer.

Widespread human rights abuse presents similar challenges. Humanitarian concerns ring loud when advocates of military intervention call upon U.S. or NATO forces to secure refugee camps in Africa and protect their inhabitants from attack.[32] The military value, if any, of diverting significant numbers of troops to protect refugees and transport them to safety would pale beside the value of saving the lives of many innocent people. Such a mission would be largely a humanitarian gesture. What are our moral obligations in this case? In light of the foregoing discussion, it is important to emphasize our collective obligations. There is no room to speak, at least initially, of *my* obligations or those of any single individual. No single person could possibly protect refugees from slaughter by well-armed forces, no matter how much he was willing to risk his life. Unable to effect any change alone, he or she has no obligation to act without the cooperation of others. On the other hand, it is clear that a large group of well-equipped soldiers working together could protect, transport, and rescue a large number of refugees. When a group can attain considerable good, it incurs an obligation to act. All members of the group share this obligation because without them all, the group will fail.

The shared obligation that Red (or the pilots or soldiers) faces in these cases arises from two related factors: the claims of the weaker group and the reasonable cost of rescue. By working together, Reds aid Blue (or camp inmates or refugees) and keep the cost down. The two factors are linked and both are important. Blue claims obligate Red collectively because Blue is in need and Red, as a group, can offer significant aid. Nevertheless, the collective obligation has its limits. Clearly, no group or nation can expect to bankrupt itself or sacrifice its best and brightest for the sake of another, just as no individual need give his life to save a drowning child. At one point, the obligation to rescue dissipates if costs to the group become too high. The shared obligations of the Reds, or the pilots or the soldiers in Darfur must consider this. As they share their burden, they not only command the wherewithal to rescue others successfully but also find the means to keep the costs of meeting their obligation within moral bounds. Reds will die, but close cooperation and widespread participation can help allay the risk that each Red faces. With this, the emphasis now shifts to a different question: What cost would a powerful nation consider reasonable and how should it distribute this burden among its citizens as it considers intervention?

HUMANITARIAN INTERVENTION: REASONABLE COSTS FOR NATIONS AND CITIZENS

When a bystander considers his obligation to rescue a person in distress, his assessment of reasonable risk is subjective. Bentham may have pretended that it is not when he ridicules a person's failure to pull a drunk from a puddle or extinguish a fire when water is at hand, but anyone failing to answer the call of duty would try to convince others that offering aid was not as easy as first appears. Any number of mitigating circumstances is imaginable, but the point is that any reasonable perception of inconvenience is sufficient to deflate the duty to rescue. Alternatively, if rescue appears difficult, but a would-be rescuer insists it is easy, then the obligation to aid reasserts itself.

This insight is helpful once we return to the idea of collective obligation. A nation in a position to help must determine whether costs are reasonable and whether it is willing to sacrifice some of its members to rescue many others. If so, and the chances of success are good, then the group is obligated to intervene. This is analogous to individual bystanders who find themselves obligated to extend aid when the risk, as they see it, is reasonable. The process of assessing reasonable costs proceeds from deliberation through implementation and evaluation. A nation must first decide that it is willing to tolerate a certain number of casualties in defense of victims of massive human rights abuses just as they might deliberate about the costs of war when less-than-vital national interests are at stake. It has been said, for example, that the Israeli public was willing to tolerate the deaths of 25 soldiers annually to sustain their presence in southern Lebanon in the 1990s, just as the American public seems willing to tolerate the deaths of eight hundred soldiers annually to implement U.S. policy in Iraq and Afghanistan.[33] Tolerance for losses in humanitarian missions can vary. Both the United States and the UN left Somalia when losses were relatively light, approximately 50 and 150 fatalities respectively between 1992 and 1995. However, the futility of fighting a limited military operation to restore order in a failed state magnifies these losses. When intervention proves more successful, the public will tolerate similar or higher losses and show greater support for humanitarian intervention than political leaders sometimes appreciate.[34] The 250 fatalities among UN- and NATO-led forces in Bosnia (1992–1996) provoked little public outcry.[35] By 2007, NATO forces in Afghanistan were taking on an increasingly hazardous role in the fighting there and although the public's reaction remains to be gauged, the EU continues to focus squarely on humanitarian intervention as it plans force deployments for the future. With the 2005 UN World Summit Agreement, one might expect similar contingency plans among UN members.

Public response to these events will depend upon the actual losses that intervening forces suffer and the success they achieve. In some cases, the costs the public will tolerate emerge from a process of active consent: public debate, the electoral process, legislative deliberation, social action, and judicial activism. In other cases, general apathy and lack of discussion may reflect tacit consent while attempts to exceed reasonable costs rouse public indignation. Neither process of consent can be construed as volunteering. Those citizens participating in intervention forces might comprise a silent and politically inactive majority, or have voted against legislators supporting military intervention, or have been minors when policymakers decided to go to war.

Reasonable costs remain highly subjective. It is not simply a matter of risking fewer lives to save more. It is doubtful, for example, that any nation would risk 900 lives to save a thousand (although they certainly might in defense of their own country). Rather, the decision to intervene appears to be a function of relative costs and risks. The intervening group will surely lose lives, but will consider sacrificing some when a) human rights abuses are great and the group can accomplish considerable good by intervening, b) the number of lives at risk is small relative to the size of the group, and c) the risk to any individual member is tolerably low. Assessing likelihood of success is particularly difficult. Intervening with the possibility of bringing radical change is not usually in the offing. Instead, intervening forces aim to ameliorate and then contain the worst of the damage and destruction. Aid workers attend to amelioration, while containment requires only moderate force to preserve the status quo and forestall deterioration; neither offers a military or political solution. A solution only comes, if at all, with a long period of reconstruction. Intervention is often a thankless task that wears down even the most enthusiastic body politic who sees no vital interest at stake, no prospect or even intention of "winning," and no ability to define military and political objectives clearly.[36]

In this environment of uncertain goals and high costs, nations must continually evaluate the good they hope to accomplish and the lives they will risk. This is the subject of constant debate and reevaluation. No numbers are hard-and-fast; nevertheless, humanitarian military aid imposes built-in restrictions. First, the military has an absolute duty not to exceed the cost the body politic imposes. There is no room to appeal to military necessity or reason of state to secure greater resources, or to escalate hostilities in a way that might bring greater casualties. Once it appears necessary to mobilize additional resources to successfully safeguard a persecuted people's human rights, the body politic of the intervening nation, not the military exclusively, must again consider reasonable costs. In this respect, wars of humanitarian intervention are unlike conventional or asymmetric wars of national self-defense where few constraints limit the number of lives a nation will risk to defend national interests.

Moreover, wars of humanitarian intervention demand that the state distribute costs fairly. War by its nature forces some citizens to bear a disproportionate share of the burden. Nevertheless, group members owe it to one another not to overburden those who risk their lives. Fairness demands as proportionate a distribution of the risk as possible. In Kutz's example, each Red contributes a small amount of water to aid Blue. No one would think of sacrificing one or more individuals by taking all their water and giving it to Blue. Since lives are not divisible in the same way that water is, only the burden of risk can be distributed more or less fairly. "More fairly" means spreading the risk and reducing the odds that those endangered, that is the soldiers, will die.

Reducing the risk to some demands greater participation from others. Considering the obligations of Reds, I noted how cooperation is obligatory to accomplish rescue and to hold costs down. While effective rescue requires a certain critical mass to be successful, the obligation to hold down and fairly distribute the costs of humanitarian wars demands much more. Distributing the burden of war fairly requires the means necessary to reduce the risk of death by protecting soldiers and rotating troops from the theatre of operations with increased frequency to lessen their exposure to deadly harm. Reducing risk by fifty percent, for example, demands twice as many soldiers on the ground or tours of duty half as long. Doing both cuts the risk further still. Obviously, there are limits that efficiency imposes, but the point is that humanitarian intervention, unlike other types of asymmetric war, is a form of armed conflict that demands a considerable infusion of resources beyond what is necessary to simply get the job done.

The imperative to reduce risk broadens the idea of necessity in military ethics. When national interests are at stake, military and political leaders may face legitimate criticism for sacrificing more lives than necessary to accomplish their military goals. They face no special obligation, however, to reduce the risk soldiers face if resources are scarce. If a nation fighting to protect vital interests is unable to spare more than the minimal number of troops and equipment necessary to secure a particular goal, then those sent to fight may bear very high costs. A war of humanitarian intervention cannot make this demand on soldiers. Apart from stipulating that the state may risk no more lives than necessary, the state must also hold down the risk each soldier faces. If a nation cannot bring the costs down to reasonable levels, then it may not undertake intervention. Mitigating costs may require a nation to build a conscript army to mobilize the forces necessary to reduce risk to soldiers. A conscripted, non-volunteer army is, therefore, the first, and not the last resort that states should turn to as they consider wars of humanitarian intervention. This reverses our earlier order of thinking. From the perspective of individual obligations, intervening troops must comprise voluntary forces; otherwise, there is no way to justify their obligation to risk their lives for others. From a collective perspective, these forces may very well build on conscripts to spread the risk combatants will face following a decision to go to war.

One can see how many of these considerations play out when the world community confronts nations inflicting unbridled persecution or intense suffering upon their people. Fleeing the conflict zone, many refugees find a temporary haven in camps for displaced persons. But marauding troops constantly threaten these camps and security is precarious. This is the lesson from Darfur. Protecting refugee camps and providing a safe corridor to bring thousands of refugees to safety in neighboring countries would pose considerable risk to intervening troops. Some would most certainly die and be wounded in the effort. On the other hand, many refugees would undoubtedly be saved. The collective obligation to aid, like the individual obligation to aid, cannot come at unreasonably high costs. One would not expect the United States, for example, to sacrifice a thousand soldiers to save a similar number of refugees. Where it draws the line, however, is a collective decision about what the body politic is willing to bear. Once the collective agrees to bear a certain cost (x billions of dollars and y number of lives) it must spread the risk as broadly as possible. At this point, the risk becomes tolerable.

Tolerable risk varies from case to case. Reducing risk, as noted, demands either more troops with the initial deployment and/or large numbers of troops available for rotation. In a humanitarian emergency of the kind that will result from a Sudanese attack on refugee camps, rapid response would be the first priority of any contingency plan. While this would require sufficient numbers of troops to stave off an attack, it may preclude a large-scale and time-consuming mobilization. Here, then, the emphasis shifts from large numbers of boots on the ground to frequent troop rotation to relieve those who are in extreme danger. Collective responsibility coupled with the imperative to reduce the risk to those rescuing others, demands a relatively large pool of manpower. To meet this need, those leading the effort, whether the United States, the United Nations, or the European Union, may ask for volunteers. But if they cannot get them in sufficient numbers to reasonably reduce the risk each soldier faces, then a conscript army deserves careful consideration to meet the practical and moral demands of humanitarian intervention.

The EU's European Security and Defense Policy illustrates the problematic role of conscript armies in humanitarian intervention. Envisioning the need to project force beyond that required for national defense, the EU laid plans for a sixty-thousand-man European Rapid Response Force whose principle duties comprise "humanitarian and rescue tasks."[37] For some observers writing in 2000, conscription was the biggest *obstacle* to the establishment of

a rapid response force because "for political reasons, conscripts in
most countries can only be deployed for collective self-defense."[38]
As a result, humanitarian intervention would require volunteers. By
2004, however, EU forces were successfully fulfilling humanitarian
missions in Bosnia-Herzegovina, Macedonia, and the Democratic
Republic of Congo. In spite of their modest scale – eighteen hundred troops went to protect refugees in the Congo in 2003, for
example – military planners began to understand that an effective response force would require sixty thousand *combat* soldiers
and therefore a pool of one hundred fifty to two hundred thousand troops. With initial plans to raise only one hundred thousand
troops, where would the extra personnel come from? Planners
certainly advocate expanding professional armies but, at the same
time, also realize that "only if member states adapt conscription
can this shortfall be remedied."[39] "Deployability capabilities," conclude the authors of a five-year review of the EU's defense policy,
"should be enhanced as legal barriers limiting the availability of
conscripts are lifted."[40]

The obstacles that limit the role of conscripts are those I have discussed here. Only national defense can obligate individuals to risk
their lives; anything else requires volunteers. In practice, however,
reliance on volunteering, that is, on individually imposed obligations,
breaks down. Facing insufficient number of volunteers, EU nations
must adapt conscription to undertake humanitarian intervention.
That is, they will have to release conscripts for duties that may have
little or nothing to do with national defense. Underlying the EU's
determination is operational necessity: without conscripted troops,
EU nations cannot fulfill their collective obligation to rescue victims of genocide or ethnic cleansing. But conscription can do more
than meet operational demands. If two hundred thousand signify
the number necessary to get the job done, the argument presented
here calls for even larger numbers of troops to ease the burden of
risk. Otherwise, the EU runs the risk of incurring unreasonable
costs and might face political pressure to use its troops solely for
national defense. Conscription is not necessarily a dying vestige of
conventional war and nation-state politics, but a necessary condition
for modern states to enforce international law through multilateral
military organizations.[41]

Apart from fairly implementing their decision to go to war when they deem costs reasonable, nations must also think about ceasing military activity when costs become too high. When a nation can no longer intervene at reasonable costs (and withdrawing aid does not make subject populations considerably worse off than before intervention), the moral duty to intervene diminishes, just as it does when a nation no longer commands sufficient financial resources to extend material assistance. Assessing costs and utilizing the courts and legislature to monitor the distribution of risk among one's soldiers is imperative during wars of humanitarian intervention in a way that is not necessary, and may even be harmful, when national interests are at stake. The muses are only silent, if ever, when nations fight to protect vital interests. During wars of humanitarian intervention, on the other hand, constant public monitoring is desirable, if not mandatory.

Once the citizens of a wealthy, powerful nation believe that they can relieve distress at costs they consider reasonable and that intervention does not irreparably harm vital national interests, they incur a double obligation that demands they act collectively on behalf of others and, at the same time, take care to protect the welfare of those they send to war. It would be a mistake, however, to ask too much about the individual's obligation to die for humanity. While one might imagine a super-state entity, today the EU and tomorrow the world, whose members feel joined in fellow feeling just as they do in the nation-state, similarly intense ties remain conspicuously absent among those requiring intervention and those best able to provide it. While the global civil society that Stanley Hoffmann envisions, one where "*raison d'etat* and *raison des individus* will compete and partially blend," may provide the bond to undergird an obligation to die for humanity, it is, at best, a distant hope.[42] In the meantime, we have to content ourselves with a hard look at the collective obligations we impose upon ourselves simply because we are in a position to help. Once we say that we should do it because the claims against us are just and the cost is reasonable, then it is time that we set ourselves to work and make certain that we all share in the burden that may cost some of us, or our children, their lives.

PART III

CONCLUSION AND AFTERWORD

10

Conclusion
Torture, Assassination, and Blackmail

New Norms for Asymmetric Conflict?

There is much talk today about the transformation of war or new wars or changing paradigms of war.[1] Observers point to asymmetric war as a prime arena for changing rules as two sides, one strong and one relatively weak, fight one another while undermining many of the conventions of war that the international community cultivated so assiduously. In many ways, the arguments of the previous chapters support this contention. Fighting asymmetric war leads participants to discount the idea of combatant equality while ascribing criminal behavior and moral liability to many of their adversaries. The close-quarters conditions of asymmetric war, widespread civilian participation, the inability to distinguish combatants from noncombatants, and the prospect that each side can adopt tactics without fear of "payment in kind" has brought belligerents to consider nonlethal weapons (NLWs), targeted killings, and a narrow view of noncombatant immunity, that puts previously protected civilians in the line of fire.

At the same time, however, the international community is scrutinizing rogue and despotic regimes for gross human rights violations, acts of genocide, and crimes against humanity. Eventually, these acts prompt calls for military intervention. As states wage asymmetric war, longstanding interpretations of "superfluous injury and unnecessary suffering," proportionality, collateral damage, and state sovereignty fall by the wayside. For some nations, targeted killing, enhanced interrogation techniques, attacks on associated targets, and humanitarian intervention are legitimate exceptions to standing conventions, for others they are signs of entirely new rules. This raises two interrelated questions. First, are new norms of warfare now emerging, and second, do they improve on those they are replacing?

TORTURE, ASSASSINATION, AND BLACKMAIL: EXCEPTIONALISM OR THE RULE?

Exceptionalism can have several meanings. For some, it refers to *American* exceptionalism, that is, the tendency of the United States to exempt itself from various human rights conventions when it no longer serves American interests. Here critics cite disregard for the Convention Against Torture (CAT), the international criminal court, or the more stringent humanitarian requirements of Protocol I.[2] However, I want to use the idea of exceptionalism more broadly. In this regard, some nations may agree that torture, assassination, and blackmail are pernicious, but remain nonetheless defensible as lesser evils when compared to alternative forms of warfare that may harm considerably more noncombatants. Generally, this is not a test of simple utility. It is not enough that exceptional methods result in somewhat less harm. Instead, the advantage must be overwhelming and obvious to most observers. This is the ethics of exceptionalism: torture, assassination, and blackmail remain outside the law but are defensible practices during national emergencies. Emergencies do not overturn or repudiate the laws of war, they simply allow for exceptions. Supporters of terrorism often make the same claim.

While torture, assassination, and blackmail may have started their lives as exceptions to the established norms of conventional warfare, there are many signs that they are evolving into rules. Exceptions violate rules. They are prima facie unlawful acts that require perpetrators to defend themselves after the fact. The best the community can then do is excuse their actions. Rules, on the other hand, lawfully guide behavior in a well-ordered society. Consider torture. The exception says that hooding or stress positions constitute torture or ill-treatment. Interrogational torture remains unlawful but recognizes that overwhelming circumstances – ticking bombs or catastrophic threats, for example – may require extreme measures to save lives. Interrogators must then defend themselves after the fact and prove that their acts were necessary to save many lives each time they used prohibited means of questioning. This is the crux of the necessity defense described in Chapter 6. Enforcing or acting on a rule, on the other hand, requires no defense. A rule simply stipulates that stress positions or waterboarding are permissible forms of interrogation in the hands of those entrusted with national security. This was the force behind the second Bush Administration's blanket approval of exceptional methods of interrogation for the CIA. Here, CIA interrogators have no need to defend themselves. Assuming they follow the guidelines that the authorities establish, their actions are always justified.

Because there is often a sense that too many excuses undermine existing rules, it is important to ask, When do too many exceptions become a *new* rule or norm? One way to answer this question is to look at the language of the debate and another is to examine the behavior of states. Exceptions use the language of excuse and defense, while rules invoke justification. To distinguish between the two, consider a simple test that turns on the victim's rights. Killing in self-defense, for example, is justifiable, not merely excusable, because it vindicates the killer's rights and does not violate the victim's rights. Excusable killing, on the other hand, is wrong because it violates the victim's rights but is, nevertheless, an "understandable though regrettable human reaction."[3] Are torture, terror, assassination, and blackmail excusable, justifiable, or neither? If they do not violate the victim's rights but vindicate the killer's, torturer's, or attacker's, then they are justifiable, a rule rather than a defensible exception. But if any of these actions violate the victim's rights, then the best anyone can do is to mount a successful defense for the community to judge.

Here, the growing emphasis to fight (or wage) terrorism on the presumption of guilt, rather than the innocence accorded conventional combatants, for example, points to emerging rules rather than exceptions. Targeted killing, aggressive interrogation, and attacks on associated targets gain their force because they aim at those who bear some measure of responsibility. Targeted killing aims at those directly affiliated with a hostile military organization or civilian combatants posing an immediate threat. Every justification of torture rests on getting the "right" person (or in the case of humanitarian intervention, the "right" nation or leader.) Attacks on associated structures target those who support or contribute to their nation's or group's war-fighting capability. In each of these cases, the targets will lose all or some of their immunity. As a result, their rights do not suffer. The hard part is to pinpoint and identify responsibility in the fog of asymmetric war. For this reason, as noted, the role of oversight and transparency is paramount.

A similar slide from exceptionalism to the rule is apparent from state behavior and support among many nations for rendition, aggressive interrogation, assassination, and the use of nonlethal chemical weapons to fight guerrillas and terrorists. Support for rendition, for example, extends far beyond the United States and draws in governments in Eastern and Western Europe, the Middle East, and Southeast Asia. These nations arrested and transferred suspects to U.S. jurisdiction (or to other locations); took custody of prisoners that the United States did not transfer to its detention facility at Guantanamo Bay, Cuba; and/or permitted the United States to apprehend suspects on their soil or transport detainees through their airspace.[4] These nations do not condone torture, but by supporting U.S. requests for rendition, they slowly placed U.S. interrogation practices outside the pale of condemnation. By their actions, members of the international community allowed the United States to stake out a sphere of lawful forms of moderate physical pressure that are distinct from torture.

Terrorism, too, has moved slowly from a prohibited to an excusable and now, with many reservations, to a justifiable form of warfare. Although long prohibited as criminal behavior, I described in Chapter 6 how the international community is uncomfortable with an absolute ban on terrorism. Many contemporary moral philosophers, too, observes C.A.J. Coady, allow for exceptions to the ban on terror "in extreme circumstances."[5] These occur as guerrillas fight the gross injustice of colonial, alien, and racist regimes. Terrorism remains wrong but excusable. In contrast, terrorism is justifiable when it aims at those responsible for injustice. This occurs as the scope of responsibility widens to include an array of traditional noncombatants ranging from political leaders to those who support the fighting indirectly. Once terror victims are ascribed a measure of responsibility, their immunity attenuates. Terrorism has not yet morphed into a rule, but it may if subsumed under the justification of attacks on associated targets. In the previous chapters, I have argued for symmetry of just this kind that will permit either party to attack civilians whose participation in hostile activity is less than direct. This breaches the traditional bounds of noncombatant immunity and allows both sides a wider range of permissible targets. At the same time, however, it also limits the force either side may use against these targets to nonlethal weapons, attacks on infrastructure, and curtailment of civil liberties. This restrains but does not prohibit what many regard as terrorism.

Similarly, international behavior is beginning to stake out justifiable grounds for using nonlethal weapons. Fifteen years after the Chemical Weapons Convention (CWC) banned all chemical weapons except the use of riot control agents by law enforcement officials, the international community now finds itself unable to implement this policy coherently. When the Russians used calmatives to subdue Chechnyan rebels threatening the lives of hundreds of civilians in a Moscow theatre in 2002, Russia made an important statement: the use of nonlethal chemical weapons is permissible in armed conflict. Until then, the international conventions were not clear about whether the CWC prohibited calmatives or whether the fight against terrorists, rebels, or militants belonged to the sphere of law enforcement or armed conflict. But the Russians, having previously defined their war in Chechnya as an armed conflict (rather than a police action against terrorists and criminals), set a precedent that was quickly endorsed by the muted reaction of world leaders.[6] Aggressive state behavior coupled with international acquiescence is a solid sign of norm change. Then, there are ripple effects of nonlethal warfare. Intentionally harming civilians is one of the most entrenched prohibitions of just war theory and international humanitarian law, but nonlethal warfare deliberately harms combatants and noncombatants as one. Accommodating nonlethal warfare will necessarily demand major changes in the war conventions and set the stage for a new norm that permits the introduction of nonlethal weapons on the battlefield.

Assassination, too, is looking increasingly like a new rule. Long frowned upon, assassination, now renamed targeted killing, straddles the paradigms of self-defense and law enforcement and highlights the inadequacy of each to excuse or justify the practice. When the Israeli Defense Forces initiated targeted killing in 2000, the Advocate General argued for "the legal right to fight hostile elements in the Occupied Territories in exceptional and extraordinary cases, when the purpose is to save lives and in the absence of any other alternative."[7] This is the language of exceptionalism: the targets of assassination find their rights grossly violated in the name of a greater good and lesser evil. Following 9/11, however, the picture is changing. Beginning with strikes against the guerrillas that attacked the USS Cole in 2000 and continuing to this day in Iraq, Pakistan, and Afghanistan, targeted killing is shifting from an excusable exception to the rules of law enforcement to a justifiable form of self-defense during armed conflict. As in the other cases described, the presumption of guilt or liability is central. Variously described as terrorists, civilians taking an active part in the hostilities or combatants party to non-international armed conflict, the targets of assassination have no immunity from attack. That is, they do not find their rights violated when attacked.

Based on state behavior and the substance of the arguments that justify rather than excuse, there is preliminary evidence that targeted killings, aggressive interrogation, nonlethal weapons, and attacks on participating civilians (by either side) reflect emerging norms of warfare. Whether these norms are new rules or acceptable exceptions, they are far from the prohibitions and severe restrictions that currently characterize the laws of war. Still, the question remains: Are these good rules and norms or do torture, assassination, and blackmail simply embrace military necessity and ignore humanitarianism? Are they, in other words, the barbaric means some think necessary to wage and win asymmetric war?

TORTURE, ASSASSINATION, AND BLACKMAIL: BETWEEN MILITARY NECESSITY AND HUMANITARIANISM

The practice of war is always subject to the exigencies of conflict, military technology, and the interests and capabilities of its participants. These change constantly because neither science nor politics remains static for long. The shift toward asymmetric war emerged forcefully as colonial conflict occupied the great powers for more than a quarter century following World War II. The great surprise was, perhaps, that the resolution of colonial grievances brought no respite from conflict. Although isolated national liberation conflicts linger, the attention of many nations has moved to the war on international terrorism, local insurgencies, humanitarian intervention, and, more recently, proxy guerrilla wars. But if war has changed, the underlying logic of settling political disputes by force of arms has not: war remains a costly last-resort means to secure vital national interests when other means fail. As such, the principles that govern any emerging practices and conventions remain in place. One of these is military necessity. Nations or groups that pursue legitimate interests warrant a fighting chance. Exercising this right, in turn, requires a constant assessment of the means a nation or nonstate actor needs to press its claims by armed force. Those it requires are militarily necessary.

At the same time, the choice of tactics or weapons remains anchored in humanitarianism. Here, there are really only two rules of warfare: avoid harming combatants unnecessarily and avoid harming noncombatants directly. From the first rule, we derive the injunction to avoid causing superfluous injury and unnecessary suffering. This plays out in the weapons systems that belligerents permit themselves to use as well as in the way they treat captured soldiers. The former generally limits weapons to various forms of high explosives while discouraging chemical, biological, and electromagnetic technologies. The latter frowns on assassination and prohibits the torture and execution of prisoners of war. From the second rule, which speaks to the rights of noncombatants, we derive the principle of noncombatant immunity, the prohibition of terrorism, and the subsidiary principles of discrimination, proportionality, and collateral harm.

During war, and asymmetric war is no exception, two moral imperatives clash: the right to wage war for legitimate purposes – whether self-defense, national liberation, or humanitarian intervention – and the duty to protect combatants from unnecessary injury and noncombatants from direct harm. This is the crux of every dilemma of asymmetric war discussed in this book and highlights the friction between military necessity and humanitarianism. Resolving these dilemmas is paramount to understanding the moral and lawful limits of waging war. As adversaries fight, the sides will always ask whether they might violate humanitarian imperatives to gain a military advantage. As they address this question, they challenge old conventions and generate new norms of conduct. The particulars of the dilemma are new; its form is not. Assessing new modes of warfare always requires a careful test of military necessity and humanitarianism. The question is: do torture, assassination, and blackmail pass the tests? The short answer is "yes, but." What begins as torture, terror, assassination, and blackmail ends up as enhanced interrogation, targeted killing, nonlethal warfare, and attacks on associated targets. On the way, the concepts of noncombatant immunity, superfluous injury, unnecessary suffering, and proportionality undergo significant revision.

Navigating Military Necessity and Humanitarianism

When military necessity and humanitarianism conflict, it is common to point out that unless explicitly specified, international humanitarian law (IHL) has already accounted for military necessity. The oft-cited example, surprisingly enough, comes from the 1907 Hague Conventions, Article 23:

It is especially forbidden:

(a) To employ poison or poisoned weapons;
(b) To kill or wound treacherously;
(c) To kill or wound an enemy who ... has surrendered;
(d) To declare that no quarter will be given;
(e) To ... cause unnecessary suffering;
(f) To make improper use of a flag of truce;
(g) To destroy or seize the enemy's property, *unless such destruction or seizure be imperatively demanded by the necessities of war.*[8]

The first five prohibitions (a–e) reflect the fundamental humanitarian rule that forbids harming combatants unnecessarily. These, together with the sixth prohibiting treachery (f), are absolute. That is, they already account for military necessity; even if such tactics confer a military advantage, humanitarianism prohibits their use. This conclusion draws from a two-stage distillation process that first filters any military practice through the sieve of military necessity and then through the sieve of humanitarianism. Poison, treachery, and execution may pass the first but not the second. 23(g), however is the exception. Seizing and destroying enemy property can be as useful as treachery or poison but is not always inhuman and, sometimes, may be necessary. Seizing and destroying property, in other words, passes through the filter of military necessity and humanitarianism. It is only "especially" prohibited when not militarily necessary. This should not be surprising. No tactic is permissible if unnecessary. The problem is with those that are necessary, that is, offer a military advantage.

In general, a two-stage distillation process is the best way to reconcile military necessity and humanitarianism; but I want to be more specific about the filtering components and, at the same time, try to update our understanding of military necessity. The Hague Convention is, after all, more than a century old. It preceded the establishment of most modern nations, two world wars, a raft of lesser wars, the airplane, the tank, and a wealth of modern military technology. Nevertheless, the core idea of military necessity and humanitarianism remains compelling, but in contexts far different from what anyone at The Hague might have envisioned. Looking more closely at this model allows us to step back and see how the dilemmas in the book resolve, dilemmas that reflect the tension between military necessity and humanitarianism.

Navigating Military Necessity and Humanitarianism:
A Two-Stage Distillation Model

Figure 10.1 presents a distillation model for evaluating modern warfare. It starts with a proposed tactic, weapon, or practice and then passes it through the twin filters of military necessity and humanitarianism.

Proposing Tactics, Weapons, and Military Practices
Given free rein, there is probably no end to a person's capacity to envision new and interesting ways to disable an enemy. Generally, these are all variations on the theme of "if force doesn't work, just use a bigger hammer." However, it is a peculiar aspect of asymmetric warfare to combine very big, precision hammers (precision-guided munitions and bunker busting bombs) with very little hammers be they nonlethal weapons or something as low-tech as targeted killing. Despite the surfeit of possible means to wage war, not all meet the test of military necessity. Here, I want to understand military necessity in terms of the means required for a nation to weaken the military forces of the enemy and disable the greatest number of men. This, as noted in Chapter 3, is a mainstay of the law of armed conflict since St. Petersburg. This declaration, consistent with the times, emphasizes the words "weaken," "disable," and "men" (that is, soldiers). It assumes that every state knows who its enemies are and who among

Proposed Tactic, Practice, or Weapon
- Nonlethal Weapons
- Targeted Killing
- Enhanced Interrogation
- Attacks on Associated Targets
- Humanitarian Intervention

Filter One: Military Necessity
- Exercising the right to a fighting chance

Filter Two: Humanitarianism
- Combatants' right to freedom from unnecessary suffering
- Noncombatants' right to freedom from unnecessary, direct, and disproportionate harm

Approved Tactic, Practice, or Weapon

FIGURE 10.1 Evaluating tactics and practices of war: a two-stage distillation model.

them has the right to fight. Buried here, in other words, is an early version of a belligerent's right to a fighting chance. Finding itself at war, any nation will seek the means it requires to disable and weaken its enemy. Weapons or practices that do so are militarily necessary.

The St. Petersburg Declaration limited itself to states. Charles Chaumont, however, pushes the envelope. Restating the right that "must allow every party an equal chance in combat" raises hard questions of justice that the international community could ignore in 1868 and for a long while thereafter. But the question today is whether any party that shows up to fight has any rights whatsoever. The answer, of course, is no, and this shows how closely the principle of military necessity is tied to that of a nation's just cause. Prior to asking about which weapons and practices are necessary to allow a belligerent to disable its enemies, comes the question about its right to wage war. The conventional answer was relatively simple: only states acting in self-defense are legitimate parties to an armed conflict and only they can think about the means necessary to disable their enemies.

Understanding that it was extraordinarily difficult and impractical to work through the question of just cause, international law dodged the question and was content to limit military participants to nation-states. Any other party threatening the security of a nation-state was criminal. This view held sway until the world community grasped the gross injustice of colonialism.

The view today is both broader and narrower. In Chapter 1 I described four kinds of asymmetric conflict: insurgencies and wars of national liberation, wars of humanitarian intervention, the war on international terror, and proxy guerrilla wars. Only the last approximates the inability in conventional war to decide the justice issue firmly. The Second Lebanon War is complex, but few claim that Syria and Iran, no less than Israel, were not pursuing legitimate geopolitical and strategic interests. The fact that the war probably helped none of these parties does not detract from the justice of their cause, narrowly defined as pursuit of national interests. In the other types of wars, however, issues are less complex. Protocol I and customary international law grant a large measure of just cause to parties fighting for national liberation while restricting their state adversaries to complaints about whether guerrillas use war as a last resort or fight by just means. Similarly, the norms of humanitarian intervention and the UN's right-to-protect go far to criminalize any state or nonstate actor that resists humanitarian forces. Targeted states, too, are limited to complaints about whether intervening states use war as a last resort or fight by just means. The same is true for international terrorists and insurgencies affiliated with international terrorism. They, like rogue and genocidal states, are beyond the pale of just cause. Having no room to speak of just cause, there is no place to speak of military necessity. Only once a party establishes its right to a fighting chance, does it move on to a detailed evaluation of military necessity.

The Filter of Military Necessity

Throughout this book I have asked whether a proposed tactic, practice, or weapons system is necessary and effective. Effectiveness has many components but it is important to evaluate effectiveness using the criteria that the side proposing the tactic or weapon uses. Are they necessary or can other weapons or tactics do the same job better? Do nonlethal weapons achieve what its proponents expect? Do they save civilian lives while disabling enemy combatants or only raise the cost of war by intentionally harming civilians and opening the door to more terrible and devastating weapons of mass destruction? Do targeted killings prevent future attacks and deplete the enemy's ranks or exacerbate hostilities and lead to the extrajudicial execution of combatants? Similar questions arise about interrogational torture or when assessing tactics that target civilians who directly or indirectly support the war effort.

Addressing the question of effectiveness is never easy, particularly when wars founder and the parties grope for alternative methods. In modern, asymmetric wars, however, and in contrast to war in 1907, a number of factors impinge upon assessments of effectiveness and military necessity. These include lack of uniforms on the weaker side, a growing role for civilian combatants, little fear of reciprocity, and the influence of the media. None of these factors counted for much in 1907 or in the aftermath of two world wars, but they are vitally important today. Lack of uniforms and the growing participation of civilians make it difficult for the stronger side to weaken an enemy without disabling certain classes of civilians who enjoy protection under the traditional law of armed conflict. Similarly, lack of access to military targets, together with civilianization of state military organizations, make it difficult for the weaker side to disable its enemy without attacking associated targets. Lack of reciprocity, that is, the inability of either side to respond to an attack in kind, also impinges upon calculations of military necessity. When sides are similarly armed, such practices as treachery, assassination, or chemical warfare are disadvantageous because each side can reciprocate. If this concern raises the cost of military action beyond what most sides will consider advantageous, they will abandon the practice for reasons of necessity, not humanitarian concern.

Without the prospect of coming under attack with the same weapons and tactics, each side has a freer rein to assess military necessity and effectiveness, and it is for this reason precisely that torture, assassination, and blackmail enjoy renewed interest. As we have seen, the results are decidedly mixed. Nonlethal weapons remain untested in battle. While there is growing evidence that targeted killings can significantly hamstring guerrilla organizations, they also arouse fierce indignation and outrage as civilians and militants die with the help of traitors and collaborators. Assassinations, like reprisals before them, may easily deteriorate into a vicious cycle of violence. Attacks on associated targets whether by the stronger or weaker side have yet to prove their worth. There is little evidence that strikes on civilians taking an indirect part in the fighting have immediate impact, at least in a war of short duration. Whether and how they will affect long-term or future fighting remains to be seen. Torture recast in terms of aggressive or enhanced interrogation has its proponents when ticking bombs threaten numerous innocent civilians and oversight committees carefully monitor interrogation and incarceration. But the cost, relative to the few potential ticking bomb cases, can be overwhelming in terms of adverse public opinion and fear of encroaching state power in democratic societies. Finally consider humanitarian intervention. Violating state sovereignty and risking soldiers' lives for the welfare of those who live far beyond one's borders may save significant numbers of lives. But will it work? Precisely because states remain reluctant to violate the sovereignty of other nations or risk their soldiers' lives for the sake of others, the entire idea remains mired in reluctance. Missions in Somalia, Bosnia, Sudan, and the Congo have fallen short of expectations. Nevertheless, humanitarian crises cannot but call upon the stronger nations for resolution.

For these reasons, assessing military necessity in asymmetric war and, in particular, evaluating the effectiveness of tactics like enhanced interrogation, targeted killing, nonlethal warfare, attacks on associated targets, and humanitarian intervention is a constant challenge. One of the recurring themes throughout this book is the call for oversight and reevaluation to ascertain effectiveness and to ascertain that weapons or tactics are used properly. If liability is a crucial criterion for targeted killing, interrogation, or intervention, then prior and postmortem assessments are crucial. Suspects are targeted, rendered to justice, interrogated, and incarcerated in response to threats before they materialize. The counterfactual weighs heavy. It is very difficult to prove that without the arrest, detention, assassination, or torture of certain individuals, many innocent people would have died. Nevertheless, only a transparent and institutionalized assessment process can even begin to consider whether a weapon or tactic or practice performed as expected.

Similar mechanisms can assess liability during asymmetric war. International law, for example, allows for status tribunals to determine or at least review combatant status. This is particularly important if one aim of nonlethal warfare is to incapacitate individuals indiscriminately and then sort out combatants from noncombatants. Public review and scrutiny are indispensible during wars of humanitarian intervention to assure that the costs in men and materiel do not surpass limits the citizens have imposed upon themselves. In contrast to conventional war, the muses are not silent during asymmetric conflict. Chief among these muses are the media; and in asymmetric warfare no state can forget that it must use the media to "shape the political, perceptual, ideological and media dimensions of war within the terms that other nations and cultures can understand, or risk losing every advantage that their military victories gain."[9]

With these remarks in mind, it should be clear that although an assessment of military necessity is the first order of business, it is necessarily incomplete. At one point, battlefield testing is essential. When a weapon or practice proves problematic, it is time to reconsider and rectify its costs. Then, back it will go into battle. Before it does, however, it must pass the test of humanitarianism.

The Filter of Humanitarianism

Armed with a reasonable expectation that a tactic, practice, or weapon will effectively disable an enemy or otherwise secure a military advantage, policymakers will then consider its humanitarian implications. Despite its age, The Hague article 23 nicely sums up the humanitarian duties toward soldiers. The duties belligerents owe to noncombatants are twice as heavy. Humanitarianism prohibits unnecessary harm to combatants and unnecessary and direct harm to noncombatants. Nonetheless, humanitarianism also allows proportionate and often lethal harm to befall noncombatants.

Asymmetric war does not change these principles, but it does strongly affect how we define their terms. The absence of uniforms and large, standing armies, combined with a growing military role for civilians on both sides, leads the parties to asymmetric war to jettison affiliation in favor of participation. Gone is the once hallowed distinction between combatant and noncombatant based on formal affiliation with a military organization. In its place come hosts of civilian combatant actors who take a direct or indirect role in the fighting. In place of absolute immunity, civilian participants find themselves at risk for various degrees of harm. Those directly participating are at risk for lethal harm; those indirectly participating find themselves at risk for nonlethal bodily harm or severe but temporary deprivation of civil and political rights. The principle of noncombatant immunity protects civilian noncombatants from direct lethal harm but may expose them to nonlethal injuries. Moreover, any tactic designed to inflict disproportionate harm on civilians whether to demoralize them, pressure their government, or deter future hostilities, remains far outside the pale. The same is true about masking disproportionate harm behind a veil of collateral damage for the same purposes. Innocent civilians have not lost the right that protects them from direct lethal harm. Asymmetric war contracts the scope of innocence and excludes many of those who once enjoyed full immunity. This is a significant departure from the traditional idea of noncombatant immunity, but is not fatal.

Second, asymmetric warfare impinges upon two important components of humanitarianism: unnecessary suffering and proportionality. The prohibition against unnecessary suffering is the lynchpin of combatant rights, one of the few concessions made to humanitarianism when the welfare of armed combatants is at stake. Yet the concept is notoriously ill defined. Content with prohibiting a handful of weapons – poison gas, barbed lances, or blinding lasers, for example – the international community has no clear definition of unnecessary suffering. Criteria are lacking but the notable attempt by the International Committee of the Red Cross (ICRC) should not go unnoticed. Here, researchers attempted to establish a baseline of field mortality, reasoning that any weapon causing more than twenty-five percent field mortality brings unnecessary suffering.[10] In the ensuing discussion (Chapter 3), it became clear just where this figure came from: it was somewhat more than the field mortality of many of the major nineteenth- and twentieth-century conflicts. These data are important and reflect the mortality necessary to wage a just and lawful war. In this way, the humanitarian principle is closely linked to the concept of military necessity. And, this is how it should be. There is no way to gauge unnecessary suffering without understanding the limits of necessary suffering, that is, the suffering necessary to disable an enemy or achieve a military advantage.

The same principle applies to the idea of proportionality. Proportionality is the exception to harming civilians. Understanding that war necessarily harms civilians, the principle of proportionality allows incidental, necessary and unavoidable harm as long as it is not excessive. "Not excessive" like "unnecessary suffering" knows no definition other than the intuitive, gut feeling of a reasonable person. But this is far from definitive. Following the ICRC's line of thought about unnecessary suffering, it should be possible to delineate the level of casualties necessary to disable an enemy under conditions of asymmetric warfare. The data are only preliminary but suggest some vague level of consensus about when casualties become excessive as a strong party fights against an un-uniformed enemy positioned among civilians and as the weaker side fights with relatively unsophisticated weapons. Armed with different capabilities and fighting under different conditions, each side may also find itself subject to a different standard of proportionality. Less-sophisticated weapons will inevitably take greater numbers of civilian lives as they destroy military targets. Technologically superior armaments can limit collateral harm but must contend with the difficulties of firing into dense, built-up areas where guerrillas often make their stand.

With these examples, one sees a close connection between military necessity and the application of humanitarian principles. Specifically, an evaluation of a new weapon, tactic, or practice is not a discrete two-step process but one that toggles between military necessity and humanitarianism. This works in several ways. First, the humanitarian impact of a weapon, practice, or tactic may not be clear until used in practice. Some nonlethal weapons may work as predicted, others as feared. There are concerns, for example, that the Active Denial System may invite charges of torture as it inflicts excruciating pain without damaging tissue or may, in general, cause more harm than it prevents. The humanitarian evaluation, therefore, is not just a theoretical exercise, but requires field data. Second, definitions of key humanitarian terms such as unnecessary suffering, excessive harm, and proportionality require an empirical assessment of what is militarily necessary in specific situations. Third, assessments of military necessity are impossible without considering prevailing humanitarian norms. This is particularly true of costs. The cost of violating a deeply held norm about noncombatant immunity or dignity or honor can be significant and necessarily affects any evaluation of military necessity. Respect for certain moral principles defines a state's ethos, which it cannot wantonly violate without undermining its own identity. Independent of the threat of "payment in kind," there are costs when a nation violates it own, deeply held moral code. This may render a tactic or practice militarily untenable from the very beginning. Nations constantly struggle to maintain fidelity to fundamental norms while trying to adjust to new security challenges.[11] This puts military necessity and humanitarianism in constant interaction.

Acceptable practices, tactics, and weapons of asymmetric war emerge following a deliberative process of give-and-take between the two filtering components. Many practices, and probably more than most people think, fall on the grounds of military necessity. When war goes astray and cries of injustice fill the air, the first charge is often disproportionate harm to noncombatants and vicious harm to combatants. In many cases, this charge misses the mark, not because the harm inflicted was disproportionate or extreme but because it was never necessary to begin with. In the Second Lebanon War, poor intelligence led to the wrong choice of targets, and unfeasible military goals led to needless casualties. Given their high dud rate, cluster munitions fired in a vain attempt to destroy short-range launchers took lives well after the conflict ended when, clearly, the loss of life could have no possible military value. None of these tactics, practices, or weapons crossed the threshold of military necessity.

Other tactics or weapons pass the test of necessity but do not pass the test of humanitarianism. Landmines, incendiary weapons, torture, demoralization bombing, and weapons of mass destruction might all be useful in war. In some cases, terrorism, murder, and rape have proved an effective means to drive civilians from their homes. Some weapons fall before the limits we impose on necessary suffering and proportionate harm. Others fall before the imperative to avoid inflicting direct harm on noncombatants. Moreover, any side waging a war to rout civilians from their homes, or cleanse a territory of one minority group or another, does not merit a fighting chance. For them, the question of military necessity does not arise.

TORTURE, ASSASSINATION, AND BLACKMAIL: A DESCENT
INTO BARBARISM?

For those tactics, practices, and weapons that emerge from the
dynamic process of distillation and evaluation, military necessity
remains tethered to humanitarianism. This might dismay those who
believe that torture, assassination, and blackmail are sufficiently
barbaric to win an asymmetric war. I noted in the first chapter how
many of the emerging practices and tactics of asymmetric war often,
though certainly not always, entail a judicious use of force, and how
proponents of such tactics hope to strike at targets that bear responsibility for an armed threat. The changing rules, definitions, weapons,
and tactics of asymmetric war do not offer one side or the other overwhelmingly brutal methods to crush its adversaries. On the contrary,
targeted killing, nonlethal warfare, strikes on associated targets, and
humanitarian intervention labor under evolving restrictions that
continue to safeguard noncombatant immunity, contain disproportionate harm, and limit unnecessary suffering. Terrorism, too, must
confront the demands of military necessity and humanitarianism,
and the result, surprising to some, is some level of parity or symmetry
between the weaker and stronger sides. Just as the stronger side may
strike at associated targets and modify the principle of proportionality to meet field conditions characterized by civilian combatants and
lack of uniforms, so may the weaker. Their weapons may be different but their targets are similar, and the weaker side, too, may adjust
the threshold of proportionality to account for relatively inaccurate
weaponry. Both sides may target associated targets but not innocent
noncombatants. As they do, they must adjust the level of harm they
inflict accordingly and use only the minimal harm necessary to disable indirect participants. This places firm limits on what guerrillas
may do. It rules out many targets and tactics of terrorism but at the
same time, expands the scope of permissible targets to preserve guerrillas' fighting chance.

Evaluating emerging practices, weapons, and tactics through the
twin lens of military necessity and humanitarianism goes a long way
to insure that they are necessary and useful, generally cause less
harm than they hope to prevent, and meet the test of proportionality and noncombatant immunity as the terms redefine themselves
in the context of asymmetric warfare. The process of evaluation is

continuous: military planners may begin it, but the public, media, and transparent oversight mechanisms continue it.

Asymmetric warfare, therefore, is not barbarism. Nor are the tactics, practices, and weapons that gain approval after confronting the demands of military necessity and humanitarianism, barbaric. Rather, they protect the right of each side to a fighting chance. At the same time, however, it is clear that asymmetric warfare opens the door to many reinterpretations. There are certainly fears that nonlethal weaponry, for example, may pave the way for nations looking to develop lethal chemical weapons. Humanitarian intervention may turn into adventurism or a crusade. Torture, even torture lite, already skirts the margins of acceptability because it is rarely effective or necessary and often is objectionable; while assassination flirts with vigilantism, death squads, and extra-legal execution. Attacking associated targets, like other practices of asymmetric war, is a tactical slippery slope along which the lives of those who have no truck with war making are endangered.

The slippery slope is an ever-present concern when nations take up arms and confront the fundamental dilemma posed by military necessity and humanitarianism. Nevertheless, attempts to restrain war cannot remain static. If nothing else, technology and circumstance are going to force reevaluation and conflicting interpretations. This not only affects very basic notions of suffering, proportionality, and combatant/noncombatant identity, but the contextual framework of armed conflict. There is currently no consensus about the scope of law enforcement or "military operations other than war" just as there is no universally acceptable definition of rogue regime or unlawful combatant. As the international community wrestles with this challenge, there is no reason to assume it will slide down a slippery slope rather than make every effort to construct firm red lines about the use of different weapons or practices in various situations. Near-unanimous unease with practices as ancient as reprisal and as modern as nuclear warfare point the way, as do prohibitions or restrictions on the use of chemical and biological weapons, landmines, blinding lasers, incendiary weapons, and, more recently, cluster bombs. The most significant change, however, comes from the international community's willingness to undertake armed humanitarian intervention on behalf of helpless individuals facing the threat of genocide and crimes against humanity. No change in this direction can be ignored.

Working through the moral dilemmas of asymmetric war should encourage a healthy respect for international humanitarian law. By "international humanitarian law," I mean the laws, conventions, and practices that guide nations during war and strive to protect the welfare of combatants and noncombatants alike. By healthy I mean critical, that is, something between mocking disrespect and zealous devotion. Both attitudes are rampant. The former is a mark of impatience among those frustrated with any attempt to make sense of humanitarianism during armed conflict. The latter, excessive zeal, also bears the mark of impatience and reflects a reluctance to recognize how military necessity and humanitarianism necessarily interact. But dogmatism is not the answer. Describing current challenges to military medicine, I once wrote how the need for medical expertise to build nonlethal chemical weapons poses a hard dilemma for military surgeons. Many physicians quickly shot back: there is no dilemma; doctors should just say no. It does not matter whether these weapons are necessary and effective. Throughout this book, I have noted similarly inflexible reactions to any attempt to reconsider the merits of targeted killing, chemical warfare, humanitarian intervention, or attacks on previously protected groups of noncombatants. Some observers can afford to be dogmatic and it keeps the rest of us squarely focused on the dilemma at hand. But such dogmatism, no less than any outright rejection of humanitarianism in war, denies the force of any dilemma that by its nature presents hard and sometimes tragic choices that we are all required to confront. Drawing the line between the acceptable and unacceptable, navigating the straits between military necessity and humanitarian imperatives while avoiding the pitfall of the slippery slope is the hard work of applied ethics during war.

11

Afterword
The War in Gaza, December 2008 to
January 2009

Though short, the war in Gaza touched on nearly every dilemma of
asymmetric conflict raised in the preceding chapters. Searching for
a military solution to the threat posed by long-range Grad missiles,
Israel struggled with the boundaries of disproportionate harm; the
ever-present danger of unnecessary civilian suffering; the inability
to distinguish between combatants, noncombatants, and participating civilians; the lure of new weapons; the complexity of fighting in built-up areas; and a less than friendly media. Facing massive
firepower and no chance of fighting anything close to a conventional war, the Palestinians confronted dilemmas of their own as
they deployed their fighters among the civilian population, stored
military supplies in mosques, placed command and control centers
in hospitals and civilian enclaves, mounted indiscriminate attacks
on mixed civilian/military targets, and manipulated the media.
These dilemmas are emblematic of asymmetric conflict, displayed
in all their complexity in the Gaza War. But there was more to this
war. In Gaza, and in contrast to the conduct of many earlier asymmetric conflicts, the state power tried to fight a ground war with
zero tolerance for military casualties. Remarkably, the attempt was
largely successful, but the cost to noncombatants may have been
intolerable.

FIGHTING A ZERO-TOLERANCE GROUND WAR

Sensitive to public concern for military casualties, NATO forces fighting in Yugoslavia in mid-1999 successfully waged a zero-tolerance *air* war as they flew thousands of sorties without the loss of a single pilot. Similarly sensitive to public opinion, particularly following the relatively heavy military casualties of the Second Lebanon War, the Israeli Army laid plans to wage a zero-tolerance *ground* war.

The results were impressive. Table 11.1 shows the percentage of soldiers killed in combat in some recent conventional and asymmetric conflicts.[1] In recent conventional wars, close to 25 percent of all soldiers hit during combat die. In asymmetric war, this drops to about 15 percent owing to superior firepower, improved body armor, and speedy evacuation of the wounded. Astonishingly, this percentage dropped to less than 3 percent in the Gaza War. Considering that about half of those killed fell to friendly fire, the numbers are even more impressive. But the war was not a cakewalk; 300 wounded soldiers in 15 days of combat attest to the ferocity of fighting a complex ground operation in a built-up area. Hamas did not avoid fighting, yet was unable to kill more than a handful of soldiers. What explains the ability to wage a zero-tolerance ground war?

Soldiers fighting a guerrilla army do not lose their lives to long-range artillery or aerial attacks, but to improvised explosive devices (IEDs), shoulder-launched anti-tank missiles, and snipers. Effectively employing these requires proximity, good cover and line of sight. Thwarting them requires the attacking soldiers to obscure visibility, remove buildings providing cover, and aggressively pursue enemy targets under conditions where civilians are close at hand and indistinguishable from combatants. These efforts characterized the fighting in Gaza and prompted two contentious debates. The first, which received enormous publicity, centered on the question of proportionality and the limits of acceptable civilian casualties in a zero-tolerance ground war. The second but less well-publicized debate addressed the underlying ethical question of a zero-tolerance ground war, namely, Is it permissible for a modern army to strive to protect its soldiers at any cost?

TABLE 11.1 Percentage of Soldiers Killed in Combat

Type of Conflict	Conflict	Killed	Wounded	% Killed
Conventional Conflict	Korea (1950–1953)*	21,310	75,831	22%
	6-Day War (1967)**	759	2,563	23%
	Arab-Israel War (1973)**	2,656	7,250	27%
	Falklands War (1982)***	252	777	25%
Asymmetric Conflict	Iraq (2003–4/2009)*	3,429	31,153	10%
	Afghanistan (2001–4/2009)*	448	2,689	14%
	Second Lebanon War (2006)**	121	628	16%
	Gaza (2009)**	9	336	3%

* American casualties; ** Israeli casualties; *** British casualties.

PROPORTIONALITY AND ACCEPTABLE HARM TO CIVILIANS IN THE GAZA WAR

As in most asymmetric wars, charges of disproportionate harm flew unrestrained. Addressing these charges, however, requires information that neither side is quick to supply. As each side jockeys to put on its best face, it must answer a number of hard and uncomfortable questions to allow observers to evaluate allegations of excessive harm to civilians and improper conduct during war.

Because any assessment of disproportionality requires an accurate count of civilian casualties, it is first important to ask, How many civilians died in the Gaza War? By March 2009, the Israelis and Palestinians published conflicting casualty figures. The Palestinians counted 1,434 dead, while Israeli figures range from 1,166 to 1,370 dead. Despite these discrepancies, the real difference was in the number of civilian casualties. The Palestinians count over 900 civilians among the dead, while Israeli figures number only 300 to 400.[2] Obviously, this makes a huge difference when assessing proportionality. The problem is not one of identification; authorities knew the *names* of most of the dead. Rather, the dispute turns on *affiliation*.

Who, exactly, counts as a civilian or combatant? This is a recurring question of asymmetric conflict and the Gaza War sharpened differences of opinion.

Identifying civilian noncombatants depended upon the status of associated targets, that is, those civilians who directly or indirectly supported the war but were not members of Hamas. Throughout the preceding chapters, I noted the tendency to broaden the scope of vulnerable civilians. The Gaza War was no exception. Among the over 900 Palestinian civilians who lost their lives were members of the Hamas political wing and nearly 300 police officers and cadets.[3] Are they vulnerable combatants or protected noncombatants? Palestinian human rights organizations claim the latter and, indeed, were this a conventional war, they might be right. But in an asymmetric war, guerrilla forces cannot fight effectively, if at all, unless they can call on armed police officers or specialized civilian personnel to aid them. This is their right, but recruiting these adjunct forces places them in harm's way, just as fighting without uniforms and in heavily populated areas places all civilians in danger.

Police officers bearing arms and taking a direct part in the fighting are vulnerable to lethal harm. Civilians associated with Hamas's political wing include those who work in its government, educational, financial, welfare, and charitable agencies.[4] These are the same associated targets that surfaced in Lebanon and in other counterinsurgency operations. They are civilian combatants or quasi-combatants whose vulnerability is subject to their level of participation. While there is no blanket justification for lethal force, most associated targets are vulnerable to nonlethal harm, capture, or incarceration. Assessing the level of permissible force Israel used against associated targets demands a case-by-case examination that requires information about each person's behavior that both sides must provide.

Although police officers are vulnerable to lethal harm and associated targets are at risk for some measure of nonlethal harm, civilian noncombatants remain protected by the principle of proportionality. They are at risk for incidental harm that is not excessive. Evaluating excessive harm demands that each side answer the same questions: Did the military benefits they sought outweigh the death and destruction that befell civilians? Did the sides cause more harm than necessary?

Was sufficient care taken to protect noncombatants? Answering these questions requires a closer look at the fighting on the ground.

Fighting on the Ground (Israel)

Fighting to keep the enemy at a distance, removing structures that provide cover, and obscuring troop movements found Israel employing an array of weapons that were both powerful and discriminating. Drones provided ground units with close air support to identify ambushes and destroy missile sites. Heavy-duty mine-clearing equipment destroyed buildings, tunnels, and booby traps by setting off underground explosions. Smart bunker-busting bombs destroyed arms-smuggling tunnels, white phosphorus shells provided cover for troops, and new, limited-lethality weapons aimed to neutralize militants with little collateral damage by setting off controlled explosions in tightly confined areas. At the same time, advancing military forces also tried to warn civilians of impending danger by calling their cell phones, distributing leaflets, and setting off small but loud explosive charges on rooftops to scare people out of the battle zone prior to an aerial attack.[5]

Before asking whether these weapons and tactics violated humanitarian principles and wrought excessive harm, it is essential to first assess their effectiveness. This is keeping with the general plan of this book to evaluate effectiveness first and humanitarianism second. Warnings, for example, have two purposes. Most obviously, they look to save innocent lives. Second, they strive to ascertain combatant status in the absence of uniforms on the assumption that noncombatants will clear the field if properly warned. But warnings are not always as helpful or compelling as one might think. Once warned, many militants flee while many civilians remain stranded in the battle zone. This was the lesson from Lebanon.[6] Warnings can create an aura of false responsibility by assuming that those who don't flee are either militants or, in the very least, civilians prepared to accept the risk of death. In reality, however, many do not flee because they cannot. Roads clog, while the sick and elderly are simply unable to go elsewhere. Moreover, the entire idea of warnings is problematic because it suggests that civilians have an obligation to distinguish themselves from combatants and, therefore, flee. Any such obligation, however, contradicts a guerrilla's option to remain indistinguishable from, and to fight with the support and cover of, the civilian population. As a result, it is neither possible nor obligatory to remove civilians from the combat zone. With civilians constantly at risk, both sides must ask whether the military gains they seek outweigh the harm befalling civilian noncombatants.

The effectiveness of the new weapons introduced in Gaza also calls for careful assessment. Human rights organizations cannot do this. They assume that the weapons an army places in service serve an important military need. Amnesty International, for example, can only document the harm weapons cause civilians. They may conclude that the harm is inhuman but they cannot assess proportionality in the absence of any data about a weapon's effectiveness. It remains, therefore, for the stronger power, in this case Israel, to explain the shielding benefits of white phosphorus smoke bombs or the tactical success of limited-lethality weapons, for example.[7] Only then, can one ask the hard questions: Did the benefits of white phosphorus outweigh the cost to civilians harmed by its use? Were other, effective methods of obscuring troop movement available? Did the benefits of using mine-clearing equipment to rid large swaths of open areas of IEDs outweigh the damage to adjacent structures? Unconfirmed reports of DIME (dense inert metal explosive) munitions raise similar questions.[8] DIME munitions release a highly charged cloud of micro-shrapnel that is lethal to anyone within a 4-meter radius. On paper, DIME munitions, when combined with good intelligence, cause less collateral harm than high-explosive shells. However, the shrapnel is difficult to detect and the chemical components of the weapon may bring long-term and as yet undetermined harm to the injured. Like phosphorus, they may cause fearsome wounds. Do these overwhelm the military advantages they confer? This question applies to any tactic, however effective it may prove. For those tactics and weapons that were ineffective, the question of proportionality does not apply. These merely caused unnecessary death and destruction.

Charges of disproportionate harm are easy to level but difficult to assess in the absence of information about a weapon's or tactic's use and effectiveness. In most cases, this information can only come from the military organizations that use them. For obvious reasons, some of this information is classified. Nevertheless, there is considerable room for governments to provide pertinent information about the general effectiveness and purpose of the weapons and tactics they employ. The importance of working with investigating agencies and striving for transparency in asymmetric war is a lesson many governments have yet to grasp. By failing to cooperate with UN committees, human rights organizations, and other nongovernmental organizations, Israel risks losing the media war that inevitably accompanies, and sometimes overshadows, the war on the ground.

Fighting on the Ground (Hamas)

Many of the foregoing questions about proportionality and effectiveness apply with equal force to the tactics and weapons that Hamas chose. As the war escalated, Hamas used increasingly powerful missiles to attack large population centers. Even assuming these attacks aimed at military targets still leaves Hamas to justify collateral harm. Few Israeli civilians died, but the potential for devastation was great. What military advantage did Hamas expect to achieve? What costs did they expect to impose? Answering these questions is necessary before one can ask whether the harm they wrought was proportionate.

Ironically, Hamas must also weigh the harm they brought to their own civilian population. The right of the weaker power to wage war without uniforms and under the cover of their civilian population does not exempt them from answering hard questions about the tactics they choose and the proportionality of the attendant civilian casualties among their compatriots.[9] As it went to war to reopen its borders, demoralize the Israeli population, and simply restore a sense of honor, Hamas was keenly aware of the ensuing devastation that would result. They, and their supporters, now need to ask whether the chances of achieving these political goals outweighed the harm that followed. They must ask whether the benefit of stationing snipers in residential buildings or constructing, and booby-trapping, an elaborate underground tunnel system throughout heavily populated neighborhoods outweigh the risk and ultimate cost to the noncombatants who live there. Is the benefit of storing weapons in a mosque more important than the safety of those who worship there? Does asking children to ferry weapons provide a military advantage that offsets the harm minors may suffer?

Some or all of these tactics may be necessary given the fact that otherwise Hamas cannot fight at all. But necessity is only one important question. Militants must ask if these tactics are effective and whether they help achieve tactical or strategic military aims. Then they must ask whether they justify the cost in civilian lives and property that is sure to come. These questions are little different from those that Israel must answer as it went to war in an attempt to remove the threat of the long-range missiles, prevent arms smuggling, and deter future attacks.

As both sides fought, Hamas built its tactics around an implicit understanding that Israeli military actions were not entirely unrestrained. It is unlikely that Hamas would have placed their command centers in hospitals or used children to transport arms if they believed that the Israelis would ruthlessly attack any of these targets. Israel's norms of conduct were precisely those that allowed Hamas to feel secure about adopting tactics that might easily invite catastrophe in other circumstances. Nevertheless, Israel's response was probably greater than in previous wars. It may yet prove disproportionate or simply unnecessary, particularly if its war aims go unrealized. But the war also introduced a new wrinkle in the proportionality debate, namely whether reducing military casualties to close to zero counts as a justifiable military goal. If it does, then permissible, proportionate harm to civilians becomes that much greater.

SAVING SOLDIERS' LIVES: AT WHAT COST?

During war, belligerents profess a strong desire to minimize casualties among those whose lives they are prepared to sacrifice. At one point, they ask whether their soldiers must assume additional risk to protect the lives of enemy noncombatants. In Gaza, as in many prior wars, the question arises when troops call in air support or artillery fire to destroy an enemy position knowing that many civilians may die in the attack. These civilian deaths are collateral. Nevertheless, must soldiers seek alternative and perhaps riskier means of warfare before endangering civilian noncombatants?

For many observers, the answer is yes. Michael Walzer states the argument plainly:

There are obligations that go with [soldiers'] war rights, and the first of these is the obligation to attend to the rights of civilians – more precisely, of those civilians whose lives they themselves endanger. ... If saving civilian lives means risking soldiers' lives, the risk must be accepted. But there is a limit to the risks that we require. ... We can only ask soldiers to minimize the dangers they impose.[10]

If Walzer is correct, then each side to the Gaza War must ask whether its soldiers assessed the merits of alternative forms of fighting and did what they could to minimize risk to civilian noncombatants. Alternatively, Israeli philosopher Asa Kasher does not ask soldiers to minimize the dangers they impose on civilian noncombatants. On the contrary, writes Kasher, "We should consider the possibility of qualifying the immunity of civilians when decreasing collateral damage means increasing jeopardy to combatants when they fight terrorists or other agents of *unjust threats*."[11] If this is correct, close air or artillery cover to protect combatants is morally obligatory even when civilian casualties are high and/or alternative but riskier avenues of attack are available. Kasher's view is not idiosyncratic but a staple of the public debate in Israel during and after the war.

The key to understanding, and refuting, the argument's appeal lies in the caveat "unjust threats," tacked on at the end. In conventional warfare, there would be no talk of reducing risk to soldiers by increasing risk to civilians. But something happens when threats are unjust. My students, for example, are more than willing to demand that Americans fighting in Germany in 1945 take care to protect German civilians even if it means risking soldiers' lives. However, they are extremely reluctant to consider that Israeli soldiers fighting in Gaza owe the same obligation to Palestinian civilians. When nations or groups believe they face an unjust threat, they tend to draw two complementary conclusions. First, adversaries readily believe that everyone on the other side, regardless of status, is part of the threat they face and, therefore, a legitimate target. Second, belligerents absolve themselves of responsibility: whatever risk civilians face is the sole responsibility of their own government who chose to pursue an unjust war or adopt unjust means of warfare. By this reasoning, Israelis have no obligation to risk their soldiers' lives to protect noncombatants because it was the Hamas government that first fired missiles at Israel and then put its own citizens in danger by waging a guerrilla war in their midst. In other words, a nation responding to an unjust threat need give but scant thought to the rights of noncombatants.

Similarly, proponents of disproportionate force argue for their right to target civilians directly in an effort to deter their government from future, unjust wars.[12]

These arguments are problematic for several reasons. First, the charge of posing an unjust threat is difficult to attach to either party in the Gaza War. On the face of it, both sides have legitimate military and political interests that they chose to pursue by force of arms. Second, an unjust threat does nothing to curtail the rights of noncombatants. While those who directly or indirectly support the war are at risk for direct harm, and lack of uniforms places the innocent in danger, civilian noncombatants retain their immunity. Part of this immunity, or right to be protected from the ravages of war, demands some element of caution from all those who make war. When a nation or group goes to war, it has to decide how much risk it is willing to shoulder to achieve its political aims. If a society is unwilling to risk the lives of its soldiers in armed conflict, then it must search for alternative means to realize its goals. While combating armies have an obligation to protect their soldiers to the greatest extent possible, no army can mitigate risk on the back of innocent noncombatants.

Accepting reasonable risk to combatants to save innocent noncombatants is also at the heart of humanitarian intervention (Chapter 9). Without the shared obligation to accept some risk, no nation would ever find cause to intervene militarily on behalf of others. Here, an intervening force is facing an unjust threat of the most blatant kind. Yet few suggest that a humanitarian force should not reasonably risk the lives of some of its soldiers to save those facing abject persecution at the hands of their own government. Civilian noncombatants in Gaza are no less innocent than those in Sudan or Myanmar.

Any attempt to qualify the rights of innocent noncombatant should be met with caution and no mean measure of concern. Nevertheless, I have argued throughout this book to broaden the scope of civilian vulnerability and adjust the standards of proportionality in asymmetric war. This has nothing to do with fighting a just or unjust war, but recognizes that many more civilians participate directly or indirectly in asymmetric than in conventional war, and that conditions on the ground make it nearly impossible to distinguish between combatants and noncombatants. At the same time, many guerrillas require active civilian aid and civilian garb if they are to fight at all. The enduring dilemma, for both sides, is to wage asymmetric war without undue harm to noncombatants. The doctrine of disproportionate force is not the answer. Disproportionality, by its very nature, knows no restraint. It has no built-in limits that invoke the imperatives of humanitarianism nor does it offer any guidance to soldiers in the field. A critical study of noncombatant immunity, proportionality, and unnecessary suffering in asymmetric war, on the other hand, urges us to search for those limits among the new challenges these wars present.

Notes

1 **Torture, Assassination, and Blackmail in an Age of Asymmetric Conflict**

1 Martin van Creveld, "The Persian Gulf Crises and the Future of Morally Restrained War," *Parameters* 22:2 (1992), 21–40.

2 Jean Pictet, *Development and Principles of International Humanitarian Law* (Dordrecht/Geneva, Martinus Nijhoff and Henry Dunant Institute, 1985): 62.

3 Gil Merom, *How Democracies Lose Small Wars* (Cambridge: Cambridge University Press, 2003):15.

4 Ivan Arreguin-Toft, *How the Weak Win Wars: A Theory of Asymmetric Conflict* (Cambridge: Cambridge University Press, 2005): 213.

5 Merom, *How Democracies Lose Small Wars*, 47 (emphasis added); see also Rupert Smith, *The Utility of Force: The Art of War in the Modern World* (New York: Vintage, 2008): 274–5.

6 Henry Shue, "Torture," *Philosophy and Public Affairs* 7:2 (1978), 124–43.

7 David Weissbrodt and Amy Bergquist, "Extraordinary Rendition: A Human Rights Analysis," *Harvard Human Rights Journal* 19:123 (2006), 123–60; Stephen Grey, *Ghost Plane: The True Story of the CIA Torture Program* (New York: St. Martin's Press, 2006); Doug Cassel, "Washington's 'War Against Terrorism' and Human Rights: The View from Abroad," *Human Rights* 33:1 (2006), 1–9; Michael John Garcia, "Renditions: Constraints Imposed by the Laws on Torture," *CRS Report for Congress* (Washington, DC: Congressional Research Service, The Library of Congress, April 2006); Jane Mayer, "Outsourcing Torture, The Secret History of America's 'extraordinary rendition' Program," *The New Yorker* (February 15, 2005).

8 See Michael Gross, 'Assassination and Targeted Killing: Law Enforcement, Execution or Self-Defense?" *Journal of Applied Philosophy* 23:3 (2006).

9 Neil Davison, "The Development of 'Nonlethal' Weapons During the 1990's," Occasional Paper No. 2. *Bradford Nonlethal Weapons Research Project* (Department of Peace Studies, University of Bradford, UK, March 2007); Nick Lewer and Neil Davison, "Nonlethal Technologies – An Overview," *Disarmament* 1 (2005), 36–51; David A. Koplow, *Nonlethal Weapons: The Law and Policy of Revolutionary Technologies for the Military and Law Enforcement* (Cambridge: Cambridge University Press, 2006).

10 See, for example, Asa Kasher and Amos Yadlin, "Military Ethics of Fighting Terror: An Israeli Perspective," *Journal of Military Ethics* 4:1 (2005), 3–32.

11 See, for example, Bard E. O'Neill, *Insurgency and Terrorism: Inside Modern Revolutionary Warfare* (Washington, DC: Brassey's, 1990); Ian F. W. Beckett, *Modern Insurgencies and Counter Insurgencies: Guerrillas and their Opponents since 1750* (London: Routledge, 2001); John A. Nagl, *Counterinsurgency Lessons from Malaya and Vietnam: Learning to Eat Soup with a Knife* (Westport, CT: Praeger, 2002).

12 See, for example, Protocol Additional to the Geneva Conventions of 12 August 1949, and Relating to the Protection of Victims of International Armed Conflicts (Protocol I, June 8, 1977), Article 51. Also referred to as Additional Protocol I.

13 See, for example, Additional Protocol I, Commentary, Article 57, paragraph 2218, p. 685.

14 Joseph Giordono and Lisa Burgess, "Insurgent 'Body Count' Records Released," *Stars and Stripes*, October 1, 2007. In other conflicts, too, far more enemy combatants are captured rather than killed. Although in Algeria, French forces killed nearly 150,000 insurgents, the numbers elsewhere were generally far less. For example, in Kenya, 12,000 insurgents were killed in the fighting (1952–1960); in Israel, 1,600 (2000–2008); and in Northern Ireland, 400 IRA members died in the fighting (1969–2001). In Kenya, upwards of 80,000 were interned (including anyone taking the Mau Mau oath), in Israel, 8,500 (in August 2008, but many thousands more from 2000–2008); and in Northern Ireland, approximately 17,000 sat in prison. (Sources: **Israel**: B'Tselem, The Israeli Information Center for Human Rights in the Occupied Territories (http://www.btselem.org/English/Statistics/Casualties.asp) and (http://www.btselem.org/English/Statistics/Detainees_and_Prisoners.asp). **Kenya:** Neal Ascherson, "The Breaking of the Mau Mau," *The New York Review of Books* 52:6 (April 7, 2005) cites official figures in Caroline Elkins, *Imperial Reckoning: The Untold Story of Britain's Gulag in Kenya* (New York: Henry Holt, 2005), xvi, and her alternative figures of hundreds of thousands killed and incarcerated. **Ireland:** CAIN Web Service (Conflict Archive on the Internet) University of Ulster (http://cain.ulst.ac.uk/sutton/tables/Status_Summary.html); Henry McDonald, "300 IRA

Members to Fight Convictions and Seek Compensation," *The Guardian*, August 25, 2008; and personal communication with Michael Culbert of Coiste na n-Iarchimi, the umbrella organization of current and former Republican prisoners.

15 See Chapter 5 (p. 111), "Targeted Killing: An Effective Tactic of Asymmetric War?"

16 B. Jenkins, "The Future Course of International Terrorism," P. Wilkinson and A. Stewart (eds.), *Contemporary Research on Terrorism* (Aberdeen: Aberdeen University Press, 1987): 581–89.

17 For Algeria see Todd Shepard, *The Invention of Decolonization: The Algerian War and the Remaking of France* (Ithaca, NY: Cornell University Press, 2006): 44; for Malaya see O'Neil, *Insurgency and Terrorism*, 79; for Kenya see Robert B. Asprey, *War in the Shadows: The Guerilla in History* (New York: William Morrow and Company, 1994): 640; for Ireland see Malcolm Sutton, *An Index of Deaths from the Conflict in Ireland 1969–1993* (Belfast: Beyond the Pale Publications, 1994); for Israel see B'Tselem, Israeli Information Center for Human Rights in the Occupied Territories, "Statistics: Israeli Civilians Killed by Palestinians" (http://www.btselem.org/english/statistics/Casualties.asp); and for Cyprus see John L. Scherer, *Blocking the Sun: The Cyprus Conflict* (Minneapolis, MN: University of Minnesota Press, 1997): 110.

18 Additional Protocol I, Article 1(4).

19 Smith, *The Utility of Force*, 272.

20 Robin M. Frost, *Nuclear Terrorism After 9/11*; Adelphi Paper 378 (London: International Institute of Strategic Studies, 2006); Anthony Cordesman, *Terrorism, Asymmetric Warfare and Weapons of Mass Destruction* (Westport, CT: Praeger, 2002); Richard Posner, *Countering Terrorism: Blurred Focus, Halting Steps*, Hoover Studies in Politics, Economics, and Society (New York: Rowman & Littlefield, 2007).

21 Philip Bobbitt, *Terrorism and Consent*, Chapter 1.

22 Yossi Melman, "Blame Game in India/Dancing on Graves," *Ha'aretz*, November 30, 2008; Animesh Roul and Jen Alic, "India, Pakistan: Peace Set Back Again" (Zurich: International Relations and Security Network, Center for Security Studies at the Swiss Federal Institute of Technology, July 25, 2006); Bruce Crumley, "The Mumbai Attacks: Terror's Tactical Shift," *Time*, November 29, 2008.

23 Additional Protocol I, Commentary, Article 35, pages 392–393, paragraph 1389.

2 Friends, Foes, or Brothers in Arms?

1 Leo Tolstoy, *War and Peace* (trans. Louise and Aylmer Maude) (New York: Simon and Schuster, 1958): Book 10, Chapter 25, 860–7.

2 UN General Assembly Resolution 3314 (XXIX), Definition of Aggression (General Assembly 29th Session, December 14, 1974): 142–4.

3 Erich Maria Remarque, *All Quiet on the Western Front* (New York: Ballantine Books, 1982): 203–4.

4 Hugo Grotius, *Rights of War and Peace* (trans. A. C. Campbell) (New York: Walter Dunne, 1901) Book 11, Chapter 23 (13): 278.

5 United Nations Security Council Resolution 502 (Question concerning the situation in the region of the Falkland Islands (Malvinas) April 3, 1982); UN Security Council Resolution 660 (Condemning the Invasion of Kuwait by Iraq, August 2, 1990).

6 On the role of duress and ignorance see Judith Lichtenberg, "How to Judge Soldiers Whose Cause is Unjust," in David Rodin and Henry Shue, *Just and Unjust Warriors: The Moral and Legal Status of Soldiers* (Oxford: Oxford University Press, 2008): 112–30.

7 Kurt Vonnegut *Slaughterhouse Five* (New York: Dell Publishing, 1969): 106.

8 "An act performed pursuant to an unlawful order is excused unless the accused knew it to be unlawful or a person of ordinary sense and understanding would have known it to be unlawful." *Manual for Courts-Martial, United States* 2000 edition, Joint Service Committee on Military Justice, paragraph 916d, II–111; see also Leslie C. Green, "Superior Orders and the Reasonable Man," Leslie C. Green, *The Modern Law of War*, Second Edition (New York: Transnational Publishers, 1999): 245–82.

9 Shannon E. French, *The Code of the Warrior, Exploring Warrior Values Past and Present* (Lanham, MD: Rowman & Littlefield, 2003): 7, 10.

10 Yitzhak Benbaji, "A Defense of the Traditional War Convention," *Ethics* 118 (April 2008): 464–95.

11 Jeff McMahan, "The Morality of War and the Law of War," in Rodin and Shue, *Just and Unjust Warriors*, 19–43 at 30.

12 Francoise J. Hampton, "Detention, the 'War on Terror' and International Law," Howard Hensel (ed.), *The Law of Armed Conflict, Constraints on the Contemporary Use of Military Force* (Aldershot, Hampshire UK Ashgate, 2007): 131–70 at 146, 148.

13 "Protocol Additional to the Geneva Conventions of 12 August 1949, and Relating to the Protection of Victims of International Armed Conflicts" (Protocol I, June 8, 1977), Article 44(3).

14 Michael R. Gordon and Bernard E. Trainor, *Cobra II, The Inside Story of the Invasion and Occupation of Iraq* (New York: Pantheon, 2006): 500.

15 Amos Harel and Avi Issacharoff, "Winter Waiting Game," *Ha'aretz*, March 13, 2008.

16 Amos Harel and Avi Issacharoff, *34 Days: Israel, Hezbollah and the War in Lebanon* (New York: Palgrave Macmillan, 2008): 131.

17	Uri Bar-Joseph, "Israel's Military Intelligence Performance in the Second Lebanon War," *International Journal of Intelligence and Counterintelligence* 20:4 (December 2007), 583–601 at 589; see also Anthony Cordesman, *Lessons of the 2006 Israeli–Hezbollah War* (Washington, DC: Center for Strategic and International Studies, 2007): 43; Reuven Erlich, *Hezbollah's Use of Lebanese Civilians as Human Shields* (Tel Aviv: Intelligence and Terrorism Information Center at the Center for Special Studies, December 5, 2006); Harel and Issacharoff, *34 Days*, 272, note 9.

18	Military Commissions Act of 2006, 120 Stat. 2600 Public Law 109–366, October 17, 2006, 948a. Similarly, Israel (which also rejects Protocol I) defines an unlawful combatant as a "person who has participated either directly or indirectly in hostile acts against the State of Israel or is a member of a force perpetrating hostile acts against the State of Israel, where the conditions prescribed in Article 4 of the Third Geneva Convention of 12th August 1949 with respect to prisoners-of-war and granting prisoner-of-war status in international humanitarian law, do not apply to him." Incarceration of Unlawful Combatants Law, 5762–2002 (http://www.justice.gov.il/NR/rdonlyres/7E86D098-0463-4F37-A38D-8AEBE770BDE6/0/IncarcerationLawedited140302.doc.)

19	Additional Protocol I, Commentary, Article 44, p. 529, paragraph 1698.

20	Additional Protocol I, Commentary, Article 44, p. 529, note 40; Charles Chaumont, "La recherche d'un critère pour l'intégration de la guérilla au droit international humanitaire contemporain," 'Mélanges offerts à Charles Rousseau' (Paris, 1974): 43, 50, quoted by J. J. A. Salmon (trans. International Committee of the Red Cross) (emphasis added).

21	European Union, "Council Decision of 15 July 2008, implementing Article 2(3) of Regulation (EC) No 2580/2001 on Specific Restrictive Measures Directed Against Certain Persons and Entities with a View to Combating Terrorism and Repealing Decision 2007/868/EC" (2008/583/EC) (http://eur-lex.europa.eu/LexUriServ/LexUriServ.do?uri=OJ:L:2008:188:0021:0025:EN:PDF).

22	International Committee of the Red Cross, Third Expert Meeting on the Notion of Direct Participation in Hostilities, Summary Report, Geneva, ICRC, October 23–25, 2005.

23	International Committee of the Red Cross, Third Expert Meeting, 21.

24	Additional Protocol I, Commentary, Article 43, paragraph 1679.

25	Gordon L. Graham, *Ethics and International Relations* (London: Blackwell, 1997): 48–71.

26	*Counterinsurgency*, U.S. Army Field Manual FM 3–24 (2006).

27	Public Committee against Torture in Israel and Palestinian Society for the Protection of Human Rights and the Environment v. The Government of Israel (High Court of Justice 769/02, December 11, 2005), paragraph 34–37.

28 See David Kretzmer, "Civilian Immunity: Legal Aspects," Igor Primoratz (ed.), *Civilian Immunity in War* (Oxford: Oxford University Press, 2007): 88–94.

29 For a more detailed discussion see Chapters 4 (p. 85), "Can They Work? The Role of Nonlethal Weapons in Asymmetric War," and 7 (p. 154), "Noncombatant Immunity and Civilian Vulnerability in Asymmetric War."

30 For a more detailed discussion of the limits of justifiable terrorism see Chapter 8 (p. 182), "Justifying the Heinous."

31 Rome Statute of the International Criminal Court, Article 5(2), July 17, 1998.

32 Jeevan Vasagar, "Sudan Throws anti-UN Rally," Slate.com, August 5, 2004 (http://archive.salon.com/news/feature/2004/08/05/sudan/index.html). Cited in Paul D. Williams and Alex J. Bellamy, "The Responsibility To Protect and the Crisis in Darfur, *Security Dialogue 36* (2005): 27–47.

3 Shooting to Kill

1 Paddy Griffith, *Battle Tactics of the American Civil War* (Wiltshire, UK: The Crowood Press, 2001): 25.

2 "Declaration Renouncing the Use, in Time of War, of Explosive Projectiles Under 400 Grammes Weight, Saint Petersburg, November 29 and December 11, 1868.

3 Ulysses S. Grant, *The Memoirs of General Ulysses S. Grant*, Part 3, Chapter 37, Project Guttenberg (http://infomotions.com/etexts/gutenberg/dirs/5/8/6/5862/5862.htm) (emphasis added).

4 *The SIrUS Project: Towards a Determination of Which Weapons Cause "Superfluous Injury or Unnecessary Suffering"* (Geneva: International Committee of the Red Cross, 1997): 23; see also Robin M. Coupland, "The Effect of Weapons: Defining Superfluous Injury and Unnecessary Suffering," *Medicine and Global Survival* 3 (1996): A1; Robin M. Coupland, "The SIrUS Project: Progress Report on 'Superfluous Injury or Unnecessary Suffering' in Relation to the Legality of Weapons," *International Review of the Red Cross* 835 (1999): 583–92; Robin M. Coupland, "Abhorrent Weapons and 'Superfluous Injury or Unnecessary Suffering': From Field Surgery to Law," *British Medical Journal* 315 (1997): 1450–2.

5 See Chapter 7 (p. 163), "Reassessing Proportionality in Asymmetric Conflict: The Problem of Human Shields and Inaccurate Weaponry."

6 Hospital mortality in WWII was 4.5%, Korea 2.5%, and Vietnam 2.6%. T. N. Dupuy, *Attrition: Forecasting Battle Casualties and Equipment Losses in Modern War* (Falls Church, VA: Nova Publications, 1990): 53.

7 Larry May makes this point when he links the use of poison to "the magic arts … . It is not honorable, or consistent with humanness," he

writes, "for a person to behave like a demon," *War Crimes and Just War* (Cambridge: Cambridge University Press, 2007): 126.

8 Geoffrey Best, *Humanity in Warfare* (New York: Columbia University Press, 1983): 162.

9 Erich Maria Remarque, *All Quiet on the Western Front* (New York: Ballantine Books, 1982): 103.

10 Antonio Cassese, "Weapons Causing Unnecessary Suffering: Are They Prohibited?" *Rivista di Diritto Internazionale* LVIII (1975): 12–42 at 23.

11 Similarly, a weapon that "*always* results in *killing all* persons who in some way happen to be struck by it" is contrary to international law. All things being equal, it is always better to disable rather than kill another person and a weapon designed solely to kill does not offer this option. Cassese, "Weapons Causing Unnecessary Suffering, 18 (emphasis in the original).

12 Michael L. Gross, *Bioethics and Armed Conflict: Moral Dilemmas of Medicine and War* (Cambridge, MA: MIT Press, 2006): 228.

13 See Chapter 7 (p. 163), "Reassessing Proportionality in Asymmetric Conflict."

14 See Dupuy, *Attrition*, 140–1; Holcomb, John B., et. al., "Understanding Casualty Combat Care Statistics," *The Journal of Trauma: Injury, Infection and Critical Care* 60: 2 (2006): 397–401; K. G. Swan and K. G. Swan, Jr., "Triage, the Past Revisited," *Military Medicine* 161:8 (1996): 448–52; R. H. Koehler, R. S. Smith, and T. Bacaner, "Triage of American Combat Casualties: The Need for Change," *Military Medicine* 159:8 (1994): 541–7; J. B. Peake, "Beyond the Purple Heart – Continuity of Care for the Wounded in Iraq," *New England Journal of Medicine* 352:3 (2005): 219–22; John B. Holcomb, Lynn Stansbury, Howard R. Champion, Charles Wade, and Ronald Bellamy, "Understanding Combat Casualty Care Statistics," *The Journal of Trauma: Injury, Infection and Critical Care* 60: 2 (2006): 397–401.

15 For a comparison of casualties in conventional and asymmetric war see Chapter 11 (p. 255), Table 11.1.

16 Holcomb, et. al., "Understanding Casualty Combat Care Statistics."

17 Protocol on Blinding Laser Weapons 1995 (Protocol IV to the 1980 Convention, October 13).

18 See W. Hays Parks, "The ICRC Customary Law Study: A Preliminary Assessment," ASIL Proceedings 99 (2005);" Ove Bring, "Regulating Conventional Weapons in the Future – Humanitarian Law or Arms Control?" *Journal of Peace Research* 24:3 (1987): 275–86; David Turns, "Weapons in the ICRC Study on Customary Humanitarian Law," *Journal of Conflict and Security Law* 11:2 (2006): 201–37; Burrus M. Carnahan and Marjorie Robertson, "The Protocol on 'Blinding Laser Weapons': A New Direction for International Humanitarian

Law," *American Journal of International Law* 90 (1996): 484–90; Jeffrey S. Morton, "The Legal Status of Laser Weapons that Blind," *Journal of Peace Research* 35:6 (1998): 697–705; Louise Doswald-Beck, "New Protocol on Blinding Lasers," *International Journal of the Red Cross* 312 (1996): 272–99.

19 International Committee of the Red Cross, *Blinding Laser Weapons: Questions and Answers* (Geneva: ICRC, November 16, 1994).

20 See Chapter 6 (p. 124), "The Torture Debate Today."

21 Rosser and Kind, *Map of Health States.* This is an excerpt from their full map. For the full map see P. T. Menzel, *Strong Medicine: The Ethical Rationing of Health Care* (Oxford: Oxford University Press, 1990): 82–3.

22 For similar tables and criteria see Dan Brock, "Quality of Life Measures," *Life and Death, Philosophical Essays in Biomedical Ethics* (Cambridge: Cambridge University Press, 1993): 268–324.

23 Anita Silvers, "Predicting Genetic Disability," in David Wasserman, Jerome Bickenbach, and Robert Wachbroit (eds.), *Quality of Life and Human Difference: Genetic Testing, Health Care, and Disability* (Cambridge: Cambridge Studies in Philosophy and Public Policy, 2005): 43–66 at 53, 60.

24 Kevin D. Frick, Emily W. Gower, John H. Kempen, Jennifer L. Wolff, "Economic Impact of Visual Impairment and Blindness in the United States," *Archives of Ophthalmology* 125 (2007):544–50 at 549; Furlong, William, et al., "Multiplicative Multi-Attribute Utility Function for the Health Utilities Index Mark 3 (HUI3) System: A Technical Report," McMaster University Centre for Health Economics and Policy Analysis Working Paper No. 98–11, December 11, 1998.

25 Calculation based on Health Utilities Index Mark 3 (HUI3) (note 24).

26 W. Hays Parks, "Conventional Weapons and Weapons Review," *Yearbook of International Humanitarian Law – 2005* Volume 8, A. McDonald (ed.) (Cambridge: Cambridge University Press, 2007): 85. There were also fears that the Chinese had developed a portable blinding laser that they were prepared to sell to rogue regimes. See Nick Cook, "Chinese Laser 'Blinder' Weapon for Export," *Janes's Defence Weekly,* May 27, 1995. My thanks to Dr. Eitan Barak for these useful references.

27 H. Blix, Swedish delegate to the II Conference of Government Experts on the Reaffirmation and Development of International Humanitarian Law Applicable in Armed Conflict, Geneva, May 4, 1972, cited in Cassese, "Weapons Causing Unnecessary Suffering," 12.

28 Malvern Lumsden, *Incendiary Weapons*, Stockholm International Peace Research Institute (Cambridge: MIT Press, 1975): 148. For a detailed description of burn wounds see pages 122–87.

29 G. Birke and S.O. Liljedahl, "Studies on Burns: XV, Treatment with warm dry air, clinical results compared with those of earlier treatment

series," *Acta Chirurgica Scandinavioca*, Supplement 337 (1971), 5, cited in Lumsden, *Incendiary Weapons*, 136.

30 Protocol III, Protocol on Prohibitions or Restrictions on the Use of Incendiary Weapons, Geneva, October 10, 1980, Article 2.

31 For a more extensive discussion of proportionality, collateral damage and the idea of excessive harm, see Chapter 7 (p. 163), "Reassessing Proportionality in Asymmetric Conflict: The Problem of Human Shields and Inaccurate Weaponry."

32 Message from the U.S. President transmitting Protocols II, III, and IV to the Certain Conventional Weapons (CCW) to the Senate, Treaty Document 105–1, Washington, DC, January 7, 1997: 37–40; see also U.S. Department of Defense, CCW: "Article by Article Analysis of the Protocol on Use of Incendiary Weapons," Office of the Under Secretary of Defense for Acquisition, Technology, and Logistics, nd (http://www.dod.mil/acq/acic/treaties/ccwapl/artbyart_pro3.htm).

33 Jean Marie Henckaerts and Louise Doswald-Beck, *Customary International Humanitarian Law* Volume 1, Rule 85, 289 (Cambridge: Cambridge University Press, 2005).

34 "It is generally admitted that [incendiary weapons] should not be used in such a way that they will cause unnecessary suffering, which means that in particular they should not be used against individuals without cover." Military manuals for armies in such nations as Austria, Norway, Mexico, Indonesia, and others have similar rules. Henckaerts and Doswald-Beck, *Customary International Humanitarian Law* Volume 1: 290, note 16.

35 Henckaerts and Doswald-Beck, *Customary International Humanitarian Law* Volume 1: 290.

36 Roman O. Reyhani, "The Legality of the Use of White Phosphorus by the United States Military during the 2004 Fallujah Assaults," Bepress Legal Series 2007, Paper 1959. Israel also used them in the Second Lebanon War; see Meron Rappaport, "Israel Admits Using Phosphorus Bombs during War in Lebanon," *Ha'aretz*, October 22, 2006.

37 On the use of chemical weapons by the Russians against Chechnyan guerrillas see Chapter 4 (p. 85), "Can They Work? The Role of Nonlethal Weapons in Asymmetric War."

38 For some analysts, norm internalization, not simple self-interest, explains the persistence of the ban on chemical and biological weapons during World War II. See Richard Price and Nina Tannenwald, "Norms and Deterrence: The Nuclear and Chemical Weapons Taboos," Peter J. Katzenstein (ed.), *The Culture of National Security: Norms and Identity in World Politics* (New York: Columbia University Press, 1996): 114–52.

4   Shooting to Stun

1   Brad Knickerbocker, "The Fuzzy Ethics of Nonlethal Weapons," *The Christian Science Monitor*, February 14, 2003.

2   Jürgen Altmann, "Acoustic Weapons – A Prospective Assessment," *Science & Global Security* 9 (2001), 165–234.

3   For recent studies see David Koplow, *Nonlethal Weapons: The Law and Policy of Revolutionary Technologies for the Military and Law Enforcement* (Cambridge: Cambridge University Press, 2006); and Neil Davison, "'Off the Rocker' and 'On the Floor': The Continued Development of Biochemical Incapacitating Weapons," Bradford Science and Technology Report 8, August 2007, Bradford Disarmament Research Centre, Department of Peace Studies, University of Bradford, UK. For the ADS system see Joint Nonlethal Weapons Program, "Active Denial System, Fact Sheet," and "Frequently Asked Questions Regarding the Active Denial System" (https://www.jnlwp.com/ads.asp).

4   Steven Metz, *Learning from Iraq: Counterinsurgency in American Strategy* (Carlisle, PA: The Strategic Studies Institute of the U.S. Army War College, 2007): 65.

5   For a complete clinical description see *Public Health Response to Biological and Chemical Weapons: WHO Guidance*, Annex 3, *Biological Agents* (Geneva: World Health Organization, 2004): 229–76.

6   Eric Croddy, *Chemical and Biological Warfare: A Comprehensive Survey for the Concerned Citizen* (New York: Springer, 2002): 208–11.

7   World Health Organization, *Health Aspects of Chemical and Biological Weapons* (Geneva: WHO, 1970). Estimates based on the release of 50 kg of agent by an aircraft along a 2-km line upwind of a population of five hundred thousand.

8   Conventional Weapons Convention, 1993, Article II, paragraph 9d.

9   World Health Organization, *Public Health Response to Biological and Chemical Weapons*, 44.

10 Julian Perry Robinson and Milton Leitenberg, *The Rise of CB Weapons* (Stockholm: Stockholm International Peace Research Institute, 1971): 189.

11 World Health Organization, *Public Health Response to Biological and Chemical Weapons*, 44.

12 National Research Council, *An Assessment of Nonlethal Weapons Science and Technology*, Committee for an Assessment of Nonlethal Weapons Science and Technology, Naval Studies Board Division on Engineering and Physical Sciences (Washington, DC: The National Academies Press, 2003): 81.

13 Article 5 of the Geneva Convention relative to the Treatment of Prisoners of War (1949) provides for tribunals to determine a person's status when

it is in doubt. Figures from the Gulf War from: Final Report to Congress, Conduct of the Persian Gulf War, Pursuant to Title V of the Persian Gulf Conflict Supplemental Authorization and Personnel Benefits Act of 1991 (Public Law 102–25), April 1992: 663.

14 Protocol FWR 2005–0037-H. Military Utility Assessment of the Active Denial System (ADS) in an Urban Environment, 6. According to the literature cited by one protocol, the threshold for pain is 47–48° C while tissue damage occurs after 8 minutes at 49° and after 20–25 seconds at 55°. A. R. Moritz and F. C. Henriques, Jr., "Studies of Thermal Injury II. The Relative Importance of Time and Surface Temperature in the Causation of Cutaneous Burns," *American Journal of Pathology*,(September 1947): 23(5): 695–720. Cited in Protocol FWR–2002–0046-H: Perceptual and Thermal Effects of Millimeter Waves, 1. Copies of the experimental protocols are available from the author.

15 Massimo Annati, "Nonlethal Weapons Revisited," *Military Technology* 31:3 (March 2007), 82–7.

16 Protocol FWR–2005–0037-H.

17 Neil Davison and Nick Lewer, Bradford Nonlethal Weapons Research Project, Research Report No. 8 (Centre for Conflict Resolution, Department of Peace Studies, University of Bradford, UK, March 2006): 16.

18 Turhan Canil, et. al., "Neuroethics and National Security," *American Journal of Bioethics* 7:5 (2007): 3–13.

19 Neil Davison and Nick Lewer, Research Report No. 8, 37.

20 Jonathan Moreno, *Mind Wars: Brain Research and National Defense* (New York: Dana Press, 2006): 112.

21 Canil, et. al., "Neuroethics and National Security," 9.

22 Moreno, *Mind Wars*, 107–8.

23 UN Human Rights Council, *Report of the Commission of Inquiry on Lebanon Pursuant to Human Rights Council Resolution S-2/1*, 23 November 2006, A/HRC/3/2, available at: http://www.unhcr.org/refworld/docid/45c30b6e0.html, paragraph 127; Human Rights Watch, "*Why They Died: Civilian Casualties in Lebanon during the 2006 War* (September 2007, Volume 19, No. 5(E)). Available at: http://www.hrw.org/en/reports/2007/09/05/why-they-died.

24 United Nations Human Rights Council, Report of the Commission of Inquiry on Lebanon, paragraph 135.

25 See Chapter 7 (p. 163), "Reassessing Proportionality in Asymmetric Conflict: The Problem of Human Shields and Inaccurate Weaponry," for a detailed discussion of proportionality in asymmetric war.

26 For the Israeli response to attacks on convoys see Israel Ministry of Foreign Affairs: "IDF Response on Convoy Hit in South Lebanon," August 12, 2006 (http://www.mfa.gov.il/MFA/Government/Communiques/2006/

IDF+response+on+convoy+hit+in+south+Lebanon+12-Aug-2006.htm);
and Sabrina Tavernise, "Before Attack, Confusion Over Clearance for
Convoy," *New York Times*, August 13, 2006. For a complete discussion of
proportionality see Michael L. Gross, "The Second Lebanon War: The
Question of Proportionality and the Prospect of Nonlethal Warfare,"
Journal of Military Ethics 7 (2008), 1–22.

27 John P. Alexander, "An Overview of the Future of Nonlethal Weapons,"
Medicine, Conflict and Survival 17 (2001): 180–93; Margaret-Anne
Coppernoll, "The Nonlethal Weapons Debate," *Naval War College Review*
52:2 (1999): 112–31; Nick Lewer and Tobias Feakin, "Perspectives and
Implications for the Proliferation of Nonlethal Weapons in the Context
of Contemporary Conflict, Security Interests and Arms Control,"
Medicine, Conflict and Survival 17 (2001): 227–86.

28 Julian Perry Robinson and Milton Leitenberg, *The Rise of CB Weapons*.

29 Neil Davison and Nick Lewer, Research Report No. 8, 38–44.

30 Amos Harel and Gideon Alon, "Chief of Staff Orders Investigation of
'Confirmed Killing,'" *Ha'aretz*, November 24, 2004.

31 Paul M. Wax, Charles E. Becker, and Steven C. Curry, "Unexpected
'Gas' Casualties in Moscow: A Medical Toxicology Perspective," *Annals
of Emergency Medicine* 41 (2003): 700–5.

32 David P. Fidler, "The Meaning of Moscow: 'Nonlethal' Weapons and
International Law in the Early 21st Century," *International Review of the
Red Cross* 87 (2005): 525–52; Koplow, *Nonlethal Weapons*, 100–12.

33 Davison, *Off the Rocker*, 14. To date, the attempt is not successful because
the pad could not penetrate protective clothing.

34 Robinson and Leitenberg, *The Rise of CB Weapons*, 187.

35 Joint Chiefs of Staff (USA), *Joint Doctrine for Military Operations Other Than
War*, Publication JP 3–07, 1995, I–1.

36 Joint Chiefs of Staff (USA), JP 3–0, *Joint Operations*, 17 September 2006,
Incorporating Change 1, 13 February 2008.

37 Chemical Weapons Convention, 1993, Article II, paragraph 7.

38 Fidler, "The Meaning of Moscow."

39 Executive Order 11850, Renunciation of Certain Uses in War of Chemical
Herbicides and Riot Control Agents (1975).

40 M. A. Coppernoll and X. K Maruyama, "Legal and Ethical Guiding
Principles and Constraints Concerning Nonlethal Weapons Technology
and Employment" (Monterey, CA: Defense Manpower Data Center,
1998); The Sunshine Project, Backgrounder Series 8 (July 2001),
Nonlethal Weapons Research in the US: Calmatives and Malodorants (http://
www.sunshineproject.org/publications/bk/bk8en.html).

41 Paola Gaeta, "The Armed Conflict in Chechnya before the Russian
Constitutional Court," *European Journal of International Law* 7 (1996),
563–70.

42 *The SIrUS Project: Towards a Determination of Which Weapons Cause "Superfluous Injury or Unnecessary Suffering"* (Geneva: International Committee of the Red Cross, 1997): 23; see also Robin M. Coupland, "The Effect Of Weapons: Defining Superfluous Injury and Unnecessary Suffering," *Medicine and Global Survival* 3 (1996): A1; Robin M. Coupland, "The SIrUS Project: Progress Report on 'Superfluous Injury or Unnecessary Suffering' in Relation to the Legality of Weapons," *International Review of the Red Cross* 835 (1999): 583–92.

43 Robin M. Coupland, "The Effect Of Weapons: Defining Superfluous Injury and Unnecessary Suffering."

44 International Committee of the Red Cross, *Guide to the Legal Review of New Weapons, Means and Methods of Warfare: Measures to Implement Article 36 of Additional Protocol I of 1977* (Geneva: ICRC, 2006) (emphasis added).

45 Although the 1997 SIrUS project recommendations (note 42) preclude nonlethal weapons, the 2006 guidelines (note 44) link superfluous injury and unnecessary suffering to weapons that cause "*long term or permanent* alteration to the victim's psychology or physiology" (19). While this does not exclude weapons that cause other kinds of harm, there is no specific mention of short-term or transient harm in this discussion.

46 Council on Foreign Relations, *Nonlethal Weapons and Capability, Report of an Independent Task Force Sponsored by the Council on Foreign Relations* (New York: Council on Foreign Relations, 2004): 30–2.

47 See also Nick Lewer and S. Schofield, *Nonlethal Weapons: A Fatal Attraction?* (London: Zed Books, 1997); Malcolm Dando, *A New Form of Warfare: The Rise of Nonlethal Weapons* (London: Brassey's, 1996): 191–205.

48 Ian McEwan, *Saturday* (New York: Doubleday, 2005): 95.

49 Moreno, *Mind Wars*, 19.

50 See Michael L Gross, "Medicalized Weapons and Modern War," *The Hastings Center Report* (Garrison, NY: in press).

5 Murder, Self-Defense, or Execution?

1 Lieber Code, 1863, paragraph 148.

2 See Leslie C. Green, *The Contemporary Law of Armed Conflict* Second Edition (Manchester: Manchester University Press, 2000):144, note 148.

3 Reports of early targeted killing programs appear in Seymour Hirsch, *Chain of Command: The Road from 9/11 to Abu Ghraib* (New York: Harper Collins, 2005): 273–86; and Douglas Jehl and Thom Shanker, "Congress Is Reviewing Pentagon on Intelligence Activities," *New York Times*, February 4, 2005. Reports of programs designed to target al-Qaeda in Iraq appear in Bob Woodward, *The War Within: A Secret White House History 2006–2008* (New York: Simon and Schuster, 2008); Bob Woodward on *60 Minutes,* September 7, 2008; Bob Woodward, "Why Did Violence Plummet? It Wasn't Just the Surge," *Washington Post* September 8, 2008; Joby Warrick

and Robin Wright, "U.S. Teams Weaken Insurgency in Iraq," *Washington Post*, September 6, 2008.

4 Jane Mayer, *The Dark Side: The Inside Story of How The War on Terror Turned into a War on American Ideals* (New York: Doubleday, 2008): 39.

5 J. M. Spaight, *War Rights on Land* (London: Macmillan, 1911): 8 (emphasis added).

6 Louis Rene Beres, "Assassination and the Law, A Policy Memorandum," *Studies in Conflict and Terrorism* 18(1995), 299–315.

7 John Toland, *The Rising Sun, The Decline and Fall of the Japanese Empire 1936–45* (London: Cassell and Company, 1970): 441.

8 Yael Stein, "By Any Name Illegal and Immoral," (Response to "Israel's Policy of Targeted Killing," Steven R. David), *Ethics & International Affairs* 17:1(2003): 127–40.

9 Public Committee against Torture in Israel and Palestinian Society for the Protection of Human Rights and the Environment v. The Government of Israel (High Court of Justice 769/02, December 11, 2005, paragraph 40).

10 Philip B. Heymann and Juliette N. Kayyem, *Protecting Liberty in an Age of Terror*, Belfer Center for Science and International Affairs, Studies in International Security (Cambridge: MIT Press, 2005): 66.

11 See *Basic Principles on the Use of Force and Firearms by Law Enforcement Officials*, adopted by the Eighth United Nations Congress on the Prevention of Crime and Treatment of Offenders, Havana Cuba, August 27 to September 7, 1990; Nigel S. Rodley, *The Treatment of Prisoners Under International Law* (Oxford: Clarendon Press, 1999): 440–4.

12 My thanks to Daniel Statman for taking me to task on this point in his "Targeted Killing," *Theoretical Inquiries in Law* 5 (2004), 179–98, and showing how naming emphasizes a combatant's role.

13 Helmut Nickel, "The Round Table, About the Saxon Rebellion and the Massacre at Amesbury," *Arthuriana* 16:1 (Spring 2006), 65–70 at 67.

14 Emer de Vattel, *The Law of Nations or the Principles of Natural Law* (trans. Charles G Fenwick) The Classics of International Law (Geneva: Slatkine Reprints – Henry Dunant Institute, 1983), [1758], III, 8, 155.

15 Statman, "Targeted Killing," 179–98 at 193.

16 Michael L. Gross, "Fighting by Other Means in the Mideast: A Critical Analysis of Israel's Assassination Policy," *Political Studies* 51 (2003), 350–68; Michael L. Gross, "Assassination: Killing in the Shadow of Self-Defense," J. Irwin (ed.), *War and Virtual War: The Challenges to Communities* (Amsterdam: Rodopi, 2004): 99–116.

17 Andrew Rigby, *The Legacy of the Past: The Problem of Collaborators and the Palestinian Case* (Jerusalem: Palestinian Academic Society for the Study of International Affairs, 1997).

18 Bruce R. Pirnie and Edward O'Connell, *Counterinsurgency in Iraq (2003–2006)* (Santa Monica , CA: Rand Corporation, 2008): 84.

19 Rupert Smith, *The Utility of Force: The Art of War in the Modern World* (New York: Vintage, 2008): 383.

20 Pirnie and O'Connell, *Counterinsurgency in Iraq (2003–2006)*, 84.

21 Physicians for Human Rights, Israel, "Holding Health to Ransom: GSS Interrogation and Extortion of Palestinian Patients at Erez Crossing" (Tel Aviv: Physicians for Human Rights, August 2008).

22 Rigby, *The Legacy of the Past*, 4; Yizhar Be'er and Saleh Abd al-Jawad, *Collaborators in the Occupied Territories: Human Rights Abuses and Violations* (Jerusalem: B'Tselem, 1994): 199); see also Aviel Linder, "Family Matters: Using Family Members to Pressure Detainees Under GSS Interrogation" (Jerusalem: Public Committee against Torture in Israel, 2008); Physicians for Human Rights, *Holding Health to Ransom.*

23 Saleh Abd al-Jawad, "The Classification and Recruitment of Collaborators," *The Phenomenon of Collaborators in Palestine: Proceedings of a Passia Workshop* (Jerusalem: Palestinian Academic Society for the Study of International Affairs, 2001): 18.

24 Yizhar Be'er and Saleh Abd al-Jawad, *Collaborators in the Occupied Territories*, 164.

25 Figures from B'Tselem, Israeli Information Center for Human Rights in the Occupied Territories (http://www.btselem.org/English/Statistics/Casualties.asp).

26 See also Chapter 7 (p. 166), "Reassessing Proportionality in Asymmetric Conflict: The Problem of Human Shields and Inaccurate Weaponry."

27 For example, one of the most widely condemned missions took place on July 23, 2002 as 15 civilians died in a strike killing Salah Shehadeh, the head of the Hamas military wing.

28 Woodward, *The War Within*, 379–80.

29 Statman, "Targeted Killing," 192.

30 Yael Stein, Position Paper: "Israel's Assassination Policy: Extra-judicial Executions" (Jerusalem: B'Tselem, Israeli Information Center for Human Rights in the Occupied Territories, 2001).

31 B'Tselem, Israeli Information Center for Human Rights in the Occupied Territories, "Israeli Civilians Killed by Palestinians within the Green Line" (http://www.btselem.org/english/statistics/Casualties.asp).

32 Daniel Byman has suggested that the fence and targeted killings go hand in hand: Daniel Byman, "Do Targeted Killings Work?" *Foreign Affairs* 85:2 (2006), 95–111.

33 Levy Gideon, "The Price of Liquidation," *Ha'aretz*, October 21, 2001; Uzi, Benziman, "Thinking Again about Assassination Policy," *Ha'aretz*, October 21, 2001; Amos Harel, "Security Brass: Targeted Killings Don't Work: No Military Solution to Terror," *Ha'aretz*, December 19, 2001; Vincent Cannistraro, "Assassination is Wrong – and Dumb," *Washington Post*, August 30, 2001.

34 Lahoud Lamia, "PA: Hamas, Back by Popular Support, Will Take Revenge," *Jerusalem Post*, November 2001.

35 Lawrence Freedman, *A Choice of Enemies: America Confronts the Middle East* (New York: Public Affairs, 2008): 461–2.

36 "Targeted assassinations have no significant impact on rates of Palestinian attacks." Mohammed M. Hafez and Joseph M. Hatfield, "Do Targeted Assassinations Work? A Multivariate Analysis of Israel's Controversial Tactic during Al-Aqsa Uprising," *Studies in Conflict & Terrorism* 29:4 (July 2006): 359–82). "When we examine how targeted killings affect *intended* violence, we find that at low levels, targeted killings actually increase the Palestinian efforts to respond with suicide attacks." David A. Jaeger and M. Daniele Paserman, "The Shape of Things to Come? Assessing the Effectiveness of Suicide Attacks and Targeted Killings," *Forschungsinstitut zur Zukunft der Arbeit*, Institute for the Study of Labor, Discussion Paper 2890, June 2007 (http://ftp.iza.org/dp2890.pdf). "The [stock] market perceives [the assassination of senior *political* leaders] as counterproductive, but sees the [assassination of senior *military* leaders] as an effective measure in combating terrorism." Asaf Zussman and Noam Zussman, "Assassinations: Evaluating the Effectiveness of an Israeli Counterterrorism Policy Using Stock Market Data," *Journal of Economic Perspectives* 20:2 (Spring 2006), 193–206; Also Hillel Frisch, "Motivation or Capabilities? Israeli Counterterrorism against Palestinian Suicide Bombings and Violence," *The Journal of Strategic Studies* 29:4 (October 2006): 843–69.

37 Edward Kaplan, et al. "What Happened to Suicide Bombings in Israel? Insights from a Terror Stock Model," *Studies in Conflict and Terrorism* 28:3 (2005): 225–35.

38 Daniel Jacobson and Edward H. Kaplan, "Suicide Bombings and Targeted Killings in (Counter-) Terror Games," *Journal of Conflict Resolution* 51:5 (October 2007): 772–92.

39 Guy Bechor, "Liquidating the Liquidations," *Yidiot Aharonot* (Hebrew), November 27, 2000.

40 Stathis N. Kalyvas and Matthew Adam Kocher, "How 'Free' Is Free Riding in Civil Wars? Violence, Insurgency, and the Collective Action Problem," *World Politics* 59:2 (2007): 177–216 at 202–3.

41 B'Tselem, Israeli Information Center for Human Rights in the Occupied Territories, "Palestinians Killed During the Course of a Targeted Killing" (http://www.btselem.org/English/Statistics/Casualties.asp).

6   Human Dignity or Human Life

1 George Tenet, *At the Center of the Storm: My Years at the CIA* (New York: HarperCollins, 2007): 497.

2 See, for example, Darius Rejali, *Torture and Democracy* (Princeton, NJ: Princeton University Press, 2007); and Jane Mayer, *The Dark Side: The Inside Story of How The War on Terror Turned into a War on American Ideals* (New York: Doubleday, 2008).

3 Committee against Torture, *Consideration of Reports Submitted by States Parties under Article 19 of the Convention*, "Concluding Observations of the Committee against Torture, Israel," CAT/C/ISR/CO/4 (Geneva: Committee against Torture, May 14, 2009): 4; Amos Harel and Avi Issacharoff, *The Seventh War: How We Won and Why We Lost the War with the Palestinians* (Hebrew) (Tel Aviv: Mishkal Publishing House, 2005): 162. This covers the period between September 1999 and July 2002. There are no figures for subsequent years.

4 This includes three cases of waterboarding. See Pamela Hess/Associated Press, "CIA Director, Michael Hayden, Says Coercive and Harsh Interrogations Worked," Cleveland Plain Dealer, January 15, 2009. For more detailed descriptions of waterboarding see memo dated August 1, 2002, from Jay Bybee, Assistant Attorney General, Office of Legal Counsel, to John A. Rizzo, General Counsel, Central Intelligence Agency, "Interrogation of al Qaeda Operative" (http://luxmedia.vo.llnwd.net/o10/ clients/aclu/olc_08012002_bybee.pdf); Steven Bradbury, Acting Assistant Attorney General, Memorandum to John A. Rizzo, General Counsel, CIA, "Re: Application of 18 U.S.C. §§ 2340–2340A to the Combined Use of Certain Techniques in the Interrogation of a High Value al Qaeda Detainee," May 10, 2005 (http://luxmedia.vo.llnwd.net/o10/clients/aclu/ olc_05102005_bradbury_20pg.pdf); Steven Bradbury, Acting Assistant Attorney General, Memorandum for John Rizzo, Senior General Counsel, CIA, "Re: Application of 18 U.S.C. §§ 2340–2340A, that may be used in the interrogation of a high value al Qaeda Detainee," May 10, 2005 (http:// luxmedia.vo.llnwd.net/o10/clients/aclu/olc_05102005_bradbury46pg. pdf); Steven Bradbury, Acting Assistant Attorney General, Memorandum for John Rizzo, Senior General Counsel, CIA, "Re: Application of United States Obligations Under Article 16 of the Convention Against Torture to Certain Techniques that May Be Used in the Interrogation of High Value al Qaeda Detainees," 30 May 2005 (http://luxmedia.vo.llnwd.net/o10/ clients/aclu/olc_05302005_bradbury.pdf).

5 Daniel Statman, "The Absoluteness of the Prohibition Against Torture" (Hebrew) *Mishpat u-memshal* 4 (1997): 161–98; Yuval Ginbar, *Why Not Torture Terrorists? Moral, Practical and Legal Aspects of the "Ticking Bomb" Justification for Torture* (Oxford: Oxford University Press, 2008); Bob Brecher, *Torture and the Ticking Bomb* (Malden, MA: Blackwell, 2007).

6 Richard Posner, *Not a Suicide Pact: The Constitution in Time of National Emergency* (Oxford: Oxford University Press, 2006): 83 (emphasis added). See also Richard Posner, "Torture, Terrorism and Interrogation,"

Sanford Levinson (ed.), *Torture, A Collection* (Oxford: Oxford University Press, 2004): 291–8.

7 Philip Bobbit, *Terror and Consent: The Wars for the Twenty-First Century* (New York: Knopf, 2008): 92.

8 See Rupert Smith, *The Utility of Force: The Art of War in the Modern World* (New York: Vintage, 2008): 331.

9 Bob Woodward, *The War Within: A Secret White House History 2006–2008* (New York: Simon and Schuster, 2008), 137.

10 See, for example, U.S. Army Field Manual FM 2-22.3 (FM 34–52) *Human Intelligence Collector Operations* (Washington, DC: Department of The Army, September 2006); Fein, Robert (ed.) "Educing Information. Interrogation: Science and Art. Foundations for the Future," Intelligence Science Board, Phase 1 Report (Washington, DC: National Defense Intelligence College Press), Center for Strategic Intelligence Research, December 2006.

11 FM 2-22.3, Human Intelligence Collector Operations, 8–3.

12 FM 2-22.3, Human Intelligence Collector Operations (sections 8–8, 8–36, 8–37, 8–47, 8–65, 8–69). For similar Israeli techniques see B'Tselem, *Absolute Prohibition The Torture and Ill-treatment of Palestinian Detainees* (Jerusalem: B'Tselem, May 2007).

13 Daniel Levin, Memorandum for James B. Comey, Deputy Attorney General, "Re: Legal Standards Applicable Under 18 U.S.C. §§ 2340–2340A," December 30, 2004 (http://www.usdoj.gov/olc/18usc23402340a2.htm); Steven Bradbury, Memorandum, May 10, 2005; Steven Bradbury, Memorandum, May 30, 2005. See also Mayer, *The Dark Side*, 306.

14 Ian Brownlie, "Interrogation in Depth: The Compton and Parker Reports," *The Modern Law Review* 35 (5) (September 1972): 501–7.

15 "Ireland vs. the United Kingdom," *Yearbook of the European Conventions on Human Rights* 19 (1976): 512–928, paragraph 96, note 83.

16 "Ireland vs. the United Kingdom," paragraph 167.

17 In addition to waterboarding, sensory and sleep deprivation, and exposure to extreme temperatures, CIA memos released in 2009 (note 4) also describe "walling" or slamming detainees against a false flexible wall while cushioning their necks to prevent serious injury. In Israel, the techniques approved for use by the GSS are similar (although there is no mention of waterboarding or walling). See B'Tselem, *Absolute Prohibition: The Torture and Ill-treatment of Palestinian Detainees*, May 2007.

18 On the other hand, some human rights organizations, distinguish between "direct violence" (beatings, slapping, kicking, painful stress positions, intentional tightening of shackles, and shaking) and sleep deprivation, exposure to heat and cold, handcuffing behind the back, cursing, threats, and humiliation. See "Back to a Routine of Torture: Torture and Ill-treatment of Palestinian Detainees, during Arrest, Detention

and Interrogation, September 2001–April 2003" (Jerusalem: Public Committee against Torture in Israel, nd): 10, 88 (http://www.stoptorture.org.il/files/back%20to%20routine.pdf).

19 Rejali, *Torture and Democracy*, 355–6 (emphasis added).

20 See note 13.

21 "Horrifying and Unnecessary Treatment of Prisoners," Editorial, *New York Times/International Herald Tribune*, March 3, 2008.

22 Peter Baker, "Banned Techniques Yielded 'High Value Information' Memo Says," *New York Times*, April 21, 2009.

23 Rejali, *Torture and Democracy*, 480–518; Meyers, *The Dark Side*.

24 Stathis N. Kalyvas and Matthew Adam Kocher, "How 'Free' Is Free Riding in Civil Wars?," *World Politics* 59:2 (2007): 177–216 at 202–3.

25 Figures from B'Tselem (http://www.btselem.org/English/Statistics/Casualties.asp). Staffers assume the civilians who died were collateral casualties and that the militants the IDF targeted were, in fact, armed and members of guerrilla organizations. Personal conversation August 7, 2008.

26 President George W. Bush, Executive Order, "Interpretation of the Geneva Conventions Common Article 3 as Applied to a Program of Detention and Interrogation Operated by the Central Intelligence Agency," July 20, 2007, Section 3. On January 22, 2009 President Barack Obama rescinded this order and suspended enhanced techniques. (Executive Order – Ensuring Lawful Interrogations, Section 5e).

27 Dignity refers to a person's fundamental worth and respect for self-esteem. Self-esteem is a primary good without which human endeavor is crippled. Degradation, humiliation, ill-treatment, and debasement all impair self-esteem. See Gross, *Bioethics and Armed Conflict*, 49–56.

28 Public Committee against Torture in Israel v. The State of Israel (High Court of Justice, 5100/94, September 6, 1999).

29 As framed in the Israel Penal Code, section 22.

30 "Of 550 examinations of torture allegations initiated by the General Security Services inspector [Israel's domestic intelligence agency] between 2002 and 2007, only four resulted in disciplinary measures and none in prosecution." (Committee against Torture, *Consideration of Reports Submitted by States Parties under Article 19*, 2009, 6). U.S. officials report that between 2001 and 2009 "more than 400 military members charged with detainee abuse were found to be guilty of some form of misconduct." It is not known how many were CIA interrogators. Gerry J. Gilmore, "Pentagon to Release Photos From Detainee Custody Investigations," *American Forces Press Service*, April 24, 2009.

31 Amos Harel, "Shin Bet Tested by Legal Restraints and a Growing Caseload," *Ha'aretz*, July 25, 2002 (emphasis added).

32 B'Tselem, *Absolute Prohibition* (May 2007); Public Committee against Torture in Israel, "Breaches in the Defense: Torture and Ill-treatment during GSS [General Security Services] Investigations Following the Verdict of the High Court of Justice, 6 September 1999" (Jerusalem: Public Committee against Torture in Israel, 2001).

33 Michael Moore, "Torture and the Balance of Evils," *Israel Law Review* 23: 2, 3 (1989): 280–344.

34 Press reports indicate relatively small numbers of U.S. soldiers captured and then killed or tortured. In January and June 2007, insurgents captured and executed four and three soldiers, respectively. In June 2006, two soldiers were captured and reportedly tortured and killed. "Military confirms 4 soldiers were abducted during attack in Karbala," USA Today, January 26, 2007; Damien Cave, "Iraq Insurgent Group Claims It Killed Missing U.S. Soldiers," *New York Times*, June 5, 2007; Dexter Filkins, "Bodies of G.I.'s Show Signs of Torture, Iraqi General Says," *New York Times*, June 20, 2006.

35 In contrast to French forces in Algeria, the Portuguese prohibited and never sanctioned torture in their colonial wars in Angola and Mozambique. The Portuguese were convinced that torture was not effective, gave unreliable information, and unnecessarily alienated the local population. See John P. Cann, *Counterinsurgency in Africa, The Portuguese Way of War 1961–1974* (Westport, CT: Greenwood Press, 1997): 117–20. For the French use of torture in Algeria see Rejali, *Torture and Democracy;* and Alistair Horne, *A Savage War of Peace: Algeria 1954–1962* (New York: Viking, 1978). In the British colonies, torture was rampant. In Kenya, the British used harsh brutal methods to force Kenyans to confess and repudiate the Mau Mau oath. The British were not after information but rehabilitation. See Caroline Elkins, *Imperial Reckoning: The Untold Story of Britain's Gulag in Kenya* (New York: Henry Holt, 2005): 152, 319–27. Nevertheless, the British distinguished between legal compelling force and illegal punitive force. Compelling force could be used "when immediately necessary to restrain or overpower a refractory detained person, or to compel compliance with a lawful order to prevent disorder." Punitive force was apparently used to describe any kind of unlawful physical punishment." (Elkins, *Imperial Reckoning*, 324). The British also practiced interrogational torture in Cyprus, Malaya, Palestine, Aden, British Cameroon. See Ian Brownlie, "Interrogation in Depth" 501–7.

36 David Weissbrodt and Amy Bergquist, "Extraordinary Rendition: A Human Rights Analysis," *Harvard Human Rights Journal* 19:123 (2006): 123–60 at 136.

37 Michael John Garcia, "Renditions: Constraints Imposed by the Laws on Torture," CRS Report for Congress (Washington, DC: Congressional Research Service, The Library of Congress, April 2006).

38 Garcia, "Renditions," 19.

39 Stephen Grey, *Ghost Plane: The True Story of the CIA Torture Program* (New York: St. Martin's Press, 2006): 267–83; Weissbrodt and Bergquist, "Extraordinary Rendition;" Amnesty International, *United States of America, Below the Radar: Secret Flights to Torture and 'Disappearance,'* AI Index: AMR 51/051/2006, April 5, 2006: 26–7; Godfrey Hodgson, "The U.S.–European Torture Dispute: An Autopsy," *World Policy Journal* (Winter 2005/06): 7–14; Richard Norton-Taylor, "CIA Tried to Silence EU on Torture Flights," *The Guardian*, October 26, 2006; Mayer, *The Dark Side*, 275.

40 Francoise J. Hampson, "Detention, The War on Terror and International Law," Howard Hensel (ed.), *The Law of Armed Conflict, Constraints on the Contemporary Use of Force* (Aldershot, Hampshire, UK: Ashgate, 2007): 131–70 at 143–4; see also Weissbrodt and Bergquist for a more conservative interpretation.

41 Agiza v. Sweden, Communication No. 233/2003, United Nations Document CAT/C/34/D/233/2003, 2005, paragraph 13.8.

42 "Judge Accuses Spies of Kidnapping Terrorist Suspects," *ABC News*, May 21, 2005; see also Grey, *Ghost Plane*.

43 "Germany Issues Arrest Warrants for 13 CIA Agents in El-Masri Case," *Spiegel Online*, January 31, 2007.

44 *"Government Response to the Intelligence and Security Committee's Report on Rendition"* (Colegate, Norwich, UK: Crown Copyright, July 2007): 6–7; see also Doug Cassel, "Washington's 'War Against Terrorism' and Human Rights: The View from Abroad," *Human Rights* 33:1 (2006), 1–9, for criticism leveled by European jurists for conditions at Guantanamo Bay.

45 President George W. Bush, Executive Order: Interpretation of the Geneva Conventions Common Article 3 as Applied to a Program of Detention and Interrogation Operated by the Central Intelligence Agency, July 20, 2007, Section 3.

46 Posner, *Not a Suicide Pact*, 83.

47 WorldPublicOpinion.org. "World Publics Reject Torture" (June 24, 2008) (http://www.worldpublicopinion.org/pipa/articles/btjusticehuman_rightsra/496.php?lb=bthr&pnt=496&nid=&id=); "World Citizens Reject Torture, BBC Global Poll Reveals" (October 18, 2006) (http://www.worldpublicopinion.org/pipa/articles/btjusticehuman_rightsra/261.php?nid=&). In 2006 29 percent supported torture while 59 percent opposed. Support grew in those nations experiencing or fighting terrorism and dropped in those nations enjoying relative quiet since 2006.

48 When a detainee was suspected of terrorism, 20 percent of respondents supported torture, 30 percent supported humiliating treatment, 33 percent supported mental torture, and 38 percent supported the

threat of torture (http://www.worldpublicopinion.org/pipa/pdf/jul06/
TerrSuspect_Jul06_quaire.pdf). Pew Research Center polls consistently
put support for torture among Americans at just under 50 percent. Pew
Research Center, "Public Remains Divided Over Use of Torture, April
23, 2009 (http://people-press.org/report/510/public-remains-divided-
over-use-of-torture). In a 2004 poll there was also majority support for
sleep deprivation, loud noise, hooding, and stress positions (http://www.
worldpublicopinion.org/pipa/articles/btjusticehuman_rightsra/111.
php?lb=bthr&pnt=111&nid=&id=).

49 WorldPublicOpinion.org. "Publics Around the World Say Governments
Should Act to Prevent Racial Discrimination" (March 20, 2008)
(http://www.worldpublicopinion.org/pipa/articles/btjusticehuman_
rightsra/460.php?lb=bthr&pnt=460&nid=&id=); "International Poll
Finds Large Majorities in All Countries Favor Equal Rights for Women"
(March 6, 2008) (http://www.worldpublicopinion.org/pipa/articles/
btjusticehuman_rightsra/453.php?lb=bthr&pnt=453&nid=&id=);
Reuters, "Poll Finds Global Support for Press Freedom," May 1, 2008.

50 Jeffrey Gettleman, "In Ethiopian Desert, Horrors of a Hidden War,"
International Herald Tribune, June 17, 2007. For other reports on human
rights abuses in Ethiopia, see U.S. Department of State, *Ethiopia,
Country Reports on Human Rights Practices, 2006* (Washington, D.C: U.S.
Department of State, Bureau of Democracy, Human Rights, and Labor,
March 6, 2007); and Amnesty International, *Ethiopia: No Progress on
Human Rights,* Congressional Testimony, Presented by Lynn Fredriksson,
Advocacy Director for Africa, Amnesty International USA, November
16, 2006 (http://www.amnestyusa.org/document.php?lang=e&id=ENG
USA20061116001).

51 *Absolute Prohibition: The Torture and Ill-treatment of Palestinian Detainees*
(Jerusalem: B'Tselem, May 2007).

52 Statman, "The Absoluteness of the Prohibition Against Torture."

53 Bruce R. Pirnie and Edward O'Connell, *Counterinsurgency in Iraq (2003–
2006)* (Santa Monica , CA: Rand Corporation, 2008):46–8.

7   Blackmailing the Innocent

1   I thank Saul Smilansky for drawing my attention to the difference between blackmail and extortion. Blackmail involves the threat to do what is
permitted (disclose embarrassing information, for example). Extortion,
on the other hand, "is a coercive request accompanied by the threat to
perform an illegal action (for example, to use violence against someone)."
See Saul Smilansky, *10 Moral Paradoxes* (Oxford: Blackwell, 2007): 42–3.

2   Yitzchak Benbaji, "A Defense of the Traditional War Convention," *Ethics*
118 (April 2008): 464–95; see also George Mavrodes, "Conventions

and the Morality of War," Charles R. Beitz (ed.), *International Ethics* (Princeton, NJ: Princeton University Press, 1985): 75–89; Robert K. Fullinwider, "War and Innocence," Beitz, *International Ethics*, 90–7; Ward Thomas, *The Ethics of Destruction: Norms and Force in International Relations* (Ithaca, NY: Cornell University Press, 2001): 95–6); and Uwe Steinhoff, "Civilians and Soldiers," Igor Primoratz (ed.), *Civilian Immunity in War* (Oxford: Oxford University Press, 2007): 42–61.

3   Andrew Exum, *Hizballah at War, A Military Assessment*, Policy Focus No. 63 (Washington, DC: The Washington Institute for Near East Policy, December 2006): 10–11.

4   Amos Harel and Avi Issacharoff, "The Northern Command Ran Out of Targets," *Ha'aretz*, April 2, 2007; Human Rights Watch, *Why They Died: Civilian Casualties in Lebanon during the 2006 War* (September 2007, Volume 19, No. 5(E)): 77. Available at: http://www.hrw.org/en/reports/2007/09/05/why-they-died.

5   Report of the Winograd Committee Investigation the Second Lebanon War (Hebrew) (Jerusalem, Office of the Prime Minister, 2008): 490, 481, note 5. The Winograd Committee made no attempt to answer "complicated questions of identifying 'military' targets or those supporting the fighting in a way that justifies attacking them."

6   Human Rights Watch, *Why They Died*, 72–8.

7   Hamza Hendawi, "Israel Targeting Hezbollah Infrastructure," Associated Press, July 26, 2006.

8   Amos Harel and Avi Issacharoff, *34 Days: Israel, Hezbollah and the War in Lebanon* (New York, Palgrave Macmillan, 2008).

9   See Chapter 2 (p. 34), "Combatant (In)Equality in Asymmetric War." For a recent summary of this discussion see Public Committee against Torture in Israel and Palestinian Society for the Protection of Human Rights and the Environment v. The Government of Israel, et. al. (High Court of Justice 769/02, December 11, 2005).

10 UN Human Rights Council, *Report of the Commission of Inquiry on Lebanon Pursuant to Human Rights Council Resolution S-2/1*, 23 November 2006, A/HRC/3/2, available at: http://www.unhcr.org/refworld/docid/45c30b6e0.html.

11 Harel and Issacharoff, *34 Days*, 118.

12 A. P. V. Rogers, "The Principle of Proportionality," Howard Hensel (ed.), *The Legitimate Use of Military Force: The Just War Tradition and the Customary Law of Armed Conflict* (Aldershot, Hampshire, UK: Ashgate Publishing, 2008): 189–218; Wesley Moore, "A War-Crimes Commission for the Hizbollah-Israel War?" *Middle East Policy* 13:4 (2006), 61–90.

13 T. Hurka, "Proportionality in the Morality of War," *Philosophy and Public Affairs* 33 (2005): 34–66 at 63 (emphasis added).

14   For a more detailed discussion of manifestly unlawful orders see Chapter 2 (p. 27), "The Idea of Combatant Equality;" Geoffrey Best, *War and Law Since 1945* (Oxford: Oxford University Press, 1997): 280.

15   Hezbollah launched 3,970 missiles killing 42 civilians. Anthony Cordesman, *Lessons of the 2006 Israeli-Hezbollah War* (Washington, DC: Center for Strategic and International Studies, 2007): 157.

16   Protocol Additional to the Geneva Conventions of 12 August 1949, and Relating to the Protection of Victims of International Armed Conflicts (Protocol I, June 8, 1977). Commentary, p. 684, paragraph 2213.

17   Joint Service Committee on Military Justice, *Manual for Courts-Martial, United States* 2000 edition, Paragraph 916d, II–111; see also Leslie C. Green, "Superior Orders and the Reasonable Man;" Leslie C. Green, *The Modern Law of War*, Second Edition (New York: Transnational Publishers, 1999): 245–82.

18   See Protocol Additional to the Geneva Conventions of 12 August 1949, and Relating to the Protection of Victims of International Armed Conflicts (Protocol I, June 8, 1977), Article 52 and Commentary 636, paragraphs 2012–23.

19   Dual-use casualties from Human Rights Watch, *Why They Died*, 75, 166-170; long-range casualties from Harel and Issacharoff, *34 Days*, 91.

20   Cordesman, *Lessons of the 2006 Israeli–Hezbollah War*, 42.

21   Protocol Additional to the Geneva Conventions of 12 August 1949, and Relating to the Protection of Victims of International Armed Conflicts (Protocol I, June 8, 1977), Article 51 (7).

22   Human Rights Watch, *Off Target: The Conduct of the War and Civilian Casualties in Iraq* December 2003): 67-9. Available at: http://humanrightswatch.net/reports/2003/usa1203/index.htm.

23   Human Rights Watch, *Why They Died*, 52–6; Hugh White, "Civilians in the Precision-Guidance Age," in Primoratz, *Civilian Immunity in War*, 182–200, especially 193–196.

24   Uri Bar-Joseph, "Israel's Military Intelligence Performance in the Second Lebanon War," *International Journal of Intelligence and Counterintelligence* 20:4 (December 2007), 583–601; see also Cordesman, *Lessons of the 2006 Israeli–Hezbollah War*, 43; Reuven Erlich, *Hezbollah's Use of Lebanese Civilians as Human Shields* (Tel Aviv: Intelligence and Terrorism Information Center at the Center for Special Studies, December 5, 2006). In other cases, IDF films show "categorical proof that Hezbollah fired rockets in the near vicinity of houses." (Harel and Issacharoff, *34 Days*, 272, note 9).

25   See Daniel P. Schoenekase, "Targeting Decisions Regarding Human Shields," *Military Review* 84:5 (September–October 2004), 26–31.

26   United Nations, Mine Action Co-ordination Center Southern Lebanon, 2008 (http://www.maccsl.org/reports/Monthly%20Reports/Monthly%202008/Monthly%20Report%20Nov-Dec%2008.pdf).

27   Human Rights Watch, *Why They Died*, 144.

28   Marwahine (July 15, 2006), Qana (July 30), Beka (August 4), and Rweiss
     (August 13), Human Rights Watch, *Why They Died*, 147, 130, 119, 144. For
     the Israeli response acknowledging erroneous intelligence in the Qana
     attack see Israel Ministry of Foreign Affairs, "Completion of Inquiry into
     July 30th Incident in Qana," August 2, 2006 (http://www.mfa.gov.il/
     MFA/Government/Communiques/2006/Completion+of+inquiry+into
     +July+30+incident+in+Qana+2-Aug-2006.htm). For anecdotal evidence
     suggesting a "mistake" at Marwahine see *The New York Review of Books*,
     "Human Rights Watch and Israel: An Exchange by Seymour Feshbach,
     reply by Aryeh Neier," 53, No. 20 (December 21, 2006).

29   United Nations Press Release, "Special Rapporteur Calls on the
     Government and the International Community to Make Renewed Efforts
     to Prevent Unlawful Killings," May 15, 2008; UN High Commissioner
     for Human Rights, *Armed Conflict and Civilian Casualties, Afghanistan
     Trends and Developments 01 January–31 August 2008*, September 10, 2008
     (www2.ohchr.org/SPdocs/Afg-UNAMAstats10sept08.doc). In several
     reports, Oxfam and Amnesty International have charged NATO forces
     with the use of disproportionate force. But these appear to be instances
     of unnecessary force (attacks based on erroneous information) or in-
     discriminate attacks (failure to distinguish between combatants and
     noncombatants). See Agency Coordinating Body for Afghan Relief,
     Protecting Afghan Civilians: Statement on the Conduct of Military
     Operations, June 19, 2007 (http://www.oxfam.ca/news-and-publica-
     tions/publications-and-reports/protecting-afghan-civilians-statement-
     on-the-conduct-of-military-operations/file); Amnesty International,
     2008 Annual Report for Afghanistan (http://www.amnestyusa.org/
     annualreport.php?id=ar&yr=2008&c=AFG). The Oxfam report, for ex-
     ample, condemns 10 NATO raids that killed 127 people. They do not say
     how many were militants.

30   In October 2008, for example, a second U.S. inquiry into an attack in
     Afghanistan revealed that an American airstrike killed far more civil-
     ians than originally claimed. Instead of collateral casualties of five to
     seven civilians in an attack that killed 30–35 militants, it appears that
     more than 30 civilians died to kill fewer than 20 militants. Nevertheless,
     the United States maintained that the attacks were legitimate (that is,
     a proportionate attack against a military target). The report was not
     released to the public but did challenge the Army's initial report. See
     Eric Schmitt, "30 Civilians Died in Afghan Raid, U.S. Inquiry Finds,"
     New York Times, October 7, 2008.

31   Yaakov Amidror, "Misreading the Second Lebanon War," *Jerusalem Issue
     Brief*, 6:16 (Jerusalem: Institute for Contemporary Affairs, January
     16, 2007); see also Gabriel Siboni, "Disproportionate Force: Israel's

Concept of Response in Light of the Second Lebanon War," *INSS Insight* 74 (Tel Aviv: Institute for National Security Studies, October 2, 2008). Disproportionate force was also on the lips of commentators and government leaders after the fighting in Gaza broke out in December 2008. See, for example, "Ethan Bronner, "Israel Reminds Its Foes It Has Teeth," *International Herald Tribune*, December 29, 2008. "Israel Vows 'Disproportionate' Response to Gaza Rocket Attacks," *The Telegraph*, February 1, 2009.

32 Amos Harel, "Analysis: IDF Plans to Use Disproportionate Force in Next War," *Ha'aretz*, October 5, 2008.

33 Daniel Statman, "Supreme Emergencies Revisited," *Ethics* 117 (2006), 58–79.

34 Additional Protocol I, Commentary, Article 57, 685, paragraph 2218 (emphasis added).

35 Geoffrey Best, *Humanity in Warfare* (London: Methuen, 1980): 242–85; Tami Davis Biddle, "Air Power" in *The Laws of War: Constraints on Warfare in the Western World*, Michael Howard, George J. Andreopoulos, and Mark R. Shulman (eds.) (New Haven, CT: Yale University Press, 1994):140–59; Frits Kalshoven, *Belligerent Reprisals* (Leyden: A. W. Sijthoff, 1971); George H. Quester, "The Psychological Effects of Bombing Civilian Populations: Wars of the Past," Betty Glad (ed.), *The Psychological Dimensions of War* (Newbury Park, CA: Sage Publications, 1990): 201–35; see also Stathis N. Kalyvas and Matthew Adam Kocher, "How 'Free' is Free Riding In Civil Wars? Violence, Insurgency, and the Collective Action Problem," *World Politics* 59 (January 2007), 177–216 at 188–9.

36 Exum, *Hizballah at War*, 12.

37 Richard Price and Nina Tannenwald, "Norms and Deterrence: The Nuclear and Chemical Weapons Taboos," Peter J. Katzenstein (ed.), *The Culture of National Security: Norms and Identity in World Politics* (New York: Columbia University Press, 1996): 114–52.

38 On the battle for public opinion in the Second Lebanon War see Cordesman, *Lessons of the 2006 Israeli–Hezbollah War*, 42; and Harel and Issacharoff, *34 Days*, 162.

8   Killing the Innocent

1   CNN, February 2, 2008 (http://us.cnn.com/2008/WORLD/meast/02/01/iraq.main/index.html).

2   See Elizabeth Rubin, "The Most Wanted Palestinian," *The New York Times Magazine*, June 30, 2002, 26–31, 42, 51–5; Ami Pedahzur, Arie Perliger, and Leonard Weinberg, "Altruism and Fatalism: The Characteristics of Palestinian Suicide Terrorists," *Deviant Behavior* 24 (2003): 421; Robert Pape, *Dying to Win: The Strategic Logic of Suicide Terrorism* (New York: Random House, 2005): 216.

3 Albert Camus, *The Just Assassins in Caligula and Three Other Plays* (New York: Vintage, 1958): 237, 246.

4 Daniel Williams, "No Regrets for an ex-Algerian Rebel Immortalized in Film," *International Herald Tribune*, June 19, 2007.

5 There are many definitions of terrorism. Common to most is intentional harm to innocent civilians for political gain. See C. W. Kegley, Jr., "The Characteristics of Contemporary International Terrorism," C. W. Kegley, Jr. (ed.), *International Terrorism: Characteristics, Causes, Controls* (New York: St. Martin's Press, 1990): 11–26. Terrorism, as a UN report defines it, is "any action intended to cause death or serious bodily harm to civilians or noncombatants, when the purpose of such an act, by its nature or context, is to intimidate a population or to compel a government or international organization to do or abstain from doing any act." *A More Secure World: Our Shared Responsibility, Report of the High-level Panel on Threats, Challenges and Change* (New York: The United Nations, 2004), paragraph 164d.

6 Bard E. O'Neill, *Insurgency and Terrorism: Inside Modern Revolutionary Warfare* (Washington, DC: Brassey's, 1990): 45–7; Ian F. W. Beckett, *Modern Insurgencies and Counter Insurgencies: Guerrillas and their Opponents since 1750* (London: Routledge, 2001):151–82.

7 See, for example, O'Neill, *Insurgency and Terrorism*; Ian F. W. Beckett, *Modern Insurgencies and Counter Insurgencies*; John A. Nagl, *Counterinsurgency Lessons from Malaya and Vietnam: Learning to Eat Soup with a Knife* (Westport, CT: Praeger, 2002).

8 Beckett, *Modern Insurgencies and Counter Insurgencies*, 177.

9 This is what Buchanan describes as a remedial right to secede. Allen Buchanan, "Theories of Secession," *Philosophy and Public Affairs* 26: 1 (1997), 31–61.

10 Paul Gilbert, *New Terror, New Wars* (Washington, DC: Georgetown University Press, 2003): 39–42; Jeff Goodwin, "A Theory of Categorical Terrorism," *Social Forces* 84:4 (2006): 2027–46.

11 Robert O. Keohane, "The Public Delegitimation of Terrorism and the Coalition Politics," Ken Booth and Tim Dunne (eds.), *Worlds In Collision: Terror and the Future of the Global Order* (New York: Palgrave Macmillan, 2002): 141–50.

12 Abraham Sofaer, "Agora, The US Decision not to Ratify Protocol I to the Geneva Conventions on the Protection of War Victims (con'd), The Rationale for the United States Decision," *American Journal of International Law* 82 (1987), 784–87 at 785–6.

13 UN General Assembly Resolution A/RES/42/159 (December 7, 1987); UN General Assembly Resolution A/RES/40/61 (December 9, 1985).

14 Jan Klabbers, "Rebel with a Cause? Terrorists and Humanitarian Law," *European Journal of International Law* 14:2 (2003): 299–312 at 307; see also Alan M. Dershowitz, *Why Terrorism Works* (New Haven, CT: Yale University

Press, 2002): 54. Here Dershowitz points to the International Convention Against the Taking of Hostages adopted by the UN General Assembly, December 18, 1979, article 12, which permitted hostage taking by "peoples [who] are fighting against colonial domination and alien occupation and against racist regimes in the exercise of their right of self-determination."

15 For a selection of views that justify terrorism see Igor Primoratz, *Terrorism: The Philosophical Issues* (New York: Palgrave Macmillan, 2004). Readers should note that although this was published in 2004, most of the articles originally appeared before the events of 9/11. As such, many of the justifications of terrorism pertain to nationalist terrorism and not post-9/11 international terrorism.

16 Serge Schmemann, "US Peace Envoy Arrives in Israel as Fighting Rages," *Ha'aretz*, March 15, 2002. For al-Qaeda see, for example, Mohammad Sidique Khan, one of the four 7 July bombers in England who stated, "Your democratically elected governments continuously perpetuate atrocities against my people all over the world. And your support of them makes you directly responsible." (*London Bomber: Text in full*, BBC News, September 1, 2005) available at http://news.bbc.co.uk/2/hi/uk_news/4206800.stm.

17 Isabel Kershner, "2 Boys, 2 Sides, 2 Beds in an Israeli Hospital Ward," *New York Times*, February 13, 2008.

18 Gregory M. Reichberg, Henrik Syse, and Endre Begby, "Paul Ramsey: Nuclear Weapons and Legitimate Defense," Gregory Reichberg, et al. (eds.), *The Ethics of War: Classic and Contemporary Readings* (Malden, MA: Wiley Blackwell, 2006): 614–24.

19 Reuvan Pedazur, "The Wrong Way to Fight Terrorism," *Ha'aretz*, December 11, 2002.

20 H. L. A. Hart, "Intention and Punishment," *Punishment and Responsibility, Essays in the Philosophy of Law* (Oxford: Oxford University Press, 1968): 119–27; Alison MacIntyre, "Doing Away with Double Effect," *Ethics* 111 (January 2001): 219–55; Robert L. Holmes, *On War and Morality* (Princeton, NJ: Princeton University Press, 1989); Warren S. Quinn, "Actions, Intentions and Consequences: The Doctrine of the Double Effect," *Philosophy and Public Affairs* 18 (Fall 1989): 334–51; Jeff McMahan, "Revising the Doctrine of Double Effect," *Journal of Applied Philosophy* 11:2 (1994): 201–212; Susan Uniacke, "Double Effect, Principle of," Edward Craig (ed.), *Routledge Encyclopedia of Philosophy* (London: Routledge, 1989).

21 A. J. Coates, *The Ethics of War* (Manchester: Manchester University Press, 1997): 244.

22 Uniacke, "Double Effect."

23 David Rodin, "Terrorism without Intentions," *Ethics* 114: 4 (July 2004): 752–71; Virginia Held, "Terrorism and War," *The Journal of Ethics*

8 (2004): 59–75. Both condemn state and nonstate terror for abusing the DDE.

24 This city is Sderot in the Western Negev, Israel. (http://sderotmedia. com/?page_id=11).

25 Human Rights Watch, "Palestinian Authority: End Rocket Attacks on Civilians, Use of Indiscriminate Homemade Rockets Violates Laws of War," *Human Rights News*, November 17, 2006. Available at: http://www.hrw.org/en/news/2006/11/17/palestinian-authority-end-rocket-attacks-civilians.

26 This city is Ashkelon, Israel, on the coastal plain periodically shelled since 2006. The military response was Operation Hot Winter in 2008, which took over one hundred Palestinian lives.

27 Human Rights Watch, *Civilians under Assault: Hezbollah's Rocket Attacks on Israel in the 2006 War* (August 2007, Volume 10, No. 3(E)). Available at: http://www.hrw.org/en/reports/2007/08/28/civilians-under-assault.

28 Frits Kalshoven, *Belligerent Reprisals* (Leyden: A. W. Sijthoff, 1971); Michael Walzer, *Just and Unjust Wars* (New York: Basic Books, 1977): 207–22; Burton M. Leiser, "The Morality of Reprisals," *Ethics* 85 (January 1975): 159–63; Andrew D. Mitchell, "Does One Illegality Merit Another? The Law of Belligerent Reprisals in International Law," *Military Law Review* 170 (December 2001): 155–77.

29 Sofaer, "Agora," 784–7.

30 See API, State Parties, (www.icrc.org/ihl.nsf/WebSign?ReadForm&id= 470&ps=P); see also Frits Kalshoven, "Belligerent Reprisals Revisited," *Netherlands Yearbook of International Law* 21(1990): 43–80 at 67; Christopher Greenwood, "The Twilight of the Law of Belligerent Reprisals," *Netherlands Yearbook of International Law* 20 (1989): 35–69 at 61, 65.

31 Jean-Marie Henckaerts and Louise Doswald-Beck, *Customary International Humanitarian Law* Volume 1, *Rules* (Cambridge: Cambridge University Press, 2005): 523.

32 See also Geoffrey Best, *Humanity in Warfare* (London: Methuen, 1980): 167. Bryan Brophy-Baermann, and John A. Conybeare, "Retaliating against Terrorism: Rational Expectations and the Optimality of Rules vs. Discretion," *American Journal of Political Science* 38:1 (February 1994): 196–210.

33 See Chapter 7, note 35.

34 Dershowitz, *Why Terrorism Works*; Andrew Valls – "Can Terrorism Be Justified," Andrew Valls (ed.), *Ethics in International Affairs* (Lanham, MD: Rowman & Littlefield, 2000): 65–80 – suggests that terrorism in Algeria, Kenya, Mandatory Palestine, and, more recently, in Beirut (when U.S. marines were attacked in 1983) was successful.

35　Michael Walzer, "Terrorism: A Critique of Excuses (1988)," Michael Walzer (ed.), *Arguing About War* (New Haven, CT: Yale University Press, 2004): 51–66 at 55–6.

36　Michael Ignatieff, *The Lesser Evil: Political Ethics in an Age of Terror* (Princeton, NJ: Princeton University Press, 2004): 111.

37　Rupert Smith, *The Utility of Force: The Art of War in the Modern World* (New York: Vintage, 2008).

38　J. Angelo Corlett, *Terrorism, A Philosophical Analysis* (Heidelberg: Springer, 2003): 127

39　Goodwin, "A Theory of Categorical Terrorism," 2037.

40　Barry Buzan, "Who May we Bomb?" Booth and Dunne, *Worlds in Collision*, 85–94; Uwe Steinhoff, "How Can Terrorism Be Justified?" Primoratz, *Terrorism*, 97–112.

41　Goodwin, "A Theory of Categorical Terrorism."

42　Michael Ignatieff, "Human Rights, the Laws of War and Terrorism," *Social Research* 69:4 (2002): 1137–58 at 1153.

43　Recall Charles Chaumont's observation in Chapter 2 (p. 38), "Shedding Uniforms in Asymmetric Warfare."

44　Between 2004 and 2009, roughly 90 percent of Palestinians surveyed supported armed attacks on Israeli soldiers or settlers while roughly 50 to 55 percent supported armed attacks on Israeli civilians living in Israel (pre-1967 borders). Palestinian Center for Policy and Survey Research, Palestinian Public Opinion Poll No (31), March 5–7, 2009; Poll # 11, March 14–17, 2004.

45　See discussion in Chapter 8 (p. 182), "Justifying the Heinous."

46　International Committee of the Red Cross, Third Expert Meeting on the Notion of Direct Participation in Hostilities, Summary Report (Geneva: ICRC, October 23–25, 2005). See also discussion in Chapter 2 (pp. 40–41), "Shedding Uniforms in Asymmetric Warfare."

9　Risking Our Lives to Save Others

1　Carnegie Council, "Myanmar: Reviewing the Argument for Humanitarian Intervention," May 8, 2008 (http://www.cceia.org/resources/picks/0007. html).

2　Samuel P. Huntington, "New Contingencies, Old Roles," *Joint Forces Quarterly* 34 (Autumn 1993): 38–43 at 42.

3　Joseph P. Bialke, "United Nations Peace Operations: Applicable Norms and the Application of the Law of Armed Conflict," *The Air Force Law Review* 50:1 (2001), 1–63. For a complete list see the UN's peacekeeping website at http://www.un.org/Depts/dpko/dpko/index.asp. For the distinction between peacekeeping and peace enforcing see Jules Lobel and Michael Ratner, "Bypassing the Security Council: Ambiguous Authorizations to Use Force, Cease-Fires and the Iraqi Inspection Regime," *The American*

Journal of International Law 93 (1999), 124–55; Carsten Stahn, "Future Implication of The Iraq Conflict: Enforcement of the Collective Will after Iraq," *The American Journal of International Law* 97 (2003), 804–23; Adam Roberts, "NATO's 'Humanitarian War' over Kosovo," *Survival* 41:3 (Autumn 1999): 102–23 at 107.

4   Fernando R. Tesón, "The Liberal Case for Humanitarian Intervention," J. L. Holzgrefe and Robert O. Keohane (eds.), *Humanitarian Intervention: Ethical, Legal and Political Dilemmas* (Cambridge: Cambridge University Press, 2003): 93–129 at 129; see also Chris Brown, "Selective Humanitarianism: In Defense of Inconsistency"; Deen K. Chatterjee and Don E. Scheid (eds.), *Ethics and Foreign Intervention* (Cambridge: Cambridge University Press, 2003): 31–52.

5   See also Allen Buchanan, "The Internal Legitimacy of Humanitarian Intervention," *Journal of Political Philosophy* 7 (1999): 71–87; Stanley Hoffmann, "Intervention: Should it Go On, Can It Go On?"; Chatterjee and Scheid, *Ethics and Foreign Intervention*, 21–30.

6   UN General Assembly, 2005 World Summit Outcome, A/60/L1, paragraph 139. See also Alicia L. Bannon, "The Responsibility to Protect: The UN World Summit and the Question of Unilateralism," *The Yale Law Journal* 115:5 (2006): 1157–65; Frederic L. Kirgis, "International Law Aspects of the 2005 World Summit Outcome Document," *American Society for International Law, Insights,* October 4, 2005 (http://www.asil.org/insights/2005/10/insights051004.html#author).

7   Robert Kaplan, "Aid at the Point of a Gun," *New York Times,* May 14, 2008; Jayshree Bajora, "The Dilemma of Humanitarian Intervention," Council on Foreign Relations, June 12, 2008 (http://www.cfr.org/publication/16524/dilemma_of_humanitarian_intervention.html).

8   "Our Friends in the North," *The Economist,* February 7, 2008; Ian James Storey, "Living with the Colossus: How Southeast Asian Countries Cope with China," *Parameters* (1999–2000): 115–25; Marek Pietschmann and Jeremy J. Sarkin, "Legitimate Humanitarian Intervention under International Law in the Context of the Current Human Rights and Humanitarian Crisis in Burma (Myanmar)," *Hong Kong Law Journal* 33 (2003): 371–416; Andrew Selth, "Burma and Superpower Rivalries in the Asia-Pacific," *Naval War College Review* 55:2 (2002), 43–60.

9   See Amnesty International, 2008 Annual Report for Myanmar (Burma) (http://www.amnestyusa.org/annualreport.php?id=ar&yr=2008&c=MMR).

10 Pietschmann and Sarkin, "Legitimate Humanitarian Intervention under International Law," 371.

11 "Burma Cyclone," Fact Sheet 24 (U.S. Agency for International Development, July 9, 2008).

12   International Commission of Inquiry on Darfur, Report to the United Nations Secretary-General Pursuant to Security Council Resolution 1564 of 18 September 2004 (Geneva, January 25, 2005): 3; International Criminal Court, "ICC Issues a Warrant of Arrest for Omar Al Bashir, President of Sudan," press release, March 4, 2009 (http://www.icc-cpi. int/NR/exeres/0EF62173-05ED-403A-80C8-F15EE1D25BB3.htm).

13   Ian Taylor, "China's Oil Diplomacy in Africa," *International Affairs* 82:5 (2006): 937–59.

14   Moira Herbst, "Oil for China, Guns for Darfur," *Business Week Asia*, March 14, 2008.

15   Denis M. Tull, "China's Engagement in Africa: Scope, Significance and Consequences," *The Journal of Modern African Studies* 44:3 (2006): 459–79.

16   Stephanie Kleine-Ahlbrandt and Andrew Small, "China's New Dictatorship Diplomacy: Is Beijing Parting with Pariahs? (Changing China)," *Foreign Affairs* 87:1 (January/February 2008). See also, Stephanie Hanson, "China, Africa, and Oil," Council on Foreign Relations, June 6, 2008 (http://www.cfr.org/publication/9557/).

17   Portions of the next section appeared previously in Michael L. Gross, "Is There a Duty to Die for Humanity? Humanitarian Intervention, Military Service and Political Obligation," *Public Affairs Quarterly* 2008, 22 (3): 213–30. My thanks to the editors for their permission to use this material.

18   International Commission on Intervention and State Sovereignty, *The Responsibility To Protect* (2001), 36 (http://www.iciss.ca/pdf/Commission-Report.pdf).

19   Fernando R Tesón, "The Liberal Case for Humanitarian Intervention," Holzgrefe and Keohane, *Humanitarian Intervention* 129; see also Chris Brown, "Selective Humanitarianism: In Defense of Inconsistency;" Chatterjee and Scheid, *Ethics and Foreign Intervention*, 31–52.

20   Buchanan, "The Internal Legitimacy of Humanitarian Intervention."

21   Hoffmann, "Intervention: Should it Go On, Can It Go On?" 28 (emphasis added).

22   John Lango, "Is Armed Humanitarian Intervention to Stop Mass Killing Morally Obligatory?" *Public Affairs Quarterly* 15:3 (2001), 187.

23   Jeremy Bentham, "Specimen of a Penal Code," *Works* Volume I, J. Bowring (ed.) (Edinburgh: Tait, 1843): 164.

24   Ernest J. Weinrib, "The Duty to Rescue," *The Yale Law Journal* 90 (1980): 247–293; see also Michael A. Menlowe," The Philosophical Foundations of the Duty to Rescue," Michael A. Menlowe and Alexander McCall Smith, *The Duty to Rescue: The Jurisprudence of Aid* (Aldershot, UK: Dartmouth Publishing, 1993): 5–54; Onora O'Neill, *Constructions of Reason: Explorations of Kant's Practical Philosophy* (Cambridge: Cambridge University Press, 1989): Chapter 12.

25 Michael Walzer, "The Obligation to Die for the State," Michael Walzer, *Obligations: Essays on Disobedience, War and Citizenship* (New York: Simon and Shuster, 1970): 77–98.

26 Patrick Riley, "Rousseau's General Will," Patrick Riley (ed.), *The Cambridge Companion to Rousseau* (Cambridge: Cambridge University Press, 2001): 124–53.

27 Allen Buchanan, *Justice, Legitimacy, and Self-Determination: Moral Foundations for International Law* (Oxford: Oxford University Press, 2003): 471 (emphasis added); see also Fernando R. Tesón, "The Liberal Case for Humanitarian Intervention," Holzgrefe and Keohane, *Humanitarian Intervention*, 128.

28 *The World Factbook* published by the CIA provides up-to-date information on conscription and volunteer armies by nation (Washington, D.C: The Central Intelligence Agency, 2009).

29 Christopher Kutz, "The Collective Work of Citizenship," *Legal Theory* 8 (2002), 471–94.

30 Kutz, "The Collective Work of Citizenship," 488.

31 Kutz, "The Collective Work of Citizenship," 488.

32 For example, see Nicholas D. Kristof, "What's to Be Done About Darfur? Plenty," *New York Times*, November 29, 2005; "Mr. Bush, Here's a Plan for Darfur," *New York Times*, August 6, 2007.

33 Through May 18, 2009, American military casualties (total deaths) numbered 4,279 in Iraq and 679 in Afghanistan. U.S. Department of Defense, DefenseLink (http://www.defenselink.mil/news/casualty.pdf).

34 Walter Clarke and Jeffrey Herbst, "Somalia and the Future of Humanitarian Intervention," *Foreign Affairs* 73 (1996), 70–85.

35 Denis McLean, *Peace Operations and Common Sense: Replacing Rhetoric with Realism* (Washington, DC: United States Institute of Peace, 1996): 13.

36 Rupert Smith, *The Utility of Force: The Art of War in the Modern World* (New York: Vintage, 2008): 317–34; Wesley Clark, *Waging Modern War: Bosnia, Kosovo, and the Future of Combat* (New York: Public Affairs, 2001).

37 Petersberg Declaration, Western European Union (June 19, 1992), II, 4 (http://www.weu.int/documents/920619peten.pdf).

38 Francois Heisbourg, *European Defence: Making it Work* (Paris: Institute for Security Studies, Western European Union, 2000): 81–2, 85 (emphasis added).

39 Institute for Security Studies Task Force, European Defense: A Proposal for a White Paper, Report of an Independent Task Force (Paris: European Union, 2004): 102.

40 Nicole Gnesotto, *EU Security and Defence Policy: The First Five Years (1999–2004)* (Paris: Institute for Security Studies, European Union, 2004): 124.

41 For a survey of modern trends of conscription (and what Joenniemi calls neo-conscription) see Pertti Joenniemi, "Introduction: Unpacking Conscription," Pertti Joenniemi (ed.), *The Changing Face of European Conscription* (Aldershot, Hampshire, UK: Ashgate, 2006): 1–12.

42 Hoffmann, *Intervention*, 29.

10 Torture, Assassination, and Blackmail

1 Martin van Creveld, *The Transformation of War* (New York: Free Press, 1991); Mary Kaldor, Mary. *New and Old Wars: Organized Violence in a Global Era* (Oxford: Polity Press, 2001); Rupert Smith, *The Utility of Force: The Art of War in the Modern World* (New York: Vintage, 2008).

2 Michael Ignatieff, *American Exceptionalism and Human Rights* (Princeton, NJ: Princeton University Press, 2005).

3 Larry Alexander, "Self-Defense, Justification and Excuse," *Philosophy and Public Affairs* 22:1 (Winter 1993), 53–66 at 53. Alexander comments on the philosophy of Judith Jarvis Thomson, "Self-Defense," *Philosophy and Public Affairs* 20:4 (Fall 1991), 283–310; see also George Fletcher, *Rethinking Criminal Law* (Boston: Little Brown, 1978): 760–2; Kent Greenwald, "The Perplexing Borders of Justification and Excuse," *Colombia Law Review* 84:8 (1984): 1897–1927 at 1918–21.

4 See Chapter 6 (p. 139), "Rendition and Interrogation: International Cooperation and Support."

5 C. A. J. Coady, "Terrorism and Innocence," *The Journal of Ethics* 8 (2004): 37–58 at 58.

6 Paola Gaeta, "The Armed Conflict in Chechnya before the Russian Constitutional Court," *European Journal of International Law* 7:4 (1996): 563–70.

7 Gideon Alon, "Mofaz: IDF Jurist Approves Killings," *Ha'aretz*, January 1, 2001; Yael Stein, Position Paper: "Israel's Assassination Policy: Extra-judicial Executions," (Jerusalem: B'Tselem, The Israeli Information Center for Human Rights in the Occupied Territories, 2001): 2.

8 Convention (IV) respecting the Laws and Customs of War on Land and its annex: Regulations concerning the Laws and Customs of War on Land. (The Hague, October 18, 1907) (emphasis added).

9 Anthony Cordesman, *Lessons from the 2006 Israeli–Hezbollah War* (Washington, DC: Center for Strategic and International Studies, 2007): 40–1; see also Smith, *The Utility of Force*, 286ff, 355ff, 400–4, for a similar assessment.

10 International Committee of the Red Cross, *The SIrUS Project: Towards a Determination of Which Weapons Cause "Superfluous Injury or Unnecessary Suffering"* (Geneva: ICRC, 1997): 23.

11   This thesis is central to the constructivist school of international rela-
     tions. For a constructivist account of norms of warfare see Ward Thomas,
     The Ethics of Destruction: Norms and Force in International Relations (Ithaca,
     NY: Cornell University Press, 2001).

11   The War in Gaza, December 2008 to January 2009

1   Sources: **Korean War:** T. N. Dupuy, *Attrition: Forecasting Battle Casualties
     and Equipment Losses in Modern War* (Falls Church, VA: Nova Publications,
     1995):141. **Six Day War (Israeli Casualties):** Israel Ministry of Foreign
     Affairs, The Six-Day War – Introduction, November 3, 2003 (http://
     www.mfa.gov.il/MFA/Foreign+Relations/Israels+Foreign+Relations+
     since+1947/1947-1974/THE+SIX-DAY+WAR+-+INTRODUCTION.
     htm). **1973 October War (Israeli casualties):** Netanel Lorch, *The Arab–
     Israeli Wars*, Israel Ministry of Foreign Affairs (http://www.mfa.gov.il/
     MFA/History/Modern+History/Centenary+of+Zionism/The+Arab-
     Israeli+Wars.htm). **Falklands War (British casualties):** Imperial War
     Museum, "Falklands War 1982, Casualty Statistics" (http://www.iwm.
     org.uk/server/show/ConWebDoc.2477). **Iraq War (Operation Iraqi
     Freedom) and Afghanistan War (Operation Enduring Freedom), U.S.
     casualties (killed or wounded in combat) through April 2009:** U.S.
     Department of Defense, DefenseLink (http://www.defenselink.mil/
     news/casualty.pdf). **Gaza War:** Israel Ministry of Foreign Affairs (http://
     www.mfa.gov.il/MFA/Terrorism-+Obstacle+to+Peace/Terrorism+and+
     Islamic+Fundamentalism-/Aerial_strike_weapon_development_
     center+_Gaza_28-Dec-2008.htm). These figures do not reflect the in-
     tensity or deadliness of war directly. They do not indicate, for example,
     whether the number of soldiers hit is high or low relative to the number
     of soldiers deployed. Instead, they focus on field and hospital mortality,
     that is, the absolute number of dead and wounded. They show that field
     mortality (the percentage of soldiers who are hit and then die in the
     field) and hospital mortality (the percentage of soldiers who die of their
     wounds in the hospital) are lower in asymmetric war than in conven-
     tional war and lower still in the Gaza War.

2   Palestinian Centre for Human Rights, press release, March 12, 2009,
     reference 36/2009 (http://www.pchrgaza.org/files/PressR/English/
     2008/36-2009.html); Sagi Or, "How Many Palestinians Were Killed?"
     Ha'aretz, March 19, 2009; Israel Ministry of Foreign Affairs, "Vast
     Majority of Palestinians Killed in Operation Cast Lead Terror
     Operatives," press release, March 26, 2009 (http://www.mfa.gov.il/
     MFA/Terrorism-+Obstacle+to+Peace/Hamas+war+against+Israel/
     Vast_majority_Palestinians_killed_Operation_Cast_Lead_terror_
     operatives_26-Mar-2009.htm); Amos Harel, "IDF: 600 Hamas Men, 309
     Civilians Died in Gaza Offensive," *Ha'aretz*, March 25, 2009.

3   For a preliminary description of attacks on civilians and civilian objects associated with Hamas see B'Tselem, *Guidelines for Israel's Investigation into Operation Cast Lead, 27 December 2008–18 January 2009* (Jerusalem: B'Tselem, 2009): 11–14.

4   Israel Ministry of Foreign Affairs, *The Operation in Gaza: Factual and Legal Aspects* (Jerusalem: Ministry of Foreign Affairs, July 2009): 86–89.

5   Amos Harel and Avi Issacharoff, "The IDF Model that Failed in Lebanon Succeeded in Gaza," *Ha'aretz*, January 24, 2009; David Eshel, "New Tactics Yield Solid Victory in Gaza," *Aviation Week*, March 11, 2009; Amnesty International, *Fuelling conflict: Foreign Arms Supplies to Israel/ Gaza*, AI Index: MDE 15/012/2009, February 23, 2009; Steven Erlanger, "A Gaza War Full of Traps and Trickery," *New York Times*, January 10, 2009.

6   See William M. Arkin, *Divining Victory, Airpower in the 2006 Israel– Hezbollah War* (Maxwell Air Force Base, Alabama: Air University Press, July 2007): 110.

7   For a partial assessment of the effectiveness of phosphorus shells see "IDF Releases Information on Military Investigations," April 22, 2009 (http://dover.idf.il/IDF/English/News/today/09/4/2201.htm? print=true). The report does not assess the effectiveness of alternative means to obscure troop movement.

8   Amnesty International, *Fueling Conflict*: 14–15.

9   See discussion of human shields and the right to fight without uniforms in Chapter 7 (p. 163), "Reassessing Proportionality in Asymmetric Conflict: The Problem of Human Shields and Inaccurate Weaponry."

10 Michael Walzer, *Just and Unjust Wars* (New York: Basic Books, 1977): 155–6.

11 Asa Kasher, "Combatants' Life: A Plea for a Major Change," presented at a public conference, "The Morality of Warfare during Operation Cast Lead," Jerusalem, February 22, 2009 (emphasis added).

12 See Chapter 7 (p. 174), "Deterrence, Demoralization, and Punishment: The Doctrine of Disproportionate Force."

Selected Bibliography

Abd al-Jawad, Saleh. "The Classification and Recruitment of Collaborators" in *The Phenomenon of Collaborators in Palestine: Proceedings of a Passia Workshop* (Jerusalem: Palestinian Academic Society for the Study of International Affairs, 2001).

Alexander, John P. "An Overview of the Future of Nonlethal Weapons," in *Medicine, Conflict and Survival* **17** (2001), 180–93.

Amnesty International. *United States of America, Below the Radar: Secret Flights to Torture and 'Disappearance'*, AI Index: AMR 51/051/2006 (April 2006).

Annati, Massimo. "Nonlethal Weapons Revisited," *Military Technology* **31**:3 (March 2007), 82–7.

Arreguin-Toft, Ivan. *How the Weak Win Wars: A Theory of Asymmetric Conflict* (Cambridge: Cambridge University Press, 2005).

B'Tselem. *Absolute Prohibition: The Torture and Ill-treatment of Palestinian Detainees* (Jerusalem: B'Tselem, May 2007).

Bar-Joseph, Uri. "Israel's Military Intelligence Performance in the Second Lebanon War," *International Journal of Intelligence and Counterintelligence* **20**:4 (December 2007), 583–601.

Beckett, Ian F. W. *Modern Insurgencies and Counter Insurgencies: Guerrillas and their Opponents since 1750* (London: Routledge, 2001).

Be'er, Yizhar and Saleh Abd al-Jawad, *Collaborators in the Occupied Territories: Human Rights Abuses and Violations* (Jerusalem: B'Tselem, 1994).

Beitz, Charles R. (ed). *International Ethics* (Princeton, NJ: Princeton University Press, 1985).

Benbaji, Yitzchak. "A Defense of the Traditional War Convention," *Ethics* **118** (April 2008): 464–95.

Best, Geoffrey. *Humanity in Warfare* (London: Methuen, 1980)
War and Law since 1945 (Oxford: Oxford University Press, 1997).

Bobbitt, Philip. *Terrorism and Consent: The Wars for the 21st Century* (New York: Knopf, 2008).

Brecher, Bob. *Torture and the Ticking Bomb* (Malden, MA: Blackwell, 2007).

Bring, Ove. "Regulating Conventional Weapons in the Future – Humanitarian Law or Arms Control?" *Journal of Peace Research* **24**:3 (1987), 275–86.

Brophy-Baermann, Bryan and John A. Conybeare. "Retaliating against Terrorism: Rational Expectations and the Optimality of Rules vs. Discretion," *American Journal of Political Science* **38**:1 (February 1994), 196–210.

Brownlie, Ian. "Interrogation in Depth: The Compton and Parker Reports," *The Modern Law Review* **35**(5) (September 1972), 501–7.

Buchanan, Allen. "The Internal Legitimacy of Humanitarian Intervention," *Journal of Political Philosophy* **7** (1999), 71–87.

Byman, Daniel. "Do Targeted Killings Work?" *Foreign Affairs* **85**:2 (2006), 95–111.

Canil, Turhan, et. al., "Neuroethics and National Security," *American Journal of Bioethics* **7**:5 (2007), 3–13.

Cann, John, P. *Counterinsurgency in Africa, The Portuguese Way of War 1961– 1974* (Westport, CT, Greenwood Press, 1997).

Carnahan, Burrus M. and Marjorie Robertson. "The Protocol on 'Blinding Laser Weapons': A New Direction for International Humanitarian Law," *American Journal of International Law* **90** (1996), 484–90.

Cassel, Doug. "Washington's 'War Against Terrorism' and Human Rights: The View from Abroad," *Human Rights* **33**:1 (2006), 1–9, 11–14, 22.

Cassese, Antonio. "Weapons Causing Unnecessary Suffering: Are They Prohibited?" *Rivista di Diritto Internazionale* LVIII (1975), 12–42.

Chatterjee, Deen K. and Don E. Scheid (eds.), *Ethics and Foreign Intervention* (Cambridge: Cambridge University Press, 2003).

Clark, Wesley. *Waging Modern War: Bosnia, Kosovo, and the Future of Combat* (New York: Public Affairs, 2001).

Clarke, Walter and Jeffrey Herbst. "Somalia and the Future of Humanitarian Intervention," *Foreign Affairs* **73** (1996), 70–85.

Coady, C.A.J. "Terrorism and Innocence," *The Journal of Ethics* **8** (2004), 37–58.

Coates, A.J. *The Ethics of War* (Manchester: Manchester University Press, 1997).

Geneva Convention (IV) Relative to the Protection of Civilian Persons in Time of War (4th Geneva Convention), August 12, 1949.

Coppernoll, Margaret-Anne, "The Nonlethal Weapons Debate," *Naval War College Review* **52**:2 (1999), 112–31.

Cordesman, Anthony. *Lessons of the 2006 Israeli-Hezbollah War* (Washington, DC: Center for Strategic and International Studies, 2007).

   Terrorism, Asymmetric Warfare and Weapons of Mass Destruction (Westport, CT: Praeger, 2002).

Corlett, J. Angelo. *Terrorism, A Philosophical Analysis* (Heidelberg: Springer, 2003).

Council on Foreign Relations. "*Nonlethal Weapons and Capability*" (New York: Council on Foreign Relations, 2004).

Coupland, Robin M. "The Effect of Weapons: Defining Superfluous Injury and Unnecessary Suffering," *Medicine and Global Survival* 3 (1996), A1.

"Abhorrent Weapons and 'Superfluous Injury or Unnecessary Suffering': from Field Surgery to Law," *British Medical Journal* 315 (1997), 1450–2.

"The SIrUS Project: Progress Report on 'Superfluous Injury or Unnecessary Suffering' in Relation to the Legality of Weapons," *International Review of the Red Cross* 835 (1999), 583–92.

Croddy, Eric. *Chemical and Biological Warfare: A Comprehensive Survey for the Concerned Citizen* (New York: Springer Verlag, 2002).

Dando, Malcolm. *A New Form of Warfare: The Rise of Nonlethal Weapons* (London: Brassey's, 1996).

Davison, Neil and Nick Lewer. Bradford Nonlethal Weapons Research Project, Research Report No. 8 (Centre for Conflict Resolution, Department of Peace Studies, University of Bradford, UK, March 2006).

Davison, Neil "'Off the Rocker' and 'On the Floor': The Continued Development of Biochemical Incapacitating Weapons," Bradford Science and Technology Report 8 (Bradford Disarmament Research Centre, Department of Peace Studies, University of Bradford, UK, August 2007).

Dershowitz, Alan M. *Why Terrorism Works* (New Haven, CT: Yale University Press, 2002).

Doswald-Beck, Louise. "New Protocol on Blinding Lasers," *International Journal of the Red Cross* 312 (1996), 272–99.

Dupuy, T.N. *Attrition: Forecasting Battle Casualties and Equipment Losses in Modern War* (Falls Church, VA: Nova Publications, 1995).

Elkins, Caroline. *Imperial Reckoning: The Untold Story of Britain's Gulag in Kenya* (New York: Henry Holt, 2005).

Exum, Andrew. *Hizballah at War, A Military Assessment*, Policy Focus No. 63 (Washington, DC: The Washington Institute for Near East Policy, December 2006).

Fein, Robert. (ed.) "Educing Information. Interrogation: Science and Art. Foundations for the Future," Intelligence Science Board, Phase 1 Report (Washington, DC: National Defense Intelligence College Press), Center for Strategic Intelligence Research, December 2006.

Fidler, David P. "The Meaning of Moscow: 'Nonlethal' Weapons and International Law in the Early 21st Century," *International Review of the Red Cross* 87 (2005), 525–52.

Freedman, Lawrence. *A Choice of Enemies: America Confronts the Middle East* (New York: Public Affairs, 2008).

Garcia, Michael John. *Renditions: Constraints Imposed by the Laws on Torture*, CRS Report for Congress (Washington, DC: Congressional Research Service, The Library of Congress, April 2006).

Gilbert, Paul. *New Terror, New Wars* (Washington, DC: Georgetown University Press, 2003).

Ginbar, Yuval. *Why Not Torture Terrorists? Moral, Practical and Legal Aspects of the "Ticking Bomb" Justification for Torture* (Oxford: Oxford University Press, 2008).

Goodwin, Jeff. "A Theory of Categorical Terrorism," *Social Forces* **84**:4 (2006), 2027–46.

Graham, Gordon L. *Ethics and International Relations* (London: Blackwell, 1997).

Green, Leslie C. "Superior Orders and the Reasonable Man," in Leslie C. Green (ed.), *The Modern Law of War*, Second Edition (New York: Transnational Publishers, 1999), 245–82.

   The Contemporary Law of Armed Conflict, Second Edition (Manchester: Manchester University Press, 2000).

Greenwood, Christopher. "The Twilight of the Law of Belligerent Reprisals." *Netherlands Yearbook of International Law* **20** (1989), 35–69.

Grey, Stephen. *Ghost Plane: The True Story of the CIA Torture Program* (New York: St. Martin's Press, 2006).

Gross, Michael L. "Fighting by Other Means in the Mideast: A Critical Analysis of Israel's Assassination Policy," *Political Studies* **51** (2003), 350–68.

   "Assassination: Killing in the Shadow of Self-Defense," in J. Irwin (ed.), *War and Virtual War: The Challenges to Communities* (Amsterdam: Rodopi, 2004), 99–116.

   "Assassination and Targeted Killing: Law Enforcement, Execution or Self-Defense?" *Journal of Applied Philosophy* **23**:3 (2006), 323–35.

   Bioethics and Armed Conflict: Moral Dilemmas of Medicine and War (Cambridge, MA: MIT Press, 2006).

   "Is There a Duty to Die for Humanity? Humanitarian Intervention, Military Service and Political Obligation," *Public Affairs Quarterly* 2008, **22** (3), 213–30.

   "The Second Lebanon War: The Question of Proportionality and the Prospect of Nonlethal Warfare," *Journal of Military Ethics* **7** (2008), 1–22.

Hafez, Mohammed M. and Joseph M. Hatfield. "Do Targeted Assassinations Work? A Multivariate Analysis of Israel's Controversial Tactic during Al-Aqsa Uprising," *Studies in Conflict & Terrorism* **29**:4 (July 2006), 359–82.

Harel, Amos and Avi Issacharoff. *34 Days: Israel, Hezbollah and the War in Lebanon* (New York: Palgrave Macmillan, 2008).

Heisbourg, Francois. *European Defence: Making it Work* (Paris: Institute for Security Studies, Western European Union, 2000).

Held, Virginia. "Terrorism and War," *The Journal of Ethics* **8** (2004), 59–75.

Henckaerts Jean-Marie and Louise Doswald-Beck. *Customary International Humanitarian Law* (Cambridge: Cambridge University Press, 2005).

Hensel, Howard (ed). *The Law of Armed Conflict, Constraints on the Contemporary Use of Force* (Aldershot, Hampshire, UK: Ashgate, 2007).

Heymann, Philip B. and Juliette N. Kayyem. *Protecting Liberty in an Age of Terror* (Belfer Center for Science and International Affairs, Studies in International Security) (Cambridge, MA: MIT Press, 2005).

Hirsch, Seymour. *Chain of Command: The Road from 9/11 to Abu Ghraib* (New York: HarperCollins, 2005).

Hodgson, Godfrey. "The U.S.–European Torture Dispute: An Autopsy," *World Policy Journal* (Winter 2005/06), 7–14.

Holcomb, John B., Lynn Stansbury, Howard R. Champion, Charles Wade, and Ronald Bellamy. "Understanding Combat Casualty Care Statistics," *The Journal of Trauma: Injury, Infection and Critical Care* **60**:2 (2006), 397–401.

Holmes, Robert L. *On War and Morality* (Princeton, NJ: Princeton University Press, 1989).

Holzgrefe, J.L. and Robert O. Keohane (eds.). *Humanitarian Intervention: Ethical, Legal and Political Dilemmas* (Cambridge: Cambridge University Press, 2003).

Horne, Alistair. *A Savage War of Peace: Algeria 1954–1962* (New York: Viking, 1978).

Howard, Michael, George J. Andreopoulos, and Mark R. Shulman (eds.). *The Laws of War: Constraints on Warfare in the Western World* (New Haven, CT: Yale University Press, 1994).

Human Rights Watch. *Off Target: The Conduct of the War and Civilian Casualties in Iraq* (December 2003). Available at: http://humanrightswatch.net/reports/2003/usa1203/index.htm.

Civilians under Assault: Hezbollah's Rocket Attacks on Israel in the 2006 War (August 2007, Volume 10, No. 3E). Available at: http://www.hrw.org/en/reports/2007/08/28/civilians-under-assault.

Why They Died: Civilian Casualties in Lebanon during the 2006 War (September 2007, Volume 19, No. 5E). Available at: http://www.hrw.org/en/reports/2007/09/05/why-they-died.

Huntington, Samuel P. "New Contingencies, Old Roles," *Joint Forces Quarterly* **34** (Autumn 1993), 38–43.

Hurka, Thomas. "Proportionality in the Morality of War," *Philosophy and Public Affairs* **33** (2005), 34–66.

Ignatieff, Michael. "Human Rights, the Laws of War and Terrorism," *Social Research* **69**:4 (2002), 1137–58.

The Lesser Evil: Political Ethics in an Age of Terror (Princeton, NJ: Princeton University Press, 2004).

American Exceptionalism and Human Rights (Princeton, NJ: Princeton University Press, 2005).

International Committee of the Red Cross. *The SIrUS Project: Towards a Determination of Which Weapons Cause "Superfluous Injury or Unnecessary Suffering"* (Geneva: ICRC, 1997).

Third Expert Meeting on the Notion of Direct Participation in Hostilities, Summary Report (Geneva: ICRC, October 23–25, 2005).

Guide to the Legal Review of New Weapons, Means and Methods of Warfare: Measures to Implement Article 36 of Additional Protocol I of 1977 (Geneva: ICRC, 2006).

Ireland vs. the United Kingdom. *Yearbook of the European Conventions on Human Rights* **19** (1976), 512–928.

Jacobson, Daniel and Edward H. Kaplan. "Suicide Bombings and Targeted Killings in (Counter-) Terror Games," *Journal of Conflict Resolution* **51**: 5 (October 2007), 772–92.

Joenniemi, Pertti (ed.). *The Changing Face of European Conscription* (Aldershot, Hampshire, UK: Ashgate, 2006)

Johnson, James Turner. *The War to Oust Saddam Hussein* (Lanham, MD: Rowman & Littlefield, 2005).

Joint Chiefs of Staff (USA). *Joint Doctrine for Military Operations Other Than War*, Publication JP 3–07, 1995.

　　JP 3-0, *Joint Operations*, 17 September 2006, Incorporating Change 1, 13 February 2008.

Kaldor, Mary. *New and Old Wars: Organized Violence in a Global Era* (Oxford: Polity Press, 2001).

Kalshoven, Frits. *Belligerent Reprisals* (Leyden: A. W. Sijthoff, 1971).

　　"Belligerent Reprisals Revisited," *Netherlands Yearbook of International Law* **21** (1990), 43–80.

Kaplan, Edward, et al. "What Happened to Suicide Bombings in Israel? Insights from a Terror Stock Model," *Studies in Conflict and Terrorism* **28**:3 (2005), 225–35.

Kasher, Asa and Amos Yadlin. "Military Ethics of Fighting Terror: An Israeli Perspective," *Journal of Military Ethics* **4**:1 (2005), 3–32.

Klabbers, Jan. "Rebel with a Cause? Terrorists and Humanitarian Law," *European Journal of International Law* **14**:2 (2003), 299–312.

Koplow, David. *Nonlethal Weapons: The Law and Policy of Revolutionary Technologies for the Military and Law Enforcement* (Cambridge: Cambridge University Press, 2006).

Kutz, Christopher. "The Collective Work of Citizenship," *Legal Theory* **8** (2002), 471–94.

Lango, John. "Is Armed Humanitarian Intervention to Stop Mass Killing Morally Obligatory?" *Public Affairs Quarterly* **15**:3 (2001), 173–91.

Levinson, Sanford (ed.). *Torture: A Collection* (Oxford: Oxford University Press, 2004).

Lewer, Nick and Neil Davison. "Nonlethal Technologies – An Overview," *Disarmament* **1** (2005), 36–51.

Lewer, Nick and S. Schofield. *Nonlethal Weapons: A Fatal Attraction?* (London: Zed Books, 1997).

Linder, Aviel. *Family Matters: Using Family Members to Pressure Detainees Under GSS Interrogation* (Jerusalem: Public Committee Against Torture in Israel, 2008).

Lumsden, Malvern. *Incendiary Weapons*, Stockholm International Peace Research Institute (Cambridge, MA: MIT Press, 1975).

May, Larry. *War Crimes and Just War* (Cambridge: Cambridge University Press, 2007).

Mayer, Jane. *The Dark Side: The Inside Story of How The War on Terror Turned into a War on American Ideals* (New York: Doubleday, 2008).

McMahan, Jeff. "Revising the Doctrine of Double Effect," *Journal of Applied Philosophy* **11**:2 (1994), 201–12.

Killing in War (Oxford: Oxford University Press, 2009).

Merom, Gil. *How Democracies Lose Small Wars* (Cambridge: Cambridge University Press, 2003).

Metz, Steven. *Learning from Iraq: Counterinsurgency in American Strategy* (Carlisle, PA: The Strategic Studies Institute of the U.S. Army War College, 2007).

Mitchell, Andrew D. "Does One Illegality Merit Another? The Law of Belligerent Reprisals in International Law," *Military Law Review* **170** (December 2001), 155–77.

Moore, Michael. "Torture and the Balance of Evils," *Israel Law Review* **23**: 2, 3 (1989), 280–344.

Moreno, Jonathan. *Mind Wars: Brain Research and National Defense* (New York: Dana Press, 2006).

Morton, Jeffrey S. "The Legal Status of Laser Weapons that Blind," *Journal of Peace Research* **35**:6 (1998), 697–705.

Nagl, John A. *Counterinsurgency Lessons from Malaya and Vietnam: Learning to Eat Soup with a Spoon* (Westport, CT: Praeger, 2002).

National Research Council. *An Assessment of Nonlethal Weapons Science and Technology*, Committee for an Assessment of Nonlethal Weapons Science and Technology, Naval Studies Board Division on Engineering and Physical Sciences (Washington, DC: The National Academies Press, 2003).

O'Neill, Bard E. *Insurgency and Terrorism: Inside Modern Revolutionary Warfare* (Washington, DC: Brassey's, 1990).

Pape, Robert. *Dying to Win: The Strategic Logic of Suicide Terrorism* (New York: Random House, 2005).

Parks, W. Hays. "The ICRC Customary Law Study: A Preliminary Assessment," *ASIL Proceedings* **99** (2005), 208–12.

Pedahzur, Ami, Arie Perliger, and Leonard Weinberg. "Altruism and Fatalism: The Characteristics of Palestinian Suicide Terrorists," *Deviant Behavior* **24** (2003): 405–423.

Physicians for Human Rights, Israel. *Holding Health to Ransom: GSS Interrogation and Extortion of Palestinian Patients at Erez Crossing* (Tel Aviv: Physicians for Human Rights, August 2008).

Pictet, Jean. *Development and Principles of International Humanitarian Law* (Dordrecht/Geneva, Martinus Nijhoff and Henry Dunant Institute, 1985).

Pirnie, Bruce R. and Edward O'Connell. *Counterinsurgency in Iraq (2003–2006)* (Santa Monica, CA: Rand Corporation, 2008).

Posner, Richard. *Not a Suicide Pact: The Constitution in Time of National Emergency* (Oxford: Oxford University Press, 2006).

   Countering Terrorism: Blurred Focus, Halting Steps, Hoover Studies in Politics, Economics, and Society (New York: Rowman & Littlefield, 2007).

Price, Richard and Nina Tannenwald. "Norms and Deterrence: The Nuclear and Chemical Weapons Taboos," in Peter J. Katzenstein (ed.),

The Culture of National Security: Norms and Identity in World Politics (New York: Columbia University Press, 1996), 114–52.

Primoratz, Igor (ed). *Terrorism: The Philosophical Issues* (New York: Palgrave Macmillan, 2004).

Civilian Immunity in War (Oxford: Oxford University Press, 2007).

Protocol Additional to the Geneva Conventions of 12 August 1949, and Relating to the Protection of Victims of International Armed Conflicts (Protocol I, June 8, 1977).

Protocol Additional to the Geneva Conventions of 12 August 1949, and Relating to the Protection of Victims of International Armed Conflicts (Protocol I, June 8, 1977). Commentary.

Protocol on Blinding Laser Weapons 1995. (Protocol IV to the 1980 Convention, October 13).

Public Committee against Torture in Israel v. The State of Israel (High Court of Justice 5100/94, September 6, 1999).

"Breaches in the Defense: Torture and Ill-treatment during GSS [General Security Services] Investigations Following the Verdict of the High Court of Justice, 6 September 1999" (Jerusalem: Public Committee against Torture in Israel, 2001).

"Back to a Routine of Torture: Torture and Ill-treatment of Palestinian Detainees, during Arrest, Detention and Interrogation, September 2001– April 2003" (Jerusalem: Public Committee against Torture in Israel).

Public Committee against Torture in Israel and Palestinian Society for the Protection of Human Rights and the Environment v. The Government of Israel (High Court of Justice 769/02, December 11, 2005).

Rejali, Darius. *Torture and Democracy* (Princeton, NJ: Princeton University Press, 2007).

Rigby, Andrew. *The Legacy of the Past: The Problem of Collaborators and the Palestinian Case* (Jerusalem: Palestinian Academic Society for the Study of International Affairs, 1997).

Roberts, Adam. "NATO's 'Humanitarian War' over Kosovo," *Survival* **41**:3 (Autumn 1999), 102–23.

Rodin, David. "Terrorism without Intentions," *Ethics* **114**:4 (July 2004), 752–71.

Rodin, David and Henry Shue. *Just and Unjust Warriors: The Moral and Legal Status of Soldiers* (Oxford: Oxford University Press, 2008).

Rodley, Nigel S. *The Treatment of Prisoners Under International Law* (Oxford: Clarendon Press, 1999).

Rogers, A. P. V. "The Principle of Proportionality," in Howard Hensel (ed.), *The Legitimate Use of Military Force: The Just War Tradition and the Customary Law of Armed Conflict* (Aldershot, Hampshire, UK: Ashgate Publishing, 2008), 189–218.

Shue, Henry. "Torture," *Philosophy and Public Affairs* **7**:2 (1978), 124–43.

Smilansky, Saul. *10 Moral Paradoxes* (Oxford: Blackwell, 2007).

Smith, Rupert. *The Utility of Force: The Art of War in the Modern World* (New York: Vintage, 2008).

Sofaer, Abraham. "Agora, The US Decision not to Ratify Protocol I to the Geneva Conventions on the Protection of War Victims (con'd), The Rationale for the United States Decision," *American Journal of International Law* **82** (1987), 784–87.

Statman, Daniel. "The Absoluteness of the Prohibition Against Torture" (Hebrew) *Mishpat u-memshal* **4** (1997), 161–98.

"Targeted Killing," *Theoretical Inquiries in Law* **5** (2004), 179–98.

Stein, Yael. "By Any Name Illegal and Immoral" (Response to "Israel's Policy of Targeted Killing" by Steven R. David). *Ethics & International Affairs* **17**:1 (2003), 127–40.

Stockholm International Peace Research Institute. *The Problem of Chemical and Biological Warfare*, 6 volumes (Stockholm: Stockholm International Peace Research Institute, 1971–1975).

Tenet, George. *At the Center of the Storm: My Years at the CIA* (New York: HarperCollins, 2007).

Thomas, Ward. *The Ethics of Destruction: Norms and Force in International Relations* (Ithaca, NY: Cornell University Press, 2001).

Turns, David. "Weapons in the ICRC Study on Customary Humanitarian Law," *Journal of Conflict and Security Law* **11**:2 (2006), 201–37.

United Nations. *A More Secure World: Our Shared Responsibility, Report of the High-level Panel on Threats, Challenges and Change* (New York: The United Nations, 2004).

United Nations Human Rights Council, *Report of the Commission of Inquiry on Lebanon Pursuant to Human Rights Council Resolution S-2/1*, November 23, 2006, A/HRC/3/2, available at: http://www.unhcr.org/refworld/docid/45c30b6e0.html.

U.S. Army, Field Manual FM 2-22.3 (FM 34-52), *Human Intelligence Collector Operations* (Washington, DC: Department of the Army, September 2006).

U.S. Army, Field Manual FM 3-24, *Counterinsurgency* (Washington, DC: Department of the Army, 2006).

Valls, Andrew (ed.). *Ethics in International Affairs* (Lanham, MD: Rowman & Littlefield, 2000).

van Creveld, Martin. *The Transformation of War* (New York: Free Press, 1991).

"The Persian Gulf Crises and the Future of Morally Restrained War," *Parameters* **22**:2 (1992), 21–40.

Walzer, Michael. *Just and Unjust Wars* (New York: Basic Books, 1977).

Arguing About War (New Haven, CT: Yale University Press, 2004).

Weinrib, Ernest J. "The Duty to Rescue," *The Yale Law Journal* **90** (1980), 247–93.

Weissbrodt, David and Amy Bergquist. "Extraordinary Rendition: A Human Rights Analysis," *Harvard Human Rights Journal* **19**:123 (2006), 123–60.

Woodward, Bob. *The War Within: A Secret White House History 2006–2008* (New York: Simon and Schuster, 2008).

INDEX

Breinigsville, PA USA
13 September 2010
245237BV0000

U 22 .G76 2010
Gross, Michael L., 1954-
Moral dilemmas of modern war